D0288015

The Market Process

For our friends at CSMP

Bliss was it in that dawn to be alive, but to be young was very heaven!
(Wordsworth)

The Market Process

Essays in Contemporary Austrian Economics

Edited by

Peter J. Boettke

Department of Economics
New York University, US

and

David L. Prychitko

Department of Economics
State University of New York – Oswego, US

Edward Elgar

Published by
Edward Elgar Publishing Limited
Gower House
Croft Road
Aldershot
Hants GU11 3HR
England

Edward Elgar Publishing Company
Old Post Road
Brookfield
Vermont 05036
USA

British Library Cataloguing in Publication Data
Market Process: Essays in Contemporary
Austrian Economics.
I. Boettke, Peter J. II. Prychitko,
David L. III. Series
330.15

Library of Congress Cataloguing in Publication Data
The Market process: essays in contemporary Austrian economics/
edited by Peter J. Boettke and David L. Prychitko.
p. cm.
1. Economics—Austria. 2. Economics—Methodology. I. Boettke,
Peter J. II. Prychitko, David L. III. Series.
HB101.A2M37 1994
330.15'7—dc20 94–322
CIP

ISBN 1 85278 854 2

Printed and bound in Great Britain by
Hartnolls Limited, Bodmin, Cornwall

Contents

Contributors

Peter J. Boettke, Department of Economics, New York University.
Don Boudreaux, Department of Legal Studies, Clemson University.
James M. Buchanan, Center for the Study of Public Choice, George Mason University.
Tyler Cowen, Department of Economics, George Mason University.
Richard M. Ebeling, Department of Economics, Hillsdale College.
Jack High, Harvard Business School and Center for Market Process, George Mason University.
Steven Horwitz, Department of Economics, St Lawrence University.
Matthew B. Kibbe, Economic Advisor, US Congress.
Israel M. Kirzner, Department of Economics, New York University.
Ludwig M. Lachmann, formerly Professor Emeritus, University of Witwatersrand.
Richard N. Langlois, Department of Economics, University of Connecticut–Storrs.
Don Lavoie, Program on Social and Organization Learning, George Mason University.
Donald N. McCloskey, Departments of Economics and History, University of Iowa.
G.B. Madison, Department of Philosophy, McMaster University.
David L. Prychitko, Department of Economics, State University of New York at Oswego.
George A. Selgin, Department of Economics, University of Georgia.
G.L.S. Shackle, formerly Professor Emeritus, University of Liverpool.
Viktor Vanberg, Department of Economics, George Mason University.
Karen I. Vaughn, Department of Economics, George Mason University.
Jack Wiseman, formerly Department of Economics, University of York.
Leland B. Yeager, Department of Economics, Auburn University.

Preface: The meaning of 'Market Process'

Don Lavoie

The decade of the 1980s can in retrospect be seen as a crucial period in the evolution of the Austrian School of economics, a period in which the younger contributors to the school came out from under several different limiting constraints that had handicapped them over the previous decades. There were, for example, dogmatisms the school needed to overcome, or at least learn to live with, not only on the part of mainstream neoclassical economists, who tend to dismiss the Austrians on methodological grounds, but also on the part of leading contributors to the Austrian School itself, who tend to exhibit an all-too confident air about the traditional ideas of the school. Although important theoretical innovations were beginning to be made in the 1970s, almost no empirical work informed by these theories was being done. The school was not exerting influence over any substantive field in economics other than the history of economic thought. There were preconceptions that deserved to be challenged about who the appropriate audience for the school's contributions were, and about what scholarly literatures the school ought to be drawing from for its insights. There were well-worn controversies into which factions of the school appeared to have gotten stuck, such as the one over whether the dynamic processes of markets are best described in terms of movements toward equilibrium.

A burst of energy had carried the school through the previous decade, propelled by the profound challenges Ludwig Lachmann had injected into the American Austrian movement, through his regular visits to New York University. But there was some danger in the early 1980s that the school would be unable to maintain its momentum, that its Pro-Lachmann and Anti-Lachmann factions had settled into hardened positions, and that the school would continue to cycle back over the issues that had arisen in the 1970s.

The formation in 1980 of the Center for the Study of Market Processes in the Economics department at George Mason University enabled a small group of scholars to take a fresh look at what this thing called "Austrian economics" was really all about. Indeed, it turns out that having opened the question, they found themselves wondering whether it was best conceived of as a school of “economics” in the first place. At issue was the very *meaning* of market process analysis.

The scholars at the Market Process Center did not at first think of themselves as revolutionaries within the Austrian School, but as merely providing a safe haven from neoclassical and Austrian dogmatisms, a place where the great ideas of the classic contributors, such as Carl Menger, Ludwig Mises, and Friedrich Hayek, could be examined in a spirit of open-minded inquiry. To be sure, there were specific themes that Rich Fink, the founder of the Center, had articulated from the outset which represented a distinctly new emphasis in the school. In particular Professor Fink encouraged Austrians to “get their hands dirty” with empirical work, and to refuse to remain on the plain of abstract theorizing and intellectual history. Yet even this was not really seen at the outset as a radical move, as something that might lead to any fundamental rethinking of theoretical ideas that had been inherited from the classic Austrians. Only now can it be seen just how radically the school has changed on the basis of research it began during the 1980s.

By the end of the 1980s, market process analysis was beginning to have a distinct if modest influence within several fields of economics, including comparative systems, industrial organization, methodology, and money and banking. Perhaps more importantly, it was beginning to be thought of more as a broad, interdisciplinary social theory rather than merely as a branch of economics. The scholars at the Market Process Center came to see their audience as not exclusively the economics profession, but as a variety of social scientists, management and organizational theorists, historians, philosophers, and even software engineers, who took an interest in the way knowledge is discovered and conveyed in market processes. Their methods were being reconsidered in relation to the other social sciences, their philosophical underpinnings were being reformulated in relation to evolutionary theory and continental philosophy, and their conception of empirical work was being articulated in relation to history and anthropology. Whereas around 1980 most new dissertations being developed in the school were strictly theoretical contributions to intellectual history, around 1990 most involved original empirical research.

Two theoretical innovations during this period deserve special mention. A group of graduate students and professors began studying hermeneutics, especially the work of the German philosopher, Hans-Georg Gadamer, and became very excited about the implications of this approach for market process economics. Hermeneutics can be described as a philosophy of *meaning*, and studying it gave the market process school a deeper appreciation of what distinguishes its “subjectivistic” approach to economics from the “objectivism” of neoclassicism. Regular readings groups were conducted, a conference was held, and numerous contributions to *Market Process* were written to elaborate on the implications of this philosophy for economics. Hermeneutics not only strengthens the school's methodological critique of mainstream neoclassical economics, it also points the way toward a resolution of many of the internal methodological stalemates over equilibrium in which the school had gotten stuck in the 1970s. And it has given market process scholars a rationale to develop their own distinctive way of doing empirical research, which they call "interpretive" empirical work, based on the methods of archival history and ethnography.

The other significant new theoretical development to arise at this time involved relating ideas from software engineering to market process economics. A group of programmers in Silicon Valley had been using Hayek's work on spontaneous order and complex systems to rethink software production, and had linked the emerging interest in what is called "object-oriented programming" with market process ideas. A group of graduate students at the Market Process Center took up this work and began to find several fascinating insights for market process thinking in this object-oriented literature. In particular the concepts surrounding the idea of "modularity" have proven valuable in rethinking the nature of property rights and evolutionary change in market systems.

These forays into philosophy and software engineering represented a profound revitalization of market process thinking, and led to several extraordinarily innovative dissertations in the economics department. The changes propelled the market process approach into a whole new self-understanding, where it no longer thinks of itself as a subset of the economics profession, but as a radically new way of thinking about society and organizations.

These changes have recently led the Center to move out of the Economics department and establish in 1992 a new department in the College of Arts and Sciences at George Mason University, called the *Program on Social and Organizational Learning*. This department is working with the graduate programs of the Economics department, the Institute of Public Policy, the Sociology and Anthropology department, and the Cultural Studies Program, to develop cross-disciplinary courses in "social learning" and "organizational learning." Social learning is taken to refer to the way markets, language, culture, and other social processes embody distributed knowledge, and the way such knowledge comes to be improved, that is, the way society in some sense learns. Organizational learning in turn is taken to refer to the empirical focus of the department. The faculty are involved in taking social learning theory out into the real world, applying the ideas it gets from market process economics, hermeneutical philosophy, interpretive social science, evolutionary theory, and object-oriented software engineering, to concrete problems of management and organizational change.

The changes in self-understanding at the Market Process Center undoubtedly represented a revitalization of Austrian research. Looking back now at the beginning of the 1980s the school seems then to have been too defensive, perhaps somewhat intimidated by the dominance of neoclassical thinking in economics, maybe a bit frustrated by its inability to get itself heard by mainstream economists. By the end of the decade the school had gained a new self-confidence, and had taken the offensive. Although it has never given up trying to get a fair hearing by mainstream economists, the school has looked around for other more sympathetic audiences, and has found them. Social scientists, organizational theorists, policy makers, philosophers, and managers in the software, telecommunication, and energy industries, are truly listening to the message market process analysts are trying to articulate.

The scholarly publication *Market Process* played the central role in the transformation of the market process school from a hesitant subset of traditional Austrian economics into a bold new research program. It served the function of an incubator for new ideas. It gave the embattled school a chance to sort out its own thinking in internal controversies, free from the dismissive dogmatisms of neoclassical and orthodox Austrian communities. The publication began as a modest "newsletter" reporting on various events in the economics graduate program, gradually including more and more book reviews and short articles, and ended up as an ambitious 148-page multidisciplinary scholarly journal. It was one of the few forums in which the more radical wing of Austrian economics was able to spell out its theoretical vision, and it witnessed the transformation of the school into a vibrant new research program.

The Market Process Center stopped publishing *Market Process* just when it was arguably at its peak. The decision was made that it was time to turn publication efforts out into the many new scholarly communities which market process scholars had located, both within and outside the economics profession. The flourishing that the school is now enjoying owes much to the efforts made in the 1980s to figure out just what market process analysis is all about. The articles included here are among the best of contributions the Austrian school has ever made, and deserve to be given a wider readership.

Acknowledgements

We both entered George Mason University's graduate economics program in 1984. Boettke, a 1983 graduate of Grove City College, was introduced to Austrian economics by Hans Sennholz (a student of Ludwig von Mises and translator of Eugen Boehm-Bawerk's multivolume *Capital and Interest*). Prychitko, a 1984 graduate of Northern Michigan University, became interested in Austrian economics indirectly from the property-rights emphasis of his undergraduate advisor Phil May, and directly through a study of the socialist calculation debate for the department chair, Howard Swaine (students of Armen Alchian). We both came to GMU to participate at the Center for the Study of Market Processes, an Austrian-School research center, and with Don Lavoie in particular, since we held a deep interest in comparative economic systems.

Looking back, our timing was ideal. Because we shared so many philosophical, political and technical economic interests, going through the program together enabled us to openly discuss problems of standard neoclassical theory, which would not have been the case with students in other graduate economics programs. This was, in fact, common among many graduate students at George Mason University at that time. Debates about the nature of economic theory and appropriate methodology were sometimes quite intense and enjoyable, especially those centered around the concepts of market equilibrium and radical subjectivism. We discovered, very shortly, that it was not only neoclassical theory that had problems; soon we began critically assessing the theory and methodology behind the Austrian-School understanding of the market process.

The Center's academic newsletter, *Market Process*, quickly matured into a serious, scholarly journal, which questioned not only the mainstream, but challenged received Austrian economics as well. Published between 1983 and 1990, *Market Process* became the forum for an exploratory dialogue about the nature and scope of Austrian economics, whose contributors ranged from graduate students to tenure-seeking assistant professors to well-established giants in the profession. Don Lavoie acted as the *Market Process* editor and the Center for the Study of Market Process faculty (Richard Fink, Jack High, Karen Vaughn, George Selgin, and Don Boudreaux) formed the editorial-advisory board, while the production staff consisted of graduate students. Karen Palasek and Roy Cordato served as the first team of managing editors from 1983 to 1984. In the fall of 1984, Boettke took over the duties of managing editor. During the 1984–5 and 1985–6 academic years, Boettke served alone as the managing editor, and in 1986–7 Prychitko became co-managing editor. They were succeeded by Kurt Schuler (1987–8), Matthew B. Kibbe (1988–9), and then Emily Chamlee (1990). From 1983 to 1990, *Market Process* evolved from a 12-page newsletter with book reviews and reports on activities at the Center to a 148-page academic journal. The main vehicle of the change in format and content was the long review essay on a recent book or books and the writings of graduate students and junior professors.

We believe that the research appearing in *Market Process*, as well as the Center's Working Paper Series, represents a turning point in Austrian School economics. For the first time in decades, Austrian economists, and those sympathetic to Austrian economics, are starting to assess critically the traditional Austrian research program. The articles gathered in this book reflect, for the most part, an expanded dialogue over the value and limits of Austrian economics, and they raise important challenges and insights in such diverse fields as methodology and choice theory, to monetary theory and political economy.

Market Process was published twice a year for several years, and was freely distributed to a relatively small group of sympathetic economists. We feel these essays deserve a much broader readership, not only because non-Austrian economists and other researchers in the human sciences and organization theory may find them worthwhile, but, and perhaps most importantly, because a research program needs to be exposed to the challenges and criticism of the broader scholarly community in order to advance. We hope this book will help expand the dialogue between Austrians and other economists and social scientists who are disenchanted with mainstream social theory.

We would like to thank the contributors to this book and the Center for the Study of Market Processes for cheerfully allowing us to reprint the *Market Process* essays. Mrs Colleen Morretta deserves a special thanks for her work at the Center and for preserving its wonderful atmosphere. Edward Elgar and Mark Blaug deserve special credit for their enthusiastic support of this project, and we thank Mario Rizzo, Karen Vaughn and Peter Klein for their insightful comments and criticisms. Becky Truax (SUNY), Dena Teeter (SUNY), and Jennifer Medveckis (Hoover) provided valuable secretarial services, and Kevin Blair's (SUNY) research assistance tied up some last-minute loose ends. Prychitko thanks the Institute for Humane Studies at George Mason University for an F. Leroy Hill fellowship, a portion of which was used to fund this project. Boettke thanks the Austrian Economics Program at New York University and the Sarah Scaife Foundation, the Earhart Foundation, and the National Fellows program at the Hoover Institution on War, Revolution and Peace at Stanford University for financial assistance, a portion of which was used to fund this project. We thank our wives, Rosemary Boettke and Julie Prychitko, for allowing us to indulge (yet again) in this project, and we promise our children, Matthew and Stephen Boettke, and Sonja Joanne Prychitko, that they do not have to grow up to become academic economists, not even Austrian economists, if they do not so desire.

Introduction: The present status of Austrian economics: some (perhaps biased) institutional history behind market process theory

Peter J. Boettke and David L. Prychitko

THE EMERGENCE OF THE AUSTRIAN SCHOOL (1870s–1920s)

Published in 1871, Carl Menger's *Principles of Economics* challenged both the German Historical School and orthodox English political economy. His development of economic theory was interpreted, however, as a contribution to a new, neoclassical orthodoxy, as opposed to a different, if not altogether pathbreaking, research program. Menger's contemporaries credited him as a marginal revolutionary, along with France's Leon Walras (*Elements of Pure Economics*, 1871) and Britain's William Stanley Jevons (*Principles of Political Economy*, 1873), who sought to root economic analysis in individual decision-making at the margin. Generations of economists would interpret the three revolutionaries as offering an identical analysis, whose differences, if any, were merely matters of analytical rigor and style.

Even Menger's students, Eugen von Böhm-Bawerk and Friedrich von Wieser, viewed their own work (*Capital and Interest* (1884–1912) and *Natural Value* (1889), respectively) as refinements in the growing school of neoclassical economics. The antagonists of economic science at the time were Marxism (considered a hold-out from classical economics), and historicism and institutionalism (considered anti-theoretical and methodologically unsophisticated). Neoclassical economics was "scientific" economics, while other approaches were, at best, frowned upon as pseudo-scientific, or outdated.

Menger and his students were not fully aware of the uniqueness of their own contribution. The Austrians were, indeed, about to launch a new school of thought. Austrians differed from their colleagues in many respects. They deliberately avoided formal mathematical modelling, for example. Menger rejected mathematics for philosophical reasons, rather than a distaste for equations: mathematics, he believed, could not successfully penetrate the "essence" of human behavior. Compared to their neoclassical colleagues, the Austrians had a more radical understanding of "subjectivism" and value theory. This created incommensurable differences in price theory (e.g., Austrians argued that subjective evaluation explains both market demand *and* supply, rejecting the "Marshallian scissors" metaphor), as well as capital and interest theory (e.g., witness the debates between Böhm-Bawerk and Clark over the marginal productivity theory of interest), and monetary theory (e.g., recall Ludwig von Mises's attempt to secure a microfoundation for monetary economics as far back as 1912, thus rejecting the micro–macro split that characterized neoclassical economics). Long before Sir John Hicks's development of indifference analysis, Mises and Franz Čuhel provided an ordinal concept of utility that held a purposive, rather than mathematical, meaning. For Menger and his students, economics was not so much the application of calculus to questions regarding production and distribution, but, instead, it was supposed to offer an understanding of the way knowledge, ignorance, time, and uncertainty influence human activity and the overall market process.

Decades passed before the Austrian School clashed with neoclassicism. And then two grand debates raged over events of the 1930s and 1940s: with the Great Crash of 1929 and the ensuing Great Depression, economists rushed headlong to determine not only the cause but, more importantly, the cure for the economic malaise. In 1931, Mises's student and close colleague, F. A. Hayek, left Vienna, to visit (and then later to assume the Tooke Chair in Economics and Statistics at) the London School of Economics. Immediately, he became John Maynard Keynes's arch-rival. Applying the Austrian theory of the trade cycle, which had been first developed by Mises, Hayek offered an interpretation of the Great Depression which focused on the monetary policies of the US and UK governments. Hayek's pro-market conclusions were unpopular among government officials – since he called for government to stay out and to develop binding constraints on future credit expansion – and among the general lay population – since Hayek interpreted unemployment and mass bankruptcy as necessary correctives to a malinvested capital order. The fundamental issue at stake in the Keynes–Hayek debate, however, was theoretical, and centered around differences in Austrian and Anglo-Saxon capital and monetary theory.[1]

CRASH AND BURN: AUSTRIANS AS ORTHODOX ECONOMISTS…AND IDEOLOGISTS (1930s–60s)

Despite its controversy, the debate with Keynes nevertheless failed to challenge the Austrians' self-understanding of their place among the mainstream economics profession. Mises and Hayek misinterpreted Keynes's *General Theory* (1936) as simply a return to the inflationist fallacies of the past (which even crude versions of the quantity theory had denounced) and an economics of abundance (which denied that capital resources are scarce). That, too, was a rhetorical ploy. Orthodox economics, according to the Austrians, was all that was needed to expose the fundamental problems with Keynes.[2]

The Great Depression influenced not only Keynes. It also legitimized appeals for socialism. A new wave of criticism damned capitalism as inherently chaotic and unjust – subjecting people to forces beyond their control. Despite growing research in Austrian cycle theory, business fluctuations were reaffirmed as inherent features of capitalism.

Yet nothing in the popular proposals of socialism would challenge the self-understanding of Austrian economists as orthodox members of the economics community. In the 1890s Böhm-Bawerk marshalled neoclassical economic theory to offer a criticism of Marx's analytical arguments about value and prices under capitalism. In 1920, Mises turned to socialist proposals for economic planning, demonstrating that without private ownership in the means of production socialist planners could not rationally calculate the alternative use of scarce resources. But, by the 1930s, Oskar Lange used the techniques of neoclassical economics to demonstrate that Mises's criticism was invalid under the normal assumptions of general equilibrium. In Lange's model, a central planning board was substituted for Walras's fictional auctioneer. By trial and error methods, central planners can discover general equilibrium prices, which state-owned enterprises take as given parameters. The enterprises are bound by two simple rules – minimize average total costs and produce to the point such that marginal cost equals price. Lange demonstrates that a socialist society can achieve a general equilibrium that is both allocatively and productively efficient.

Lange's criticism of Mises took the Austrians by surprise. A remarkable achievement in neoclassical theory, Lange's model was also widely accepted by the economics profession. Frank Knight and Joseph Schumpeter concurred, in principle, with Lange's assessment of the analytical issue, and younger economists, such as Abba Lerner, began to develop Lange's argument further.[3] Later, both Mises and Hayek tried to articulate more clearly the main tenets of Austrian economics. But, by this time (the 1940s) it was too late for the contemporary generation of economists. Most agreed that the

Austrians lost… and the debate was relegated to historians of economic thought.

Austrian economics was soundly defeated by both Keynesianism and neoclassical socialism. These arguments were not as disconnected as the Austrians may have believed. Neoclassical socialism challenged the efficiency arguments of the private market. In its weakest form, the argument of Lange and Lerner could be interpreted as demonstrating that socialism could perform as well as the private market. But there was a stronger argument. In the face of monopoly power under capitalism – that is, a lack of real, perfectly competitive markets – socialism would be even more efficient than real existing markets. Thus, neoclassical socialism devastated the formal microeconomic efficiency claims for the market economy. Keynesian economics swung from the other side, and challenged the macroeconomic stability claims of the market.

The Austrians were not idle during this period. Mises had published his magnum opus, *Human Action: A Treatise on Economics*, in 1949 and Hayek published *The Pure Theory of Capital* in 1941, *Individualism and Economic Order* in 1948 and *The Counter-Revolution of Science* in 1952, yet hardly anyone in the economics profession listened. The arguments of Mises and Hayek about the effectiveness of free markets (as espoused in their popular policy books such as Mises's *Bureaucracy* and *Omnipotent Government* in 1944, and Hayek's *Road to Serfdom* in 1944) were interpreted as ideologically motivated polemics, rather than serious scientific contributions. Mises and Hayek were no longer viewed as formidable economists, but rather as political pundits on the far right. From 1950 to 1975, Austrian economics sunk so far from the mainstream that it became subterranean, at best.

A few emigrant Austrians did enjoy professional success in the 1950s (Fritz Machlup and Oskar Morgenstern leap to mind), but they did not stress their "Austrianism," and avoided policy issues. On the other hand, Milton Friedman and George Stigler grew in professional prominence in the 1950s developing arguments favorable to the free market, but from an entirely different analytical perspective than the Austrians. The "crash and burn" of Austrian economics in the late 1940s cannot be solely explained simply by the policy positions. The professional successes of Friedman and Stigler, and the entire Chicago School of Economics, counter the policy bias. Nor can the Austrians' failure be explained by some ignorance of the intellectual scene in the United States (at least Machlup and Morgenstern counter the cultural gap explanation – they both rose to professional prominence at Princeton). The real problem, as we interpret it, is that Mises and Hayek were closely wedded to a certain methodological tradition in economics, an anti-positivism that was completely rejected by the 1950s. Their work simply appeared anachronistic to the majority of economists, who preached positivism and formal modelling.

Mises emigrated to the United States in 1940. He originally accepted a position at the National Bureau of Economic Research and offered a graduate seminar as a visiting professor in the Graduate School of Business at New York University. In 1945, Mises left the NBER and taught at NYU full-time (though with a salary provided by outside foundations after 1949), which lasted until his retirement in 1969.[4] Hayek, on the other hand, left the LSE and the economics profession in 1950 to assume a professorship on the interdisciplinary Committee on Social Thought at the University of Chicago.[5] A self-consciously Austrian School of economics failed to take root in the graduate education of economists or social scientists in the United States. Hayek did not teach economics students, but rather political and intellectual historians (such as Ralph Raico or Ronald Hamowy). Mises taught a handful of doctoral economics students during his 25 years at NYU, most notably Louis Spadaro, Hans Sennholz, George Reisman, Israel Kirzner and Murray Rothbard (who was not technically his student but pursuing a Ph.D. at Columbia under the supervision of Joseph Dorfman).

Except for Kirzner and Rothbard, neither Mises's nor Hayek's students pushed or challenged the frontiers of economic theory. Instead, they contributed, in their own way, to a resurgence of classical liberal political theory. Raico and Hamowy, for example, edited the *New Individualist Review*, and Spadaro, Sennholz and Reisman pursued teaching careers at Fordham, Grove City College, and Pepperdine, respectively. Sennholz, in particular, produced a stream of undergraduate students from Grove City College who later pursued their Ph.D.s and/or became leaders in American classical liberal foundations and think-tanks. These individuals, however, remained uninterested in refining and testing Austrian economic theory. Gone was the one ingredient that assists scientific growth in a body of thought: curiosity of the subject matter, independent of its political and ideological consequences. Austrian economics was now part of a subculture that was mainly interested in resuscitating the argument for a free society based on classical liberal principles.

The main institutional components of this "movement" were the Foundation for Economic Education in New York, founded by Leonard Read in 1946, and the Mont Pélèrin Society, founded by Hayek to gather an international group of scholars and intellectuals working on developing arguments for the free society. The Mont Pélèrin Society was designed to downplay analytical and methodological differences amongst the scholars and forge cooperation between them to further the argument for a free society.[6]

The Foundation for Economic Education, while uniquely Austrian in outlook, pursued a strategy of persuading the common man and did not try to affect the scholarly community concerning the nature of economic reasoning. The free market ideology was seen as important, not the analytical understanding of the market process. FEE became the intellectual home of Mises and Henry Hazlitt.

Since Austrian economics, however, was seen by some as providing the most consistent and uncompromising defense of the free society, some foundations and institutes did target research along Austrian lines. The William Volker Fund, for example, did try to affect change in the scholarly community, but, similar to the Mont Pelerin Society, it was not so much concerned with Austrian economics as such. It, too, explored classical liberalism, and therefore, supported research among those schools with definite classical liberal traditions: Chicago, Austrian and Public Choice. The same was also true for the Institute for Humane Studies, founded by F. A. Harper in the early 1960s when the Volker Fund dissolved – though IHS was much more closely associated with Austrian economics. Harper's mission was to forge an interdisciplinary approach to social theory that would resurrect classical liberalism and place it on a firm foundation of economics, ethics, politics and history. Austrian economic theory, he thought, must play a significant role in this endeavor.

In the meantime, standard economic theory had become increasingly technical, following Paul Samuelson's impressive *Foundations of Economic Analysis* (1947). In fact, this technical revolution was wedded to the previous developments of neoclassical economics that emerged in the debates with the Austrians: Samuelson pioneered the neoclassical synthesis with Keynesian economics and endorsed the Lange–Lerner position on market socialism. Moreover, Samuelson further developed the case against the free market with his formalization of the theory of market failure. In this intellectual environment, it would be difficult for younger Austrian economists to know how to even begin addressing the economics profession.

Younger Austrians during the 1950s and 1960s would instead try to communicate with the general public through seminars and publications like *The Freeman* and to lure particularly bright young people into the college classroom through an ideological defense of the market process. But we believe this was a self-defeating strategy: without further analytical developments of an Austrian theory of the market process, mere ideological defenses would collapse under the argumentative weight of the economics profession and, as a consequence, even further marginalize Austrian economics. Austrian economics, by the 1960s, was neither developed enough nor strategically placed to precipitate a change in the profession. It amounted to little more than a bombardment of soap bubbles against the mainstream establishment.[7]

In retrospect, the Austrians needed to embark upon a radical paradigmatic challenge against the core of neoclassicism, regardless of its ideological consequences. Ideally, a sustainable *scholarly* movement should instill in individuals the desire to *understand* the world *first*, independently of their ideological desire to change the world (students of Marx will recognize a modification of Marx's eleventh thesis on Feuerbach here). Unfortunately, Austrian economics, as interpreted by its handful of students in the 1950s, needed no refinement, critical reflection, nor change: it was considered free-market wisdom to be dispensed to anybody who would listen, in the hope of rebuilding a political program for laissez faire.

TOWARD PARADIGMATIC CHALLENGE: AUSTRIANS AS RADICAL ECONOMISTS (1960s–80s)

Hints of an Austrian counter-revolution in economics surfaced in the early 1960s with the work of Murray Rothbard and Israel Kirzner. Their paths differed somewhat, but their message was the same: the time had come for a reconsideration of the basic questions about the nature and scope of economic theory. Kirzner pursued this re-orientation through a series of tightly focused monographs: first, a book on the meaning of the subject matter of economic science (*The Economic Point of View*, 1960, his Ph.D. thesis written under Mises at NYU), followed by an enquiry into price theory (*Market Theory and the Price System*, 1963) and capital theory (*An Essay on Capital*, 1966). Then, in 1973, Kirzner published his landmark study, *Competition and Entrepreneurship*. If economic theory was an apple, Kirzner sought to get at the core with the paring knife of careful analysis.

Murray Rothbard used an ideological sledge hammer. At the age of 32, Rothbard offered the economics profession not a carefully focused monograph, but a formidable treatise which tried to recast neoclassical economics along Misesian lines. *Man, Economy and State*, published in 1962, was a *tour de force* over 900 pages long. Rothbard's book gave students the impression that he simply read and digested everything in the economics journals (and history and politics). The book covered every field, from basic choice theory to business cycle theory, from the failures of wage and price controls to the problems of socialism.

Considering the impact of their two different approaches, it seems that the skilled use of the analytical knife worked better than an indiscriminately swung sledge hammer. Kirzner's careful analysis of price theory and especially the fundamental role of entrepreneurship in a systematic theory of the market process captured the attention of neoclassical microeconomists. Kirzner was too good a scholar and had too careful a mind to be simply ignored (although even he too would be dismissed by some).[8] Rothbard, on the other hand, was jettisoned as a wild-eyed ideologue. Rothbard had embraced from the beginning of his career an interdisciplinary and ideological turn, writing a series of works beyond technical economics which, nevertheless, proved to be fundamental for the resurgence of Austrian economics. He hoped to build a comprehensive scientific defense of the free society that included not only economics, but history, politics and philosophy as well. *The Panic of 1819* (his doctoral thesis at Columbia, published 1962) and *America's Great Depression* (1963) employed Austrian trade cycle theory to interpret crucial historical events. *Power and Market* (1970) provided some important ideas for the economic analysis of public policy. And, *For a New Liberty* (1973) became the manifesto of a new libertarian movement which rejuvenated classical liberalism and lifted it from a conservative stagnation.

Rothbard's libertarian polemics did inspire an entire generation of young scholars to study Austrian economics in depth. Rothbard was a necessary, though not sufficient, component of the renewed interest in Austrian economics as a scholarly vocation. Once students and young professors were enticed to examine the analytical foundations of Austrian economics, most turned to Kirzner, who was quietly working on the intricacies of theory at New York University. In the fall of 1974, Hayek was awarded the Nobel Prize in Economics for his contributions to monetary and trade cycle theory. Combined with the libertarian intellectual movement Rothbard had created, and the analytical puzzles Kirzner worked on, the awarding of the Nobel Prize to Hayek created the conditions for an Austrian resurgence from the underground of the economics profession.

In the summer of 1974 the Institute for Humane Studies and the Liberty Fund undertook a series of initiatives to help place Austrian economics within the mainstream of the economics profession. A conference in South Royalton, Vermont was held, at which a new generation of young economists was introduced to Rothbard, Kirzner and Ludwig Lachmann. Lachmann, Hayek's student at the LSE in the 1930s, was teaching in South Africa and had done work in the 1940s and 1950s on Austrian capital theory, leading to the publication of *Capital and Its Structure* in 1956, and had recently been reexamining the implications of radical subjectivism for economic theory under the influence of G.L.S. Shackle (also a student of Hayek's at the LSE), especially Shackle's *Epistemics and Economics* which was published in 1972.[9]

The conference was successful and produced a volume, *The Foundations of Modern Austrian Economics* (1976), edited by Ed Dolan. During the same year of the South Royalton conference, Larry Moss organized a fruitful session on Mises for the Southern Economic Association, and later published those conference papers and comments in *The Economics of Ludwig von Mises: Toward a Critical Reappraisal* (1976). Other annual conferences followed, which in turn produced additional volumes: *New Directions in Austrian Economics* (1978), edited by Louis Spadaro, *Time, Uncertainty and Disequilibrium* (1979), edited by Mario Rizzo, and *Method, Process and Austrian Economics* (1982) and *Subjectivism, Intelligibility and Economic*

Understanding (1986), both edited by Israel Kirzner. Kirzner's ability to establish the Austrian Economics Program at New York University was key to the resurgence. This program allowed Ph.D. students to work on dissertations in the Austrian tradition that would not be possible at other institutions. Also, Kirzner arranged with Ludwig Lachmann an annual visit to the NYU department for each spring semester, where he would teach a graduate seminar on economic theory. A regular workshop was established, and Kirzner and Lachmann were joined on the faculty by Mario Rizzo and Gerald O'Driscoll and later Lawrence H. White.

Kirzner also brought in several visiting faculty members (such as Stephen Littlechild, Leland Yeager, Don Bellante, Roger Garrison, Uskali Mäki, and Stephan Boehm), and the weekly workshop in Austrian economics soon became the leading forum for new Austrian research not only in the United States, but throughout the world. New collections from research conferences mentioned above were produced, classic works in the Austrian tradition were reprinted, and new books published. O'Driscoll published a monograph on Hayek's contributions to economics, *Economics as a Coordination Problem* (1977, based on his Ph.D. thesis at UCLA). Kirzner continued his analysis of the entrepreneurial process in *Perception, Opportunity and Profit* (1979) and *Discovery and the Capitalist Process* (1985).

Don Lavoie, Richard Fink, John Egger, and George Selgin were among doctoral graduates of the Austrian Economics Program at NYU. Several other students spent extended periods of time at the NYU program as visitors while they completed their studies elsewhere. Jack High, for example, while a Ph.D. student at UCLA, spent a year at NYU studying in the Austrian program. Richard Ebeling also spent a considerable amount of time in the NYU program and has pursued an academic career, accepting the Ludwig von Mises Professorship at Hillsdale College. And, Walter Grinder (who is currently the vice president of the Institute for Humane Studies), was one of Kirzner's graduate students in the 1960s, and played a significant role in the resurgence of Austrian economics in the 1970s. In particular, Grinder was largely responsible for introducing Ludwig Lachmann's work to modern Austrian economics through his collection of Lachmann's papers, *Capital, Expectations and the Market Process* (1977), which included a lengthy and highly informative introductory essay on Lachmann's research program of radical subjectivism.

THE ROLE OF THE CENTER FOR THE STUDY OF MARKET PROCESSES IN THE RESURGENCE

This next generation of Austrian economists embarked upon an innovative scholarly movement. Our history, however, will only deal with one strand of these developments in the 1970s.[10] In 1979 Richard Fink founded an undergraduate program in Austrian economics at Rutgers University. Fink had himself been an undergraduate student at Rutgers, where he was introduced to Austrian economics by Walter Grinder, when Grinder worked as a professor at Rutgers for several years. Fink then went on to graduate school at UCLA, receiving an MA in economics, and then pursued and obtained his Ph.D. at NYU. Fink brought Joe Salerno (a new Ph.D. from Rutgers who was working on aspects of Austrian monetary theory), Richard Ebeling, and Don Lavoie to teach in the program at Rutgers. But Rutgers did not prove to be the right environment for a fledgling Austrian program. In 1980, through the insightful initiative of Karen Vaughn, a deal was engineered so that Fink could move his center to George Mason University in Fairfax, Virginia. Lavoie and Jack High made the move with Fink to GMU, and, along with Karen Vaughn, founded the Center for the Study of Market Processes.

In addition to the four core faculty members, Tom DiLorenzo was also a young faculty member in the economics department at George Mason University. DiLorenzo was a recent graduate of the doctoral program at Virginia Tech and a scholar of Public Choice economics and industrial organization. He was interested in Austrian ideas such as competition as a process and quite sympathetic to the general philosophical thrust of the Austrian school.

At first, Fink's center was intended as an undergraduate training center from which young graduates could pursue their doctoral studies at either NYU or other top research universities or go on to careers in law or public policy. Fink's program was quite successful: Tyler Cowen went on to Harvard to receive his Ph.D., Dan Klein received his Ph.D. from NYU, and Kathy Curtis went on to law school where she excelled. But something happened shortly after the Center moved to GMU that would significantly change its purpose.

James Buchanan, the leader of the Virginia School of Political Economy who, along with Gordon Tullock, pioneered public choice economics, had grown restless at Virginia Tech. Buchanan was also sympathetic to Austrian economics and shared with Austrians many of the same concerns (for example, Buchanan forged a consistently subjectivist notion of opportunity cost in his 1969 monograph, *Cost and Choice*, and further promoted subjective cost theory in a book edited with G.F. Thirlby, *LSE Essays on Cost* [1973]). Vaughn (who would become department chair in the fall of 1982) seized another entrepreneurial opportunity by luring Buchanan, Tullock and their Center for Study of Public Choice to George Mason University in the spring of 1982. George Johnson, GMU's maverick president, jumped at the chance to grab a group of scholars of the caliber of Buchanan and Tullock, realizing Mason's fledgling Ph.D. program would be instantly successful with the addition of Buchanan, Tullock, and the Public Choice Center entourage.

GMU indeed became a major American research center for public choice and Austrian economics by 1983. In addition to Buchanan and Tullock, Kenneth Boulding also arrived at George Mason University as a Visiting Robinson Professor. Yet another boost for Austrian graduate students: Boulding's tutor was Lionel Robbins, and like Buchanan, he was a student of Frank Knight (in fact, Boulding made his professional debut in defending Austrian capital theory against Knight's criticisms). Moreover, Boulding was deeply sympathetic to thorough-going subjectivism and questions of the role of knowledge in sustaining social coordination (as is evident in his book, *The Image* (1956)). If ever there was an ideal teacher and role model for young Ph.D. students, then Boulding was it. His sparkling sense of humor matched his passion for peaceful cooperation among people and nations. He invited students to his house for cookies and cider, and to read from Adam Smith, and went to lunch to talk about economics, life and nuclear disarmament, and even joined the students in an informal readings group on general systems theory.

What was most impressive about Buchanan, Tullock and Boulding was their genuine love of ideas and the encouragement they gave students to pursue ideas wherever they may lead. Their presence at GMU during our time there enhanced the educational experience immeasurably. And the fact that "The Great Unwashed" – Buchanan – was awarded the Nobel Prize in 1986 added to our sense that we were at the right place at the right time.

Fink transformed the Center for the Study of Market Processes into a graduate research and teaching program and actively recruited new doctoral students. Two formal courses in the Austrian theory of the market process were created, and a field in Austrian economics was established – the first at any university in the US or UK. In addition, a weekly colloquium for the presentation of Austrian research brought in visitors and allowed graduate students to test out their ideas. A working paper series was established, and *Market Process*, under the editorship of Don Lavoie, and the managing editorship of a series of graduate students, was established as a combination newsletter for the Center, forum for new ideas, and quasi-journal for graduate students in Austrian economics.

Fink hoped that the Center's graduate students would accomplish three things (in addition, of course, to passing their field exams and completing their dissertations): first, teach a course on their own; second, present a paper at a professional meeting; and third, publish a paper in a professional journal. These were not idle wishes. The young Center faculty devoted resources (time and money) to make sure that every student accomplished those tasks. In the summer or during the year, students enjoyed many opportunities beyond their first year to teach, if they desired. Writing workshops were conducted in the summer so students would learn how to write for the professional journals, or do policy studies for the think tanks in Washington. The

Center often arranged research assistantships for the summer so students could pursue their studies and participate in these extra programs, such as the writing workshop. Conference fees and travel expenses were paid for by the Center for any student participating on a session at a professional meeting; submission fees for journal articles were often picked up by the Center. There was simply no excuse for the students not to get work done and meet Fink's expectations, and we think that for the most part all of our contemporaries met those challenges.

Although ideological overtones were still present, Center faculty were committed to the intellectual development of their students. George Mason University was in many aspects an ideal place for this. We would not deny that the unashamed commitment to Austrian economics, mixed with a strong ideological kinship among the students, created an atmosphere of excitement that would be hard to match. (Accidentally entering a room full of students embroiled in a debate about fine points of economic theory, Gordon Tullock once sneered that "You Austrians are truly nuts." Yet, as he turned and walked out the door, we heard him mumble "But at least you're enthusiastic.") Students ran study groups to help with the core courses in standard theory, reading groups in the classics of Austrian economics, reading groups in current neoclassical journal articles, and so on. Since classes met during the evenings, and our research assignments for professors were during the day (20 hours per week), Austrian students spent literally the whole day, and much of the night, engaged in serious study as well as bull sessions over such issues as the possibility of anarcho-capitalism versus libertarian socialism versus minimal statism. Within this practically anarchic intellectual arena, students working in Austrian economics could challenge not only the neoclassical mainstream, but traditional Austrians economics as well. (Boulding, for example, remarked that he enjoyed George Mason University because it seemed to have "no tradition, and therefore everything is up for grabs!") Young Austrian doctoral students would be just as likely to debate the epistemological status of Edmund Husserl's transcendental *a priori* as they would the theoretical consistency of Franklin Fisher's modelling of money in general equilibrium. Where else would one find a graduate economics student with the latest article by Joseph Stiglitz sandwiched in a dog-eared copy of Hans-Georg Gadamer's *Truth and Method*? Most of us thought that this was a natural graduate economics environment: David Colander and Arjo Klamer (who had interviewed us for their *The Making of an Economist* research), told us a very different story about orthodox graduate study in economics.

In addition to High and Lavoie, George Selgin and Don Boudreaux joined the Center in 1986. Selgin was working on his book, *The Theory of Free Banking*, which broke new ground in the examination of the economic operation of competitive note issue. His command of the history of monetary thought was truly impressive, and though he demanded rigorous argument from the students, he was always ready to work with them and discuss their ideas. He was a great intellectual asset to the program. Boudreaux was working in the area of industrial organization and the theory of the firm. His research sought to synthesize Austrian ideas with the economics of organization literature that Oliver Williamson developed. Like Selgin, he was quite open to working with the students and discussing their ideas, and was vital to the program. In addition to Selgin and Boudreaux, Tyler Cowen visited the Center as a post-doctoral fellow after completing his degree at Harvard, then later joined the department faculty. Cowen was simply interested in everything and worked with the students freely.

Visitors flowed into the Center. Both John Egger and Sudha Shenoy taught courses in Austrian economics to GMU graduate students. Leland Yeager also visited the Center, and Viktor Vanberg was a visiting scholar at the Center before moving to the Public Choice Center the following year. A long list of exciting, non-mainstream scholars, including Brian Loasby, Jack Wiseman, Ulrich Witt, Don McCloskey, Arjo Klamer, Richard Ebeling, Gary Madison, and Barry Smith, cheerfully accepted invitations to present their latest research before Center faculty and students. Seminar papers by Israel Kirzner and W.H. Hutt also stand out as memorable. And Ludwig Lachmann's annual seminar presentation was always an eagerly awaited special event.

Besides the social environment of GMU, it was generally an exciting time to work in Austrian economics, for finally a stream of research monographs was emerging from the pens of a new generation of Austrian economists and being published by leading university and academic presses. Dom Armentano's *Antitrust and Monopoly* was published in 1982, Bruce Caldwell's *Beyond Positivism* (which contained a rather lengthy discussion of the Austrians) was published in 1983, Lawrence White's *Free Banking in Britain* was published in 1984, Don Lavoie's *Rivalry and Central Planning* and *National Economic Planning: What is Left?* were published in 1985, and Gerald O'Driscoll and Mario Rizzo's *The Economics of Time and Ignorance* was published in 1985. In addition, Richard Langlois published a collection of essays in 1986, *Economics as a Process*, which promoted a synthesis of Austrian economics, transaction cost economics, positive political economy and the new economic history. George Selgin's book *The Theory of Free Banking* was published in 1988. Jack High revised his doctoral thesis throughout the 1980s to take into account new developments in market adjustment theory, and published *Maximizing, Action and Market Adjustment* in 1990, while Karen Vaughn's *Austrian Economics in America: The Migration of a Tradition* recently appeared in 1994.

Also, a new generation of students of these "students" emerged with doctoral dissertations written in the 1980s at NYU, GMU or Auburn which were transformed into published books and articles in the scholarly journals in the 1990s. Esteban Thomsen published *Prices and Knowledge* (1992). Roy Cordato published *Externalities and Welfare Economics in an Open Ended Universe* (1992). Steve Horwitz published *Monetary Evolution, Free Banking and Economic Order* (1992). Mark Thornton published *The Economics of Prohibition* (1992). Boettke published *The Political Economy of Soviet Socialism: The Formative Years, 1918–1928* (1990) and *Why Perestroika Failed: The Politics and Economics of Socialist Transformation* (1993). Prychitko published *Marxism and Workers' Self-Management* (1991). In addition, articles, comments and reviews by these last two generations of Austrian economists have appeared in professional journals such as *The Southern Economic Journal*, *The Journal of Economic Perspectives*, *Journal of the History of Economic Thought*, *Journal of Institutional and Theoretical Economics*, *Public Choice*, *Methodus*, *Global Economic Policy*, *Cultural Dynamics*, *Review of Social Economy*, *History of Political Economy*, *Research in the History of Economic Thought and Methodology*, and even *The American Economic Review* and *Journal of Political Economy*. Clearly, Austrian economics experienced tremendous growth in the 1980s, not just in numbers but in thought.

Much of this work is written by individuals who were products of the George Mason program and the Center for the Study of Market Processes. Looking back, we believe that the internal atmosphere of the Center and the overall environment at the university provided fertile ground for the next generation of Austrian economists to ask fundamental questions – a rare event. *Market Process* was one of the places where they could submit their conjectures to community review and rebuttal. *Market Process* emerged from a newsletter with book-review essays and grew to become a forum for original research. We have selected a range of articles that represent the breadth of issues discussed in its pages and its spirit from when it started in 1983 to its final issue in 1990. This was a period of intense inquisitiveness among young Austrians. Gone from contemporary Austrian economics were any notions of being part of the received orthodoxy. Gone were any notions that what was needed was simply a better spin on the traditional Austrian doctrine. It was time simply to try to understand market processes and social institutions independently of where that might lead. Fundamental questions in the methodology and method of economics were asked. New avenues of empirical research were explored. New opportunities in the mainstream economics literature were tested.

The issues discussed in the pages of *Market Process* reflect the concerns and directions of contemporary Austrian economics. Much of what one sees here is the first statement of lines of research that many individuals are now pursuing, and which should yield significant dividends in the near future in terms of a better understanding of market processes and social institutions.

Not since the 1920s had young economists been offered the opportunity to gather together to pursue questions and develop arguments in the Austrian tradition within such a nurturing environment. We hope that this collection conveys the spirit of open inquiry that characterized this period, and continues to characterize contemporary Austrian economics.

NOTES

1. Keynes was highly adept at the art of controversy during this debate: he did not really address Hayek's theoretical work, but instead he challenged Hayek's policy conclusions through a critique of the theoretical work of A.C. Pigou. In this manner, Keynes avoided addressing the fine points in Hayek's analysis of money and capital. If Hayek's policy conclusions could be wedded to a weaker theoretical structure, then Keynes could dismiss Hayek's non-interventionist policy on the basis of poorly informed theory.
2. In this regard it may be illuminating to consider the correspondence between Mises and Hayek during the period from 1939 to 1946. It is quite clear from Mises's letters that he sees the "progressive" views of Veblen–Hansen and Laski–Keynes as the major threat to economic thinking and policy in the West. In a letter dated 16 December 1941, for example, Mises wrote that he had begun work on a volume "critically dealing with the whole complex of 'anti-orthodox' doctrines and their consequences." And, in the same letter, Mises refers to an Alvin Hansen lecture he recently attended by saying that two centuries of economic theory could not dispose of the mercantilist prejudices contained in Hansen's analysis. Again, viewing himself as part of an embattled orthodox minority, Mises, in a letter dated 27 July 1944, states that he has taken to asking himself of what use is economic science, since the progressive intellectual culture disregards its teachings. Clearly Mises and (from the sense of the letters) Hayek considered themselves the pallbearers of a social and public policy wisdom that was being buried under a pile of monographs written by progressive intellectuals ignorant of the main teachings of economic science. See the Hayek Collection, Correspondence, Box 38, file 24, Hoover Archives, Stanford University. Hayek never reviewed the *General Theory*, but his reaction to that work at the time is contained in *The Pure Theory of Capital* (1941). Just as Mises had, Hayek mistakenly interpreted Keynes's analysis as not worthy of serious scientific criticism.
3. Lerner would go so far as to describe Marxism as the economics of capitalism and neoclassical theory as the economics of socialism.
4. There is no doubt that Mises was treated rather poorly by the American academic establishment. But this assessment needs to be tempered a bit by the circumstances surrounding Mises. First, in correspondence with Hayek, Mises suggests that a position for him is available at the New School for Social Research, but he does not want to take it if he can avoid it (letter dated 27 October 1940). In that same letter, Mises highlights that the real problem in finding an acceptable position is his advanced age. Also, in a letter dated 22 December 1940, Mises informs Hayek that he had already given lectures at Harvard, Fletcher School, Princeton, Columbia and NYU, and that he had decided to accept a position at NBER where he would have time to work on his own projects full-time. Hayek collection, Box 38, file 24, Hoover Archives, Stanford University.
5. So that we do not give the wrong impression, it should be pointed out that like Mises, Hayek's salary at Chicago was paid through outside foundations. There is simply no doubt that the academic culture was biased against individuals like Mises and Hayek. But the bias is not the only causal factor in their treatment.
6. This, for Mises, was a major weakness of the project from the beginning. See his criticism of the plan for the Mont Pelerin Society dated 31 December 1946. Hayek Correspondence, Box 38, file 24, Hoover Archives, Stanford University. On the founding of the Mont

Pélèrin Society see Hayek, "Opening Address to a Conference at Mont Pelerin," in *The Fortunes of Liberalism*, Peter Klein, ed., *The Collected Works of F.A. Hayek*, vol. 4 (Chicago: University of Chicago Press, 1992): 237–48.

7. It is true that the Chicago School was strategically located at a leading university. But their line of argument could not overthrow the orthodoxy of interventionist thinking. Certainly, Chicago School economists could pick holes in the mainstream Keynesian synthesis or demonstrate the empirical fallacies behind both Keynesian interpretations of the macroeconomy and the standard literature on the microeconomic inefficiency of free markets. The Chicago School, however, did not systematically challenge the neoclassical model: Chicago economists chose to play on the same (formal) turf as the rest of the profession. Even Friedman acknowledged that the debate between Chicago and Cambridge (Mass.) was empirical, not theoretical. The Chicago School headed by Friedman and Stigler was as vulnerable to "school desolation" as the Austrian School was a generation before, when they erroneously considered themselves part of the neoclassical orthodoxy. The contemporary trend in economic thinking toward interventionist policy found in the work of Stiglitz (information economics), Summers (new Keynesian economics), and Krugman (new international trade theory) simply can not be countered with the arguments associated with Chicago School economics. For a discussion of this see Boettke, "The Trend of Economic Thinking" (unpublished manuscript, Hoover Institution, 1993).
8. See, for example, Benjamin Klein, "Competition and Entrepreneurship: book review," *Journal of Political Economy*, 82 (December 1975): 1305–9.
9. Hayek and Lachmann actively corresponded throughout the 1950s and 1960s on issues ranging from methodology and capital theory to public policy. They agreed that the task of the social sciences was to view institutions and social practices as vehicles for the transmission of knowledge. Their correspondence mainly deals with how one approaches such a study and what existing literature they could harness to build the argument. See Hayek Collection, Box 32, file 2, Hoover Archives, Stanford University.
10. A comprehensive history of modern Austrian economics would need to address the founding of the Foundation for Economic Education, Center for Libertarian Studies, Ludwig von Mises Institute, the Carl Menger Institute (Vienna, Austria), the establishment of the CATO Institute and other public policy "think tanks," the development of new graduate and undergraduate programs at Auburn University, University of Nevada at Las Vegas, California State University at Hayward, Grove City College, Hillsdale College, Loyola University (New Orleans), St. Lawrence University and SUNY-Oswego, and the emergence of publications such as *Journal of Libertarian Studies*, *Review of Austrian Economics*, *Austrian Economics Newsletter*, *Critical Review*, and *Advances in Austrian Economics*, etc. We do not offer such a history. The best history to date of the Austrian revival is found in Karen Vaughn, *Austrian Economics in America: The Migration of a Tradition* (Cambridge University Press, 1994).

PART ONE

Equilibrium, Evolution and Market Process

1. The market process: an Austrian view

Jack High

INTRODUCTION

Charges against economic theory for being deficient in one way or another have become so predictable and common as to resemble a litany. We may be excused if we grow weary of the repetition, and we could rightly ask for a cessation of the charges were it not for their substance. No impartial jury could fail to be impressed by the weight and variety of the criticisms levelled against neoclassical theory. Nor could the defense take refuge in the claim that many of the criticisms cancel one another. Someone who believed all the charges against orthodox theory might conclude nothing was right; he would never conclude nothing was wrong.

The other and brighter side of the criticism is the array of alternatives being offered to replace or amend neoclassical theory. Its elements are numerous, diverse, and changing, and out of them economists may forge something that markedly improves economic theory. The competitive process of ideas does not guarantee improvement, of course, but even the competition has aroused discontent. Mark Blaug has complained that "we seem to be entering an era in which there will be too many, rather than too few, competing economic research programs" (Blaug, 1980, pp. 264–5). Even neoclassical economists, it seems, sometimes want a restricted choice set.

The critics of neoclassical theory are too diverse to qualify for anything that might be called a school. Nevertheless, many of these critics can be brought together under the heading of "market process." The (interrelated) characteristics which unite market process economists are:

1. A prominent place given to the ignorance and uncertainty that permeate most economic decisions. The plans of producers and consumers consist partly of knowledge, and partly of speculation.
2. Recognition of the complexity of a market economy. In one way or another, market process economists recognize that the market is a vast and complex order of interdependent plans of millions of agents.
3. An explanation of plan coordination (and breakdown in the coordina-

tion) that includes institutions. Institutions are used to explain the transmission of information, which goes into the formation and revision of plans.

This paper – briefly, selectively, and imperfectly – undertakes to present the modern Austrian view of the market process, to relate this view to the work of others who may be classified under this heading, and to differentiate market process from other theory. We hope to show that market process theories constitute a promising alternative to neoclassical economics.

THE MACROECONOMIC CONTEXT

Austrian economics is distinguished from neoclassical economics by a number of characteristics, one of which is that Austrian economics defines the market as a spontaneous order. This proposition is meant to convey that the market, although it is the product of human action, is decidedly *not* the product of human design. Of course, the conception of the market as a spontaneous order can be considered the common property of all economists who trace their lineage to Adam Smith. Nevertheless, this property has suffered undeserved neglect since the marginal revolution, and has been positively abused by much of neoclassical theory (cf. Loasby, 1976, p. 47). I think it fair to say that at the hands of Menger and his followers, the market as a spontaneous order has received its most explicit and systematic development since the marginal revolution.

If we take as a central proposition of our economic theory that the market is the result of an historical development which, in its entirety, was no part of anyone's intention to develop, we can derive a number of insights about individual decision-making (microtheory) and about the way these decisions interact on an economy-wide scale (macrotheory). The following pages attempt to lay out some basic features of market process analysis, all of which can, I think, be traced back to the fundamental conception of the market as a spontaneous order. (Other features of this theory, such as method, the analysis of government, the nature of property rights, will not be discussed, although these subjects, too, are influenced by the way the market is depicted as a process.)

To say that the market is a spontaneous order is to say that the individual pursuit of plans has consequences which no one can know in detail, but which do result in discernable patterns. If the consequences could be known in detail, the order would not be spontaneous; if the consequences did not result in discernable patterns, there would be no order. The tasks of the economist are to explain (a) how it is possible for an order to exist, despite the fact that no one intends it or oversees it; (b) how it develops; (c) what causes breakdowns in the order.

Institutions must play an important role in any explanation of the market order. They are the means by which agents are able to gather sufficient information to cooperate with one another, despite each agent's ignorance of so much detail. Without such established practices as using money, trading on organized markets, and producing within the structure of firms, no widespread division of labor would be possible.

Money and monetary calculation are particularly important to the operation of the market and have received much attention in the study of the market order. Carl Menger has explained how traders will develop money, despite the fact that no one invents it. Even in a market with relatively few goods (as compared to a modern market), specialized producers will find it advantageous to trade their product away for a highly marketable good, which can then be used to purchase other goods. In the early stages of market development, only a few of the more alert producers may employ indirect exchange, but through the imitation of those who succeed, the practice will spread until the highly marketable goods become generally acceptable mediums of exchange (see Menger, 1892; for a more modern statement of this process see Jones, 1972).

The process by which money emerges in a market is a prototype that can be used to help explain other social institutions, such as language and law. The basic pattern is that a few persons adopt a practice because it furthers their individual ends. If the practice can then be used advantageously by others, it spreads until it becomes an institution (Menger, 1963 [1883], pp. 223–34; Hayek, 1973, pp. 22–4, 72–93).

Institutions will often interact with one another to produce discernible patterns. For example, the division of labor on a small scale gives people an incentive to use indirect exchange, which can result in the development of money. Once the use of money is established, it becomes much easier to specialize, both because money makes it easier to exchange, and because money prices make it easier to know if resources are being used efficiently. So money leads to further specialization.

The role of money and monetary calculation were further elucidated in the socialist calculation debates of the 1920s and 1930s. Mises challenged the original socialist view that money, markets, and prices should be abolished by showing that without the use of money in resource markets, widespread division of labor would be impossible because central planners would have no way of telling if resources were being used efficiently (Mises, 1935). Lange, Taylor, and other socialists responded by conceding the need for prices, but arguing that a central planner could, in the manner of the Walrasian auctioneer, call out hypothetical prices for production goods, calculate excess demand for each good, and then adjust prices accordingly (Lange and Taylor, 1964 [1938]). Our purpose here is not to recount or adjudicate the debate (for recent contributions see Vaughn, 1980 and Lavoie, 1981), but to emphasize the degree of specialization and the complexity of a monetary economy. Even the socialist side of the debate did not argue that the central planner could gather up all the relevant information on production possibilities and resource availability and formulate an efficient production plan without the aid of prices.

Money and monetary calculation also figure into large-scale breakdowns of the market order. One example of this is the Mises–Fetter theory of the trade cycle. When the governmentally controlled central banks wish to increase the money supply, they induce the commercial bankers to loan out more money. The commercial banks do this by lowering the rate of interest on loans. To the extent that businessmen use this lowered rate of interest in their capital value calculations, they will undertake projects that they would not undertake if they used the higher rate of interest. The general undertaking of new investment projects is the upswing of the cycle. As the increased supply of money works its way through the economy, prices will rise, and so will the rate of interest. At this point, many of the new projects, which had been predicated on a lower rate of interest, will fail. The increase in bankruptcies and unemployment are the downswing of the cycle (O'Driscoll, 1980).

An explanation of business depressions must rely not only on the assumption of market complexity but also on the assumption that capital goods are heterogeneous, complementary, and unable to be easily shifted among different industries. The truth of this assumption is almost self-evident in the modern economic world; we need only watch the manifold effects of a sudden and unexpected rise in the price of oil, including the changes in capital values, to realize how interdependent capital goods are. A theory of capital that emphasizes the heterogeneity, complementarity, and specificity of capital goods will be a theory of capital *structure* rather than a theory of putty or clay, and will recognize the sensitivity of this structure to monetary influences (Lachmann, 1978 [1956]).

Market coordination, monetary calculation, and institutions have received attention from several prominent macroeconomists outside the Austrian tradition, including Axel Leijonhufvud, Robert Clower, and Paul Davidson.

In revising the orthodox interpretations of Keynes, Leijonhufvud explicitly formulated a theory of the market as a complex coordinating mechanism. Clower had already published his dual-decision hypothesis, which incorporated trading at disequilibrium prices into the budget constraint. Building on the work of Clower, Leijonhufvud interpreted Keynes as being concerned, not with "unemployment equilibrium," but with the adjustment process that brings about a large scale breakdown in the market order. Central to his reinterpretation of Keynes is the notion that the market is a coordination mechanism in which money prices transmit signals to agents. Under certain circumstances, which we will not detail here, these signals can lead to a cumulative process of unemployment and general discoordination. More recently, Clower and Leijonhufvud have stressed the importance of the institution of middlemen in helping to coordinate plans (Clower, 1969; Leijonhufvud, 1968; Clower and Leijonhufvud, 1975).

Paul Davidson has laid particular stress on the uncertainty surrounding production decisions in a market economy and the critical role that the institution of money plays in the market. The use of money, which helps us to carry general, non-specific capital into an uncertain future, has peculiarities that can lead to widespread breakdown of production in the market. If for some reason people decide to hold more money, they will cut back on their purchases of present goods, without giving any signal that they intend to increase their purchases of future goods. That is, the increased holding of money is a response to uncertainty, not an intention to increase future purchases, and will therefore not lower the rate of interest. The cutback in present purchases will induce employers to lay off workers. Since these workers are not required to produce money, nor is there an increased demand for them to produce more future goods, they will not be immediately employed elsewhere. Consequently, there can be widespread unemployment in an economy that employs paper or credit for money (Davidson, 1978 and 1981).

Quite obviously there is disagreement on the way a market works among economists who view the market as a complex order. Hayek, for example, believes that market instability is caused by government influence over money (thus disputing Leijonhufvud and Davidson) and has suggested a proposal for the market to develop its own money, free from the vagaries of politics. Lawrence H. White has argued that Hayek's insight is essentially sound, and that Scotland's long experience with free banking exemplifies the stability of free-market money (Hayek, 1976; White, 1984).

What we wish to stress here is not the difference in the particular way the market coordinates or does not coordinate individual plans, although these theoretical differences are important. Rather we wish to draw attention to the increased importance that prominent macroeconomists are attributing to the market as a complex order. This view of the market is fundamentally different from those schools of thought that believe the market is fully coordinated, or that its operation can be mechanically manipulated.

In the world of general equilibrium, for example, the market is fully coordinated. Where there is no coordinating process, there is no need for money, a monetary rate of interest, or monetary calculation. In fact, there is virtually no need for institutions. The assumptions of general equilibrium theory require agents to do nothing more than maximize subject to the conditions laid down by the auctioneer. The auctioneer himself does all the coordinating of these plans. Whatever the merits of the general equilibrium approach, it cannot describe the institutional processes by which independent agents coordinate their plans in actual markets.

Keynesian and monetarist macro-models also distort the fundamental complexity of the market through their aggregations. By lumping the complex array of consumers' goods into a C, the complex array of labor services into an N, and the capital structure into a bond market, they make it appear that the economy can be mechanically regulated simply by controlling aggregate demand or the money stock. If the market were really as simple as these models suggest, there would be no need for government policy at all, because there would be no coordination problem. How much trouble would businessmen have efficiently employing resources if there were only two producers goods and one consumption good?

Incorporating lagged expectations into macro-models does little to make them less mechanical, nor does the assumption of rational expectations capture the complexity of the market order. In a world of rational expectations, everyone is presumed to know all possible future states of the world, the probability that each of these states will occur, and the equilibrium price vector for each possible state. In other words, the complexity of the market economy has been reduced to somewhere around the level of a game of dice.

Although rational expectations models are said to incorporate uncertainty into economic theory, they really incorporate nothing more than actuarial risk. There is no Knightian uncertainty, no ignorance of possible outcomes, no process by which knowledge is transmitted, and no need for (or at least no explanation of) institutions. (For a recent criticism of the notion of a rational expectations equilibrium see Frydman, 1982).

THE MICROECONOMIC FOUNDATIONS

One of the happy trends among the macroeconomists cited in the previous section (and many others besides) is the increasing attention paid to individual decisions. Clower, Davidson, and Leijonhufvud have all traced macroeconomic coordination, or lack of it, to the individual decisions of the agents who make up the market. The rational expectations school has also stressed the importance of individual expectations, and has questioned the validity of the assumption that economists or policy makers have more accurate forecasts of particular market developments than do businessmen.

One of the implications of the market being a spontaneous order is that *no one* has particular knowledge of all the relevant conditions on which economic action is based. Consequently, ignorance and uncertainty will surround most market decisions.

The Austrian School's method of incorporating ignorance, uncertainty, and expectations into economic theory has been to stress the entrepreneurial element in human consciousness. When a person is ignorant of particular influences in his economic environment and therefore uncertain about the success of possible undertakings, he will be alert to new information, and he will mull over the information he does have in formulating his decisions. The alertness and judgment occasioned by ignorance is what Mises and Rothbard mean by entrepreneurship.

Israel Kirzner, building on the work of Mises, has devoted considerable effort to explaining how a market process develops from individual entrepreneurial activity. His basic theme is that the ignorance of particulars that are an inherent feature of a market economy open up arbitrage possibilities. Finding a good that sells for different prices in the market is the most obvious example, but Kirzner believes that the discovery of factors of production that can be transformed into consumers' goods can also be considered arbitrage if factor prices are lower than the price of the consumer's good. Kirzner has recently extended his arbitrage theory of the market process to include uncertainty (Kirzner, 1978, 1982).

Austrians are not the only economists who have stressed the importance of ignorance, uncertainty, and/or discovery to economic theory. Frank Knight's work is a classic in this field (Knight, 1976 [1921]). No one has done more to make the meaning of uncertainty clear to us and to explain the relationship between uncertainty and entrepreneurial profit. One of the most unfortunate developments of economic theory has been the equation of mathematical with epistemic uncertainty, a mistake no one should have made after Knight.

Herbert Simon has vigorously criticized the static maximizing model of decision-making. He has argued that we do not have the kind of information needed to attain the neoclassical maximizing solution to complex problems. Instead we find a "satisfactory solution" or we reduce the problem to one we can maximize. His study of decision science and its use by businessmen has led him to conclude that a theory of process is a necessary part of economics (Simon, 1979).

G.L.S. Shackle in a series of works ranging over 30 years has incorporated epistemic uncertainty and expectations into his vision of economics. Market agents do not merely maximize in the Shacklean system; they employ their "constrained imagination" to envision possible results of their actions, rank these possibilities, and base their actions on a combination of benefit and plausibility. His resulting market theory stresses the "kaleidic" interaction of these market decisions (Shackle, 1972).

Harvey Leibenstein's alternative to maximizing theory is X-efficiency. Leibenstein does not believe that agents maximize even in the sense of doing as well as they can do. He recognizes that the mind is not a machine that always functions at top efficiency. Rather it is an active originator of effort and knowledge whose degree of "productivity" is a part of our choice. He has used his idea of X-efficiency to effectively criticize the static theory of production, and his basis for microtheory is obviously congenial to the kind of economic activity that occurs in a complex market order (Leibenstein, 1976) .

Joseph Schumpeter's writings on competition and entrepreneurship are particularly important to the microfoundations of a theory of spontaneous order. The prospect of profits induces entrepreneurs to undertake those risky, innovative enterprises that revolutionize methods of production, organization, and marketing in a capitalistic economy. This entrepreneurial pursuit of profit not only provides economists with a notion of competition to replace perfect competition, but it also explains why the spontaneous order never settles into an equilibrium, why the market is in fact a process of continual "creative destruction" (Schumpeter, 1976 [1942]).

The process view of competition, i.e., profit-seeking behavior of entrepreneurs, is almost a polar opposite of perfect competition. Competition for profits requires ignorance and uncertainty in the market; perfect competition precludes them. Competition for profit is the result of alertness, judgment, imagination, and X-efficiency, none of which have any place in a perfectly competitive market.

The dynamic, Schumpeterian, vision of competition also differs markedly from such static notions of competition as the imperfect competition of Chamberlain and the perfect contestability of Baumol. Both of these variants of static competition assume the producers to know demand curves, production functions, and cost curves. There is no guesswork, no innovation, no significant change of any kind in these market structures

Models of price and quantity change that use static notions of competition do not fit within the purview of market process theory, as we are using the term here. Stability analysis, for example, although it is a theory of change, embodies none of the entrepreneurship that we find in spontaneous orders. The excess demand equations of stability analysis are derived from Walrasian maximizing experiments. The agents in these models do not innovate, they do not undertake risk, they do not try to judge future market conditions. In fact, they do not even change price; the auctioneer does that for them (Arrow and Hahn, 1971, p. 329).

Similar remarks can be made about search theory. There is a sequence of search in these models, and agents are not assumed to have perfect knowledge, but the models only introduce ignorance into the market in the way that rational expectations models do. That is, the agents maximize according to known (or nearly known) probability distributions. There is no Knightian uncertainty, or innovation, or profit and loss in these models. In fact, they are really better described as equilibrium models (Hey, 1981, p. 165).

SUMMARY AND CONCLUSION

Austrian economics is one of several modern schools of thought that approach the market as a process. Common to all these schools is recognition of the ignorance and uncertainty faced by market agents, the importance of expectations in decision making, the importance of institutions in realizing or revising those expectations, and the essential complexity of the market. These common characteristics differentiate market process theory from equilibrium theory and from theories that look on market change as mechanical.

Part of the market process approach to these problems has been to show how a market order can emerge "spontaneously," i.e., without conscious design, from the actions of agents who possess limited information, but who also possess active and creative minds. Using this method, economists have been able to show how institutions will develop and how these institutions then make possible the operation of a complex market economy.

Market process ideas are currently being extended to several specific fields of study, such as property rights, legal liability, industrial organization, antitrust law, and education. All of these efforts are part of an attempt to gain a fuller understanding of the complex and ever-changing society that, in our view, constitutes the proper subject matter of economics.

REFERENCES

Arrow, Kenneth, and Hahn, Frank (1971), *General Competitive Analysis*, San Francisco: Holden-Day.

Blaug, Mark (1980), *The Methodology of Economics*, Cambridge: Cambridge University Press.

Clower, Robert A. (1969), "The Keynesian Counter-Revolution: A Theoretical Appraisal," in R.A. Clower, (ed.), *Monetary Theory,* Baltimore: Penguin Books.

Clower, Robert and Leijonhufvud, Axel (1975), "The Coordination of Economic Activities: A Keynesian Perspective," *American Economic Review*, May.

Davidson, Paul, (1978), *Money and The Real World*, New York: Macmillan, chs 6–9.

—— (1981), "Post Keynesian Economics," in Irving Kristol and Daniel Bell, (ed.), *The Crisis in Economic Theory*, New York: Basic Books.

Frydman, Roman (1982), "Towards an Understanding of Market Processes," *American Economic Review*, September.

Hayek, Friedrich (ed.) (1935), "Economic Calculation in the Socialist Commonwealth," *Collectivist Economic Planning*, London: George Routledge and Sons.

—— (1973), *Law Legislation and Liberty*, vol. 1, Chicago: University of Chicago Press.

—— (1976), *Denationalization of Money*, Sussex: IEA.

Hey, John D. (1981), *Economics in Disequilibrium*, New York: New York University Press.

Jones, Robert (1972), "On the Origin and Development of Media of Exchange," *Journal of Political Economy*, August.

Kirzner, Israel (1978), "Economics and Error", in Louis Spadaro (ed.), *New Directions in Austrian Economics*, Kansas City: Sheed Andrews & McMeel, Inc.

—— (ed.) (1982), *Method, Process, and Austrian Economics*, Lexington, MA: Lexington Books.

Knight, Frank (1971 [1921]), *Risk, Uncertainty, and Profit*, Chicago: University of Chicago Press.

Lachmann, Ludwig (1978 [1956]), *Capital and Its Structure,* New York: New York University Press.

Lange, Oskar, and Taylor, Fred M. (1964 [1938]), *On the Economic Theory of Socialism*, New York: McGraw-Hill.

Lavoie, Donald (1981), "A Critique of the 'Standard' Account of the Socialist Calculation Debate," *Journal of Libertarian Studies*, Winter.

Leibenstein, Harvey (1976), *Beyond Economic Man*, Cambridge, MA: Harvard University Press.

Leijonhufvud, Axel (1968), *On Keynesian Economics and the Economics of Keynes*, London: Oxford University Press.

Loasby, Brian J. (1976), *Choice, Complexity and Ignorance*, Cambridge: Cambridge University Press.

Menger, Carl, (1963 [1883]), *Problems of Economics and Sociology*, Urbana: University of Illinois Press.

—— (1892), "On the Origins of Money," *Economic Journal*, June.

Mises, Ludwig (1935), "Economic Calculation in the Socialist Commonwealth" in F. Hayek (ed.), *Collectivist Economic Planning*, London: George Routledge & Sons.

O'Driscoll, Gerald P. (1980), "Frank A. Fetter and 'Austrian' Business Cycle Theory," *History of Political Economy*, **12**.

Shackle, G.L.S. (1972), *Epistemics and Economics*, Cambridge: Cambridge University Press.

Schumpeter, Joseph (1976 [1942]), *Capitalism, Socialism and Democracy*, New York: Harper Colophon.

Simon, Herbert (1979), "Rational Decision Making in Business Organizations," *American Economic Review*, September.

Vaughn, Karen (1980), "Economic Calculation Under Socialism: The Austrian Contribution," *Economic Inquiry*, October.

White, Lawrence H. (1984), *Free Banking in Britain*, Cambridge: Cambridge University Press.

2. The market process: an evolutionary view

Richard N. Langlois

"Market process" theories of economic organization have in common an underlying presumption that – as the old advertising slogan would have it – "getting there is half the fun." A market process theory is one that explicitly traces out economic action as a sequence of steps over time. This stands in contrast to "equilibrium" theories, which concern themselves with hypothetical states of logical consistency among variables. Market process theories are usually "disequilibrium" theories and "dynamic" theories; but a process theory can also be "static," in the specific sense that the process in question may have a rest state or may undergo periods of slow change – just as an equilibrium theory may be dynamic in the specific sense that a variable labelled "time" is among those whose logical consistency determines the equilibrium.

This is an important distinction between types of theory. But it is also an extremely broad distinction, one that admits of a wide range of processes – from mechanistic dynamic-systems models on the one hand (of which "cobweb" models are the familiar example) to "kaleidic" visions in the manner of Shackle (1972) on the other. This essay is an attempt to focus in on one particular mode of process theorizing – the evolutionary approach – and to suggest its power as an organizing vessel for a theory of the "market process."

Perhaps the best way to understand the evolutionary logic of explanation is by contrast with the logic implicit in the more familiar equilibrium modeling of so-called neoclassical economics. In the latter, one conceives of the economic world as a kind of allocation problem – a giant exercise in Operations Research. W.S. Jevons put the matter squarely in 1871. "The problem of economics," he wrote, "may, as it seems to me, be stated thus: – Given, a certain population, with various needs and powers of production, in possession of certain lands and other sources of material: required, the mode of employing their labour which will maximize the utility of the produce" (Jevons, 1911, p. 267). In tandem with this global allocation problem is the local allocation problem faced by each individual agent: to maximize his own utility subject to a budget constraint. In addition to such "rationality" (in the narrow sense of means/ends maximizing), what holds the system together – what aligns the local optimization problem with the global one – are some strong assumptions about the knowledge the economic agent possesses and about the cognitive processes he uses.

In an evolutionary model, the logic of the system is quite different. Rather than conceiving of a preexisting global allocation that individual economic action may (or may not) succeed in bringing about, an evolutionary portrayal is concerned with the processes by which global patterns of resource allocation come into being – with the ways in which individual action creates (rather than merely conforms to) overall orderliness. As a result, evolutionary theories are theories of "spontaneous order" in a far more real sense than are their more conventional optimizing/allocative counterparts. Indeed, F.A. Hayek writes of "twin concepts of evolution and spontaneous order" (Hayek, 1979, p. 258) in a way that makes the two ideas seem necessarily cognate.

To oversimplify a bit, one might say that an evolutionary theory relies on three interrelated factors: selection, memory, and variation or mutation.

Selection is the system-wide factor, a filtering mechanism that both results in and is itself the result of unintended consequences of human action. The interactions of agents in the system combine to create an environment that rewards some patterns of behavior (permitting or encouraging them to spread) and penalizes others (causing them to decline). In an economic model, the selection mechanism manifests itself in the form familiar to the economist's intuition: profit and loss in commercial competition. In political and sociocultural settings, the operative mechanisms would be different, even if perhaps analogous, and would likely prove more difficult to specify and analyze.

In order for a selection process to produce a persistent order, the behavior patterns subject to selection must themselves persist. That is to say, there must be memory in the system. In biological evolution, this is the province of genetics; in economic theories, the memory function is normally discussed in terms of habits, conventions, and the following of rules – rules that may often be unconscious or tacit in the manner of Michael Polanyi (1958). Talking about habitual or rule-following behavior is not an assumption that agents lack creativity or that they never alter their situations consciously; rather, it involves a recognition that, because of the immense complexity of economic life, agents cannot simultaneously attend to *all* of the many aspects of their economic condition – and that, as a result, they must rely to a very great extent on the practical knowledge condensed and stored in rules.

In fact, conscious rationality may be said to play as great a role – and creativity a far greater role – in evolutionary theories as in neoclassical ones. But, as one might guess, their role in the former case is quite different from what it is in the latter. In neoclassical theory, rationality (in a restricted sense of the term) is the very glue that holds the system together, the element that ensures alignment of the global and local allocation problems. In an evolutionary theory, selection and memory hold the system together, and the function of creativity and rationality (in the broad sense) becomes one of economic *change*. This is, of course, the function of "mutation," of generating new behavior patterns.

In an economic context, the mutation function is associated with the idea of entrepreneurship. Joseph Schumpeter, for example, writes of the "process of industrial mutation – if I may use a biological term – that incessantly revolutionizes the economic structure" (Schumpeter, 1942, p. 83). And both Schumpeter's theory (Schumpeter, 1934) and that of Israel Kirzner (1973) are distinguished from most other theories of entrepreneurship in that they are broadly consistent with this evolutionary view. Indeed, a more explicitly evolutionary perspective might help to resolve some of the controversies within the literature of entrepreneurship; for example, the distinction in evolutionary thought between "specializing" and "generalizing" adaptations (Dunn, 1971) might well clarify the debate over the "equilibrating" versus the "disequilibrating" role of the entrepreneur.

Evolutionary thought in social science is, of course, a pastime as old as the social sciences themselves. If Hayek is right, biologists got the idea from economists – notably the eighteenth-century Scottish moral philosophers – rather than the other way around (Hayek, 1973, p. 23). David Hume, in his "Dialogues Concerning Natural Religion" (published posthumously but written in 1759, a hundred years before the appearance of *The Origin of Species*), described clearly how a spontaneous order could emerge from a process of variation and selection (Hume, 1961, esp. pp. 478–9). The economics of Hume's friend Adam Smith was also arguably evolutionary, even if not so explicitly; his concern with economic development and with the increasing division of labor is very much a concern with the evolution and elaboration of economic structure – a concern very different from that implied in the allocative interpretation (or, rather, misinterpretation) conventionally accorded the "invisible hand" (O'Driscoll, 1978; Boehm, 1982).

In the nineteenth century, the principle evolutionary theorist was probably Carl Menger. His well-known theory of money is a prototype of evolutionary explanation (Menger, 1981, ch. 8); and his basic microeconomics, while not explicitly evolutionary, was arguably a disequilibrium process theory (Streissler, 1972; Jaffe, 1976; but cf. Kirzner, 1979, ch. 4). Also, Menger's methodological discussion of the "organic" explanation of institutions is very much consistent with an evolutionary approach (Menger, 1963). To a lesser extent, Alfred Marshall also deserves mention as an evolutionary economist; for, while he is best remembered for having given us partial-equilibrium comparative-static analysis, he was nonetheless conscious of and influenced by evolutionary ideas and biological analogies, perhaps to the point of being something of a Social Darwinist (Moss, 1982).

The Institutionalists of the early century made a fuss about evolutionary ideas (e.g., Veblen, 1898); but, for a variety of reasons, none was ever able to get a truly evolutionary research program off the ground (Coats, 1954; Seckler, 1975). In fact, one could argue that it was some of the strongest *antagonists* of Institutionalism – the Austrian descendents of Menger – who presented a more successfully evolutionary story. As I've already suggested, the work of Schumpeter is broadly consistent with an evolutionary approach, especially in his treatment of habit and convention (memory) and entrepreneurship (mutation). Also, the tradition of Ludwig von Mises, especially as interpreted by Kirzner, has many elements consistent with an evolutionary view.

Of the modern "Austrians," the most self-consciously evolutionary – and the most avowedly Mengerian – is Hayek. His work includes some of the most important and sophisticated discussions of evolutionary thought in the social sciences (Hayek, 1967, 1973, 1979). But his substantive concerns are directed less toward economic theory or market processes *per se* than towards issues of political and social philosophy. To put it another way, Hayek's evolutionary writings take as their focus what, following Lachmann (1971, p. 81), we might call "external" institutions – the legal and political outer skeleton of society. By contrast, studying the market process involves analyzing what goes on within a given outer framework; for example, one might be concerned with the patterns produced by competition within a particular regime of property rights, including the development of such "internal" institutions as business firms.

This is not, of course, to say that Hayek's evolutionary ideas cannot be applied at the level of economic theory. Indeed, his own early writings on the microeconomics of competition seem consistent with his later work; and such modern followers of Hayek as O'Driscoll and Rizzo (1985) have endorsed an evolutionary view of economic theory.

What would an evolutionary portrayal of economics look like? In order to paint the picture properly, one needs to return to the brief but significant discussion of marginalism-versus-natural-selection that blossomed in the early 1950s.

As I've already suggested, the intuition that evolutionary considerations lie in some manner behind the phenomena of economic competition has long been a congenial one to many economists. Some routinely go so far as to say that "natural selection" militates toward or "enforces" efficient behavior – and therefore that evolutionary ideas reinforce and justify conventional maximization formulations of theory. Even Milton Friedman – who, in his well-known 1953 article, was actually arguing that marginalist formations *need* no justification other than "usefulness" and empirical testability – paused long enough to offer, as a kind of fall-back argument, the proposition that maximizing models are more tractable ways of capturing the evolutionary process that (he admitted) is the *real* process underlying economic competition (Friedman, 1953). But, while one can still find many economists who are not excessively diffident about equating evolutionary selection with efficiency and even optimality (e.g., Hirshleifer, 1977), it is becoming increasingly clear that an optimization model can often be a very bad guide to the results of an evolutionary process.

One of the best early discussions of selection processes in economics was that by Armen Alchian (1950). In large part, his goal was to suggest the extent to which the results of an economic selection process could look as if they had been generated by conscious optimizing behavior under perfect information. Consider drivers setting out from Chicago on five different roads, with each driver choosing a road at random; suppose further that on only one of these roads are there gas stations. Drivers on the other roads would run out of gas and be "selected out". And this prediction is qualitatively the same as would have resulted from assuming that the drivers all knew which road had the gas stations and consciously chose that road.

But Alchian's intent in this article seems less to plump for optimizing models than to illustrate the interesting properties of selection models. For example, he goes on to point out the difficulties that "nonconvexities" introduce into an optimization problem: local optimizers may find themselves with what is only a "local" maximum, one inferior in light of the global optimum; by contrast, the "blanketing shotgun process" of a selection model might well attain the global optimum.

A far more telling argument about the potential cleavage between optimization and selection models was offered in a later article by Sidney Winter (1964). He suggested that, if one looks carefully at the dynamics of an evolutionary process, it becomes clear that what would have been "optimizing" behavior in an eventual equilibrium may never actually find its way to that equilibrium. The process may experience periods to which the ultimately optimal behavior is very poorly adapted; and that behavior may be selected out before the ultimate equilibrium is reached, leaving behind what are *not* in fact "optimal" forms of behavior. This is what we might call the "path dependency" problem.

In my view, the gulf between optimizing and evolutionary conceptions is larger even than these arguments would make it seem. If we take seriously the notion that we live in a world of open-ended economic knowledge, in which there always remain wholly new facts or ideas to be learned or created, then it actually becomes difficult to talk meaningfully about "optimality" in any but a limited sense. By contrast, it is always meaningful to talk about the results of a selection process in a world of radical uncertainty; indeed, the very idea of economic evolution implies such a world. My own view is that "efficiency" constructs do have a crucial place in the evolutionary analysis; but such constructs have a role rather different from the one they are usually seen as playing, and they are only part of a satisfactory economic explanation (Langlois, 1983).

What all this suggests, of course, is that one must begin to theorize in explicitly evolutionary terms rather than to rely on optimization models as a "summary" of the results of the evolutionary process. Where does economic theory stand as far as explicitly evolutionary models are concerned? The most important efforts in that direction are probably those of Richard Nelson and Sidney Winter, whose recent book (1982) is a compendium and synthesis of their work on evolutionary theory during the last decade or so.

In addition to a methodological discussion of evolutionary versus "orthodox" theorizing, the book contains – especially in chapters 4 and 5 – an extremely suggestive treatment of the organization-theoretical basis of rules, norms, and routines. In a conventional model, they point out, one implicitly draws a sharp distinction between a firm's (or agent's) knowledge and its choices: there exists a set of techniques "known" by the firm and among which it chooses; knowledge of how to choose is never considered part of the firm's repertoire of techniques, and the exercise of a technique once chosen is never portrayed as involving further choices. Drawing heavily on Polanyi's conception of tacit knowing, Nelson and Winter suggest the alternative of seeing the behavior of the firm as epistemologically akin to the exercise of a skill, a view in which knowing and choosing are closely bound up with one another.

But, for present purposes, the more significant part of the book is its presentation of explicitly evolutionary models of economic processes. Picking up on a suggestion by Alchian (1950) – that "the formulation of this [evolutionary] approach awaits the marriage of the theory of stochastic processes and economics" – Nelson and Winter construct stochastic simulation models of the market process.

In these models, all three of the elements of an evolutionary process are present: memory, variation, and selection. The economic agents (which it may be best to think of as "firms") produce according to rules; that is, the firms have input/output coefficients similar to those in the production-function model, but these coefficients are nowhere presumed to have resulted from a maximization calculation. Precisely because they are the result of rule-following behavior, the coefficients are persistent – they are not subject to continual revision – and they serve the function of memory. The function of variation or mutation is introduced by the stochastic aspect of the model. The firms can search for more profitable rules by taking a chance on a random draw of new coefficients, keeping the new coefficient if it is an improvement and rejecting it otherwise. The firms then compete to sell their output on the same market (which is usually specified by a neoclassical demand curve). Those firms that make a profit are able to expand; those that do not contract – and may eventually find themselves "selected out" through bankruptcy.

This procedure defines a stochastic process; but it is an open-ended kind of search process, one in which the agents do not know the probability distributions involved and in which there is no question of "optimal" search.

Nelson and Winter use models of this sort to reexamine some of the standard questions of economics – from simple comparative statics to growth theory – and find that they are able to replicate most of the qualitative results of the neoclassical approach while providing an explanation far richer than is conventionally possible. At the same time, they are also occasionally able to point to predictions different from those of optimization theory. For example, in an optimization model the rise in the price of a factor of production can never lead a firm to use *more* of that factor than it did before the price rise. (Not without a complicated and contrived set of ad hoc assumptions, at any rate.) But in a search-and-selection model, a firm might well end up using more of a more expensive factor – because the price rise triggered a search that led to an expansion of the firm's choice set. As a consequence, evolutionary models of this sort are not merely superior in terms of explanatory power but may also potentially produce the "excess empirical content" over conventional models that is a sign to modern philosophers of science of an advancing research program (Lakatos, 1970).

And where is this evolutionary research program heading? It seems to me that there are at least two directions which one might usefully explore. One would be to take the basic Nelson and Winter model as a paradigm (in the narrow sense) and to develop and elaborate models like it – in much the same way that the neoclassical research program has proliferated constrained maximization models. This would provide a much stronger "positive heuristic," something arguably lacking in many programs critical of neoclassical economics. Another direction I find appealing – one broader though related – would be to reexamine questions of economic organization in an evolutionary light (cf. Langlois, 1983). For example, such questions as the nature of the division of labor or the choice between market-contracting and internal (in-firm) organization – questions that have so far been examined largely with the equilibrium/optimization apparatus – might be profitably recast in more evolutionary terms.

REFERENCES

Alchian, Armen (1950), "Uncertainty, Evolution, and Economic Theory," *Journal of Political Economy*, **58**(3), 211–21.

Boehm, Stephan (1982), "Das Beispiel der unsichtbaren Hand," in Karl Acham (ed.), *Gesellschaftliche Prozesse*, Graz: Academia.

Boulding, Kenneth E. (1978), *Ecodynamics: A New Theory of Societal Evolution*, Beverley Hills, CA: Sage Publications.

—— (1981), *Evolutionary Economics*, Beverley Hills, CA: Sage Publications.

Coats, A. W. (1954), "The Influence of Veblen's Methodology," *Journal of Political Economy*, **62**, 529–37.

—— (1976) "Economics and Psychology: The Death and Resurrection of a Research Programme," in S.J. Latsis, (ed.), *Method and Appraisal in Economics*, Cambridge: Cambridge University Press.

Dunn, Edgar S. (1971), *Economic and Social Development: A Process of Social Learning*, Baltimore: Johns Hopkins Press.

Friedman, Milton (1953), "The Methodology of Positive Economics," in *Essays on Positive Economics*, Chicago: University of Chicago Press. Reprinted in William Breitt and Harold Hochman (eds), *Readings in Microeconomics*, Hinsdale, IL: Dryden Press, 2nd edn, 1977.

Gould, Stephen Jay (1977), *Ever Since Darwin*, New York: Norton.

Hayek, F.A. (1948), *Individualism and Economic Order*, Chicago: University of Chicago Press. (Gateway edn, 1972.)

—— (1967), *Studies in Philosophy, Politics, and Economics*, Chicago: University of Chicago Press.

—— (1973), *Law, Legislation, and Liberty*, vol. 1: *Rules and Order*, Chicago: University of Chicago Press.

—— (1979), "The Three Sources of Human Values," Epilogue to *Law, Legislation, and Liberty*, vol. 3, Chicago: University of Chicago Press.

Hirshleifer, Jack (1977), "Economics from a Biological Viewpoint," *Journal of Law and Economics*, **20**, 1.

Hume, David (1961), "Dialogues Concerning Natural Religion," in *The Empiricists*, Garden City, NY: Doubleday.

Jaffe, William (1976), "Menger, Jevons, and Walras Dehomogonized," *Economic Inquiry*, **14**.

Jevons, William Stanley (1911), *The Theory of Political Economy*, London: Macmillan, 4th edn.

Kirzner, Israel M. (1973), *Competition and Entrepreneurship*, Chicago: University of Chicago Press.

—— (1979), *Perception, Opportunity, and Profit*, Chicago: University of Chicago Press.

Lachmann, Ludwig (1971), *The Legacy of Max Weber*, Berkeley: The Glendessary Press.

Lakatos, Imre (1970), "Falsification and the Methodology of Scientific Research Programmes," in Lakatos and Musgrave (eds), *Criticism and the Growth of Knowledge*, Cambridge: Cambridge University Press.

Langlois, Richard N. (1983), "Economics as a Process: Notes on the New Institutional Economics," C.V. Starr Center for Applied Economics, New York University, Research Report 83–04.

Menger, Carl (1963), *Problems of Economics and Sociology*, trans. F.J. Nock, Urbana: University of Illinois Press.
—— (1981), *Principles of Economics*, trans. James Dingwall and Bert F. Hoselitz, New York: New York University Press.
Moss, Lawrence S. (1982), "Biological Theory and Technological Entrepreneurship in Marshall's Writings," *Eastern Economics Journal*, **8**, 3–13.
Nelson, Richard R. and Sidney G. Winter (1982), *An Evolutionary Theory of Economic Change*, Cambridge, MA: Harvard University Press.
O'Driscoll, Gerald P. (1978), "Spontaneous Order and the Coordination of Economic Activities," in L.M. Spadaro (ed.), *New Directions in Austrian Economics*, Kansas City: Sheed and Ward.
O'Driscoll, Gerald P. and Mario J. Rizzo (1985), *The Economics of Time and Ignorance*, Oxford: Basil Blackwell.
Polanyi, Michael (1958), *Personal Knowledge*, Chicago: University of Chicago Press.
Shackle, G.L.S. (1972), *Epistemics and Economics*, Cambridge: Cambridge University Press.
Schumpeter, Joseph A. (1934), *The Theory of Economic Development*, Cambridge: Harvard University Press. (New York: Oxford University Press, 1961.)
—— (1942), *Capitalism, Socialism, and Democracy*, New York: Harper & Brothers. (Harper Colophon edn, 1976.)
Scriven, Michael (1959), "Explanation and Prediction in Evolutionary Theory," *Science*, **130**(3374), 447–82.
Seckler, David (1975), *Thorstein Veblen and the Institutionalists*, Boulder: Colorado Associated University Press.
Streissler, Erich (1972), "To What Extent Was the Austrian School Marginalist?" *History of Political Economy*, **4**.
Veblen, Thorstein (1898), "Why Is Economics Not an Evolutionary Science?" *Quarterly Journal of Economics*, **12**.
Winter, Sidney (1964), "Economic 'Natural Selection' and the Theory of the Firm," *Yale Economic Essays*, **4**, 225–72.
—— (1971), "Satisficing, Selection, and the Innovating Remnant," *Quarterly Journal of Economics*, **85**, 237–61.
—— (1975), "Optimization and Evolution in the Theory of the Firm," in R. Day and T. Groves (eds), *Adaptive Economic Models*, New York: Academic Press.

3. On *The economics of time and ignorance**

Israel M. Kirzner

The following pages do not constitute a balanced, overall review of *The Economics of Time and Ignorance*. They consist, almost entirely, of this writer's criticisms of certain central themes of the work. No attempt has been made to offset these criticisms by applause for the many superb features of the book. To avoid any possible misunderstanding I wish to emphasize here my very great admiration for the many excellent aspects of this work. It represents a courageous, and in many respects a brilliant attempt by two distinguished Austrian scholars to re-examine the foundations of Austrian economics. All of us must be grateful for this work, and look forward to the stimulus it will hopefully provide for new work along Austrian lines.

It may be useful to introduce my criticisms of the book by reviewing the background of the work's development over a period of years. The work began, one recalls, as an attempt to restate, for the benefit of the profession at large, the main ideas of modern Austrian economics, and to set forth its grounds for dissatisfaction with the dominant core of contemporary economic understanding. As the work progressed it evolved in the direction of a more original development of the authors' own ideas concerning the course of future work stemming from the Austrian tradition. The book before us presents important elements both of the authoritative restatement and of the innovative "work at the frontiers." One hastens to add that of course the restatement and particularly the critique of the standard, mainstream view, sparkle with novelty and originality. It is here that one encounters many of the book's brilliant passages. One is particularly impressed by the breadth of the scholarship through which Austrian concerns are, in the early chapters, linked with important issues debated in the literature of other disciplines, particularly the philosophy of science and sociology. One is struck both by the verve and by the sensitivity to the history of economic doctrines that suffuse much of the book, particularly the latter half of it. But praiseworthy as these and other features of the book undoubtedly are, the reader is com-

*(by Gerald P. O'Driscoll and Mario J. Rizzo, Oxford: Basil Blackwell Press, 1985.)

pelled to base his overall appraisal of the work on what he sees as its principal function – to serve as a pacesetter for anticipated contributions within the Austrian tradition during the second decade of its revival. It is here that what this reviewer sees as the weaknesses of the book appear very serious indeed. It will be convenient to cite a theme first raised by Roger Garrison (who happens to be the contributor of a chapter in the present work – a chapter whose strengths are, it should be stated, not clouded by the weaknesses to be argued below) in his contribution to *Method, Process, and Austrian Economics* (1982)

MIDDLE-OF-THE-ROAD – OR RAZOR'S EDGE?

Roger Garrison pointed out that, although Austrian economics is often viewed as representing a radical, extreme position, the truth is almost exactly the opposite. On a whole range of issues, Garrison was able to demonstrate, the relevant spectrum of possible theoretical positions finds the Austrian view solidly on middle ground between two opposing polar views that are represented in the professional literature. One such spectrum identified by Garrison relates to the existence of equilibrating tendencies. Garrison points out that the traditional Austrian view has been somewhere between the following extremes: (a) a view of the world as embodying underlying data so stable and predictable that the existence of rapidly equilibrating tendencies can be taken entirely for granted, making the equilibrating processes themselves uninteresting; (b) a view of the world as displaying such volatility as to push any equilibrating tendencies beyond the bounds of possibility. Austrian economics has never fallen into the traps lurking at either of these two poles. And it is here that this reviewer finds *The Economics of Time and Ignorance* severely flawed.

Much of the book consists in pointing out, cogently and incisively, the fatal inadequacies of those dominant varieties of economic theory that lie at or close to the first of these just-mentioned two polar extremes. The earlier chapters most perceptively link these criticisms with subtle and profound issues discussed by philosophers, philosophers of science and other scholars. The excellence of these critical statements is unfortunately marred, it seems to this reviewer, by their having led the authors not merely to rightly reject this polar extreme, but, most regrettably, in effect to rush headlong into the abyss represented by the opposite polar extreme. It is as if the middle of the road position identified by Garrison were in fact hardly broader than a razor's edge – and as if our authors failed utterly to maintain any analytical foothold upon that edge. To establish the validity of this criticism of the book will be left to subsequent sections of this comment. At this stage we pause only to point out the very serious implications of this criticism of ours. As Roger Garrison put it (*ibid*., p. 133), in referring to this second polar extreme, to see the world as characterized by such extreme volatility is not only to deny the possibility of equilibrating tendencies; it is also to render economic science non-existent.

It would be unfortunate in the extreme if the publication of this work were to have the unintended consequence of turning the modern development of the Austrian tradition in a direction that suggests that, because of the volatility of the underlying data and of mutual expectations, the likelihood of systematic market forces must be dismissed. This would at once demote economics from the status of a theoretical discipline enunciating powerful general patterns of market causation (that manifest themselves in innumerable different concrete instances). At best, economics could then hope to become a descriptive discipline able to do not much more than catalogue the various possibilities that might occur. It would be a bizarre irony indeed if the modern revival of the Austrian tradition, begun over a century ago as a brave defense of economic theory (against a dominant tide of historicism), were to find its most sophisticated expression in the denial of any possibility for systematic market forces susceptible to general analysis.

ON "HAVING IT BOTH WAYS"

But of course our authors do *not* wish to argue the non-existence of economic science. While the author of "Spontaneous Order and the Coordination of Economic Activities" (O'Driscoll, 1978) has apparently modified his views on a number of important points, he and his co-author have certainly not abandoned the understanding of markets as embodying spontaneous coordinating forces. (It is for this reason that the preceding paragraph referred to possible "unintended consequences" of this book.) The truth is that our authors show every evidence of a lively concern that their very great emphasis on the volatility and indeterminacy of expectations, on the open-ended uncertainty associated with the passage of "real" time, and on the creativity and spontaneity of human decisions, should not be thought to imply the complete denial of systematic market processes. Our assertion that, despite all this, their book may have the unintended consequence of suggesting precisely this denial, rests on the following: (a) the authors reject the more conventional Austrian understanding of how systematic market processes occur; (b) the authors offer an alternative explanatory framework to account for the existence of such systematic processes; they believe that this suggestion "allows [them] to have it both ways" (i.e. they can reject the conventional Austrian explanations while still recognizing the existence of systematic adjusting forces); (c) this alternative framework, it seems to this reviewer is, however, susceptible to the very same critical arguments on the basis of which the more conventional Austrian understanding was rejected, so that (d) acceptance of the authors' arguments in regard to the latter, in effect, commits one to the denial of any systematic market forces altogether; in other words the authors cannot really have it both ways. From the perspective of this critical appraisal, then, (1) the root error in the volume consists in its argument that recognition of the creativity of human action in "real" time implies the denial of conventional Austrian understanding of market processes; (2) the subsidiary error consists in the belief that the notion of "pattern coordination" introduced by the authors can be maintained (apart from the conventional Austrian insights into coordinative processes) as somehow unaffected by the unpredictability of human decisions in the face of interpersonal uncertainty.

THE CONVENTIONAL AUSTRIAN POSITION

The conventional Austrian position (identified with the work of Mises and Hayek) has been that recognition of the spontaneity of human action and discovery, while it drastically diminishes the relevance of equilibrium models, does not, to put it mildly, rule out the plausibility of possible systematic processes of market coordination. (This reviewer has, in explicating this conventional Austrian position, suggested that such possibly systematic processes in fact *depend* upon the propensity of human beings to transcend the boundaries of the given, and spontaneously to discover and to create new opportunities for their betterment). In this conventional Austrian discussion, the model of market equilibrium has as its principal function the articulation of those totally unrealistic circumstances under which no scope whatever remains for the spontaneity of human action and discovery – strictly in order to enable us to understand, by contrast, the nature of the dynamic forces working towards coordination in the real world. These forces are for Mises, explicitly entrepreneurial in character. Mises repeatedly identifies entrepreneurial action as being the driving force in the market process. And "it is the competition of profit-seeking entrepreneurs that does not tolerate the preservation of *false* prices of the factors of production. The activities of the entrepreneurs are the element that would bring about the unrealizable state of the evenly rotating economy if no further changes were to occur" (1949, p. 335). Hayek has not emphasized the entrepreneurial element in the market process, but there is every reason to understand Hayek's competitive "discovery procedure" as being fully consistent with the entrepreneurial view (and Hayek has acknowledged as much in oral discussion). Why have our authors rejected this view? And what have they offered in its place?

THE ECONOMICS OF TIME AND IGNORANCE: A THUMBNAIL SKETCH

It must be confessed that this reviewer has not found, anywhere in this book, an entirely lucid statement of precisely why the authors find the Mises–Hayek view unacceptable. The discussions in the early chapters (especially Chapter 4) culminate (in several rather cryptic pages in Chapter 5) in the rejection of any equilibrating processes that take the notion of "exact equilibrium" (or "exact coordination") as their reference point. The "genuine uncertainty" associated by the authors with "real" (as distinguished from "Newtonian" time) injects unpredictable change and thus inescapable error into the individual decisions that make up social processes. These errors, it appears, preclude any coordinative processes that can be explicated by reference to "exact" (i.e. Hayekian) equilibrium. "A process in which there must be errors cannot, except by chance culminate in an errorless equilibrium" (p. 85).

In place of the offending notion of "exact equilibrium," our authors introduce that of "pattern equilibrium." This notion depends heavily on the "distinction between typical and unique aspects of future events" (p. 85). The reliability with which "typical" events are able to be anticipated can be reconciled with "genuine uncertainty" because such reliability does not affect the "time-dependent" character of the unique aspects of activities and events. Process analysis, in the "pattern coordination" sense, depends on the extent to which market participants can correctly mesh the typical aspects of their plans without restricting the open-endedness of the "actual activities" that will be "filled" into these plans (p. 86).

THE ECONOMICS OF TIME AND IGNORANCE: A THUMBNAIL CRITIQUE

A. It is one thing to recognize the open-endedness of the future and of expectations concerning the future, the paramountcy of uncertainty, genuine error, and the like. It is quite another thing to claim that these aspects of reality render as fatuous any explanations of market processes in terms of entrepreneurial anticipations of future unique events (as well as of typical aspects of future events), and that they render invalid any postulation of processes of systematic market coordination that refer to the meshing of specific activities. Despite statements by Austrian economists that entrepreneurial activity generates systematic equilibrating processes, such statements by no means *depend* on the possibility that such processes might (even in the absence of unpredictable change) culminate in the *attainment* of equilibrium.

Such statements simply recognize that the course of events over any given period of time express the systematic attempts by entrepreneurs to grasp the opportunities generated by the initially postulated violation of the conditions for equilibrium. To assert the systematic character of such attempts, and of the market consequences of such attempts, is not to deny the complications introduced by endogenous uncertainty. It simply explicates the nature of such coordinative success that markets do possess, *in the teeth of* the genuine uncertainty that pervades reality. Certainly economists, particularly Austrian economists, owe a debt of gratitude to Professors Shackle and Lachmann, and to our own authors, for their indefatigable efforts at "keeping us honest," in terms of recognizing how easily the coordinative forces of the market can be derailed by "genuine uncertainty." But to be honest, in this respect, does not require complete denial of coordinative processes identified by reference to "exact equilibrium." It merely requires that we maintain the healthy "middle-of-the-road" position discussed above.

B. Our authors' emphasis on the distinction between the typical and the unique aspects of events may prove to be of considerable value in terms of *applied* Austrian economics. It is very much to be hoped that the authors will pursue the implications of this potentially fruitful distinction. There is every reason to agree with the authors that many entrepreneurial activities do indeed seek to take advantage of anticipatory insights into the typical, rather than the unique, aspects of the future.

But to grant all this is not at all to accept the merit of what the authors appear to see as one of their principal contributions: the understanding of market processes exclusively in "pattern coordination" terms. In particular it is not at all clear why we are allowed to assume, as a matter of science, the reliability of those typicalities upon which the entire analysis depends. At one point (p. 77) it seems to be suggested that such reliability is itself the fruit of entrepreneurially-driven coordination processes. But concrete entrepreneurial activities that are postulated as being *responsible*, in "unintended" fashion, for the typicality of certain aspects of events, must presumably have been initiated with respect to what must have been seen as *unique* aspects of the future. To the extent, then, that the distinction between typical and unique aspects of reality rests upon the systematic character of entrepreneurially-driven processes, it must remain a mystery why what we have called the "conventional Austrian" position is to be rejected. On the other hand, to the extent that the latter position is rejected on grounds related, for example, to the circumstances that "entrepreneurial activity (may) create some uncertainty of its own" (p. 78) then it is not apparent why *any* aspects of reality can be relied upon to be other than "unique."

THE FUTURE OF AUSTRIAN ECONOMICS

Much recent theoretical discussion among Austrians has revolved around the implications of genuine uncertainty for the possibility of systematic market processes. This reviewer believes such discussion to be necessary, even crucial, to the future course of work being done in the Austrian tradition. At the same time he would venture to suggest that (within the context of such discussions) the more pressing immediate task is not to further elaborate on how genuine uncertainty *might* derail all systematic processes altogether, but to explicate the extent to which, *despite* genuine uncertainty, systematic processes (the empirical existence of which, after all, is so often obvious even to the most superficial observer) can be understood. As we have seen, our authors do not necessarily disagree with this assessment. This reviewer's unhappiness with the volume stems from what appears to him (a) to be the authors' lack of appreciation for the subtlety and power of the conventional Austrian position; (b) to be a less than satisfactory substitute (offered by the authors) for that position, and thus (c) to be a clear (if unintended) invitation to the reader to believe that Austrian insights suggest that market processes are affected by external reality, and by human preferences, either not at all, or in totally unsystematic fashion.

REFERENCES

Garrison, Roger (1982), "Austrian Economics as the Middle Ground: Comment on Loasby," in Israel M. Kirzner (ed.), *Method, Process, and Austrian Economics: Essays in Honor of Ludwig Von Mises*, Lexington, MA: Lexington Books, pp. 131–8.

Mises, Ludwig von (1949), *Human Action: A Treatise on Economics*, London: William Hodge & Co.

O'Driscoll, Gerald P. (1978), "Spontaneous Order and the Coordination of Economic Activities," in Louis M. Spadaro (ed.), *New Directions in Austrian Economics*, Kansas City: Sheed Andrews & McMeel, pp. 111–42.

4. On *The economics of time and ignorance**

Ludwig M. Lachmann

In 1974, in a mood of radical subjectivism, economists of the Austrian school, after many years in the wilderness, decided to launch an effort for the revival of Austrian Economic Thought. It was clear that this would have to involve the renewal of much of traditional Austrian teaching.

Some of this effort has now borne fruit. In the present volume we have an example of it. Its Chapter 2 in particular, entitled "Static versus Dynamic Subjectivism," might be described as a bold and exhilarating example of radical subjectivism. As the authors point out, this chapter establishes "a theme that will be pursued throughout most of this book" (p. 32).

Our authors have broken new ground. How far this ground will give rise to nourishing crops nobody can say now. That remains to be seen. Meanwhile all those who ten years ago committed themselves to supporting this effort, and of course all who have undertaken this commitment since, are under an obligation to ask themselves what they can do to help this endeavor.

The style of Chapter 2 is austerely analytical. Given the nature of its subject matter it could hardly be otherwise. The outline of the distinction between static and dynamic subjectivism had to be drawn firmly, the text to be written clearly and unambiguously. The fact remains that to most economists today the style is probably somewhat strange and unfamiliar. The ideas of Popper and Shackle which inspire the chapter are today probably well known, those of Schutz and Luckmann less so. Economists pay a high price for their separation from the other social sciences which neoclassical orthodoxy enforced on them for so many decades, but Austrians pay an even higher one. We can do little about this now.

In one respect, however, we may be able to ease the reader's lot a little. Subjectivism, to be sure, is a research program of the social sciences requiring analytical examination, but as such it has a history extending now over more than a century. It is surprising that the authors make so little use of this fact to illustrate their argument. To be able to show that in recent years a

*(by Gerald P. O'Driscoll and Mario J. Rizzo, Oxford: Basil Blackwell Press, 1985.)

more dynamic form of subjectivism has, as a matter of fact, come to supersede one less dynamic would have lent strength to their thesis. "From static to dynamic subjectivism" as the title might have served to make it even more explicit. It often is possible to elucidate baffling problems by setting them out in historical perspective.

TOWARD RADICAL SUBJECTIVISM

To Austrians, of all people, committed to radical subjectivism, the news of the move from static to dynamic subjectivism should be welcome news. We need only remember the famous Hayek passage that "it is probably no exaggeration to say that every important advance in economic theory during the last hundred years was a further step in the consistent application of subjectivism" (Hayek, 1955, p. 31), or the footnote appended to it according to which "this is a development which has probably been carried out most consistently by L. von Mises" (*ibid.*, n. 24) to realize that subjectivism is here conceived of as undergoing a typical development of its own which may be more or less "consistent." If, now, as seems legitimate, we identify "consistent" subjectivism with one that pays close regard to all the implications of the autonomy of the human mind, Hayek's view of the evolution of subjectivism appears to be in strict conformity with an "evolutionary" interpretation of Chapter 2's theme, viz. that, at least in the history of Austrian doctrine, subjectivism has become progressively more dynamic.

On the other hand, without being thought unduly cynical, we may suggest to our authors that they read what Hayek says about Mises in this footnote as a warning also addressed to them. "I believe that most peculiarities of his views which at first strike many readers as strange and unacceptable are due to the fact that in the consistent development of the subjectivist approach he has for a long time moved ahead of his contemporaries" (*ibid.*, n. 24). Must we not conclude from this that moving ahead of one's contemporaries, in particular "in the consistent development of the subjectivist approach," is a rash and perilous enterprise which may well lead to the result that one's views come to look "strange and unacceptable" to many readers? If Mises, for all his courage and eloquence, encountered such widespread lack of understanding, are those who follow him today in the path of the development of subjectivism less likely to have such disappointing experiences?

It is possible to view the evolution of subjectivism in economic theory as having (thus far) taken place in three stages: at each of the two lower stages the introduction of a form of it resolved some problems while also giving rise to new ones. In this sense, each form of subjectivism may be said to have "pointed beyond itself."

The introduction of subjectivism into economic theory is generally associated with the "subjective revolution" of the 1870s when the new theory of value based on marginal utility, hence on subjective evaluation by individuals, superseded the older classical cost-of-production theory of value. Correct as this is, it fails to convey the true flavor of the events recorded. It also fails to account for the fact that the infusion of so small a dose of subjectivism into the body of economic theory could have such far-reaching results.

Classical economics was a science of wealth, primarily concerned with its production and distribution. Value was the measure of this wealth. Men mattered only as producers of wealth, and as such were treated as stereotypes. Individual differences between them were abstracted from the model. There was thus no place for subjectivism. The consumer, who destroyed rather than produced wealth, was no economic agent. He appeared to lead a solitary life outside the bounds of the classical system. Markets, the efficient functioning of which was seen to affect wealth, were composed entirely of producers and merchants. Economic phenomena were not seen as utterances of individual human minds.

With the introduction of a subjective theory of value, however, all this changed. The consumer could no longer be ignored. After all, it was he who bestowed value on objects. All of a sudden the former outsider moved to the center of the stage. And equally all of a sudden, what had been the science of wealth turned into *catallactics*, the science of markets in which the consumer alongside producers occupied a prominent place (see Mises 1949, pp. 233–57). In other words, the introduction of a subjectivist theory of value into our discipline transformed the latter in many unforeseen ways. For example, the role of producers and merchants in markets had to be reconsidered in such a way as to match the action of consumers. Most important, different consumers have different wants. The consumer cannot be treated as a stereotype. Individuality came to matter.

Nevertheless, the subjectivism which during the last quarter of the century found universal acceptance was still a narrow concept, a subjectivism of wants and not of minds. These wants were typically conceived as "propensities" or "dispositions," such as might easily be thought of as properties of human bodies or other pieces of nature.

In Mises's work we reach the second stage, the subjectivism no longer of wants, but of means and ends. Mises criticizes Menger for thinking that men might commit errors in satisfying wants and points out that no man can tell another what ends he should pursue. Here choice has become the prototype of human action, and choice presupposes a mind capable of choosing between rival ends.

On the other hand, while Misesian subjectivism is one of mind, and no longer of wants, it is one of limited mind. The relation of means to ends has become problematical, but the ends themselves not; they are "given" to us, whatever that may mean.

The third stage of subjectivism finally, which we prefer to describe as the subjectivism of the active mind, is evidently identical with what our authors call "dynamic subjectivism." In a world of change, action takes the form of the execution of plans previously conceived which are couched in terms of means and ends. But plans may, and often do, fail. From time to time they have to be revised by the mind in control of action. This is not merely a matter of watching continuously the adequacy of means planned to be used to ends pursued, but also of watching the ends themselves, e.g. whether they are still worth pursuing, whether other ends have become more attractive, etc. This evidently is the form of what our authors say "views the mind as an active, creative entity in which decision-making bears no determinate relationship to what went before. Here decision-making is literally a 'cut', a new beginning." This "highest" stage of subjectivism is evidently very much Shackle's own. Here, we may say, radical subjectivism, the Austrian program of 1974, has (provisionally) reached maturity. (In particular, see Shackle, 1972.)

INTELLIGIBILITY AND THE METHOD OF SUBJECTIVISM

Having thus far endeavored to promote our authors' cause by setting their main theme within a framework of history of thought and evolution of ideas rather than of abstract analysis, we propose to devote the remainder of this review to elucidating a few points concerning the methodology appropriate to subjectivism on which we either disagree with them or may have failed to grasp the full import of their words.

On pages 22–3 we read that the determinism of "the well-known covering-law model of scientific explanation…is closely related to the 'apodictic' praxeological theorems of Mises…and the 'exact' laws of Menger…For both of these economists, there was a variant of subjectivism that had much in common with the rigidly deterministic systems of classical mechanics."

This argument seems to rest on confusion between empirical regularity and logical necessity. Classical mechanics and the covering-law model belong of course to the former category while Menger and Mises are concerned with those necessary qualities of action which result from the fact that for them *action* is *thought*, not a piece of nature.

A similar misunderstanding appears to have arisen concerning Machlup's position, whom our authors seem to regard as a determinist (p. 24). While admittedly his methodological position is under dispute, in our understanding he followed Weber in regarding ideal types as instruments of thought necessary to reduce the empirical world to intelligible order. Determinism is not a property of action as such, but our mind finds it easier to grasp some aspects of action, e.g. recurrence, if they are presented to it *as though* they were determinate. Other aspects may be more readily grasped without this property of our model.

We come to the vexed question of "pattern prediction." We understand this to mean that concerning a class of events, it is not the single events composing the class, but characteristics that the events hold in common that are predicted. From the Malthusian law of population to the Phillips curve most such predictions have in fact proved to be notorious failures. It would be helpful if supporters of the notion of pattern prediction on occasion were to support their case with a few examples of successful prediction.

It is also clear that success in pattern prediction must depend on our ability to divide properties of events clearly into unique and typical ones. But all economists know that one of the most formidable obstacles to the establishing of empirical generalizations in our discipline is that as a rule the *cetera* do not remain *paria*, i.e. the facts about which we want to make generalizations are invariably linked to, or depend on, other facts which exist in such numbers and variety that it is impossible to enumerate all of them. If so, how is pattern prediction possible without an extensive list of *cetera paria*? Or are we to understand that the patterns to be predicted are to be found on such a high level of abstraction that they remain unaffected by any change in the state of knowledge?

If, as dynamic subjectivists, we reject determinism as a principle of explanation of events observed, antecedent and consequent, we need to find another. *Intelligibility* offers itself as an alternative, but, as this is a notion peculiar to products of the mind, we must, especially in this age of post-positivism, exercise some care in its use and clarify its background. The following features of the situation call for our attention.

Lending intelligibility is a principle of ordering events applicable to products of the mind only, by making them accessible to minds other than that which originated them. Intelligible is to us that which we can understand, and what we can so understand is its meaning.

Elucidation of meaning is a typical research procedure of the social sciences. Phenomena and processes in the realm of nature have no meaning that is accessible to us. The natural sciences thus have to employ other methods. They must, as best they can, relate observable events to each other and try to fashion an order out of them. *Hermeneutic* disciplines, like the social sciences, by contrast, can and should do more than that.

To understand human action means to understand the plan which guides the observable acts to which it gives rise. The *hermeneutic* method, which aims at enabling us to understand action, rests on the parallelism between action and plan, a fact which has no parallel in nature. The plan, gradually unfolding in space and time as it is executed, contains a scheme of orientation which comprehends ends, means, and obstacles encountered. Action is orientated to them.

Choice is the prototype of human action. It presupposes a mind presented with alternatives that it is capable of weighing them. Meaning presupposes a mind capable of attributing it to events. Planning presupposes a mind capable of imagining a future different from the present. Subjectivism without the autonomy of the human mind makes very little sense.

ON MAKING INSTITUTIONS INTELLIGIBLE

Our authors rightly point out that institutions "reduce but do not eliminate uncertainty, they provide, as it were, 'points of orientation'" (p. 32; see also Lachmann, 1971, esp. pp. 49–91). In Chapter 3 on "Knowledge and Decisions" they successfully criticize Hayek's view "that institutions also convey knowledge in the sense that the routine courses of action they embody are efficient adaptations to the environment. A vague Darwinian process is postulated which weeds out institutions with inferior survival properties" (pp. 39–40). They correctly emphasize "indivisibilities" as an obstacle to such smooth adaptation. This is a point which warrants and demands elaboration, even though we would prefer to speak of the complementarity of institutions, especially those of a capitalistic market society, it appears to give rise to at least three classes of problems that call for our attention.

In the first place, such complementarity finds expression in the institutional order of society. Within it, not all institutions have the same function. Some are more fundamental than others. As the classical economists knew well, property and contract, as well as the agencies necessary to enforce their observation, are basic institutions of market society. They must exist before there can be markets which function smoothly.

Secondly, we must distinguish between what Menger called "organic" and "pragmatic" institutions, those which have been evolved by market forces and those which owe their existence to the "social will," i.e. in modern conditions, the state. Not all institutions are organic. Even so, there remain open problems. How do we classify trade unions which seem to fit into neither category?

Finally, if institutions are to remove uncertainty, they must be permanent. But if they are to be shaped by market forces they must be flexible. How, within the institutional order of modern market society, is this problem resolved? Do we have to say that it is only in the interstices between the firm and immutable parts of the edifice that market forces can operate and we find sediments of organic institutions?

CONCLUSION

For half a century now, ever since it became the fashion to emulate the ways of thought of classical mechanics, and the darkness of the age of the econometricians fell upon us, economists have suffered from a sad narrowing of outlook. Many, perhaps a majority of them, today identify rational conduct with the maximizing of functions.

Our authors have contrived to reverse this trend. This is perhaps their greatest merit. They are laying the foundations for an approach which, in true Austrian fashion, rests on a broad interpretation of the potential of human reason while, at the same time, also accounting for its practical limits. For in a world of change all our practical knowledge is always problematical, and it may happen to us that the objects of our learning become obsolete as fast as we are learning about them.

These are insights valuable to all economists. We all owe to our authors a perceptible widening of our horizon. Within the space thus gained, owing to their efforts, new areas of thought and action are coming into sight. As individualists Austrian economists will no doubt wish to explore them in various, perhaps in opposite, directions while husbanding their scarce resources.

REFERENCES

Hayek, F.A. (1955), *The Counter-Revolution of Science: Studies on the Abuse of Reason*, New York: The Free Press of Glencoe.

Lachmann, Ludwig M. (1971), *The Legacy of Max Weber*, Berkeley: The Glendessary Press.

Mises, Ludwig (1949), *Human Action: A Treatise on Economics*, New Haven: Yale University Press.

Shackle, G.L.S. (1972), *Epistemics & Economics: A Critique of Economic Doctrines*, Cambridge: Cambridge University Press.

5. Schumpeter and Kirzner on competition and equilibrium

Don Boudreaux

> There is a difference between Kirzner's theory of entrepreneurship and that of Schumpeter. Schumpeter's entrepreneur is a disequilibrating force in the economic system; he initiates economic change. Kirzner's entrepreneur plays an equilibrating role... Unlike Schumpeter's entrepreneur, he is not so much the creator of his own opportunities as a responder to the hitherto unnoticed opportunities that already exist in the market. (Paul J. McNulty, 1987, p. 537)

Israel Kirzner's *Competition and Entrepreneurship* (1973) is often credited as having influenced the resurgence of interest in Austrian economics beginning in the 1970s. This book both advanced the Austrian conception of competition as a rivalrous process and made this idea of dynamic competition more acceptable to non-Austrian economists. And as its title suggests, the entrepreneur is seen as key to the competitive process. Kirzner's concern with entrepreneurship continues a long tradition in the Austrian school that was developed most thoroughly by Joseph Schumpeter. However, as indicated by the above quotation from Professor McNulty, and as Kirzner himself notes, his theory of entrepreneurship differs from Schumpeter's theory. The main difference is that Kirzner sees the entrepreneur as an equilibrating force, whereas Schumpeter views the entrepreneur as a disequilibrator. But such terminology overstates the differences between Kirzner's theory and Schumpeter's theory. The purpose of this note is to develop a model in which the entrepreneurial activity emphasized by Kirzner is complementary to the entrepreneurial–development process as explained by Schumpeter.

SCHUMPETER'S THEORY

Paul Samuelson (1976, p. 747) neatly characterizes the entrepreneur-driven innovation process as modeled by Schumpeter: "The violin string is plucked by innovation; without innovation it dies down to stationariness, but then along comes a new innovation to pluck it back into dynamic motion again."

The Schumpeterian enterpreneur is an innovator plucking the strings and, as a consequence, a disequilibrator. In Schumpeter's theory, innovations – which are the basic stuff of entrepreneurial action – disturb the calmness of equilibrium conditions (Schumpeter, 1934, esp. pp. 128–56).

Schumpeter questioned the relative significance of the type of competition that is the main concern in standard economic theory. This is competition that brings prices into closer alignment with costs. Schumpeter did not deny that, *ceteris paribus*, prices equal to costs are better than prices not equal to costs. Nor did he deny the existence of competitive forces working to keep prices equal to costs. But he insisted that the *ceteris paribus* conditions typically invoked to explain price determination contain what in fact are the most significant features of real-world competition. According to Schumpeter (1942, p. 84), the kind of competition that "counts" is

> the competition from the new commodity, the new technology, the new source of supply, the new type of organization (the largest-scale unit of control for instance) – competition which commands a decisive cost or quality advantage and which strikes not at the margins of the profits and the outputs of the existing firms but at their foundations and their very lives.

By working with competitive models that are designed to explain only the logic of price determination, and (as a consequence?) by defining competition only as the equilibrating force in price-theoretic models, economists overlook or misinterpret the many other desirable nonprice features and outcomes of real-world competition. The problem with mainstream theories of competition is not that they take product qualities, technology, tastes, etc., as given and fixed in order to sharpen their focus on the forces of price determination. Abstraction is necessary for all theory. The problem with these theories is rather that economists forget that the heuristic assumptions of their models of price competition have neither descriptive nor normative content. Competition works in many dimensions, with the price dimension being only one. As a result, many economic phenomena other than prices require explanation. Accounting for and explaining the several dimensions of competition was for Schumpeter the task to which economic theorists should attend. Schumpeter was critical not so much of the logical consistency of the theory of perfect competition as of its relevance.

KIRZNER'S THEORY

Kirzner's criticism of neoclassical competition theory is different from Schumpeter's criticism. Whereas Schumpeter questioned the applicability of the theory, Kirzner's contribution is to fill a logical gap in mainstream theory in which competition is modeled only as a price-determining force. Kirzner's work contributes to a better understanding of the forces of price determination than can be had from the model of perfect (or pure) competition.

The correct intuition behind the theory of perfect competition is that prices are bid down to minimum costs of production by the rivalry of other actual and potential sellers. It is thus a theory of price determination that justifiably abstracts from all phenomena judged to be incidental to the task of explaining the logic of how competitive rivalry keeps prices from remaining higher or lower than costs. But as Kirzner and others note, the equilibrium outcome of the competitive process as modeled by economists came to be defined as competition: the outcome is confused with the process that leads to the outcome. Human action and choices are thus squeezed from the model and, hence, from the economist's notion of price competition. The model does not explain how particular prices actually come to be set in competitive markets.

Central to Kirzner's thesis is the recognition that acting entrepreneurs are indispensable for the changes in prices and the pattern of resource allocation that occur under competitive conditions. Kirzner's emphasis on entrepreneurship as conscious, volitional action is in the tradition of Menger (1981 [1871], 1985 [1883]), Mises (1949), Hayek (1948), and other Austrians who were skeptical of theories in which social phenomena can not be traced back to the choices and actions of individuals. The Mengerian insistence on tracing all social outcomes to their causes at the level of individual actors is now labeled "methodological individualism."[1] Of course, tracing social phenomena back to choices made at the level of the individual does not imply that these phenomena are intended or even understandable by those whose actions produce the phenomena. Austrians generally appreciate the reality of the invisible hand. However, a minimum criterion for a theory's acceptance is that the outcomes explained by the theory be understandable as the result of human action, if not necessarily of human intention.[2]

By this criterion, the standard model of competition, as it developed since the 1930s, is incomplete. Because this theory assumes that everyone is a price taker, the pattern of prices and resource allocation generated by putting the model of perfect competition through its paces is emphatically not the result of human action. Genuine choice – i.e., decision-making opportunities that contain the possibility for individual decision makers to have something more than a negligible effect on market outcomes – is thus excluded from the mainstream economists' theory of competition.

The result of this method of theorizing is that the central phenomenon to be explained by price theory, price, cannot be traced back to human action in standard models of competition. No one ever has control over price as long as markets are "competitive." Prices instead are set wholly by the impersonal forces of supply and demand with no human intervention actually to carry out the task of price setting in individual markets. As Arrow (1959) demonstrated, to give someone in the model the power to change prices in response to excess demand or supply is simultaneously to abandon competition as defined in the model. Arrow concluded that the existence of perfect competition implies equilibrium. It is at this point in the theory of competitive price determination that Kirzner's work on entrepreneurship makes its contribution.

Kirzner accepts the task of mainstream competition theory (i.e., the explanation of prices and output levels in different industries), but he reformulates the theory of competitive price determination to incorporate a plausible explanation of how prices are actually set. Although Kirzner recognizes that the tasks of competition in reality go far beyond keeping prices equal to costs, the thrust of his theory is to resurrect the role of human action in bringing about the prices that equate supply and demand. Kirznerian entrepreneurship – which is spread throughout the economy at the level of the acting person – accomplishes what the Walrasian auctioneer would accomplish were the auctioneer not a fiction. The aspect of entrepreneurship emphasized by Kirzner is that which is responsible for actually setting equilibrium prices so that given supplies and demands are equilibrated with each other.

Kirzner's theory of entrepreneurship thus explains competitive price determination in a way that allows outcomes to be traceable to individual human actions. Instead of avoiding the problem by merely asserting that prices are set by the impersonal forces of demand and supply, or instead of relying upon the auctioneer as Walras did, Kirzner's theory of price determination is consistent with methodological individualism: All prices, at each moment in every market, are the result of entrepreneurial action.

The substance of Kirzner's reformulation of price theory goes beyond making the theory consistent with the Austrian requirement of methodological individualism. An additional benefit of Kirzner's work is that it allows economists to escape the trap of having to label all real-world exchanges as monopolistic (see, e.g., Arrow 1959) simply because actual prices are set by flesh-and-blood people. By putting human decision making back into the theory of competitive price determination, the distinction between competitors and monopolists is no longer synonymous with the distinction between price takers and price makers. Kirzner's version of price theory avoids the unhelpful notion of competition in which all pricing decisions by sellers are defined as monopolistic. The search for, and the identification of, real-world monopolies can then proceed along lines that are less likely to lead to conclusions in which activities that are vital for competition in reality (e.g., price cutting, advertising, product differentiation) are perceived as monopolistic through the lens of standard price theory simply because these activities are inconsistent with price-taking behavior.[3]

Kirzner's theory goes a long way toward showing that price-setting by flesh-and-blood people does not imply that monopoly power infects markets. Nor does this notion of competition imply that entrepreneurs are free to set whatever prices they like. The decisions of what prices to set are constrained by the willingness of consumers to buy outputs and the willingness of input owners to sell the services of their factors. Monopoly power exists when an entrepreneur (or group of entrepreneurs) are artificially shielded from the would-be constraining forces generated by the actions of other entrepreneurs. It follows that no sensible general rule can be devised that enables economists or the courts to distinguish between "competitors" and "monopolists" solely by measuring elasticities of demands of different producers.[4]

Although the definition of an artificial barrier to the forces of competition is difficult to formulate (and unnecessary for purposes of this paper), under no conceivable set of circumstances will *any* real-world markets operate with prices that are not selected by someone. That someone is the Kirznerian entrepreneur, and the insight that human action is a necessary element in any theory of price determination is Kirzner's main contribution to the economic theory of competition.

EQUILIBRIUM OR DISEQUILIBRIUM?

The above discussion suggests that the common practice of labeling Schumpeter's entrepreneur as a "disequilibrator" and Kirzner's entrepreneur as an "equilibrator" is unhelpful. Kirzner himself adopts this practice by noting that

> there is one important respect – if only in emphasis – in which Schumpeter's entrepreneur differs from my own. Schumpeter's entrepreneur acts to *disturb* an existing equilibrium situation. Entrepreneurial activity *disrupts* the continuing circular flow. The entrepreneur is pictured as *initiating* change and as generating *new* opportunities. Although each burst of entrepreneurial innovation leads eventually to a new equilibrium situation, the entrepreneur is presented as a *disequilibrating* rather than an equilibrating force. … By contrast my own treatment of the entrepreneur emphasizes the equilibrating aspect of his role. (1973, pp. 72–3; emphasis in original)[5]

Schumpeter modeled the entrepreneur as a force that disrupts an equilibrium pattern of resource allocation by introducing new products, production techniques, etc., while Kirzner is emphatic that his entrepreneur is an equilibrating force. But this distinction is of little help for distinguishing between the essential properties of Schumpeter's notion of entrepreneurship and that of Kirzner. The important question here is what is meant by equilibrium. In contrast to their skepticism of the neoclassical theory of competition both Schumpeter and Kirzner too willingly accept the standard neoclassical notion of equilibrium.

Schumpeter and Kirzner both follow standard practice by defining market equilibrium as a situation in which relative prices equate the supplies and demands implied in the *given array of tastes, technology, and resource availabilities.* Whereas Schumpeter highlighted those activities that change the givens, Kirzner's focus is on the activities that actually establish equilibrium prices given the particular givens. As Kirzner says, "For me the function of the entrepreneur consists not of *shifting* the curves of cost or of revenues which face him but *of noticing that they have in fact shifted*" (1973, p. 81; emphasis in original). That is why Schumpeter saw entrepreneurship as disequilibrating (because the Schumpeter entrepreneur shifts the curves) while Kirzner sees it as equilibrating. A broader concept of the competitive market process, however, allows recognition of both functions of entrepreneurs while avoiding sterile debates on whether the entrepreneur equilibrates or disequilibrates. A broader concept of competition implies a broader concept of equilibrium. Use of such a concept allows the theorist to take into account the fact that changes in variables other than price can be equilibrating. Both Kirzner's *and* Schumpeter's entrepreneur are equilibrating in this broader context.

Figure 5.1 is useful for comparing Kirzner's entrepreneur with Schumpeter's and for broadening the concept of competitive equilibrium. The horizontal axis measures the money price of some particular good while the vertical axis measures the quality of the good. For simplicity, I reduce quality to a single dimension – e.g., expected life of the product. Although this assumption is unrealistic, the point being made applies to real-world cases in which quality is multidimensional.

Obviously, the higher the quality of the good the higher is the price that consumers are willing to pay for the good. We can thus draw in a family of hypothetical indifference curves showing some aggregate of consumers' subjective evaluation of the tradeoff of lower prices for higher quality. These curves are labeled "I." Indifference curves further to the left represent higher levels of consumer satisfaction.[6]

Of course, producers face a tradeoff between price and quality also. Because quality is not free, higher levels of quality are more costly to provide and, thus, firms must receive a greater amount of revenue from sales if they are to produce higher-quality goods and services. If we assume quantity sold per firm to be constant, higher prices are necessary for larger revenue. The tradeoffs faced by producers are represented by the isoprofit curves labeled "π."

Each of these curves shows different combinations of price and quality for which a firm's level of profits is unchanged. Isoprofit curves further to the

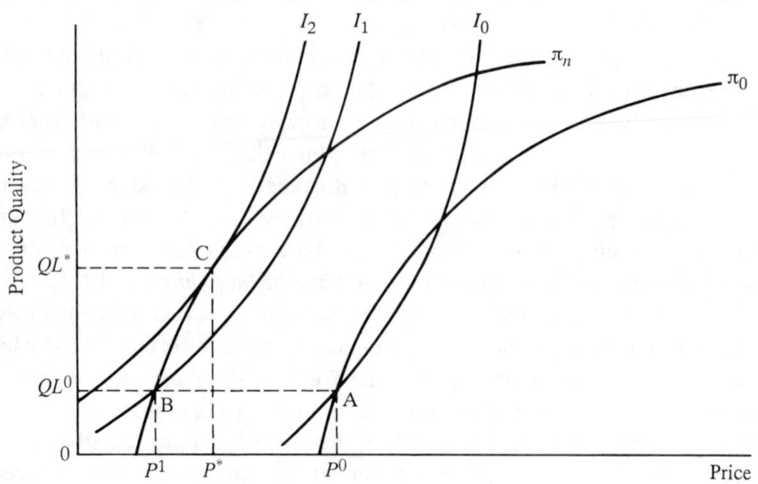

Figure 5.1

right represent higher levels of profits.[7] The curve labeled "π_n" is the normal-profit curve. Production at any point to the left of π_n will not take place because, at these points, firms do not cover their full costs; production at any point to the right of π_n yields above-normal profits which attract other competitors into the field.

Assume for now that the quality of the good is QL^0, and that the price of the good is P^0. This price-quality combination is shown as point A. Producers are earning above-normal profits (of π_0) while consumers receive an amount of satisfaction represented by I_0. Clearly, if product quality is *fixed* at QL^0, the only available task for competition is to force price down from P^0 to P^1. Consumers benefit from the price reduction because at point B consumers are on an indifference curve I_1 that represents a higher level of satisfaction than I_0. The long-run equilibrium price can fall no lower than P^1 as long as product quality is fixed at QL^0. Given QL^0, P^1 is the equilibrium price which equates supply and demand.

But notice that there are many combinations of price and quality that afford consumers even more satisfaction than they receive at point B and that allow firms to earn enough profit to remain in business in the long run. Indeed, in the hypothetical case portrayed in Figure 5.1, product quality of QL^* in combination with price P^* represents the maximum possible consumer satisfaction obtainable in this market. The price-quality combination of P^*,

QL^* is on I_2, which is the highest possible level of consumer satisfaction obtainable in this market. To insist that price P^1 is the optimal or equilibrium price simply because it is the lowest possible price given the level of product quality QL^0 is to ignore the fact that improvements in product quality are possible and desirable. To ignore the possibility of improvements in the nonprice dimensions of outputs implies an overly restricted definition of competitive equilibrium.

As shown in Figure 5.1, there are many prices that yield just-normal profits but which nevertheless leave room for welfare improvements. For a market to have "room for improvement" is for a market to be in disequilibrium. As long as disequilibrium persists, competition still has tasks to perform. Equilibrium prices, then, as conventionally defined, do not necessarily imply market equilibrium in this broader context in which product qualities are not given. Put another way, when changes in product quality are incorporated into the competitive model as an equal with price adjustments, there is no longer a reason to refer to any price that happens to equate given supply and given demand as an equilibrium price because the supply and demand functions themselves may not be in their equilibrium positions.

Both Schumpeter and Kirzner accept the definition of equilibrium as a situation in which prices equate given supplies and demands. By this reasoning, every point along π_n is an equilibrium point. Because Schumpeter understood that movements in the nonprice ("quality") dimension are at least as prevalent and as socially valuable as movements in the price dimension, and because his entrepreneur is the driving force that causes these changes in nonprice variables, Schumpeter's emphasis was on entrepreneurship as a disequilibrating force. Kirzner, in contrast, chose to explain only movements in the price dimension. Because both theorists follow common practice by implicitly defining equilibrium as the equality of given supplies and demands, which is established by prices, they both regard changes in product quality as disequilibrating and changes in prices that eliminate above- or below-normal profits as equilibrating. In terms of Figure 5.1, the task of Schumpeter's entrepreneur is to initiate "disequilibrating" changes in the vertical direction (i.e., improve product quality), while Kirzner's entrepreneur ensures the "equilibrating" movements in the horizontal direction (i.e., reducing prices to the level of normal profits). Clearly, though, the activities of both of these entrepreneurs are an important part of the market process. To label the activities of one entrepreneur "equilibrating" while the activities of the other entrepreneur are labeled "disequilibrating" is arbitrary at best. Competition is more correctly modeled as a force that moves the market from less desirable price-quality combinations (point B) to more desirable price-quality combinations (point C). Any movement toward point C is equilibrating and should be recognized as such.[8]

CONCLUSION

Economists attempting to explain the forces and results of competition can profit from a broadened concept of equilibrium. This broadened concept (and models built upon it) should include quality adjustments and technological and organizational improvements in addition to price adjustments. That is, such a broadened concept would focus on nonprice variables in addition to the price variable. Competition, and the equilibria it gives rise to, can then be modeled not simply as the consequence of the pricing behavior of sellers, but rather as the consequence of price and nonprice decisions of market participants. Both Schumpeter's and Kirzner's entrepreneurs act as an equilibrating force in this broader sense.

NOTES

The author thanks Pete Boettke, James Buchanan, Roger Garrison, Randy Holcombe, Steve Horwitz, Israel Kirzner, and E.C. Pasour for helpful comments.

1. White (1985) provides a clear discussion of this methodological principle.
2. See Hayek (1967).
3. See, e.g. Cowling and Mueller (1978, 1981). In attempting to measure the welfare loss caused by real-world monopoly power, these authors include, as a social cost of monopoly power, all costs incurred by firms in reality that would not be incurred under conditions of pure competition. Among such costs explicitly mentioned by Cowling and Mueller are advertising and research and development expenditures.
4. In addition to the writings of some Austrians, other economists such as Fisher (1979), Demsetz (1982), Benson (1984), and DiLorenzo (1984) have made important contributions to reformulating the concept of monopoly as market power that exists when market participants are artificially or arbitrarily shielded from the competition of other entrepreneurs and firms.
5. See also Kirzner, 1973, pp. 125–31; and 1979, pp. 111–19.
6. The convexity of the indifference curves with respect to the horizontal axis results from the law of diminishing marginal utility. Higher product quality, *ceteris paribus*, is worth less to consumers the greater the amount of product quality they already have. Thus, consumer indifference requires price increases to be smaller and smaller as product quality is higher and higher.
7. The concavity of the isoprofit curves results from the plausible assumption of increasing cost of quality provision.
8. Of course, if product quality is higher than QL^*, the entrepreneur improves matters by lowering the quality of the product and offering it to consumers at a reduced price.

REFERENCES

Arrow, Kenneth J. (1959), "Toward a Theory of Price Adjustment," in Moses Abramovitz (ed.), *The Allocation of Economic Resources*, Stanford, CA: Stanford University Press.

Benson, Bruce L. (1984), "Rent Seeking from a Property Rights Perspective," *Southern Economic Journal*, **51**, October, 388–400.

Cowling, Keith, and Mueller, Dennis (1978), "The Social Costs of Monopoly Power," *Economic Journal*, **88**, December, 727–48.

—— (1981), "The Social Costs of Monopoly Power Revisited," *Economic Journal*, **91**, September, 721–5.

Demsetz, Harold (1982), "Barriers to Entry," *American Economic Review*, **72**, March, 47–57.

DiLorenzo, Thomas J. (1984), "The Domain of Rent-Seeking Behavior: Private or Public Choice?," *International Review of Law and Economics*, **4**, 185–97.

Fisher, Franklin M. (1979), "Diagnosing Monopoly," *Quarterly Review of Economics and Business*, **19**, Summer, 7–33.

Hayek, Friedrich A. (1948), *Individualism and Economic Order*, Chicago: University of Chicago Press.

—— (1967), "The Results of Human Actions but not of Human Design," in F.A. Hayek, *Studies in Philosophy Politics, and Economics*, London: Routledge & Kegan Paul, pp. 96–195.

Kirzner, Israel M. (1973), *Competition and Entrepreneurship*, Chicago: University of Chicago Press.

—— (1979), *Perception, Opportunity, and Profit*, Chicago: University of Chicago Press.

McNulty, Paul J. (1987), "Competition: Austrian Conceptions," in John Eatwell, Murray Milgate, and Peter Newman (eds), *The New Palgrave: A Dictionary of Economics*, vol. 1, London: Macmillan, pp. 536–7.

Menger, Carl (1981 [1871]), *Principles of Economics*, trans. Bert Hoselitz, New York: New York University Press.

—— (1985 [1883]), *Investigations into the Method of the Social Sciences with Special Reference to Economics*, trans. Francis J. Nock, New York: New York University Press.

Mises, Ludwig von (1949), *Human Action*, New Haven: Yale University Press.

Samuelson, Paul A. (1976), *Economics*, New York: McGraw-Hill, 10th edn.

Schumpeter, Joseph A. (1934), *The Theory of Economic Development*, trans. Redvers Opie, Cambridge, MA: Harvard University Press.

—— (1942), *Capitalism, Socialism, and Democracy*, New York: Harper & Bros.

White, Lawrence H. (1985), "Introduction," in Menger, 1985.

6. Beyond equilibrium economics: reflections on the uniqueness of the Austrian tradition

Peter J. Boettke, Steven Horwitz and David L. Prychitko

> Only those entirely blinded by the prepossession that economics must be a pale replica of mechanics will underrate the weight of this objection. A very imperfect and superficial metaphor is not a substitute for the services rendered by logical economics. … Economics is not about goods and services, it is about the actions of living men. Its goal is not to dwell upon imaginary constructions such as equilibrium. These constructions are only tools of reasoning. The sole task of economics is analysis of the actions of men, is the analysis of processes. (Mises, 1966, p. 357)

INTRODUCTION

The renewed interest in Austrian economics has brought in its wake disagreement. To a large extent, the disagreement reflects a healthy state of growth. With new students come new ideas which work their way into scientific thought, and with new ideas come resistance through reflection, discussion, and debate. Fresh thought always meets resistance from established doctrine. A recent example of resistance to the new ideas has come from Murray Rothbard, who has charged some Austrians, such as Ludwig Lachmann, with nihilism. He says:

> It is one thing to say, with Mises and his followers, and in contrast to the neoclassical economists, that equilibrium does not and can never, exist on the market. It is quite another thing to say that the market does not even harbor equilibrating tendencies.
>
> The upshot is really the scrapping of economic theory all together and the Lachmannian economist becomes a mere institutionalist and historian, recording past choices and trends. There is no question that Mises would have called such a doctrine anti-economics. (1985b, p. 284)[1]

While avoiding the term nihilism, Israel Kirzner has also expressed serious misgivings about recent Austrian theorizing. He writes,

> [T]o see the world as characterized by such extreme volatility is not only to deny the possibility of equilibrating tendencies, it is also to render economic science non-existent...
>
> It would be a bizarre irony indeed if the modern revival of the Austrian tradition, begun over a century ago as a brave defense of economic theory (against a dominant tide of historicism), were to find its most sophisticated expression in the denial of any possibility of systematic market forces. (1985b, pp. 2–3)

While other economists have also recently expressed dissatisfaction with general equilibrium theory, and wondered whether it is possible to have a systematic science without it (see Hahn, 1973; 1981), this essay will concentrate on the Austrian debate.[2] We will argue that dropping general equilibrium (or the evenly rotating economy) from economic theory is not equivalent to the abandonment of science. We will further argue that dropping general equilibrium analysis opens the way to an alternative theoretical approach, which we call "order analysis," which we believe captures what is most distinctive and promising about Austrian economic theory. Although order analysis gives history and empirical work a more prominent place, the analysis itself is not historicism. It is theory at its relevant best.

EQUILIBRIUM AND ORDER

To question the value of equilibrium analysis is not to question the value of economic science. Systematic thought is not equivalent to equilibrium analysis. The Austrian debate blurred the distinction. One can have a theory of the market without postulating that the market is always moving toward general equilibrium. One point we wish to emphasize is that this particular debate is one over methods, not over the status of economic science. "The specific method of economics," as Mises says, "is the method of imaginary constructions" (1966, p. 236). Since there is no justification for any imaginary construction except for its success in aiding science, any particular construct can be questioned without destroying the scientific nature of analysis. The debate, therefore, turns on whether or not the imaginary construction of general equilibrium is an appropriate and helpful tool for understanding the world. It is our belief that much of the current confusion results from the failure to remember the metaphorical status of general competitive equilibrium.

In science, as in everyday life, we rely on metaphors to express our ideas (McCloskey 1983). Economic equilibrium is a metaphor, developed under the influence of the physical sciences, in particular Newtonian mechanics and nineteenth-century physics. In the attempt to explain the interconnectedness of market activity, economists developed the imaginary state of system-wide equilibrium. The metaphor describes a logically consistent system, but the conditions necessary, such as full relevant knowledge and zero transaction costs, never exist. If they did, there would be no market process as the Austrians understand that term.

Rather than simply a metaphor, Rothbard claims that equilibrium "is an ever-present force, since it is the goal toward which the actual system is always moving, … [the] concept, then, is of legitimate and *realistic* importance" (1970 [1961], p. 236: emphasis added).[3] But is this position tenable? The Austrian emphasis has always been on changing market conditions. Movement toward the evenly rotating economy is only imaginable if value scales are fixed and technology and resources are held constant. Cowen and Fink (1985), however, have argued that freezing tastes, technology and resources is an exercise which illegitimately restricts the full force of the market process. Such a restricted view says little about the actual course of market adjustments.

If one argues that the equilibrating tendencies of markets are an empirical regularity, then human society must be tending toward a state of affairs without money, without firms, without any market institutions. As Fehl (1986) has argued, the very existence of coordinating processes in markets depends upon non-equilibrium situations. Moreover, the closer one gets to an equilibrium state the less effective the coordinating role of institutions becomes. What, then, does this say about the theory of spontaneous order? It seems that the very ordering processes that arise spontaneously in a market are undermined by the mechanical metaphor of equilibration.

If the imaginary construction of the evenly rotating economy (ERE) is useful at all, it is only as a foil where the theorist contrasts this imaginary world with the real world in order to elucidate the complexity of reality.[4] As Mises states, "The main formula for designing of imaginary constructions is to abstract from the operation of some conditions present in actual action. Then we are in a position to grasp the hypothetical consequences of the absence of these conditions and to conceive the effects of their existence" (1966 [1949], p. 237). While Mises characterizes the use of such imaginary constructs as indispensable, he also warns of the danger of their careless use. "It leads along a sharp edge; on both sides yawns the chasm of absurdity and nonsense. Only merciless self-criticism can prevent a man from falling headlong into these abysmal depths" (ibid.).

Much of neoclassical economics has fallen into one of these chasms with an exclusive concentration on equilibrium states. By forgetting the metaphorical nature of equilibrium, neoclassicists often view economic theory and equilibrium as synonymous.[5] In other words, economics has become "equilibriumics" (Woo, 1986, pp. 79–101). This "mechanomorphism" of economics is also found in what might be called neoclassical Austrianism.[6] When Austrians refer to proximity to an end state in their treatment of entrepreneurship they may be relying too much on the equilibrium construct.[7] In analyzing entrepreneurship, Austrians have traditionally postulated a world of Robbinsian maximizers, and allowed the entrepreneur to seek arbitrage opportunities which equilibrate the market. Such an entrepreneur need only exercise alertness to profit opportunities. But entrepreneurship is also characterized by *judgments* about imagined future opportunities (High, 1982). Once the role of judgment is added to alertness, expectations are granted full force and the satisfaction of some individuals' expectations can come only at the expense of the disappointment of others'.[8] While High rightly stresses that equilibration is inadequate to explain the endogeneity of market change, he too seems to fall back on an implicit equilibrium benchmark.

The equilibrium benchmark can only be justified if we take "equilibrium" to mean market clearing, rather than general equilibrium. Certainly *market clearing* is essential for a theory of market order. In any given market there is a tendency for supply to meet demand, but this is quite different from the mechanical metaphor of equilibration.[9] While equilibrium implies market clearing, market clearing does not imply equilibrium, with all of its questionable assumptions.[10] It appears to us that the equilibrium metaphor has proven misleading and that the time has come to seek a less mechanical metaphor, one that does not trivialize the incessant change of market processes.

"Logical economics," states Mises, "is essentially a theory of processes and changes. It resorts to the imaginary constructions of changelessness merely for the elucidation of the phenomena of change" (1966, [1949] p. 356). Following a Misesian research program, one is led to question any mechanical analogy to market processes. In particular, given the "mechanomorphism" of modern economics, Austrians need to move beyond the neoclassical paradigm, rather than try to fit into it. Neoclassical Austrianism merely attacks the status quo for concentrating on the long-run solution to the exclusion of the processes by which the result is achieved. Unfortunately, we do not fully reject the notion of an artificial and mechanical approach to the end state. We do not fully reject the mechanical metaphor. Underlying our reluctance may be an undue fear of destroying the scientific nature of economics.

Rejection of the equilibrium metaphor does not destroy the scientific status of economic theory. The development of a medium of exchange, the evolution of law, a growing division of labor, the relative price effects of the inflation process, and the calculation problem under socialism,[11] are but a few of the Austrian insights that do not depend on the idea of proximity to general equilibrium. Rather they characterize order analysis.[12]

CREATIVITY, COMPLEXITY, AND COORDINATION

Consider the development of a complex economy. Starting in a barter economy, people realize the gains to be made by the division of labor. Because this division increases productivity, people stand to benefit through specialization and exchange. However, coordinating barter exchanges becomes progressively more difficult because of the lack of double coincidences of wants, thus opening the door to the development of money.

Once a money is established, it facilitates further division of labor by making exchange easier and by permitting monetary calculation. Entrepreneurship drives this whole process. Not only does money emerge from exploiting the opportunities for indirect exchange, but the extensive division of labor results from attempts to capture profits. Increased specialization will continue until the added benefits of divided labor are outweighed by the increasing costs of complexity (High, 1986, p. 117).

In this story one clearly sees what Tyler Cowen has called the three characteristics of an ordering process. Creativity is the entrepreneurial element, both in the increased division of labor and in the development of money. The complexity aspect flows from the further division of labor. As economists have known since Smith, the division of labor increases the productive possibilities of a society and in so doing increases its complexity. Finally, the role of money is seen as a coordinating influence. By allowing profit and loss calculation, money enables entrepreneurs to use resources efficiently, and allows the division of labor to increase by facilitating the necessary exchanges. All of these three characteristics intertwine to form the "marvel" of the market (Hayek, 1980 [1948], p 87).

Most important though is the nature of this account. It is an evolutionary ordering process. It is a scientific alternative that works without reference to any equilibrium construct. An evolutionary process is open-ended, in that the process does not tend toward any end-state.

Consider what it would mean for human evolution to tend toward a final state. No biologist would ever say that we need to have a concept of a "fully evolved" human to understand the process of evolution. It would also seem questionable to attempt to explain evolution as a process "tending toward" such a being. That would necessitate both constructing the being *and* explaining the process. Similarly, the evolutionary process in economics does not refer to an end-state, but instead explains how creativity leads to complexity, while retaining a sufficient degree of coordination to make the complexity beneficial.

A serious concern raised by the preceding analysis is that by following this approach to studying market processes the economist will have trouble defending the market economy. For example, Kirzner has worried that by denying that market activity is strictly equilibrating one loses the ability to defend free markets. It seems to us, however, that the defense of the market becomes stronger when based upon analyses such as the above, without reference to any notion of equilibrium.

First of all, as scientists we must question our free market policy conclusions if they rely on an impossible world like the construct of the evenly rotating economy. If defending the market depends on movement towards general equilibrium, the case for the market would have to be declared both unrealistic and unpersuasive.[13]

Any defense of the free market which relies on the equilibrium state of market affairs misrepresents the ordering aspect of market activity and sets up an easy target for opponents.[14] For example, the spread of Keynesian economics was facilitated by the confusion of Say's Law with Walras's Law's.[15] If J.B. Say had meant by his Law of Markets that supply always equals demand, then Austrians would have joined Keynes in its rejection. Say's Law, however, can be understood as an ordering principle rather than an equilibrium condition.

An ordering principle describes the processes in market activity that produce mutually reinforcing sets of expectations, but does not deny that some expectations will be wrong. In the example of Say's Law, the ordering principle is that production is the source of demand. As Say states: "A man who applies his labor to the investing of objects with value by the creation of utility of some sort, cannot expect such a value to be appreciated and paid for, unless where other men have the means of purchasing it" (Say, 1971 [1880], p. 133). Viewing market activity this way "leads us to a conclusion that may at first sight appear paradoxical, namely, that it is production which opens a demand for products" (*ibid.*). In this form Say's Law does not rely on the assumption of perfect markets.

Profits, losses, bankruptcies, and money are necessary to the market process. They do not indicate inefficiency or market failure. The ordering principle view of Say's Law is an example of a way of understanding these phenomena without recourse to equilibrium constructions.

The equilibration language also led to theoretical conclusions that had profoundly misleading policy implications during the socialist calculation debate of the 1920s and 30s. The lack of emphasis on the non-equilibrium nature of the Austrian argument allowed Lange *et al.* to answer Mises in the eyes of the profession (Lavoie, 1985b). The failure of both the orthodoxy and the Austrians to realize the unique contribution of Austrian spontaneous order theory led to this confusion. The real Austrian theoretical contribution, and its policy implications, lie between mere institutionalism and the arid formalism of much neoclassical economics (Lavoie, 1986b).

BETWEEN INSTITUTIONALISM AND FORMALISM

The challenge that Austrians face today is to show that Austrian theory lies between non-theoretical institutionalism and non-historical formalism, that its value lies in opening its theory to being informed by history, and in its ability to use theory to interpret history. The challenge is to show that Austrian economics is empirical theory.

Rothbard has criticized young Austrians for the way they defend the relationship between theory and history. It leads, he says, to an "abandonment of theory altogether in behalf of a vaguely empirical institutionalism" (Rothbard, 1985a).

Recognizing that history informs theory is not nihilistic. It does not deny the importance of theory. Rather, it corrects the insufficient attention Austrians have paid to history. This is why the charges of nihilism are so dangerous; they miss the point of the problem with modern economics, both Austrian and neoclassical. It is not that economists undervalue theory; it is that they undervalue history.

Theory and its relationship to history have long concerned Austrian economists. Menger (1985 [1883]), launching the famous methodological debates known as the *methodenstreit*, argued that an economic theory of "exact laws" was necessary for understanding the complex historical record, a point which is now generally understood. The particulars of economic phenomena can only be made intelligible through a background of general, abstract theory.[16]

Austrians have progressed since Menger, and over time the rivals have changed from the German historicists to the contemporary modernists. In the interim, a bold defense of Austrian theory was put forward by Mises. He pointed out that Austrian economics is a product of Continental thought. Mises was strongly influenced by this tradition, as evidenced by his favorable references to Bergson, Collingwood, Croce, Dilthey, Husserl, and Schutz.[17] Unfortunately, Rothbard fails to understand these Continental roots, and recently dismissed these philosophers as "muzzy minded nihilists."[18]

But it is not possible to dissociate Mises from his continental roots. Austrian economics cannot be defended as a linearly deductive apodictally certain string of syllogisms, a Euclidean system presumed to be free from all the prejudices and ambiguities of historical research.[19] To claim apodictic certainty for an entire science is to claim the end of discussion, for either one believes in logic or one doesn't. Indeed, once one realizes the primordial fact of human action, one need only deduce to one's heart's content, never once confronting the real world.[20] The claim that theory is completely immune from historical refutation is a particular understanding of what theory is, and represents only one variant in the diverse Austrian methodological tradition.[21]

Mises, for example, says that "Reasoning and scientific inquiry can never bring full ease of mind, apodictic certainty, and perfect cognition of all things" (1966, [1949] p. 25). Instead, "All that man can do is submit his theories again and again to the most critical reexamination" (*ibid.*, p. 68).

Deductive logic is a necessary component of scientific inquiry, but it is not sufficient to establish a theory's relevance. What if, for instance, we are confronted with another theory which purports to be logically tight, but rests on a different set of axioms, say, like that of Debreu, or of Hollis and Nell?[22] As Bruce Caldwell (1984) rightly observes, "apodictic certainty" is not the issue. He asks: "How does one choose between competing theories, all of which claim to be logically deduced from true premises?" Theory choice depends on which questions scientists consider fruitful, and therefore which theories are more pragmatic, i.e., more successful at answering the questions scientists consider interesting and worthwhile. Mises, in fact, defends praxeology on pragmatic grounds stating that: "The practice of considering fellow men as beings who think and act as I, the Ego, do has turned out well; on the other hand, the prospect seems hopeless of getting a similar pragmatic verification for the postulate requiring them to be treated in the same manner as the objects of the natural sciences" (1966, [1949], p. 24).

In addition to appealing, internally, to the formal structure and validity of a theory, Austrians must also appeal to its relevance. That is, theory choice should be contextual.[23] Austrians must risk comparing their theory to other approaches, past and present. To judge the worth of a theory requires a process of interpretation and reflection, as well as logical ratiocination. This process is the means by which scientists persuade their contemporaries about the usefulness of their theory. Science succeeds when the guiding idea of the scientific process is the free flow of ideas in a reasonable communicative environment.[24]

One important method of keeping theory relevant is to employ its principles in the interpretation of concrete events. Mises's classic work of 1912 stands as a shining example of the integration of theory and history. *The Theory of Money and Credit* shows that theory and history are complements, not substitutes.[25] There is nothing nihilistic in recognizing this. On the contrary, using theory to interpret history, and history to inform theory, can only improve both. It is thus high time to reconsider our description of the relationship between theory and history. There is a distinction between theory and history, not a dichotomy. Thus Austrians lie somewhere between anti-theoretical institutionalism and ahistorical formalism.

CONCLUSION

Much of modern economics is trapped in an ahistorical equilibrium world, unable to render intelligible the purposive action of human beings in the real world.[26] The value of Austrian analysis has always been its realism. It is a human-centred approach, recognizing fallible humans acting in a world of constant flux. By moving beyond equilibrium theorizing and the dichotomization of theory and history, Austrians can advance the heritage passed on to us by Menger, Mises and Hayek.

As Austrians examine and debate these issues, we should recall Hayek's neglected *The Sensory Order* (1976, [1952]), and recognize that the mind is always in the process of becoming. The way we understand our theory, the way we put it to use, and the way we defend it changes as the nature of our knowledge and the problems we want answered change. Theoretical knowledge, like the market process, is neither equilibrating nor disequilibrating; it is rather an orderly process of change.

As Mises said:

> It is customary for many people to blame economics for being backward. Now it is quite obvious that our economic theory is not perfect. There is no such thing as perfection in human knowledge nor for that matter in any other human achievement. Omniscience is denied to man. The most elaborate theory that seems to satisfy completely our thirst for knowledge may one day be amended or supplanted by a new theory. Science does not give us absolute and final certainty. It only gives us assurance within the limits of our mental abilities and the prevailing state of scientific thought. A scientific system is but one station in an endlessly progressing search for knowledge. It is necessarily affected by the insufficiency inherent in every human effort. But to acknowledge these facts does not mean that present-day economics is backward. It merely means that economics is a living thing – *and to live implies both imperfection and change*. (1966, p. 7: emphasis added)

NOTES

The authors would like to express more than the usual thanks to Don Lavoie and Jack High for their detailed and extremely helpful comments on earlier drafts. In addition, we would like to thank the members of the Austrian Economics colloquium at the Center for the Study of Market Processes for their comments and suggestions. Notwithstanding, the opinions expressed within and any responsibility for remaining errors are exclusively our own.

1. More recently Rothbard (1986b, p. 17) has stated his concern in the following manner:

> In recent years, there has been an attempt by nihilists within Austrian theory to downgrade Boehm-Bawerk and pay allegiance to Menger alone. The nihilists, who in the name of subjectivism deny objective reality and therefore all economic law, are dead wrong, however. Boehm-Bawerk, like Menger, saw Austrian theory as analyzing indi-

vidual human beings subjectively evaluating objective reality. But Menger's work was fragmentary and therefore subject to misinterpretation; Boehm-Bawerk's mighty architectonic stands as undying testimony to the ability of Austrian methodology and subjective value theory to arrive at objective economic law. And Mises' great work stands, alongside Boehm-Bawerk's, as the Twin Towers of the Austrian system. He who denies Boehm-Bawerk, denies Mises, and repudiates the best of what economics has to offer.

It appears to us, however, that this is a misinterpretation on Rothbard's part of the modern developments in Austrian theory. No one is denying objective reality or truth. On the contrary, modern developments in Austrian economics are truth seeking. To the Austrian the emphasis is "individual human beings subjectively evaluating objective reality" as Rothbard states. The modern developments in Austrian theory, however, are attempts to refine and extend this analysis, not deny the possibility of economic science. As an economist Rothbard should realize that choices are on the margin. To find fault with Boehm-Bawerkian concepts such as the average period of production, does not mean the denial of other crucial insights made by Boehm-Bawerk, such as time preference theory of interest or his analysis of price formation in the horse market. Boehm-Bawerk does stand as one of the pillars of the Austrian system along with Mises, but so do Menger, Wieser, Hayek, Kirzner, Lachmann and Rothbard himself.

2. For a discussion of the historical origin of the debate see Lavoie (1978a, 1978b, 1979a and 1979b). Also see the exchange between Lachmann and White: White (1979) and Lachmann and White (1979).

   Some of the contributions in the Austrian literature that are relevant include: Kirzner (1973, 1978, 1979, 1981, 1982, 1985a, 1985b and 1985c), Lachmann (1976a, 1976b, 1976c, 1978, 1985 and 1986), O'Driscoll (1978), O'Driscoll and Rizzo (1985), Garrison (1982, 1985 and 1986), Littlechild (1982), Littlechild and Owen (1980), White (1981 and 1985), Cowen and Fink (1983 and 1985), Rothbard (1985a, 1985b, 1986a, 1986b and 1986c), High (1980, 1982, 1983, 1983–4 and 1986), Addelson (1984), Fehl (1986), Langlois (1983), Boettke (1986a, 1986b and 1988), Prychitko and Boettke (1985), Hayek (1967a, 1967b and 1979), Selgin (1986), Mittermaier (1986) and Buchanan (1982).
3. It is interesting that Rothbard chooses to describe market equilibration with reference to the analogy of a dog chasing a mechanical rabbit. This analogy is similar to one employed by Kenneth Boulding, who uses the story of a dog chasing a cat to describe the direction of change in an economy. Equilibrium for the dog is where the cat is, but the dog might never catch the cat. The concept, however, is useful to explain the direction in which the dog is running. Even though we don't agree with this target use of the equilibrium metaphor, it seems to us that Boulding's analogy is better, because it incorporates the changing conditions – the cat becomes aware of the dog and moves away. With the mechanical rabbit analogy, this process of endogenous change is lost.
4. Mises's description of the ERE, in fact, points to why it is of no other use in analyzing the market processes that result from purposive human action:

   [I]n the evenly rotating economy there is no choosing and the future is not uncertain as it does not differ from the present known state. Such a rigid system is not peopled with living men making choices and liable to error, it is a world of soulless unthinking automations; it is not a human society, it is an anthill. (1966, p. 248)
5. Roger Garrison in his article, "Time and Money," demonstrated this belief in the equivalence between theory and general equilibrium in the following manner "[T]he notion that 'money as veil' … allows us to identify the underlying general equilibrium relationships with which any theory, macroeconomic or otherwise, must ultimately be reconciled" (1984, p. 203, fn). While we consider Garrison's article one of the most important contributions to modern developments in Austrian economics, we cannot follow him on this equivalence of theory and general equilibrium, if general equilibrium is understood as it usually is within the modern literature. If, however, Garrison is merely suggesting that all economic theories must recognize the interconnectedness of economic activities and

that changes in real variables have real effects while changes in nominals effect nominals, then we would have no disagreement.

6. Mittermaier explains the adoption of mechanomorphism by the human sciences in the following manner:

> Mechanomorphism has emerged in economics due to the high respect held for the physical sciences. The physical sciences have largely succeeded in purging anthropomorphism from within their domain. That is, eliminating reference to mind and purpose in physical phenomena. Social scientists, who dwell in the phenomena of mind and purpose, have ironically attempted to purge the human sciences of their very object of study, the plans and purposes of human actors.
>
> A scientist engages in anthropomorphism when he ascribes human attributes to what is otherwise recognized as inanimate or at least not human. By analogy we may say that an economist engages in mechanomorphism when he ascribes mechanical properties to what is otherwise recognized as an aspect of human affairs or when he treats an economic system as though it were a mechanical system. (Mittermaier, 1986, p 237)

   It is a paradox that Austrian economics, which has always stressed human purposes and plans in economic analysis, would fall prey to the mechanistic language of equilibration. As Menger states: "The so-called social organisms ... simply cannot be viewed and interpreted as the product of purely mechanical force effects. They are rather the result of human efforts, the efforts of thinking, feeling, acting human beings" (1985 [1883], p. 133). See also Mises (1966 [1949]) and Hayek (1964 [1955]).

7. See the relevant sections of Mises (1966 [1949]), Rothbard (1970 [1961], Kirzner (1973, 1979 and 1985a) and High (1980, 1982 and 1986).
8. Ironically, in his recent work on the history of thought Rothbard finds "brilliance" in the very anticipation by theorists, such as Turgot, of these Austrian insights into market processes. As Rothbard states "in his [Turgot's] analysis of human action as the result of *expectations*, rather than in equilibrium or as possessing perfect knowledge, Turgot anticipates the Austrian emphasis on expectations as the key to actions on the market. Turgot's very emphasis on expectations of course implies that they can be and often are disappointed in the market" (1986c, p. 11).
9. This may be called a "partial market clearing" analysis as opposed to a partial equilibrium analysis.
10. Market clearing arises when quantity supplied equals quantity demanded. Market equilibrium is achieved when the above holds, as well as an equality of marginal rates of substitution across all goods and factors, thus allowing price to equal marginal cost.

    Viewed as such, partial equilibrium is essentially sectoral general equilibrium theory. States Hirshliefer (1984, p. 19), "microeconomics concentrates mainly upon equilibrium states of particular markets, presuming an equilibrium of the market system as a whole." Also, consider Friedman's interpretation:

> The distinction commonly drawn between Marshall and Walras is that Marshall dealt with 'partial equilibrium,' Walras with 'general equilibrium.' This distinction is, I believe, false and unimportant. Marshall and Walras alike dealt with general equilibrium; partial equilibrium as usually conceived is but a special kind of general equilibrium analysis – unless, indeed, partial equilibrium analysis is taken to mean erroneous general equilibrium analysis. (1953, p. 89)

    To the extent, however, that partial equilibrium theorists are analyzing markets consisting of firms, the use of money, etc., their analysis is inconsistent given the (at least implicit) assumptions of general equilibrium theory. For more on this see Fink (1983, 1984–5 and 1989) and High (1983–4 and 1984–5).

11. The calculation debate suggests a way in which we can defend the market as the best way of organizing society. As we discuss later in the essay, the equilibrium defense is inad-

equate. That argument is, however, simply a criticism. Though space does not permit us to delve deeply into it, an alternative positive defense of the market can be hinted at.

The thrust of this argument is that the reason the market generates a high degree of order is that it effectively processes the bits of knowledge scattered among market participants (Hayek, 1980 [1948]). Since much of this knowledge is of particular circumstances (*ibid.*), or even tacit (Polanyi, 1958), it cannot be accessed by, or articulated to, government agents (Lavoie, 1985a, p. 54ff.). Without such knowledge, no government action can improve upon the order generated in the market.

12. We argued above that there is a definite difference between order and equilibrium. The point we wish to add here is that though the notions of order and coordination are similar, they are also quite distinct. Both concepts concern themselves with *ex ante* expectations. While coordination emphasizes the limit where individual plans actually dovetail, order reflects the broader notion of internal predictability of the elements of an order to the individuals who are part of that order. As Hayek states, "Order with reference to society thus means essentially that individual action is guided by successful foresight, that people not only make effective use of their knowledge but can also foresee with a high degree of confidence what collaboration they can expect from others" (1972 [1960] p. 160).

Coordination implies that the plans and actions of different individuals are mutually compatible. The internal predictability necessary for social order, on the other hand, corresponds to the less limiting notion that individuals are capable of forming more or less correct expectations about the actions of others. Order encompasses, but is not synonymous with, coordination.

Thus, spontaneous order explanations of market activity are not concerned solely with the coordination of economic phenomena. Rather, spontaneous order explanations attempt to explain the being, becoming, and maintenance of social institutions that bring about order, with all of their diversity and complexity. For a fuller elaboration of these ideas see Cowen and Fink (1983).

13. For example, the Clark–Wicksteed exhaustion theorem can be viewed as a quick response to Marxian exploitation theory. This theorem, however, makes an equilibrium solution to the problem of wage earners receiving wages below their marginal product. An answer based on this line of reasoning merely substitutes a long-run state for the present and does not explain the processes by which wages equate with the value of the marginal product. Essentially, the exhaustion theorem apologizes for current discrepancies by asserting that in the long run such inequities will disappear. In reality, however, it is the very existence of such discrepancies that drives the market process. Rather than apologize for the existence of differing prices and wages, economists could analyze the importance of wage and price inequities in the processes which bring about social order.

14. That such an eminent theorist as Professor Lachmann could fall under the sway of such arguments is tribute to their power:

> It puzzles me that White fails to see that, by pretending to see 'spontaneous order' everywhere, we are playing right into the hands of our opponents who merely have to point to obvious instances of malcoordination to win debating points. Every case of malinvestment can be held against the market economy. Does it not show malcoordination? The 'absence of universal future markets' in Arrow and Hahn as an argument against the market economy makes sense only, but, alas, does make sense, against such 'universal affirmations' as I am now asked to subscribe to. (Lachmann and White, 1979, p. 7)

The difficulty here is that Lachmann is confusing the concepts of equilibrium and spontaneous order. It is not inconsistent with the notion of spontaneous order that there is malcoordination and no universal future markets. Spontaneous order describes the processes which bring about degrees of order, it does not describe an equilibrium. Lachmann's confusion perhaps stems from an earlier article by O'Driscoll (1978), in which he makes a similar mistake.

15. The point is demonstrated by Keynes's exclusive concentration in *The General Theory* (1936) upon the Cambridge economists, for example Marshall and Pigou, as the representatives of the Classical School, and his lack of references to the monetary disequilibrium economists, such as Thornton, Brown, Davenport, and Warburton). On the different understandings of Say's Law see Leijonhufvud (1981), Cowen (1982), and Garrison (1984). Also see Mises (1980 [1912]) and Say (1971 [1880], pp. 132–40).
16. By saying, however, that one's theory is composed of "exact" laws seems to free it, unjustifiably, of any criticism. Thus Knut Wicksell, although an admirer of the Austrian school, complained that exact "means finished or complete, and a science is not finished until it has completed all its tasks; so it is never really exact in the strictest sense of the word" (1904, p. 57). Certainly Menger did not consider economic theory to be finished, but the way he defended it seemed to render the existing, incomplete theory immune from criticism.
17. The specific citations in Mises are (1976 [1960] p. 46; 1966 pp. 24, 33, 100, 219; 1985 [1957], pp. 308, 312; 1978 [1962] pp. 47, 135–6). In addition to these citations, it must also be noted that Mises organized and led a seminar in the philosophy of Husserl while living in Vienna. Mises was also good friends with Schutz and it was Schutz who met Mises at the dock when Mises arrived in the United States.
18. It is interesting to note that Rothbard also relies upon the Continental tradition in his defense of Austrian economics. For example, he relies upon the Schutzian conception of the "life-world" to ground the action axiom (cf. Rothbard, 1979, pp. 31–61). Thus, this is another example where Rothbard in "pointing beyond himself" has influenced the direction of research which he now considers nihilistic. These developments, however, are not nihilistic, but are rather the consistent extension of the Austrian tradition, a tradition to which Rothbard has contributed greatly.
19. Admittedly, Mises himself often reads like this (see, for example, 1966 [1949] p. 39). This presents the theorist with the difficulty of interpreting "what Mises really meant." Bettina Bien Greaves shed light on Mises's view of interpretations of his work when she described the atmosphere at his New York seminar: "Mises encouraged participants in his seminar to ask questions. They should not accept his every statement as absolute truth, or, he said, he might as well be a dictator" (Greaves, 1981, p. 24).

    In choosing between the different interpretations of Mises, it seems plausible to seek that understanding of his meaning that best fits within his general theory of human action. It is the "spirit of the text" which speaks to us, and it is within this context that we hope to understand the Misesian system.
20. Though admittedly starting from a different set of axioms, namely, utility maximization, economists have in a way witnessed this in the works of such mathematical economists as Debreu, whose *Theory of Value* (1959) exemplifies the Euclidean position.
21. Austrian economists have never had a homogeneous methodological position. For example, Menger could be described as an Aristotlean essentialist, Mises a Neo-Kantian apriorist, Hayek a Popperian, Lachmann a Weberian hermeneutist and Rothbard a "radically empirical" neo-Thomist Euclidean. Each member of the school has put forward their own defense of a subjectivist approach to the social sciences. For a survey of the different Austrian methodological positions see White (1984). More recently, new defenses of the Austrian approach have come from Lavoie (1985c and 1986a), Ebeling (1986), O'Driscoll and Rizzo (1985) and Prychitko (1986), some of which is influenced by Bernstein (1983) and Gadamer (1985).
22. While Austrian theory is based on the "fundamental axiom" of human action, Hollis and Nell (1975) deduce their theory from the "primary fact" of "the reproduction of the system." Both sides argue that empirical testing of the theory is out of the question. For an Austrian response see Lavoie (1977).
23. Since the value of scientific theories is imputed from their applicability in answering the questions that science considers important, it is crucial to continue discussion within the scholarly community over what constitutes a good question and a good answer. Moreover, it would be interesting to analyze the distortions or benefits that have resulted from interventions by the government within this process.

24. The primary condition for a successfully truth-seeking scientific process is that the participants are reasonable. As Van Dun (1986, p. 22) says, "That we ought to be reasonable is the most fundamental, the most indubitable fact of all – the fact without which nothing else can be a fact." To deny that we should be reasonable itself requires an attempt to be reasonable. Hans Hoppe (1988) posits a similar line of thinking based on the primacy of argumentation.

    By reasonableness, Van Dun means that scientists should follow the ethical norms of purposeful dialogue, including openness to disagreement, not using rewards or threats, not compromising one's views, and respecting all of these norms in other scientists (1986, p. 24). In sticking to the rules of dialogue, scientists allow the scientific process to achieve a high degree of truth, much like the unfettered market process generates a high degree of order. See also Lavoie (1985a), Polanyi (1969), and Prychitko (1985).
25. Among the best examples of Austrian historical work are Rothbard (1975a, 1975b), Armentano (1981), and White (1984). In addition, the Workshop in Austrian Empirical Studies at George Mason University has begun a series of historical studies which apply Austrian theory. For example, see Horwitz (1986). The White book and the historical section of Selgin (1985), are examples of historical works that have informed Austrian theory. The theory of free banking is much better articulated because of such historical investigation.
26. For instance, consider the following statements: "Economic relationships are never perfectly competitive if they involve any personal relationships between economic units" (Stigler 1946, p. 24). "Traditional equilibrium theory does best when the individual is of no importance – he is of measure zero. My theory also does best when all the given theoretical problems arising from the individual's mattering do not have to be taken into account" (Hahn 1973, p. 33). Attempts at applying such a framework to interpret the historical record have been abysmal.

REFERENCES

Addelson, M. (1984), "General Equilibrium and 'Competition': On Competition as Strategy," *The South African Journal of Economics*, **52**(2).

Armentano, D.T. (1981), *Antitrust and Monopoly*, New York: John Wiley & Sons.

Bell, Daniel and Kristol, Irving (eds) (1981), *The Crisis in Economic Theory*, New York: Basic Books.

Bernstein, Richard J. (1983), *Beyond Objectivism and Relativism: Science Hermeneutics, and Praxis*, Chicago: University of Chicago Press.

Boettke, Peter (1986a), "The Market is a Spontaneous Order Part 1," *Nomos: Studies in Spontaneous Order*, **4**(5), September/October.

—— (1986b), "The Market is a Spontaneous Order Part 2," *Nomos: Studies in Spontaneous Order*, **4**(6), November/December.

—— (1988), "Evolution and Economics: Austrians as Institutionalists," *Research in the History of Economic Thought and Methodology*, **6**.

Buchanan, James (1982), "Order Defined in the Process of Its Emergence," *Literature of Liberty*, **5**(4), Winter.

Caldwell, Bruce (1984), "Praxeology and its Critics: An Appraisal,' *History of Political Economy*, Fall.

Cowen, Tyler (1982), "Say's Law and Keynesian Economics," in Fink (ed.), 1982.

Cowen, Tyler and Fink, Richard (1983), "Order Analysis and Economic Science," unpublished ms.

—— (1985), "Inconsistent Equilibrium Constructs: The ERE of Mises and Rothbard," *American Economic Review*, **75**(4), September.

Debreu, Gerard (1959), *Theory of Value*, New York: John Wiley & Sons.
Dolan E. (ed.) (1976), *The Foundations of Modern Austrian Economics*, Kansas City: Sheed & Ward Inc.
Ebeling, Richard (1986) "Toward a Hermeneutical Economics," in Kirzner (ed.), 1986.
Fehl, U. (1986), "Spontaneous Order and the Subjectivity of Expectations: A Contribution to the Lachmann–O'Driscoll Problem," in Kirzner (ed.), 1986.
Fink, Richard (ed.) (1982), *Supply Side Economics: A Critical Reappraisal*, Frederick, MD: University Publications of America.
—— (1983), "Partial Equilibrium and the Analysis of Resale Price Maintenance," Center for the Study of Market Process Working Paper No. 9.
—— (1984–5), "General and Partial Equilibrium Theory in Bork's Antitrust Analysis," *Contemporary Policy Issues*, **III**, Winter.
—— (1989), "Resale Price Maintenance: A Market Process Approach," Ph.D. dissertation, New York University.
Friedman, Milton (1953), "The Marshallian Demand Curve," in *Essays in Positive Economics*, Chicago: University of Chicago Press.
Gadamer, Hans-Georg (1985) *Truth and Method*, New York: Crossroad Publishing Co.
Garrison, Roger (1982), "Austrian Economics as the Middle Ground: A Comment on Loasby," in Kirzner (ed.), 1982.
—— (1984), "Time and Money: The Universals of Macroeconomic Theorizing," *Journal of Macroeconomics*, Spring.
—— (1985), "Intertemporal Coordination and the Invisible Hand: An Austrian Perspective on the Keynesian Vision," *History of Political Economy*, Summer.
—— (1986), "From Lachmann to Lucas: On Institutions, Expectations, and Equilibrating Tendencies," in Kirzner (ed.), 1986.
Greaves, B. (1981), "Mises's New York University Seminar (1948–1969)," *Libertarian Review*, September.
Hahn, Frank (1973), *On the Notion of Equilibrium in Economics*, Cambridge: Cambridge University Press.
—— (1981), "General Equilibrium Theory," in Bell and Kristol (eds), 1981.
Hayek, F.A. (1964 [1955]), *The Counter-Revolution of Science*, New York: The Free Press of Glencoe.
—— (1967a), "The Theory of Complex Phenomena," in *Studies in Politics, Philosophy, and Economics*, Chicago: University of Chicago Press.
—— (1967b), "Degrees of Explanation," in *Studies in Politics, Philosophy, and Economics*, Chicago: University of Chicago Press.
—— (1972 [1960]), *The Constitution of Liberty*, Chicago: University of Chicago Press.
—— (1976 [1952]), *The Sensory Order*, Chicago: University of Chicago Press.
—— (1978a), "The Primacy of the Abstract," in *New Studies in Politics, Philosophy, Economics, and the History of Ideas*, Chicago: University of Chicago Press.
—— (1978b), "Competition as a Discovery Procedure," in *New Studies in Politics, Philosophy, Economics, and the History of Ideas*, Chicago: University of Chicago Press.
—— (1979), *Law, Legislation, and Liberty*, Chicago: University of Chicago Press, chs 2, 10 and epilogue.
—— (1980 [1948]), "The Use of Knowledge in Society," in *Individualism and Economic Order*, Chicago: University of Chicago Press.

Hirshleifer, Jack (1984), *Price Theory and Its Applications*, Englewood Cliffs, NJ: Prentice-Hall.

High, Jack (1980), "Maximizing, Action, and Market Adjustment: An Inquiry into the Theory of Economic Disequilibrium," unpublished Ph.D. dissertation, UCLA.

—— (1982), "Alertness, Judgment and Entrepreneurship: A Comment on Kirzner," in Kirzner (ed.), 1982.

—— (1983), "The Market Process: An Austrian View," *Market Process*, **1**(1), January. (Reprinted as Chapter 1 in this volume.)

—— (1983–4), "Knowledge, Maximizing, and Conjecture: A Critical Analysis of Search Theory," *Journal of Post-Keynesian Economics*, Winter.

—— (1986), "Equilibration and Disequilibration in the Market Process," in Kirzner (ed.), 1986.

Hollis, M. and Nell, E.J. (1975), *Rational Economic Man*, Cambridge: Cambridge University Press.

Hoppe, Hans-Hermann (1988), "From the Economics of Laissez-Faire to the Ethics of Libertarianism", in Walter Block and Lew Rodwell (eds) *Man, Economy, and Liberty*, Auburn: Ludwig von Mises Institute.

Horwitz, Steven (1986), "The Panic of 1907: More Evidence for Private Money," unpublished ms., Center for the Study of Market Processes.

Keynes, John Maynard (1936), *The General Theory of Employment, Interest, and Money*, New York: Harcourt, Brace & Co.

Kirzner, Israel (1973), *Competition and Entrepreneurship*, Chicago: University of Chicago Press.

—— (1978), "Economics and Error," in Spadaro (ed.), 1978.

—— (1979), *Perception, Opportunity and Profit*, Chicago: University of Chicago Press.

—— (1981), "The Austrian Perspective," in Bell and Kristol (eds), 1981.

—— (ed.) (1982), *Method, Process and Austrian Economics: Essays in Honor of Ludwig von Mises*, Lexington, MA: D.C. Heath & Co.

—— (1985a), "Princes, the Communication of Knowledge, and the Discovery Process," in K. Leube and A. Zlabinger (eds), 1985.

—— (1985b), "Review of *The Economics of Time and Ignorance*," *Market Process*, **3**(2), Fall. (Reprinted as Chapter 3 in this volume.)

—— (1985c), *Discovery and the Capitalist Process*, Chicago: University of Chicago Press.

—— (ed.) (1986), *Subjectivism, Intelligibility, and Economic Understanding*, New York: New York University Press.

Lachmann, Ludwig M. (1976a), "On the Central Concept of Austrian Economics: Market Process," in Dolan (ed.), 1976.

—— (1976b), "Austrian Economics in the Age of the Neo-Ricardian Counterrevolution," in Dolan (ed.), 1976.

—— (1976c), "From Mises to Shackle: An Essay on Austrian Economics and the Kaleidic Society," *Journal of Economic Literature*, **XIV**(1), March.

—— (1978), "An Austrian Stocktaking: Unsettled Questions and Tentative Answers," in Spadaro (ed.), 1978.

—— (1985), "Review of *The Economics of Time and Ignorance*," *Market Process*, **3**(2), Fall. (Reprinted as Chapter 4 in this volume.)

—— (1986), *The Market as an Economic Process*, London: Basil Blackwell.

Lachmann, L. and White, L. (1979), "On the Recent Controversy Concerning Equilibration," *Austrian Economics Newsletter*, **2**(1), Spring.

Langlois, Richard N. (1983), "The Market Process: An Evolutionary View," *Market Process*, **1**(2), Summer. (Reprinted as Chapter 2 in this volume.)
Lavoie, Don (1977), "From Hollis and Nell to Hollis and Mises," *Journal of Libertarian Studies*, **1**(4).
—— (1978a), "Austrian Economics Seminar, Part 1: 1975–1976," *Austrian Economics Newsletter*, **1**(2), Spring.
—— (1978b), "Austrian Economics Seminar, Part 2: 1976–77," *Austrian Economics Newsletter*, **1**(3), Fall.
—— (1979a), "Austrian Economics Seminar, Part 3: 1977–1978," *Austrian Economics Newsletter*, **2**(1), Spring.
—— (1979b), "Austrian Economics Seminar, Part 4: 1978–1979," *Austrian Economics Newsletter*, **2**(2), Fall.
—— (1985a), *National Economic Planning: What is Left?*, Cambridge, MA: Ballinger Publishing Co.
—— (1985b), *Rivalry and Central Planning: The Socialist Calculation Debate Reconsidered*, Cambridge: Cambridge University Press.
—— (1985c), "The Interpretive Dimension of Economics: Science, Hermeneutics and Praxeology," Center for the Study of Market Processes Working Paper No. 15.
—— (1986a), "Euclideanism versus Hermeneutics: A Reinterpretation of Misesian Apriorism," in Kirzner (ed.), 1986.
—— (1986b), "Between Institutionalism and Formalism: The Rise and Fall of the Austrian School's Calculation Argument, 1920–1950," Center for the Study of Market Processes Working Paper No. 21.
Leijonhufvud, Axel (1981), "Say's Principle: What it Means and Doesn't Mean," in *Information and Coordination*, Cambridge: Oxford University Press.
Leube, K. and Zlabinger, A. (eds) (1985), *The Political Economy of Freedom: Essays in Honor of F.A. Hayek*, Munchen: Philosophia Verlag.
Littlechild, S. (1982), "Equilibrium and the Market Process," in Kirzner (ed.), 1982.
Littlechild, S. and Owen G. (1980), "An Austrian Model for the Entrepreneurial Market Process," *Journal of Economic Theory*, **23**.
McCloskey, Donald (1983), "The Rhetoric of Economics," *Journal of Economic Literature*, **XXI**, June.
Menger, Carl (1985 [1883]), *Investigations into the Method of The Social Sciences with Special Reference to Economics*, New York: New York University Press.
Mises, Ludwig von (1966 [1949]), *Human Action: A Treatise on Economics*, Chicago: Henry Regnery.
—— (1976 [1960]), *Epistemological Problems of Economics*, New York: New York University Press.
—— (1978 [1962]), *The Ultimate Foundation of Economic Science*, Kansas City: Sheed Andrews & McMeel, Inc.
—— (1980 [1912]), *The Theory of Money and Credit*, Indianapolis, IN: Liberty Press.
—— (1985 [1957]), *Theory and History: An Interpretation of Social and Economic Evolution*, Auburn, AL: Ludwig von Mises Institute.
Mittermaier, K. (1986), "Mechanomorphism," in Kirzner (ed.), 1986.
O'Driscoll, Gerald P. (1978), "Spontaneous Order and the Coordination of Economic Activities," in Spadaro (ed.), 1978.
O'Driscoll, Gerald P. and Mario J. Rizzo (1985), *The Economics of Time and Ignorance*, New York: Basil Blackwell.
Polanyi, M. (1958), *Personal Knowledge*, Chicago: University of Chicago Press.

—— (1969), "The Republic of Science: Its Political and Economic Theory," in *Knowing and Being*, Chicago: University of Chicago Press.

Prychitko, David L. (1985), "The Persuasive Nature of Science," *Market Process*, **3**(2), Fall.

—— (1986), "Interpretation over Prediction," presented at the 12th Annual Convention of the Eastern Economics Association meetings, Philadelphia, 10–12 April 1986.

Prychitko, David L. and Peter Boettke (1985), "Equilibrium, Action, and Order," unpublished ms., Center for the Study of Market Processes.

Rothbard, Murray N. (1970 [1961]), *Man, Economy and State*, Los Angeles: Nash Publishing Co.

—— (1975a [1963]), *America's Great Depression*, Kansas City: Sheed & Ward.

—— (1975b), *Conceived in Liberty*, (3 vols.), New York: Arlington House Publishers.

—— (1985a), Preface in Mises, 1985 [1957].

—— (1985b), "Professor Hebert on Entrepreneurship," *Journal of Libertarian Studies*, **7**(2), Fall.

—— (1986a), "The New Kochian Economics: The Hermeneutical Twist," *American Libertarian*, Summer.

—— (1986b), "Review of Eugen Bohm-Bawerk, *Capital and Interest*," *Laissez Faire Books*, October.

—— (1986c), *The Brilliance of Turgot*, Auburn, AL: The Ludwig von Mises Institute.

Say, Jean-Baptiste (1971 [1880]), *A Treatise on Political Economy*, New York: Augustus M. Kelley.

Selgin, George A. (1985), *The Theory of Free Banking*, unpublished Ph.D. dissertation, New York University.

—— (1986), "Praxeology and Understanding," unpublished ms., George Mason University.

Spadaro, Louis (ed.) (1978), *New Directions in Austrian Economics*, Kansas City: Sheed Andrews & McMeel, Inc.

Stigler, George (1946), *The Theory of Price*, Chicago: Rand-McNally.

Van Dun, Frank (1986), "Economics and the Limits of Value-Free Science," *Reason Papers*, Spring.

White, Lawrence H. (1979), "The Austrian School and Spontaneous Order: Comment on O'Driscoll," *Austrian Economics Newsletter*, **2**(1), Spring.

—— (1981), "Mises, Hayek, Hahn and the Market Process," in Kirzner (ed.), 1982.

—— (1984), *Free Banking in Britain*, Cambridge: Cambridge University Press.

—— (1985), Introduction to Menger, 1985 [1883].

Wicksell, Knut (1904), "Ends and Means in Economics," in *Selected Papers on Economic Theory*, New York: Augustus M. Kelley.

Woo, H. (1986), *What's Wrong with Formalization in Economics?*, Newark, CA: Victoria Press.

PART TWO

Cost and Choice

7. Expectations and expectations formation in Mises's theory of the market process

Richard M. Ebeling

> The main epistemological problem of the specific understanding is: How can a man have any knowledge of the future value judgments and actions of other people? ...The task with which acting man, that is, everybody, is faced in all relations with his fellows does not refer to the past; it refers to the future. To know the future reactions of other people is the first task of acting man. Knowledge of their past value judgments and actions, although indispensable, is only a means to this end. (Ludwig von Mises, (1985 [1957]) *Theory and History*, Auburn, AL: Ludwig von Mises Institute, p. 311)

INTRODUCTION

An increasing number of historians of economic thought have pointed out the existence of significant differences in the approach and methods of the founding fathers of marginal utility theory. Carl Menger and the Austrians, it has been argued, were distinctive in their attention to and emphasis on the problems of time, process and adjustment in the market order. Unlike the neoclassical traditions that emerged from the contributions of Jevons and Walras, the Austrians were less interested in comparative static analysis and much more concerned with the dynamics of an ongoing market process.[1]

The Austrian interest in the market process extended beyond Menger and those early Austrians whose major contributions were made before the First World War. It was also of central focus for many of the Austrians of the interwar period. While it is true that several of the Austrians of this period also devoted their efforts to formalizing the meaning of and conditions for economizing behavior (a formalization that had a significant influence on Lionel Robbins in his writing of *An Essay on the Nature and Significance of Economic Science*)[2] most of their writings never drifted too far from "process" questions. This was particularly pronounced in the writings of Hans Mayer,[3] Paul N. Rosenstein-Rodan,[4] and Oskar Morgenstern.[5] And especially after publishing his essay on "Economics and Knowledge" in 1937, the analysis of market process, knowledge and interpersonal coordination became *the* problem in the writings of Friedrich A. Hayek.[6]

In many of these writings by members of the interwar generation of the Austrian school, emphasis was placed on the "anticipatory" quality of economic decision-making because of the pervasive existence of uncertainty in the field of human action. The role and problem of expectations, therefore, were considered of profound importance for the understanding of all intertemporal and interpersonal processes.[7] Yet, at the same time, while pointing to the importance of expectations and the integration of expectations into economic analysis, during this period little towards a constructive theory of expectations and expectations formation was offered by the Austrian economists.[8] (Oskar Morgenstern attempted to formulate a constructive alternative with John von Neumann in their theory of games.)[9]

The same emphasis on time, process, adjustment and expectations was just as visible in the writings of another prominent member of the Austrian school during this time, Ludwig von Mises. In both his theory of money and his critique of socialism, among the features that appear most pronounced to the reader are the appreciation of imperfect knowledge, temporal and sequential adjustment to change, and the expectational quality of all economic evaluation and appraisement by the market agents. Indeed, the attention that Mises assigned to these topics led Arthur Marget to point out that Mises's "discussion of the role of uncertainty in the calculations underlying the pricing process, like so many other elements in Mises's general theoretical position, may be said to follow directly in the path traced out by Menger."[10]

Unlike many of his fellow Austrians, however, Mises *did* attempt to formulate a constructive theory of expectations and their formation in the market process. What is curious is that later Austrians have given little attention to Mises's attempted solution. There is almost no discussion of expectations formation in the writings of either Murray N. Rothbard[11] or Israel M. Kirzner.[12] The only recent Austrian to take the problem of expectations seriously has been Ludwig M. Lachmann.[13] In his essay, "From Mises to Shackle: An Essay on Austrian Economics and the Kaleidic Society," however, Lachmann suggests that Mises limited his application of methodological subjectivism to individual tastes and preferences and did not extend his "subjectivist" approach to expectations.[14] This is a peculiar conclusion for Lachmann to reach because in his review of Mises's *Human Action* Lachmann pointed out that "we must never forget that it is the work of Max Weber that is being carried on here."[15] As we shall see, it is Max Weber's approach that is the basis for Mises's theory of expectations formation.

THE INFLUENCE OF MAX WEBER

In his methodological writings, Ludwig von Mises has long been recognized as a fervent and uncompromising critic of positivism. Mises rejected as unworkable and unscientific the attempt to reduce mind to matter and to construct a science of economics on the basis of the purely quantitative, external manifestations of human actions. It was unworkable, Mises argued, because (unlike portions of the physical environment) there were no quantitative constancies in economics independent of human volition.[16] And it was fundamentally unscientific because, since the purpose of science was to understand reality, a science of economics that denied interest in and investigation of the mental processes that generated the observed residues of human actions and choices was placing out of bounds an essential domain of that reality.[17]

The influence of some of the classical economists (especially Nassau Senior and John E. Cairnes) upon Mises on the topic of methodology has been long recognized.[18] Less well known is the influence of the phenomenological tradition in philosophy on Mises's approach.[19] Though it is difficult to document any of the influence on Mises directly from his writings except for a few scattered footnotes and passing statements,[20] it is clear that both Max Scheler and Edmund Husserl had an impact on his own ideas on the theory of knowledge in the social sciences. It is particularly the concept of intentionality as the uniquely "human" ingredient to any theory of human action and the role of "essentialism" in discerning the universal categories of purposeful conduct that bear the phenomenological mark in Mises's approach.[21]

But the greatest influence on Mises in terms of method seems to have been Max Weber. At the end of the First World War Mises developed a close friendship with Weber when the latter taught for one semester at the University of Vienna.[22] In the 1920s, Weber's *Verstehende Soziologie* was a widely discussed and debated topic in Mises's famous private seminar.[23] And one of Mises's earliest essays devoted to the methodology of the social sciences was written in the form of an immanent criticism of Max Weber's concept of ideal types.[24]

Weber's starting point for historical and sociological analysis was the concept of "action" defined as "all human behavior…insofar as the acting individual attaches a subjective meaning to it."[25] It was the meaning behind an action from the actor's point of view that gave the action an orientation or reason for its occurrence. And it was an attempt to understand that meaning that was an essential goal of the social analyst; the meaning behind the actor's external behavior was the source of intelligible interpretation. "Social action," therefore, was, in Weber's words, an action by an individual "by virtue of the subjective meaning attached to it by the acting individual (or individuals); it takes account of the behavior of others and is thereby oriented in its course."[26]

It was the reciprocal orientations of subjective meanings by actors that enabled a "meaning" to be assigned to the "social" behavior observed. What defined a social action as "exchange," for example, were the respective meanings that the individuals imputed to both their own behavior and that of the others. "Without this 'meaning,'" Weber argued, "we are inclined to say an 'exchange' is neither empirically possible nor conceptually imaginable."[27] All of the relationships, objects and patterns of social and historical investigation were seen by Weber as having meaning ultimately, and only, in terms of the meanings of the social and historical actors whose doings were the concern of the social scientist.

In the attempt to understand both history and contemporary social orders, structures and forms of behavior, Weber relied upon the concept of the "ideal type." An ideal type is meant to be a stylized reconstruction, a selection of typical traits or characteristics conceived to represent for purposes of the analysis at hand those qualities in an individual, social institution or order, or historical period that enable an interpretive understanding of that individual, institution or order, or historical period. By its very construction, given the analytical problem at hand, it represents an accentuation of certain qualities or characteristics and thus an idealization of the various attributes the individuals or objects possess or have in common.[28]

MISES, PRAXEOLOGY AND IDEAL TYPES

Max Weber's conception of meaningful action is the starting point for Mises's formulation of "praxeology," a general theory of human action. But Mises believed that Weber had remained too much the child of the German Historical school, with its theoretical relativism. Both Mises and Weber believed that theory and history were inseparably intertwined; and that in one sense theory *was* the handmaiden of historical analysis and the level of generalization in theory construction was a function of the historical questions being asked. But for Weber any universal theory of human action would be too abstract and too general; every generalization involved movement away from the unique and individual details of the nonrepeating historical drama and, therefore, a movement away from the task of the social scientist. Thus while ideal types were, obviously, stylized generalizations, they were meant to be as concrete as the analysis permitted.[29]

Mises argued that all ideal typical constructions were subsidiary formulations of a wider and more generic conception of action, one from which all ideal types were derived. The logical categories of economics, Mises argued, were not obtained through accentuations or idealizations of *aspects* of human conduct. Instead, "they are obtained through reflections having in view the comprehension of what is contained in *each* of the individual phenomena taken into consideration."[30] That is, one looked for those elements in human conduct that were so general, so ever-present in any and all human actions that they must and did represent the universal in any and all human conduct. And these most general of characteristics were what defined all purposeful behavior: dissatisfaction with existing or expected conditions or circumstances; an imagined preferred state of affairs; and beliefs that methods were or could be available to bring about the desired change. "Action" was a relationship between chosen ends, selected means and conduct or conscious behavior to achieve the ends preferred with the means available.[31]

All subjectively meaningful action had these characteristics in common. And while this level of generalization, on the one hand, emptied "action" of all specific context, on the other hand it could then serve as a universal framework within which all human activity could be ordered, arranged and *understood*. Praxeology was a *logic of action* within which the specificities of concrete human choices could be analyzed.

The task of history, as Mises saw it, was to then apply the action framework – with its categories of means and ends, costs and benefits, (subjective) profits and losses – to the interpretive understanding and explanation of the residues of past human conduct. But history never reproduced the past; rather, Mises argued, it is "a condensed representation of the past in conceptual terms." It always involved selection, arrangement and interpretation.[32] It always involved an "understanding" of complex historical phenomena in terms of an analytical schema, i.e., the historian's story was his theory of the *relevant* facts and their relationships and interdependencies.[33]

The primary tool of historical understanding, Mises argued (and in this he followed Weber completely), was the ideal type:[34]

> [A]ll historical events are described and interpreted by means of ideal types… The ideal type itself is an outcome of an understanding of the motives, ideas, and aims of the acting individuals and of the means they apply… An ideal type cannot be defined; it must be characterized by an enumeration of those features whose presence by and large decides whether in a concrete instance we are or are not faced with a specimen belonging to the ideal type in question … when the historian … speaks of Napoleon, he must refer to such ideal types as commander, dictator, revolutionary leader; and if he deals with the French Revolution he must refer to ideal types such as revolution, disintegration of an established regime, anarchy.

UNCERTAINTY, IDEAL TYPES AND EXPECTATIONS

Mises uniquely argues that ideal types are useful not only for historical understanding, but for social and economic forecasting. Indeed, the ideal type is the method by which individuals are able to form expectations concerning the prospective behavior of other actors, and without which interpersonal coordination would be impossible.

It is only in *Human Action* and *Theory and History* that we find the most explicit references to the ideal type as a method for expectations formation. His earlier works emphasize the expectational and forward-looking character of choice and action but contain no explanation of the process of how such expectations are arrived at. There is some evidence that the writings of Alfred Schutz had a significant influence on Mises's theory of expectations. Schutz had been a student of Mises in the 1920s and they remained friends until Schutz's death in 1959. Schutz, in his 1932 volume, *The Phenomenology of the Social World*, had tried to extend Weber's ideas into a much more developed theory of the process and use of ideal type construction for the understanding of both historical and contemporary action.[35]

The dilemma for human activity in a social setting, Mises argued, was that it always occurred under the shadow of uncertainty. Like Frank Knight,[36] Mises distinguished between risk and uncertainty under the respective headings of class and case probability:

> Class probability means: We know or assume to know, with regard to the problem concerned, everything about the behavior of a whole class of events or phenomena; but about the actual singular events or phenomena we know nothing but that they are elements of this class.[37]
>
> Case probability means: We know, with regard to a particular event, some of the factors which determine its outcome; but there are other determining factors about which we know nothing.[38]

For the former category all of the standard methods of statistical inference apply. The interest or concern is with the probability of an outcome within a class of events, but with no knowledge of which individual element within the class the event will happen to. Knowledge of the frequency of an outcome can then be incorporated into the decision-making process.

However, Mises's argument was that in social and market interaction it frequently was necessary for the decision-maker to judge or speculate as to what the next specific event was going to be, and not just its probability within a class. To see what Mises is trying to get at the following examples may help: (1) You are told that event *x* happened to someone you know, and before you are told how that person reacted, you say, "Don't tell me, I know exactly what he did." (2) You plan to try to increase your market share of the product you produce by lowering your price or increasing your advertising, but you stop to think, "But how will my market rival react to my actions *this time*?" (3) You're told by an investment advisor to sell your shares in a particular company because the economy is going into a downturn and the industry in which that company operates has experienced procyclical changes in demand in the past; but you sense a change in the "mood" of the buying public for that product that will result in the demand for the product rising in the very near future, so you decide to hold on to your shares.

Now if someone is rolling a die and knows that the probability of a three is one-sixth, he could say, "But I want to know what the *next* roll of this fair die will be! I have a hunch, a 'feeling' it's going to be a four!" Assuming that the die is fair, there is no way for him to make this statement. He has no way of knowing *how the die is feeling* – whether *it wants* to show a four this next time instead of a five or a three, or whether the die is watching the bets and is going to be mischevious and make everyone a loser by balancing itself on one of its corners.

But in interacting with other human beings knowledge of others can be accumulated and "out of what we know about man's past behaviour, we construct a scheme about what we call his character," Mises concluded.[39] The source of knowledge for construction of such "schemes" or composite pictures or images of individuals only come through historical experience. They did not exist *a priori*.[40] This knowledge, said Mises, is "acquired either directly from observing our fellow men and transacting business with them or indirectly from reading and from hearsay, as well as out of our special experience acquired in previous contacts with the individuals or groups concerned." And with this knowledge, "we try to form an opinion about their future conduct."[41]

The *ideal type* is a composite image of an individual or group of individuals created in the mind of a person wishing to either understand their actions in the past or anticipate their actions or reactions to various circumstances in the future. The complexity and difficulty for the individual attempting to construct and apply ideal types for the purpose of forming expectations about the possible actions of others arises from the fact that two problems confront him; first, it is necessary to enumerate the various idealized characteristics and attributes believed to be relevant for understanding what makes particular human beings "tick"; and, second, and often much more difficult, it is necessary to evaluate the relative importance (the "weight") of each of these behavioral characteristics or qualities in alternative and changing circumstances. Only success in both – an understanding of the relevant behavioral characteristics and their relative importance in an individual's actual conduct in a specific setting – enables correct expectations to be formed.[42]

Mises was conscious that, "Compared with the seemingly absolute certainty provided by some of the natural sciences, these assumptions and all their conclusions derived from them appear as rather shaky… Yet they are the only available approach to the problems concerned and indispensable for any action to be accomplished in a social environment."[43] What this process of intersubjective interpretation and ideal-type construction enables is a probability analysis by actors in the social and economic arenas that can go beneath the frequency distributions to the likelihoods of the individual and qualitatively unique events.

EXPECTATIONS, ENTREPRENEURS AND THE MARKET PROCESS

The relevance of "subjective meaning" and ideal-typical expectations in Mises's theory of the market process can best be understood in the context of his analysis of "economic calculation." The thrust of Mises's criticism of socialist central planning was that without money prices to serve as an evaluational steering rod for the comparison and appraisal of heterogeneous physical factors of production, a "rational" use of scarce resources to satisfy various human ends would be impossible. Mises concluded that market prices required private property: without private ownership there would be nothing for individuals to buy and sell; without buying and selling there can be no bids and offers; without bids and offers no ratios of exchange could emerge on the market; without ratios of exchange (prices expressed in a commonly used medium of exchange) no economic calculation concerning the relative scarcities and opportunity costs of using resources among alternative applications could be made. Thus, socialist economic planning is "impossible" and, therefore, only a private property order under free-market competition is consistent with the efficient use of scarce means among the competing ends of a multitude of individuals in the social division of labor.[44]

The socialist reply was that the markets and prices were consistent with the elimination of a private property order. The central planning authority could establish parametric prices within which the "managers" could undertake economic calculations, with any discovered "shortages" or "surpluses" corrected for through price changes introduced by the planning authority.[45]

While this has been the standard answer to Mises's "impossibility" claim, in Mises's eyes such a reply missed the point of what prices were all about. All prices on the market have their origin in valuation or appraisal. And both only have meaning in terms of the evaluating minds whose judgments they reflect. With valuation the actor estimates the significance of the commodity in question in terms of his own uses for it in the immediate or more distant future. With appraisal the actor estimates the future value of the commodity in question to others in the market arena; and his judgment as to its worth today, either as a good to resell in the future or as an input to produce such a product, is guided by his expectations of the valuations and demands of others at a future date.[46] *Real prices*, as opposed to arbitrarily designated ratios of exchange, are the outcomes of real evaluating individuals entering into exchange. Their formation results from actual valuing and appraising processes and, therefore, reflects a true composite of the circumstances, preferences and expectational judgments of the participants in the social division of labor.[47]

But this also means that prices are nothing more than these valuations and appraisals. In other words, "objective" market prices were reducible to and only the result of a plethora of "subjective meanings" and interpretations by the market participants. In themselves prices mean nothing outside of the context of the evaluating mind that uses those prices as a point of orientation, given the purposes in mind and the expectations held.[48]

In Mises's theory of the market process, the focal point of the analysis is the entrepreneur: "The driving force of the market process is provided...by the promoting and speculating entrepreneur."[49] Entrepreneurs visualize the shape of things to come in the market of the future. They conceive of ways to combine factors of production to bring potential final goods to fruition. They utilize the prices of the market to undertake economic calculations as to the *future* configuration of prices and, therefore, the relative potentials of profits and avoidances of loss. Their expectations of selling prices set the limits of their bids in the factor markets and the competitive swirl of entrepreneural activity brings about the emergence of the prices in these markets. Changes in these prices reflect back to the individual entrepreneurs as new datum for re-evaluation and adjustment.

The primary tool for the entrepreneural undertaking, Mises argued, was the interpretive tool of *Verstehen* (understanding) and the method for "understanding" the future demands and actions of others was the ideal type.

Having proposed a theory of expectations formation that emphasized the role of the ideal type for interpretive understanding; and having emphasized the pivotal role of the entrepreneur for market coordination, the next step would seem to be for Mises to have integrated these two elements – ideal-type constructs as an expectational tool and entrepreneural decision-making – into one analysis. He, however, does not do so. Left unanswered is the question of how ideal types may vary among entrepreneurs as a result of the division of labor, the limitation and dispersion of knowledge about different markets. Nor does he try to explain the process by which the ideal-typical constructions held in the minds of entrepreneurs are modified through the events experienced in the market. It is, of course, possible that Mises believed that changes in expectations, because of the creativity of the minds, could not be formally explained; but if this was the case he does not clearly express this either.

At the same time, Mises's writings on monetary theory clearly reveal a strong belief on his part that market participants do not only learn from experience, they anticipate future effects from present policies, and this anticipation modifies present behavior, thereby reinforcing or nullifying the monetary influences. But, once again, this part of his writings is not integrated into his theory of expectations formation, not even in *Human Action.*[50] His theory is incompletely developed and applied within his own system.

CONCLUSION

Austrian economists have long been concerned with the problems of the market process and interpersonal coordination of plans. While emphasizing the significance of expectations for understanding the process of market adjustment and coordination, few of the Austrians attempted to build a constructive theory of expectations and their formation.

One of the few who did was Ludwig von Mises. Similar to the other Austrians, he drew attention to the anticipatory and speculative quality of all human choice and action in an environment of change and uncertainty. However, in his later works, especially *Human Action* and *Theory and History*, Mises tried to develop a theory of expectations by using Max Weber's concept of the ideal type. The ideal type serves as a mental tool with which to integrate historical experience that has arisen from various interactions with individuals, groups and institutional structures and orders. As Mises expressed it:[51]

> The characteristic mark of an 'ideal type'...is that it implies some proposition concerning valuing and acting. If an ideal type refers to people, it implies that in some respect these men are valuing and acting in a uniform or similar way. When it refers to institutions, it implies that these institutions are products of uniform or similar ways of valuing and acting or that they influence valuing and acting in a uniform or similar way.

Ideal types, Mises argued, enabled acting man to be "the historian of the future."[52] Forming composite pictures or images of individuals in terms of characteristics, qualities, motives and meanings, ideal types enable an individual decision-maker to project himself into the future, imagine that another individual or individuals is confronted or faced with a particular event or change in their circumstance, and then ask the question, "What responses and courses of action would these individuals manifest in this situation?" It enables the formation of expectations concerning patterns or regularity or "types" of response for prediction of unique cases, and not merely a probability in terms of a class. No matter how imperfect, it introduces an additional source of knowledge for coordination of plans in the complex social setting of the market.

While viewing the entrepreneur as the focal point of the market process, and while emphasizing that it is through the tool of interpretive understanding of others in the market that entrepreneurs direct economic activity, Mises failed to fully integrate his ideal-type conception into his theory of entrepreneurship. And as a result he left his theory of the market process incomplete. It is a task that remains for the next generation of Austrian economists.[53]

NOTES

1. Enrich Streissler (1973), "To What Extent Was the Austrian School Marginalist?" in R. D. Collison Black, A. W. Coats, and Craufurd D. W. Goodwin (eds), *The Marginal Revolution in Economics*, Durham: Duke University Press, pp. 160–75. Also, William Jaffe (1976), "Menger, Jevons and Walras De-Homogenized," *Economic Inquiry*, December, 551–74.
2. Jack Wiseman (1985), "Lionel Robbins, The Austrian School and the LSE Tradition," *Research in the History of Economic Thought and Methodology*, **3**, 147–59.
3. Hans Mayer (1932), "Der Erkinntniswert der funktionellen Preistheorien," in Hans Mayer, Frank A. Fetter and Richard Reisch (eds), *Die Wirtschftstheorie der Gegenwart*, vol. II, Vienna: Julius Springer, pp. 147–239b.
4. Paul N. Rosenstein-Rodan (1929), "Das Zeitmoment in der mathematischen Theorie des wirtschaftichen Gleichgewichtes," *Zeitschrift fur Nationalokonomie*, 133ff. Also, *Idem.* (1934), "The Role of Time in Economic Theory," *Economica*, February, 77–97.
5. Oskar Morgenstern (1928), *Wirtschaftsprognose, eine Untersuchung iher Voraussetzungen und Moglichkeiten*, Vienna: Julius Springer; (1976 [1935]), "The Role of Time in Value Theory" and "Perfect Foresight and Economic Equilibrium" in *Selected Economic Writings of Oskar Morgenstern*, ed. Andrew Schotter, New York: New York University Press, pp. 151–67, 169–83.
6. Friedrich A. Hayek (1948), "Economics and Knowledge" [1937], "The Use of Knowledge in Society" [1945], "The Meaning of Competition" [1946], in *Individualism and Economic Order*, Chicago: University of Chicago Press, pp. 33–56, 77–91, 92–106.
7. Cf. Arthur Marget (1966 [1942]), *The Theory of Prices,* vol. II, New York: Augustus M. Kelley, p. 189, n. 98.
8. I have discussed this shortcoming in Hayek's writing in my (1986) essay, "Toward a Hermeneutical Economics: Expectations, Prices and the Role of Interpretation in a Theory of the Market Process," in Israel M. Kirzner (ed.), *Subjectivism, Intelligibility and Economic Understanding*, New York: New York University Press, pp. 39–55.
9. John von Neumann and Oskar Morgenstern (1944), *Theory of Games and Economic Behavior*, Princeton: Princeton University Press.
10. Marget, *The Theory of Prices*, vol. II, p. 189.
11. Murray N. Rothbard (1970 [1962]), *Man, Economy and State*, (2 vols), Los Angeles: Nash Publishing.
12. Israel M. Kirzner (1973), *Competition and Entrepreneurship*, Chicago: University of Chicago Press; (1979), *Perception, Opportunity and Profit*, Chicago: University of Chicago Press; (1985), *Discovery and the Capitalist Process*, Chicago: University of Chicago Press.
13. Ludwig M. Lachmann (1977 [1943]), "The Role of Expectations in Economics as a Social Science," in *Capital, Expectations and the Market Process*, Kansas City: Sheed, Andrews & McMeel, pp. 65–80; (1978 [1956]), *Capital and Its Structure*, Kansas City: Sheed,

Andrews & McMeel; pp. 20–34; (1971), *The Legacy of Max Weber*, Berkeley: Glendessary Press, pp. 17–48.

14. Ludwig M. Lachmann (1976), "From Mises to Shackle: An Essay on Austrian Economics and the Kaleidic Society," *Journal of Economic Literature*, March, 54–62.
15. Ludwig M. Lachmann (1977 [1951], "The Science of Human Action," in *Capital, Expectations and the Market Process,* p. 95.
16. Ludwig von Mises (1966 [1949]), *Human Action, A Treatise on Economics*, Chicago: Henry Regnery Co., 3rd rev. edn, pp. 30–52.
17. *Ibid.*, pp. 38–41.
18. Marian Bowley (1967 [1937]), *Nassau Senior and Classical Economics*, New York: Octagon Books, pp. 64–5; Murray N. Rothbard (1973), "Praxeology as the Method of Economics," in Maurice Natanson (ed.), *Phenomenology and the Social Sciences*, vol. II, Evanston: Northwestern University Press, pp. 311–39; and Mises (1976 [1933]), *Epistemological Problems of Economics*, New York: New York University Press., pp. 17–22.
19. I have tried to demonstrate the relationship between Mises's approach and Phenomenological Philosophy in my paper, "A Phenomenological Foundation for Dynamic Subjectivism" delivered at a Liberty Fund conference devoted to "The Economics of Time and Ignorance" in November 1984.
20. Cf. Mises, *Epistemological Problems*, pp. 80–81, 127, n. 67; (1944), "The Treatment of 'Irrationality' in the Social Sciences," *Philosophy and Phenomenological Research*, June; (1978), *Notes and Recollections*, South Holland: Libertarian Press, p. 104. The latter was written by Mises in 1940.
21. Mises (1966 [1949]), *Human Action*, Chicago: Henry Regnery, p. 39; *Epistemological Problems*, pp. 78–9.
22. Mises (1978), *Notes and Recollections*, South Holland, Il: Libertarian Press, pp. 69–70.
23. Gottfried Haberler (1981), "Mises's Private Seminar," *Wirtschaftspolitische Blatter*, (4), 121–4.
24. Mises [1929], "Sociology and History," in *Epistemological Problems*, pp. 68–145; cf. *Notes and Recollections*, pp. 122–3; also, Mises (1961), "Epistemological Relativism in the Sciences of Human Action" in Helmut Schoech and James W. Wiggins (eds), *Relativism and the Study of Man*, Princeton: D. Van Nostrand, Co., 117–34.
25. Max Weber (1947 [1922]), *The Theory of Social and Economic Organization*, New York: Oxford University Press, p. 88.
26. *Ibid.*
27. Max Weber (1977 [1907]), *Critique of Stammler*, New York: The Free Press, pp. 109, 112.
28. Max Weber (1949), *The Methodology of the Social Sciences*, New York: The Free Press, p. 90; also, cf. Raymond Aron (1970), *Main Currents in Sociological Thought*, vol. II Garden City, NY: Anchor Books, pp. 244–7.
29. Weber, *Methodology of the Social Sciences*, pp. 77, 173–6
30. Mises, *Epistemological Problems*, pp. 78–9.
31. Mises, *Human Action*, pp. 13–14; *Epistemological Problems*, pp. 79–80, 148.
32. Mises, *Human Action*, p. 47.
33. *Ibid.*, pp. 49, 51, 53.
34. *Ibid.*, p. 60; also Mises (1969 [1957]), *Theory and History*, New Rochelle: Arlington House, pp. 316–20.
35. Alfred Schutz (1967 [1932]), *The Phenomenology of the Social World*, Evanston: Northwestern University Press. I have tried to summarize Schutz's ideal type method and to suggest its economic applicability in my review of Helmut Wagner's *Alfred Schutz: An Intellectual Biography* in *Market Process*, Fall 1986. The earliest reference to Schutz in Mises's writings appear in the 1933 volume *Epistemological Problems of Economics*, pp. 125–6, n. 27, in which he refers to

> Schutz's penetrating investigations, based on Husserl's systems, [which] lead to findings whose importance and fruitfulness, both for epistemology and historical science itself, must be valued very highly. However, an evaluation of the concept of the ideal type, as

it is newly conceived by Schutz, would exceed the scope of this treatise. I must reserve dealing with his ideas for another work.

Other than in his own explanation and analysis of the ideal type in *Human Action* and *Theory and History*, Mises never directly analyzed Schutz's approach in print.

36. Frank Knight (1957 [1921]), *Risk, Uncertainty and Profit*, New York: Kelley & Millman, Inc., pp. 197–232. The close resemblance between the arguments in Part III of Knight's book and Mises own exposition in various parts of *Human Action* suggests the strong influence of the former upon the latter.
37. Mises, *Human Action*, p. 107.
38. *Ibid.*, p. 110.
39. Ludwig von Mises (1978 [1962]), *The Ultimate Foundations of Economic Science*, Kansas City: Sheed, Andrews & McMeel, p. 50.
40. An appreciation of this aspect of Mises's analysis of market activity offers an answer to a charge made by T. W. Hutchison, in his recent (1981) work *The Politics and Philosophy of Economics*, Oxford: Basil Blackwell, p. 209:

    It is not very illuminating for him [Mises] to insist, for example, that 'action' is always speculation… In any real and living economy every actor is always an entrepreneur and speculator when he fails to spell out just how it is possible, from his *a priori* axioms regarding such speculative actions, that non-trivial conclusions of 'apodictic certainty' can be obtained, which relate to real-world conditions of uncertainty and ignorance.

    What Mises considered as *a priori* and universal axioms were the general concepts and categories inseparable from "action" of any and all types regardless of specific context. But to anticipate or predict *actual actions* by others the "general form" of the action equation would have to be filled in with historical knowledge of the actions, motives and goals of actual actors in the past, which would serve as the material for an interpretive judgment as to the future actions of those same actors.
41. Mises, *Theory and History*, p. 313.
42. *Ibid.*, p. 314.
43. Mises, *Ultimate Foundation*, p. 50.
44. Ludwig von Mises (1969 [1936]), *Socialism, An Economic and Sociological Analysis* (London: Jonathan Cape, pp. 111–50 and 211–20; (1978 [1962]), *Liberalism*, Kansas City: Sheed, Andrews and McMeel, Inc. pp. 70–75; (1969 [1944]), *Bureaucracy*, New Rochelle: Arlington House, pp. 20–63.
45. E.g., Oskar Lange (1964 [1936]), *On the Economic Theory of Socialism*, New York: McGraw-Hill, pp. 57–143.
46. Mises, *Human Action*, pp. 331–533.
47. *Ibid.*, pp. 395–7.
48. *Ibid.*, pp. 229–30.
49. *Ibid.*, pp. 328.
50. Ludwig von Mises (1971 [1924]), *Theory of Money and Credit*, New York: Foundation for Economic Education, pp. 219–31; (1978), *On the Manipulation of Money and Credit*, Dobbs Ferry: Free Market Books, pp. 5–16; *Human Action*, pp. 455–6, 426–8; (1943), "'Elastic Expectations' and the Austrian Theory of the Trade Cycle," *Economica*, August, 251–2.
51. Mises, *Theory and History*, p. 316.
52. *Ibid.*, p. 322.
53. The first steps towards such an integration can be found in Gerald P. O'Driscoll and Mario J. Rizzo (1985), *The Economics of Time and Ignorance*, New York: Basil Blackwell. I have attempted to undertake such a task in my papers, "Hermeneutics and the Interpretive Element in the Analysis of the Market Process," Center for the Study of Market Processes Working Paper Series No. 16 (1985), and "Toward a Hermeneutical Economics," in *Subjectivism, Intelligibility and Economic Understanding*.

8. Mind, historical time and the value of money: a tale of two methods

Matthew B. Kibbe

There is no more striking symbol of the completely dynamic character of the world than that of money. (Georg Simmel 1978 [1900], p. 510)

But money is a manifestation or aspect or recourse of something in our experience which arises from the very roots of conscious being, namely, the fact that our existence consists in continually finding out what is happening. Consciousness is finding out. If there is always something to find out, it follows that we do not yet know everything, that we do not ever know everything. The things we do not, at any moment, know are the whole future near and remote, mundane and trivial or momentous. Of course our short term guesswork often comes out right. Experience is some use... There is some degree of assurance concerning the sequel to particular states of affairs and particular manipulation, which makes daily life practicable. But, we do not know, if knowing consists in the possession of demonstrable certainty. (G.L.S. Shackle, 1974, p. 3)

INTRODUCTION

F.A. Hayek has made the bold claim that "it is probably no exaggeration to say that every important advance in economic theory during the last hundred years was a further step in the consistent application of subjectivism" (1979 [1951], p. 52).[1] Given the present state of the so-called "dismal science," the implicit prediction embodied in Hayek's claim has proven quite prophetic. The breakdown of the neoclassical paradigm, or what Shackle has termed "the rational ideal," has left the established economics profession in a rather embarrassing state of disarray. Nowhere are the deficiencies of this "timeless" style of thought more evident than in monetary theory. Searching for answers within the strictures of imaginary equilibrium states, many neoclassical economists have been quite unable to explain the very existence of money (Shackle, 1974, pp. 3–4), let alone the determinants of its value.[2]

The Austrian tradition, starting with the works of Carl Menger, has followed a path quite different from that of mainstream economic thought. Central to the Austrian method is an understanding of purposeful human action imbedded in a world of historical time. Menger's conception of money is that of an essentially time-bound institution that continuously evolves through a historical process of purposeful human interaction (Menger, 1976 [1871], pp. 257–85 and 1892, pp. 239–55).[3]

Building on the subjectivist paradigm of Menger,[4] Ludwig von Mises wrote *The Theory of Money and Credit* in 1912. This book is an attempt to return money to a world imbedded in the continuous flux of historical time; a world in which purposeful actors create and carry out their plans based on their interpretations or "expectations" about an unknown future. Employing this view of the world – a view quite different from that of the neoclassical paradigm – Mises arrives at an explanation for the value of money. This explanation is chided by some as merely "historical."[5] Unfortunately, Mises's critics fail to realize that only by invoking a methodological framework which takes purposive human action in the world of historical time seriously can the problem of the value of money be solved at all.

THE CIRCULARITY PROBLEM

Economists writing at the turn of the century considered the problem of the value of money to be economic theory's foremost dilemma (Ellis, 1934, pp. 51, 64). In general, it was believed that any attempt to explain the value of money by using the theory of diminishing marginal utility resulted in a "circularity" of reasoning. The value of money could only be explained by an appeal to that value. Marginal utility analysis was hapless, "for the utility of a given nominal quantity of money depends on its real value, and this cannot itself be known until the price level has first been determined. Hence in speaking of the marginal utility, we would already be implicitly assuming what we had undertaken to explain" (Patinkin, 1965, p. 115.).

As the problem was perceived, explaining the value of money posed a serious difficulty for the whole subjectivist revolution.[6] If the theory of subjective value could not be consistently used to explain the value of money, modern economics was a theoretical dead end. It was this dilemma which Mises sought to solve with the historical regression theorem.

According to Mises, the difficulties of the vicious circle are "merely apparent."

> The purchasing power which we explain by referring to the extent of specific demand is not the same purchasing power the height of which determines this specific demand. The problem is to conceive the determination of the purchasing power of the immediate future, of the impending moment. For the solution of this problem we refer to the purchasing power of the immediate past, of the moment

> just passed. These are two distinct magnitudes. It is erroneous to object to our theorem,... that it moves in a vicious circle. (1966 [1949], pp. 408–9)

Although Menger never "touched upon the problem at all" (Mises, 1981 [1912], p. 138), Mises's solution is clearly an extension of the Mengerian notion of the evolution of money. The value of money today is based on the price of money yesterday and the expected value of money tomorrow is based on the "price" of money today. Instead of falling into an infinite regress, the "objective" or market value of money can be traced historically back to the time when money was valued as a commodity alone. In fact, Mises argues that the value of money can only be explained by appealing to its original commodity value.

> If the objective exchange value of money must always be linked with a preexisting market exchange ratio between money and other economic goods (since otherwise individuals would not be in a position to estimate the value of money), it follows that an object cannot be used as money unless, at the moment when its use as money begins, it already possesses an objective exchange value based on some other use. (*Ibid.*, p. 131)

THE PATINKIN "BOGEY"

Don Patinkin, in his influential book *Money, Interest, and Prices,* considers the whole debate over circularity to be a pointless and confusing "bogey" that "paralyzed" economic thought with its "intimidatory powers" (1965 [1951], p. 573). This unfortunate diversion from the marginal revolution, he says, attempts to deny what is now an obvious point. The value of money is determined on the margin, just like any other economic good. The supposed circularity problem "originates in a basic misunderstanding of the theory of price determination" (*Ibid.*, p. 115).

Patinkin is equally critical of Mises's historical regression theorem. Attempting to solve a bogus dilemma, Mises in fact solves nothing at all.

> It is...ironical that Mises – who is known in the literature as the advocate of the application of marginal-utility analysis to money – should have made this application solely in terms of "the marginal utility of the goods for which the money can be exchanged"... As a result, Mises was forced to base his attempted escape from the circularity charge on a historical regression to the time when "the value of money is nothing other than the value of an object that is useful in some other way than as money." (*Ibid.*, pp. 574–5)

For Patinkin, the circularity bogey is easily solved by making the simple mental distinction between demand and quantity demanded. This distinction can be shown through a series of logical experiments.

> In a market-experiment, money prices are the variables whose values must be determined... But in an individual-experiment, the amounts of excess demands are the variables to be determined, and money prices are the independent variables whose values must be given in order to conduct the experiment. Clearly, there is no circularity in stating that the market excess-demand equations derived from such individual-experiments are then used to determine the equilibrium money prices of the market experiment. (*Ibid*., p. 116)

These "experiments" require several important steps. Initially, any notion of real time must be removed from the model altogether. Also, the individual must be conceptually separated from a social or "market" setting. Given money prices, this atomistic individual is able to calculate his demand for money. The solution to this experiment can then be plugged into the market-experiment to derive the excess demand equations. The question-begging character of the circularity bogey is supposedly removed by ignoring the indeterminate variables of time, ignorance, and the social or market setting in which an individual's utility calculations are made.

THE RELEVANCE OF HISTORICAL TIME

Essential to an understanding of Patinkin's equilibrium "experiments" is the notion of what Gerald O'Driscoll and Mario Rizzo have called "Newtonian time" (1985, pp. 53–9.) This view sees time as a static quantity, similar to the way space is viewed in the physical sciences. According to Shackle, it is quite natural that economists have come to view time in this way (1967 [1958], p. 13). In an attempt to establish a quantifiable, "objective" science equal to that claimed to have been achieved in the natural sciences, many neoclassical economists are often quite willing to sacrifice the real-world characteristics of their models for analytical tidiness.

"Time as a scheme of thought contrasts in a way that must astonish us, when we examine it, with time as a vehicle of experience" (Shackle 1969 [1961], p. 16). Unlike the continuous flow of unique moments experienced by the human mind, all of Newtonian time is completely homogeneous in its moments. Moments of time are viewed as empty points in space, each one being completely interchangeable with the next. In a sense, all points in Newtonian time are out of time.

> To the mathematician all the points of an abstract space are, a priori, equally valid and equally important. They exist in the mind together, and, in the logical sense of the word, simultaneously. This remains true if he considers by itself one dimension of such a space and labels it "time." If this dimension is the range of a variable, all values of that variable are equally meaningful, equally necessary to the general validity of his theorems or his equations involving that space. The

> different points of his conceptual time co-exist. But the single momentary thought in which he can embrace all those points manifestly lies in a different time, a different world. (*Ibid.,* p. 16)

Concerning the relevance of this "mathematical" view of time to the human sciences, Wilhelm Dilthey suggests that "this framework of relationships embraces, but does not exhaust, the experience of time through which the concept of time receives its ultimate meaning" (Rickman, 1976, p. 209). Any concept of a historical process in the imaginary world of Newtonian time is nonsensical. All adjustment, if it can be discussed at all, is contained within the world from its very beginning. "The initial state of the system must contain within it all that is necessary to produce 'change'. Time adds literally nothing" (O'Driscoll and Rizzo 1985, p. 55). Problems of expectations formation and the process of price determination, for either commodities or money, are eliminated by definition in this bizarre world of Newtonian time.

Contrasted to this is an understanding of time as it is experienced by the individual human mind; what Shackle refers to as "the solitary present" (1969 [1961], p. 17). This "Bergsonian" view of time is also accepted by Mises (Lachmann 1976, p. 57). According to Dilthey,

> Here time is experienced as a restless progression, in which the present constantly becomes the past and the future the present. The present is the filling of a moment of time with reality; it is experience, in contrast to memory or ideas of the future occurring in wishes, expectations, hopes, fears and strivings. This filling with reality constantly exists while the content of experience constantly changes… The present is always there and nothing exists except what emerges in it. The ship of our life is, as it were, carried forward on a constant stream, and the present is always wherever we are on these waves – suffering, remembering or hoping, in short, living in the fullness of our reality. (Rickman, 1976, p. 209)

Forever trapped within the continuous flux of solitary moments, the fundamental task of the human mind is to bind present experience within the context of a remembered past and an expected future.

Implicit in the world of historical time is a necessary breakdown of "the rational ideal" of Newtonian time (Shackle, 1972, pp. 120–29). To be rational in this Shackleian sense, conduct must be demonstrably the best or optimal way to solve the stated problem. "To be demonstrable, [an action's] superiority must be related to a complete set of relevant circumstances" (*Ibid.*, pp. 229–30). Similar to this view – albeit in a watered-down form – is the standard for rationality proposed by Talcott Parsons in *The Structure of Social Action.* In his view, "action is rational in so far as it pursues ends possible within the conditions of the situation, and by the means which, among those available to the actor, *are intrinsically best adapted to the end for reasons understandable and verifiable"* (cited in Schutz, 1943, p. 130; emphasis added).[7]

It should be intuitively obvious that an individual's actions typically fail to meet such criteria for "rationality." As Alfred Schutz points out:

> In our daily life it is only very rarely that we act in a rational way if we understand this term in the meaning envisaged in Professor Parsons' previously quoted statement. We do not even interpret the social world surrounding us in a rational way. ... Each of us, so it seems, has naively organized his social world and his daily life in such a way that he finds himself the centre of the social cosmos surrounding him. Or, better, he was already born into an organized social cosmos. (1943, p. 134)[8]

It is important to stress the difference between Shackle's and Mises's uses of the term "rational." For Mises, rationality is equivalent to human purposiveness. In other words, man acts in order to achieve his chosen ends within the world of unknowable and continuous change. It is best to view the ideas of Shackle and Mises on this issue as complementary parts to a fuller picture of human rationality. While Shackle's thought is focused on the deconstruction of the "Rational Ideal" of the neoclassical paradigm, Mises's work is an attempt to break out of the mold of instrumental reasoning and construct a richer, positive alternative to the neoclassical view of man.

Far from being a meaningless tautology, this Misesian concept of human rationality finds its roots in the phenomenological or "life world" movement in philosophy. Influenced by social theorists such as Edmund Husserl, Wilhelm Dilthey and Alfred Schutz,[9] Mises's notion of purposeful action represents the rudiments of a far richer understanding of human reason.

THE BOUNDS OF CREATIVITY

What Mises begins to develop with his historical regression theorem is a theory of expectations formation. It is best to view his effort as a major break with the mechanical, timeless style of thought of neoclassicism – a "thrust towards subjectivism."[10] Unfortunately, Mises never made his theory of the formation of price expectations explicit (Kirzner, n.d., p. 6). To a large extent, he left such a theory implicit in his own work – the underlying theme for others to discover and build upon.[11]

Mises's failure to make the role of expectations explicit has led Ludwig Lachmann to the belief that they do not exist within the Misesian paradigm. It was not until later that subjectivism was extended into the realm of the "subjectivism of interpretations" of the human mind (Lachmann, 1982a, p. 37). This consistent extension of subjectivism was the realization "that economic action concerned with the future, so far from being strictly determined by a set of objective data, is often decided upon in a penumbra of doubt and uncertainty, vague hopes and inarticulate fears, in which ultimate decision may well depend on mental alertness, ability to read the signs of a changing world, and readiness to face the unknown" (Lachmann, 1977 [1943], p. 65). As for methodological considerations, "nothing will be achieved in the way of an inductive study of expectations until people's expectational responses to the fact of a situation are made *intelligible* to us, until we are able to understand why the acting and expecting individuals interpreted a set of facts the way they actually did. From this point of view we need not deplore unduly the indeterminateness of expectations, for it is *intelligibility* and not *determinateness* that social science should strive to achieve" (*ibid.*, p. 6; emphasis in original).

What Lachmann is objecting to is the methodological sterility of the timeless, logical allocation of a given set of information. "How can each person choose his action (for example, the quantity of goods of some kind which he will exchange) in knowledge of what each of the others is choosing?" Only through a conceptual "pooling of statements of conditional intentions and the finding of a general solution or General Equilibrium which shall prescribe for each person, as the action to be taken by him, the very action he would prefer, given that each other person is committed to perform the particular action prescribed to him" (Shackle, 1979, pp. 3–4).

In contrast with this general equilibrium solution is the creative process by which the mind actually chooses the ends it wishes to pursue. In this sense, it is proper to speak of individual actions as acts of entrepreneurship. According to Mises,

> Economics, in speaking of entrepreneurs, has in view not men, but a definite function. This function is not the particular feature of a special group or class of men; it is inherent in every action and burdens every actor. In embodying this function in an imaginary figure, we resort to a methodological makeshift. The term entrepreneur as used by catallactic theory means: acting man exclusively seen from the aspect of the uncertainty inherent in every action. In using this term one must never forget that every action is embedded in the flux of time and therefore involves a speculation. (Mises, 1966 [1949], pp. 252–3)

Human action "cannot be pressed into the standard 'maximizing' model of the decision." Instead, individual entrepreneurship is concerned with "the very identification of the ends–means configuration itself" (Kirzner, 1979, p. 158).

In this sense an individual must create his ends or goals before they can be considered as options within the realm of what is possible. "In our attitude toward the future," Dilthey points out, "we are active and free… We feel that we have infinite possibilities" (Rickman, 1976, pp. 209–10).

Entrepreneurship is not simply a discovery procedure requiring alertness. Individual entrepreneurship is essentially a creative process which emerges from the process of thought itself. As James Buchanan puts it, "not even individuals have well-defined and well-articulated objectives that exist independently of choices themselves" (1979 [1978], p. 111). As a result, the process of human choice produces indeterminate outcomes. "Imagination, the power of conceiving the unprecedented, the alchemy of thought, are liberated and ignited by mankind's elemental predicament, the human imprisonment in present time" (Shackle 1986, p. 281). "The economic problem" becomes a task far more complex than the logical task faced by Patinkin's chooser. The individual must first create an imagined future and then ask how his actions will alter such a future. He must answer the question he alone has created.

> Can the answer describe a singular, unequivocal path which, given his commitment to some specific action, the chooser supposes his affairs to follow? This would imply that he can know, when he makes his decision, just how the course of his affairs will be affected by choices of action made by others in time-to-come. Such knowledge of choices-to-come could only exist in the present, if each such choice was entirely determined by present circumstances and takings-place. To suppose that choices-to-come are thus predetermined destroys the meaning of choice, robbing human choices of all power of their own. The notion of choice would be empty and the act of choice sterile. A nondeterminist view of history requires us to suppose that a choice can be in some respects exempt from governance by antecedent thought or contemporary circumstances, that a choice can be in some respects an uncaused cause. (Shackle, 1986, p. 282)

However, as Lachmann is careful to point out, "the discontinuity of ends, stressed by Professor Shackle, do not entail that there are no continuities at all in human action" (Lachmann, 1977 [1959], p. 84). Shackle himself has described choice as being bounded by a historical understanding of "possibleness." The human imagination limits its choices between what is possible enough to be hoped for and what is far too possible to be dismissed (Shackle, 1986, p. 285). "Whatever commitments (the actor's) present choice consists of, any sequel of the present must start from the state of things in the present, including those commitments. Any imagined course of affairs that supposes a different starting-point is out of bounds" (Shackle, 1979 [1978], p. 21). In this way, the status of events in the present constrains the choices which are made.

Beyond the bounds of creativity allowed for by Shackle, there is an ordered coherence in human action which endures the continuous flux of historical time. An individual need not know with *demonstrable certainty* what the future holds in store. According to Dilthey, the individual mind itself creates a unity of moments through an ordering or "structuring" of lived experience:

> The qualitatively determinate reality which constitutes lived experience is structural coherence. To be sure, it flows in time and is experienced as a process – its temporal qualities are apprehended. But what is preserved, so to speak, as a force in the present, even though past in time, receives a peculiar quality of presence through this structure. Although lived experience is a flowing process, it is a dynamic unity – and not only objectively, but for our consciousness. (Cited in Ermarth, 1978, p. 218)

This unity is "phenomenologically irreducible." It consists of attitudes that "present themselves to us in a vast multiplicity which cannot be reduced to a specific number. Questioning, opinioning, supposing, asserting, feeling, wishing, desiring, and willing are modifications of the psychic attitude" (cited in Ermarth, 1978, p. 221). The process of an individual's actions is itself the process which creates unity. This dynamic unity of mind forms the basis for a noninstrumental understanding of human rationality.[12] However, it is only part of the story.

The creative unity of the individual mind is itself bound in an intersubjective web of historical tradition. According to Hans-Georg Gadamer, "there is always a world already interpreted, already organized in its basic relations, into which experience steps as something new, upsetting what has led our expectations and undergoing reorganization itself in the upheaval" (Gadamer, 1976, p. 15). Also recognizing the role of tradition, Mises insists that "as a thinking and acting being man emerges from his prehuman existence already as a social being" (Mises, 1966 [1949], p. 43). As a result, the "subjective" or personal perspective of the individual has already been influenced by the intersubjective meaning embodied by society *prior* to an individual's choices and actions.

The result is a mutually dependent process by which both the individual and his social context are informing to and informed by each other. Historical "tradition is not simply a precondition into which we come, but we produce it ourselves, inasmuch as we understand, participate in the evolution of tradition and hence determine it ourselves. Thus the circle of understanding is not a 'methodological' circle, but describes an ontological structural element in understanding" (Gadamer, 1985 [1960], p. 261). Knowledge itself is dependent on this open-ended process or intersubjective understanding. Given this view of human rationality and the formation of knowledge, it is clear that the process of expectations formation does not occur willy-nilly. Human expectations are strictly bounded by the process of the formation of knowledge itself; a process in which the subjective meanings of individuals produce an intersubjective understanding between individuals.

One way in which this intersubjective process of knowledge formation manifests itself is in the structure of prices. Mises argues that historical prices contribute to a common institutional basis for the solution to the problem of the value of money. Money prices convey meaning about the ever-changing values and expectations of all individuals acting within the social order. Of course, market prices do not represent given information which can systematically be uncovered. Individuals must assign meaning and significance to perceived price changes through a continuous process of interpretation.[13] Because interpretation is always a creative process, prices are as much informed by the individual mind as they are informing to it.

Arguably, this "subjectivist" view of expectations is completely compatible with and implicit in Mises's historical regression theorem. In fact, in a short response to Lachmann's article on "The Role of Expectations in Economics" (1977 [1943]), Mises claims to have no basic disagreement with Lachmann's view of expectations. He only warns against Lachmann's own insufficient subjectivism by questioning his use of the term "elastic" in his description of expectations. Such terminology "implies an inadequate and misleading mechanical metaphor" (Mises, 1943, p. 251).

THE VALUE OF MONEY

The regression theorem demonstrates that by interpreting the significance of the pattern of money prices in the present individuals are able to form what are reasonably reliable expectations about the future value of money. This does not mean that the value of money is somehow wholly determined at the moment an economic "good" becomes "money." "One day's price builds upon yesterday's. At some point, we recognize that a commodity has become money in the modern sense, but any arbitrariness derives from our perception, not the historical events themselves" (O'Driscoll and Rizzo, 1985, p. 195). Nor does the regression theorem imply, as John Hicks has suggested, that money is nothing more than "the ghost of gold" (Hicks, 1967 [1935], p. 62). As Mises himself argues, "not only its supply and demand for industrial purposes, but also its supply and demand for use as a medium of exchange, have influenced the value of gold from that point onward when it was first used as money" (Mises, 1981 [1912], p. 131). Mises never denied the value of money as a medium of exchange. His insistence that money must be somehow linked with an already valued commodity concerns an altogether separate issue – the theory of the evolution of money, which he inherited from Menger.

This evolutionary process through which money becomes valued has been described in further detail by Georg Simmel (1978 [1900], pp. 168–203).[14] According to Simmel, the historical development of money valued as a substance to money valued as a function "is much less radical than appears at first sight; for, strictly speaking, the substance value of money is also a functional value" (p. 168). The value of anything is based ultimately on its ability to satisfy the subjective "needs" of the individual. "No matter how much precious metals are appreciated as substances, they are in fact appreciated only because they adorn, distinguish, are technically useful, give aesthetic pleasure, etc., that is to say, because they perform functions" (p. 168). Substance, in itself, is meaningless.

So, when speaking of the evolution of money from substance to function, we are in fact speaking of an evolution of the individual mind's perception of money. Money, in order to have value, must first be perceived as having value by individuals.

In this light, Mises's insistence that money must somehow be linked with an already valued commodity becomes both relevant and even necessary to his theory. In order to be accepted at all, the value of money depends on the *trust* of the individuals within society (Frankel, 1977, pp. 36–41), and this can only be established through an appeal to some other already accepted value. The value of money does not magically appear out of nothingness, but rather out of the unfolding of human history itself.

But what of Patinkin's own solution to the value of money problem – do "thought experiments" also explain the value of money? Laurence Moss argues that Patinkin does indeed offer an alternate solution to the value of money problem with which Mises's regression theorem deals.

> In his assertion that the *only* way the demand for money can be consistently incorporated into the general body of utility theory is by introducing historical prices, Mises is quite mistaken. Patinkin demonstrated how to derive a demand curve for money without resorting to past price behavior by performing what is essentially a "thought experiment" in which the individual is confronted with alternative levels of commodity prices and asked how many units of money he will demand in each case. (Moss, 1976, p. 21)

The real question is whether or not Patinkin's "solution" helps explain how the value for money is determined by real individuals in the real world. Patinkin's experiments explain how individuals with given sets of preferences and a given "price" of money are able to come up with an equilibrium solution to the value for money. According to Patinkin, "what we take *as given and not subject to explanation* – the 'independent variables of the analysis' – are the individual's tastes and initial endowments, the prices with which he is confronted, and his desire to transform his initial endowment into an optimum price" (Patinkin, 1965 [1951], p. 12; emphasis added).

Such "experiments" beg the question. Obviously, if we assume answers to all the questions we are attempting to solve, the problem itself is easily assumed away. "The goal of a theory of equilibrium price, whether for bread or money, certainly extends far beyond the mere identification of that price which would, if it were ever attained, be the equilibrium price; the theory certainly implies, at least, that market forces can be relied upon to generate a *tendency toward that price*" (Kirzner, n.d., p. 4, emphasis added).[15] Mises argues that "economics has to explain the formation of prices on the market, which means how prices are really arrived at, *not how they ought to be arrived at*" (Mises, 1981, p. 97).

Patinkin, who is only concerned with the equilibrium solution to the problem of the value of money, remains unable to solve the problem of how money comes to be valued in the first place. Such a solution does not lie in some series of timeless equations – it lies within the process of human interaction itself.[16] A historical process of purposive human interaction – a process in which individual actors create and act upon their expectations about the future – offers the only relevant, real-world solution to the problem of the value of money.

CONCLUSION

The basis of this debate is method. As Hayek argues, "most peculiarities of [Mises's] views which at first strike many readers as strange and unacceptable trace to the fact that in the consistent development of the subjectivist approach he has for a long time moved ahead of his contemporaries" (1979 [1951], pp. 53–4, n.). Unfortunately, Austrians have for a long time proven quite unable to fully articulate the uniqueness of their methodology. Mises, along with Hayek, was never "able to show, with the cogency their case required, the incompatibility between the idea of planned action, the very core of Austrian economic thought, and an analytical model which knows no action, but only reaction" (Lachmann, 1977 [1969], p. 164, n.).

It will be the task of others to develop this uniquely Austrian insight to full fruition.

NOTES

I would like to express my thanks to Pete Boettke, Steve Horwitz, Don Lavoie, Dave Prychitko, and George Selgin for their respective comments on an early draft. The final responsibility for this version is mine alone.

1. For an important discussion of what Hayek means by "subjectivism," see Madison, 1987. Madison argues that Hayek's notion of subjectivism has little to do with subjectivity or objectivity as they are commonly understood. However, there are good reasons why Hayek chose this somewhat misleading terminology at the time in which he wrote.

    To attack objectivism is to attack the notion that in order to achieve valid knowledge the social scientist must take up a position which is supposed to be that of the natural

> scientist, namely that of a detached, disembodied onlooker, a pure spectator, acting in a spirit of disinterested "objectivity" eschewing all "subjective" considerations. However, in the social sciences one simply cannot...avoid taking into account in one's interpretive theorizing the interpretive activity of the acting subjects themselves. (Madison, 1987, p. 7)

It is in this sense that the method of "subjectivism' is being pursued here.

2. Neoclassical monetary theorists are often faced with a methodological dilemma. Within the analytical framework of general equilibrium, logical consistency is maintained by removing money from the model altogether. Partial equilibrium theory allows money back into the model, but sacrifices internal consistency. Once one accepts the neoclassical benchmark for economic theory, one is forced to choose between an internally consistent theory and a theory which incorporates money in some realistic sense.
3. For an extension of Menger's evolutionary approach, see Selgin and White (1986) and also O'Driscoll (1986).
4. Ludwig Lachmann (1978) argues that the Mengerian paradigm limited itself unnecessarily to the subjectivism of values. However, as Lachmann points out, it is clear that Menger's work points beyond itself, to the subjectivism of human expectations. In particular, Menger was able to plant the intellectual seeds to a fuller realization of the Austrian/subjectivist paradigm through his emphasis on the historical evolution of institutions.
5. See Patinkin (1965 [1951]), Hicks (1967 [1935]) and, most recently, Timberlake (1986). This discussion will focus primarily on Patinkin's own solution to the problem of the value of money. While there are significant similarities among Patinkin, Hicks, and Timberlake, there are also a number of important differences which prohibit lumping the ideas of the three economists together. For a treatment of Timberlake, see Selgin (1987).
6. There were in fact three separate and distinct revolutions in economic theory – the general equilibrium revolution of Walras, the marginal utility revolution of Jevons, and the subjectivist revolution of Menger. "To treat the three approaches as one would gloss over the differences, obscures the distinctiveness of each contribution" (O'Driscoll, 1986, p. 602). It is no accident that Mises, relying on the foundation built by Menger, approached the problem of the value of money in an entirely different way than other economists writing at the time.
7. What Kirzner has labeled "Robbinsian maximizing" (1973, p. 38) is quite similar to Parsons's standard for rationality. The task of the Robbinsian man is to choose between a fixed set of given ends and means – a purely logical task. In fact, to speak of human "choice" within this framework of determinate means and ends is entirely meaningless. To choose is to decide between an indeterminate "set" of options (see Kirzner, 1985, pp. 46–50).

   Presently, there is a lively debate within the Austrian school over this very issue. While Murray Rothbard (1970 [1962], p. 435, n. and 1986, p. 16) tends to side with the Parsons/ Robbins view of rational choice, both Kirzner and Lachmann have espoused the positions taken by Shackle and Schutz.
8. Lachmann argues that "we must beware...of imputing to Parsons a position similar to that held today by the neoclassical orthodoxy, even though there are some parallels between the general equilibrium model and the 'structural functionalism' he espoused." However, we must side with Schutz in this debate, for he defends "a radical subjectivism against a lukewarm one, and the claims to our attention of the participant actor against those of the outside observer" (Lachmann, 1982b, p. 12).
9. According to Mises, "Schutz's penetrating investigations, based on Husserl's system, lead to findings whose importance and fruitfulness, *both for epistemology and historical science itself*, must be valued very highly" (Mises, 1981 [1976], pp. 125–6; emphasis added). Unfortunately, "the importance of phenomenology for the solution of the epistemological problems of praxeology has not been noticed at all" (Mises, 1944, p. 530).

   For a general description of the intellectual environment in which Mises formulated his ideas, see Prendergast, 1986.

10. This phrase is taken from Lachmann (1986, p. 89). Ironically, as Roger Garrison has correctly pointed out (1987, p. 80), Lachmann virtually ignores Mises's contribution in his account of the extension of the subjectivist paradigm into the theory of money. This costly oversight forces Lachmann to glean from the altogether inferior tradition of Keynes and Hicks in monetary theory.
11. Such a theory of price expectations has been further developed by both Kirzner (n.d.) and Lachmann (see esp. 1977 [1943]; 1978 [1956], pp. 20–32).
12. This notion of the dynamic unity of the individual mind may well be what Ludwig Lachmann intends to describe when he speaks of "individual equilibrium" (Lachmann, 1986, p. 140). However, to say that an individual's actions are unified by plans through time means something far different from what most economists mean by the term equilibrium. I discuss this question in further detail in Kibbe (1987).
13. On this point, see Lachmann (1978 [1956], pp. 22–5); Lavoie (1987, pp. 596–602); and Ebeling (1986, pp. 42–4).
14. S. P. Altmann, in his 1903 review of *The Philosophy of Money*, describes Simmel's theory of value as "an eclectic combination of the theories of the Austrian school" (cited in Bottomore and Frisby, 1978, p. 10).
15. Kirzner acknowledges a comment made by Karen Vaughn as the impetus of this important insight. "Mises could not divorce the problem of the acquisition of knowledge and the formation of expectations from the problem of how equilibrium states are reached. While Patinkin was interested in defining an equilibrium condition, Mises was much more interested in explaining how human actions lead toward that equilibrium" (Vaughn, 1976, p. 103).
16. Patinkin's error is a case of misplaced concreteness – he assumes that the perfect dovetailing of preferences portrayed in the imaginary state of equilibrium depicts the actual process of price determination in the real world. Mises warns against the incorrect use of such imaginary constructions. The method of imaginary constructions is "difficult to handle because it can easily result in fallacious syllogisms. It leads along a sharp edge; on both sides yawns the chasm of absurdity and nonsense. Only merciless self-criticism can prevent a man from falling headlong into these abysmal depths" (Mises, 1966 [1949], p. 237). While imaginary constructions are only useful to the extent that they help explain the real world phenomena which the social scientist studies, Mises insists that imaginary constructions constitute the method of economics.

REFERENCES

Bottomore, Tom, and Frisby, David (1978), "Introduction to the Translation," in Georg Simmel, *The Philosophy of Money*, London: Routledge & Kegan Paul.

Buchanan, J.M. (1979 [1978]), "Natural and Artifactual Man," in *What Should Economists Do?*, Indianapolis: Liberty Press.

Ebeling, Richard (1986), "Towards a Hermeneutical Economics: Expectations, Prices, and the Role of Interpretation in a Theory of Market Processes," in Israel M. Kirzner (ed.), *Subjectivism, Intelligibility and Economic Understanding*, New York: New York University Press.

Ellis, H.S. (1934), *German Monetary Theory: 1905–1933*, Cambridge: Cambridge University Press.

Ermarth, Michael (1978), *Wilhelm Dilthey: The Critique of Historical Reason*, Chicago: University of Chicago Press.

Frankel, S. Herbert (1977), *Money: Two Philosophies*, Oxford: Basil Blackwell.

Gadamer, Hans-Georg (1985 [1960]), *Truth and Method*, New York: Crossroad Publishers.

—— (1976), *Philosophical Hermeneutics*, Berkley: University of California Press.

Garrison, Roger (1987), "The Kaleidic World of Ludwig Lachmann," *Critical Review*, Summer.

Hayek, F.A. (1979 [1951]), *The Counter-Revolution of Science*, Indianapolis: Liberty Press.

—— (1980 [1948]), *Individualism and Economic Order*, Chicago: University of Chicago Press.

Hicks, John (1967 [1935]), "A Suggestion for Simplifying the Theory of Money," in *Critical Essays in Monetary Theory*, Oxford: Oxford University Press.

Kibbe, Matthew (1987), "Escaping the Paretian Paradigm," *Market Process*, **5**(2), Fall.

Kirzner, Israel M. (1973), *Competition and Entrepreneurship,* Chicago: University of Chicago Press.

—— (n.d.), "A Note on the Circularity 'Bogey' in the History of the Marginal Utility Theory of Money," unpublished ms.

—— (1979), *Perception, Opportunity and Profit*, Chicago: University of Chicago Press.

—— (1985), *Discovery and the Capitalist Process*, Chicago: University of Chicago Press.

—— (ed.) (1986), *Subjectivism, Intelligibility and Economic Understanding*, New York: New York University Press.

Lachmann, Ludwig M. (1977 [1943]), "The Role of Expectations in Economics as a Social Science," in *Capital, Expectations and the Market Process*, Kansas City: Sheed, Andrews & McMeel.

—— (1978 [1956]), *Capital and Its Structure*, Kansas City: Sheed, Andrews & McMeel.

—— (1977 [1959]), "Professor Shackle and the Economic Significance of Time," in *Capital, Expectations and the Market Process*, Kansas City: Sheed, Andrews & McMeel.

—— (1977 [1969]), "Methodological Individualism and the Market Economy," in *Capital, Expectations and the Market Process*, Kansas City: Sheed, Andrews & McMeel.

—— (1977 [1971]), "Ludwig von Mises and the Market Process," in *Capital, Expectations and the Market Process*, Kansas City: Sheed, Andrews & McMeel.

—— (1976), "From Mises to Shackle: An Essay on Austrian Economics and the Kaleidic Society," *Journal of Economic Literature*, **14**(1), March, 54–62.

—— (1978), "Carl Menger and the Incomplete Revolution of Subjectivism," *Atlantic Economic Journal*, September.

—— (1982a), "Mises and the Extent of Subjectivism," in Israel M. Kirzner (ed.), *Method, Process and Austrian Economics*, Lexington, MA: Lexington Books.

—— (1982b), "Review of *The Theory of Social Action: The Correspondence of Alfred Schutz and Talcott Parsons*," *Austrian Economics Newsletter*, **3**(3), Summer.

—— (1986), *The Market as an Economic Process*, New York: Basil Blackwell.

—— (1987), "Austrian Economics as a Hermeneutic Approach," unpublished ms.

Lavoie, Don (1987), "The Accounting of Interpretations and the Interpretation of Accounts," *Accounting, Organizations and Society*, **12**(6).

Madison, G.B. (1987), "Hayek and the Interpretive Turn," unpublished ms., Canadian Philosophical Association.

Menger, Carl (1976 [1871]), *Principles of Economics*, New York: New York University Press.
—— (1892), "On the Origin of Money," *Economic Journal*, **2**.
Mises, Ludwig von (1944), "The Treatment of 'Irrationality' In the Social Sciences," *Philosophy and Phenomenological Research*, **4**, June.
—— (1966 [1949]), *Human Action*, Chicago: Contemporary Books.
—— (1943), "Elastic Expectations and the Austrian Theory of the Trade Cycle," *Economica*, August.
—— (1981 [1912]), *The Theory of Money and Credit,* Indianapolis: Liberty Classics.
—— (1981 [1976]), *Epistemological Problems of Economics,* New York: New York University Press.
Moss, Laurence S. (1976), "The Monetary Economics of Ludwig von Mises," in Moss (ed.), *The Economics of Ludwig von Mises,* Kansas City: Sheed & Ward.
O'Driscoll, Gerald (1986), "Money: Menger's Evolutionary Approach," *History of Political Economy*, **18**(4).
O'Driscoll, Gerald and Mario Rizzo (1985), *The Economics of Time and Ignorance*, New York: Basil Blackwell.
Patinkin, Don (1965 [1951]), *Money, Interest, and Prices*, New York: Harper & Row.
Prendergast, Christopher (1986), "Alfred Schutz and the Austrian School of Economics," *American Journal of Sociology*, **92**(1), July.
Rickman, H.P. (ed.) (1976), *W. Dilthey: Selected Writings*, Cambridge: Cambridge University Press.
Rothbard, Murray N. (1970 [1962]), *Man, Economy and State*, Los Angeles: Nash Publishing.
—— (1986), "The Hermeneutical Invasion of Philosophy and Economics," *The Salisbury Review*, September.
Schutz, Alfred (1943), "The Problem of Rationality in the Social World," *Economica,* May.
Selgin, George A. (1986), "Praxeology and Understanding," *Review of Austrian Economics*, **1**.
—— (1987), "The Yield on Money Held Revisited: Lessons for Today," *Market Process*, **5**(1), Spring. (Reprinted as Chapter 14 in this volume.)
Selgin, George A. and White, Lawrence H. (1986), "The Evolution of a Free Banking System," *Economic Inquiry*, **25**, July, 439–57.
Shackle, G.L.S. (1967 [1958]), *Time in Economics*, Amsterdam: North-Holland Publishing Company.
—— (1969 [1961]), *Decision, Order and Time in Human Affairs*, Cambridge: Cambridge University Press.
—— (1972), *Epistemics and Economics: A Critique of Economic Doctrines*, Cambridge: Cambridge University Press.
—— (1974), *Keynesian Kaleidics*, Edinburgh: Edinburgh University Press.
—— (1979 [1978]), "Imagination, Formalism, and Choice," in *Time, Uncertainty, and Disequilibrium*, Lexington, MA: Lexington Books.
—— (1986), "The Origination of Choice," in Israel M. Kirzner (ed.), *Subjectivism, Intelligibility and Economic Understanding*, New York: New York University Press.
Georg Simmel (1978 [1900]), *The Philosophy of Money*, London: Routledge & Kegan Paul.
Timberlake, Richard (1986), "A Critique of Monetarist and Austrian Doctrines on the Utility and Value of Money," *Review of Austrian Economics*, **1**.

Vaughn, Karen I. (1976), "Critical Discussion of the Four Papers," in Moss (ed.), *The Economics of Ludwig von Mises*, Kansas City: Sheed & Ward.

9. A note on the cost controversy

Jack High

> At the end of his study Professor Chapman seems to confess that his initial hypothesis is quite remote from the facts. Could he not have remained in close touch with those facts throughout his investigation if he had carried the great principle he announces boldly through? He would then, surely, have treated the whole direction of resources to ends as a continuous selection between alternatives, guided throughout by a weighing of the significance of anticipated results, in which the "cost" of adopting any alternative is simply the relinquishing of some other alternative. (Philip Wicksteed, 1933)

> Two roads diverged in a wood, and
> I-
> I took the one less travelled by,...
> (Robert Frost)

INTRODUCTION

Some economic controversies seem never to die. They fade, lie dormant, then revive in a new season, under different circumstances. Such, at least, has been the story of controversies over cost in economic theory.

Wicksteed's telling criticism of Marshall[1] won the day for opportunity costs. But victory did not settle matters. "Foregone opportunities" meant different things to different economists, and debate over the meaning and use of costs continued through the thirties and forties, with the London School arguing for a subjectivist theory of cost. The London School's contributions were largely forgotten until Buchanan's exposition in *Cost and Choice* (1969); also see Buchanan and Thirlby (1981). Buchanan's work excited interest in the subjective theory of cost, with Vaughn (1980), Kirzner (1986), and others ably extending and defending the theory.

Other respected figures argued that Buchanan has overdone the subjectivist theme. Baumol (1970, pp. 1210–11) thought so in his review of *Cost and Choice*, and Yeager (1986) recently objected to "ultrasubjectivism" and "exaggeration" in subjective cost theory. Yeager's objections merit attention. On the whole he is sympathetic to subjective ideas, and his hard-nosed common sense is a virtue in his economic writings. When he complains, subjectivists should listen.

YEAGER ON BUCHANAN AND THE LONDON SCHOOL TRADITION

Yeager raises three objections to subjective cost as expounded by Buchanan. First, he disputes the claim that costs are borne solely by the decision maker. Yeager (1986, p. 25) says:

> cost can be imposed on others in quite ordinary senses of those words; it is not always kept inside the mind of the decisionmaker. What about adverse externalities – smoke damage and the like? What about losses imposed on stockholders by an incompetent business management?... Isn't it notoriously true that a government official need not personally bear all the costs of his decisions?

Second, Yeager argues that outside observers can indeed measure costs with tolerable accuracy. He writes (p. 25), "The money costs of producing a definite amount of some product, or the marginal money cost of its production, can indeed be estimated."

Third, and most fundamentally, Yeager questions the wisdom of defining opportunity cost as "the most highly valued opportunity foregone by a decisionmaker." He says (p. 24):

> Next I turn to exaggerations in the subjectivist cost doctrines of Buchanan and the London School. These terrorists[2] interpret the cost of a particular course of action as the next-best course perceived and forgone by the decisionmaker... Well, suppose the best course of action open to me is, in my judgment, to open a restaurant of a quite specific type in a specific location. The next-best course, then, is presumably to open a restaurant identical in all but some trivial detail, such as the particular hue of green of the lampshades. If so, the cost of the precise restaurant chosen is presumably an all but identical restaurant worth to me, in my judgment, almost fully as much. Generalizing, the cost of a chosen thing or course of action is very nearly the full value that the decisionmaker attributes to it.

Yeager (p. 25) considers this objection decisive enough to conclude that "either radical error or sterile word-juggling is afoot" in the usual subjective definition of opportunity cost.

The objections amount to charging subjective cost with a kind of theoretical madness, which has lost its mental grip on evident and ordinary truth. What can be said in defense?

SOME ETIQUETTE OF AMBIGUITY

The terms of economic discourse are notoriously ambiguous. Rooted as it is in human conduct, economics has had to take its words from ordinary discourse, and give them meanings suitable to science. "Competition," "value," "utility," "demand," "welfare," and numerous other terms have been lifted from the common language and given special meanings, often with some confusion. So it is with "cost." Yeager himself (p. 17) pointed out that cost does not have "a single definite and unequivocal meaning."

When using a word in a particular sense, the writer is obliged to say what that sense is, and to show its value in theoretical discourse. He is further obliged to warn the reader, through context or some other sign, when he is switching meanings. Buchanan, Vaughn and the others have performed these tasks conscientiously. Cost as a foregone opportunity is essential to our comprehending economic choice, especially the choices that we make in complex market settings. Moreover, economists are more vulnerable to error when they forget the subjective meaning of cost.[3]

Ambiguity also obligates the reader. A term should not be taken to mean one thing when the writer obviously intends it to mean another. A specific meaning should not be faulted for its failure to solve all theoretical problems if it nevertheless helps to solve some. Much of Yeager's criticism results from not adhering to a particular meaning of cost, the importance of which Buchanan and company have persuasively argued for.

However, Yeager's fundamental criticism of subjective opportunity cost is not a mere switching of terms. If "the next-best course [of action] perceived and foregone by a decisionmaker" involves "radical error or sterile word-juggling," then the theory built around this definition is suspect. I will argue that Yeager's criticism may well apply to general equilibrium theory, which would explain why opportunity costs are not much used in that theory,[4] but does not seriously affect the sensible approach to decision-making emphasized by Buchanan.

THE COSTS OF DECISIONS AND THE EFFECTS OF DECISIONS

It is true, of course, that "costs can be imposed on others in quite ordinary senses of those words." To my knowledge, nobody in the subjectivist tradition has ever denied this. Buchanan (1969, p. viii) notes that "several uses of the word 'cost' are categorically different. Linguistic usage dictates the same word for several different things. It is little wonder that we find great confusion, especially among economists, about cost."

Buchanan and the London School emphasize the link between decision and cost. We cannot do everything we would like to do; a niggardly nature has imposed scarcity on us. In choosing one course of action, we commonly forego another. At the moment of choice, what we forego "stands together"[5] with what we actually do. The foregone alternative is an inextricable part of the decision; without it there is no deciding, no cut to be made. It is in the sense of a foregone value that costs are borne exclusively by the decision-maker.

Having chosen one course of action over another, the agent will do things that have social repercussions. A factory owner may embark on a course that will introduce a new technology or bid up the price of equipment and labor. Or he may pollute the air. These actions have effects on others, effects that may reasonably be labeled costs. The new technology or the higher prices of factors may force competitors to act in ways that they would not otherwise have done. Air pollution may force inhabitants to forego cleaner air, which they value, and which, if the external effect is "Pareto-relevant," they may act to restore. (See Buchanan and Stubblebine (1960) for a classification of external effects. Buchanan clearly recognizes that the actions of some impose "costs" or "diseconomics" on others. See also Buchanan 1969, pp. 70–74.)

The effects of actions on others are undeniably important in economic theory and economists have traditionally called harmful effects "costs." But they are costs that are categorically different from the foregone alternatives of decision-makers. This, I take it, was Buchanan's message (pp. 42–5) in distinguishing between choice-influencing and choice-influenced cost. To point out, as Yeager does, that the characteristics of one kind of cost are not characteristics of other kinds of costs does nothing to invalidate subjective cost theory. At best, Yeager reminds us of other meanings and uses of the word "cost;" at worst he confuses the issues that Buchanan *et al.* have done so much to clarify.

This is especially apparent in the dispute over the measurability of costs. Costs in the sense of monetary expenses are often measurable *ex post*, and *ex ante*. The quantification of monetary costs, and their comparison with monetary receipts, are indispensable to the functioning of a complex market order. This was the insight of Mises that originally led to his criticism of socialism. Without prices for factors of production, no monetary calculation is feasible. It is, therefore, practically impossible to allocate resources to their most highly valued uses.

However, recognizing the measurability of monetary prices should not obscure the subjective influences on the formation of market prices. In modern economics, production takes place "for the market." Enterprisers appraise the future revenues and expenses of various production plans. They adopt those plans that seem to them most promising, and forego those plans that seem less so. It is the decisions of enterprisers to carry out some plans and to forego others that create supplies, demands, and prices in factor markets. The demand and supply curves of markets, as opposed to the curves of general equilibrium, have built into them imperfect foresight, imagination, and judgment. Consequently, so do market prices. "Equilibrium" in the sense of market clearing is a rather different theoretical construct than the "equilibrium" of general equilibrium theory.

We can, of course, assume away imperfect foresight, creativity, and judgment. We can postulate that producers know what the most economical production methods are. We can assume that they know the future receipts and expenses of production decisions. We can pretend that prices for resources and output are somehow "given." This is the world of general equilibrium, where a fictitious auctioneer calls out numeraire prices, where production decisions amount to calculating the right level of output, where there are neither profits nor losses.

Whatever the value of this hypothetical construction, it ignores the complexity, uncertainty, and creativity of modern production decisions. It ignores the scope for enterprise. As Vaughn (1980) pointed out, it is the objective reality of a complex market order that gives the subjectivity of costs their fullest scope and importance.

DO SUBJECTIVE COSTS MAKE SENSE?

Our discussion so far has taken for granted that "subjective opportunity cost" may be defined sensibly. Yeager doubts this when he says that the definition implies "radical error or sterile word-juggling is afoot."

Yeager's objection to opportunity cost shows up clearly in the neoclassical theory of utility. The usual maximization of a utility function subject to a budget constraint results in a unique commodity bundle at the point of tangency between the budget constraint and an indifference curve. If we ask "What is the most highly valued foregone bundle?" we get no definite answer. For any bundle an e away from the chosen bundle, there is a more highly valued bundle at $e/2$ from the chosen bundle. The limit of this process is precisely the bundle chosen. In continuous and connected commodity space, opportunity cost does not make much sense.

This problem can be easily remedied in discrete space. In Figure 9.1, discrete points are ranked in order of preference. Given his budget constraint and commodity preferences, the person chooses (1,2) and foregoes his next most highly ranked bundle, (2,1). The subjective opportunity cost in goods is sensible and easily identified.[6]

If we are dealing with utility space, we cannot tell how "close" the utility of (2,1) is to (1,2). The numbers are rank orderings, not magnitudes; we cannot

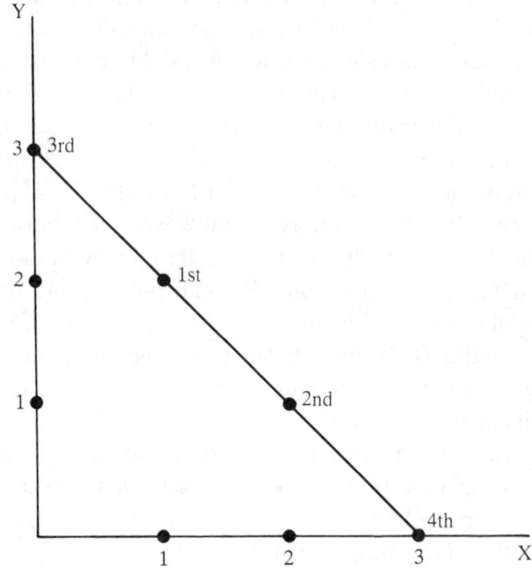

Figure 9.1

legitimately add or subtract them. But this is not true of production decisions. The discounted dollar value of investment A may indeed be very close to the value of investment B, the foregone investment. Nevertheless, as long as we are working with discrete alternatives, subjective opportunity costs make perfect sense. Whatever the dollar difference between A and B, B is the most highly valued foregone alternative. Thus it is "dense" choice space, not subjective opportunity cost, that stretches credulity and common sense.[7]

The subjectivist has two other legitimate grounds on which to criticize Yeager's restaurant example.

First, choosing between two restaurants that are identical in every respect but the color of lampshades is a logical possibility, but not a very realistic one. A more realistic description would be this:

A prospective restaurateur would decide between different kinds of restaurants – say between a steak house and a Mexican restaurant. If he chooses a Mexican restaurant, he then decides on whether to locate downtown or in a shopping mall. If he decides on locating downtown, he then decides, working within confines of space, whether layout one or layout two is better. Having chosen layout one, he then selects among decors, which can well include a decision between differently colored lampshades.

A common feature of decision-making under imperfect knowledge is that we carry out our plans using a sequence of decisions, which progress from the general to the particular. At the beginning of the month, the householder budgets so much for food, so much for housing, so much for clothing, so much for travel, so much for entertainment, and so on. Having decided to spend, say, a hundred dollars on entertainment, our householder then decides which particular plays, or concerts, or operas, or movies to see. At each stage, the costs of the decision are different. At the budgeting stage, the cost of entertainment is, say, clothes. At the stage of selecting particular entertainment, the cost of an opera may have been a play.

When we look at the sequences of decisions, the cost of a restaurant with dark green lampshades, if we want to speak of such a cost, is not simply an identical restaurant with light green ones. It is the list of foregone possibilities that the restaurateur would have pursued had he not selected the options he considered more favorable.

I might add that the choice between various hues of green may not be so trivial as Yeager believes. If the decor of the restaurant fits with one shade of green but not others, or if the owner has a particular liking for one shade of green, the decision may well be an important one. Whether a choice is trivial or not depends ultimately on the evaluation of the agent, not on physical similarity.[8]

CONCLUSION

The importance of subjective cost to economic theory is in explaining choices that take place in complex market settings. A valued foregone alternative is a necessary concomitant of economic choice. In the complex settings of modern markets, the actions chosen, as well as those relinquished, depend on the alertness, creativity, and judgment of consumers and producers. There is nothing "exaggerated" or "sterile" in studying the nature and effects of complex decisions. There is certainly nothing "nihilistic" about it.

Of course, the theory of market processes has not been formulated in mathematical terms, as have the theory of general equilibrium and the theory of *tatonnement* (see Negishi, 1962). Nor is it likely that process theory will be so formulated. But in place of the mathematical formulation, we have an impressive verbal theory, broad in scope, realistic in orientation, and founded on human nature as we know it, to use Frank Knight's phrase. One of the important achievements in this theory has been the formulation of cost theory, which explains the nature and effects of decisions in complex market settings. Subjective costs, like all parts of economic theory, deserve critical scrutiny and further development. But this doctrine is not exaggerated, or word-juggling, or nihilistic. It is, rather, an essential component of our theory of markets.

APPENDIX

A simple graphical model, which is built on Robbins's (1935) definition of economics, illuminates some of the various meanings of subjective opportunity cost.

Assume that a person has ends a, b, c, d, e, f, where a, c, e may be attained with units of good y, and b, d, f may be attained with units of good x. Further assume that the person ranks sets of ends as follows:

Set of Ends	**Rank**
(a,b,c,d,e,f)	1st
(a,b,c,d,e)	2nd
(a,b,c,d,f)	3rd
(a,b,c,d)	4th
(a,b,c,e)	5th
(a,b,c)	6th
(a,b,d,f)	7th
(a,b,d)	8th
(a,b)	9th
(a,c,e)	10th
(a,c)	11th
(b,d,f)	12th
(a)	13th
(b,d)	14th
(b)	15th

From the ranking of ends, the person will impute a ranking to bundles of goods. The ranking is shown in Figure 9.2, along with a budget constraint, BB.

With the given set of preferences and budget constraint, the person will acquire the bundle (1,2), ranked 6th in his overall set. What is the "cost" to him of doing so? There are several ways to answer, depending on what we mean by cost.

If the person had not acquired (1,2), he would have acquired (2,1), the next most highly ranked bundle available to him. This is the subjective opportunity cost expressed as a "bundle of goods."

But goods have value because they enable the person to attain his ends. With bundle (1,2) the person attains ends (a,b,c); with bundle (2,1) he attains (a,b,d). By acquiring (1,2) and foregoing (2,1), the person attains end c and foregoes end d. So we may say that end d is the cost of acquiring bundle (1,2). This is the meaning of opportunity cost in "utility space," which is fundamental in the sense that the importance of the ends determines the

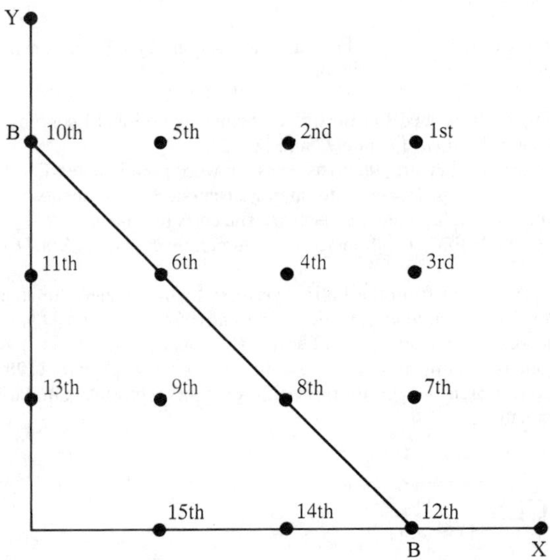

Figure 9.2

ranking of the goods. It is precisely because the person ranks end c above end d that he will acquire bundle (1,2) rather than (2,1).

This model also illustrates another kind of cost, the cost of economizing or allocating resources. Once the person has acquired bundle (1,2), he can allocate the units of x and y to attain various ends. In using his unit of x to attain end b, he foregoes attaining either d or f. Since d is the most highly valued of these, it is the subjective opportunity cost of attaining end b. Similarly, end e is the opportunity cost of attaining end c.

In the example, we can also speak of cost in the sense of price. In choosing between (1,2) and (2,1), the person is deciding whether or not to acquire a second unit of x or a second unit of y. The "cost" or "price" of choosing y is x. This cost is of course given by the slope of the budget constraint. This is objective in the sense that it is given independently of the preference scale of the chooser.

The purpose of this brief appendix has been to show some various meanings of "the most highly valuable foregone alternative" in a theory of choice. This model does not exhaust the meanings, nor does it convey the complexity and uncertainty that suffuse actual choice. However, it does show that "the most highly valuable foregone alternative" is an eminently sensible element of a theory of discrete choice.

NOTES

My thanks to James Buchanan, Pamela Heard, and Karen Vaughn for constructive criticisms. Remaining imperfections are not their fault.

1. See, for example, Wicksteed's criticism of Chapman's Political Economy, reprinted in *The Common Sense of Political Economy*, pp. 818–22.
2. This is a typographical error; "theorists" was the word used in an earlier draft of the paper.
3. See Kirzner's (1986, pp. 144–5) entertaining discussion of the man who cannot afford to marry a woman with a high income, because she costs too much .
4. Debreu, for example, only mentions costs as numeraire expenses. See *Theory of Value*, pp. 43, 62.
5. The word "cost" comes from the Latin "*constare*," which means "to stand together." See *Webster's New World Dictionary*, College Edition, 1962.
6. See the Appendix for an elaboration of costs using this model.
7. For a more general treatment of discrete utility theory see High *et al.* (1987).
8. I am indebted to Karen Vaughn for this point. Of course, physical similarity will influence subjective valuation.

REFERENCES

Alchian, A.A. (1969), "Cost," in *Encyclopedia of the Social Sciences*, vol. III, New York: Macmillan.

Baumol, William (1970), "Review of *Cost and Choice*," *Journal of Economic Literature*, December.

Buchanan, James M. (1969), *Cost and Choice*, Chicago: The University of Chicago Press.

Buchanan, James M. and Stubblebine, W. Craig (1960), "Externality," *Economica*, November, 371–84.

Buchanan, James, M. and Thirlby, G.F. (1981), *L.S.E. Essays on Cost*, New York: New York University Press.

Debreu, Gerard (1959), *Theory of Value*, New Haven: Yale University Press.

High, Jack, Alexeev, Michael and Heiner, Ron (1987), "Proving Convexity with Ordinal Marginal Utility," unpublished ms.

Kirzner, Israel M. (1986), "Another Look at the Subjectivism of Costs," in Kirzner (ed.), *Subjectivism, Intelligibility, and Understanding*, New York: New York University Press.

Negishi, Takashi (1962), "The Stability of a Competitive Economy: A Survey Article," *Econometrica*, October, 635–69.

Robbins, Lionel (1935), *An Essay on the Nature and Significance of Economics Science*, London: Macmillan, 2nd edn.

Vaughn, Karen I. (1980), "Does it Matter that Costs are Subjective?," *Southern Economic Journal*, **46**(3), January.

Webster's New World Dictionary (1962), College edn, New York: The World Publishing Company.

Wicksteed, Phillip H. (1933), *The Common Sense of Political Economy*, London: Routledge & Kegan Paul, Ltd.

Yeager, Leland (1986), "Why Subjectivism?" *The Review of Austrian Economics*, **1**, 5–31.

10. The cost controversy: a reply to Professor High

Leland B. Yeager

As Professor High (1987) briefly recognizes, my article in the first issue of the *Review of Austrian Economics* illustrated and applauded the accomplishments of subjectivism before going on to regret apparent examples of exaggeration and sterile word-juggling. Since I happened to touch on uses made of a few formulations by Professor James Buchanan, I take this opportunity to apologize to Buchanan for a grievous oversight on a related matter. Almost from the moment when it was too late to change my *RAE* article, I realized that I had unaccountably forgotten to mention one of the greatest triumphs of subjectivism, namely, Buchanan's demonstration that the burden of government deficit spending can indeed be largely shifted onto future generations. I try to atone for this oversight in my reply to a comment by Walter Block in the second issue of the *RAE*.

High chides me for my example of the restaurant's lampshades, which I used in commenting on the assertion that the cost of any particular line of action is the next-best course perceived and foregone. A corollary is Ronald Coase's remark, quoted by Buchanan (1969, p. 28), that covering costs and maximizing profits are essentially the same thing. High also questions my comments on widely quoted assertions that cost exists solely in the mind of the decision-maker and can be neither measured by nor shifted onto anyone else. He even repeats that "costs are borne exclusively by the decision-maker." Of course, he is using the word "cost" in a special sense, as Coase and Buchanan were doing (they were employing what Buchanan called a "choice-bound conception," as I noted). That is why I objected. In a confused area of discussion, it is no help to proliferate meanings of a term that already breeds misunderstanding.

I suspect that any disagreement between High and myself concerns terminology and style of discourse, not substantive questions of how the world works. Let's avoid confusion over what is the issue. When speaking of the subjectivity and nonshiftability of "cost," what one may mean is that an outsider cannot know all the considerations a decision-maker may have taken into account and what alternative courses he may have rejected and why and is therefore in a poor position to second-guess him or to lay down rules for him. If so, why not straightforwardly say just that? Why risk confusing one's reader or listener by using the word "cost" in a special way and appearing to tell him something substantive, new and even astonishing?

The subjectively perceived next-best line of action that a decision-maker foregoes in favor of his chosen course and the estimated money cost of that course do have *something* in common: both correspond to opportunity costs *in some sense or other.* The two senses are different enough, however, to require care with terminology. The first sense, which brings to mind the sorts of considerations and even the agonies involved in making a decision, is familiar to the layman and clear enough. Ever since my first college course in economics exposed me to this next-best-alternative interpretation of opportunity cost, I have been vaguely uneasy about it. Now I think I see why. It trivializes the concept; it suggests a deceptive or spurious familiarity.

Explaining the second sense of opportunity cost – the wider social significance of money cost – is what requires the economist's expertise and the student's alertness to learning something new. (Despite what High suggests, I am poles apart from objecting to the very concept of opportunity cost.) Misunderstanding still abounds. How often do we hear complaints about desired production being cut short or worthwhile projects shelved out of grubby concern with mere money cost? What still keeps needing to be explained is how money costs reflect the subjectively appraised values of the other outputs and other activities that necessarily must be foregone if resources are withheld from them for the sake of the particular output or activity in question. What further needs repeated explaining is how money costs transmit information and incentives to decision-makers through the price system. (This is not to say that the information conveyed about opportunity cost is completely accurate; for one thing, real-world prices are not general-equilibrium prices. However, the market process works to weed out gross inaccuracies more successfully than any other system of economic organization.)

The required explanation is not easy. (Even Irving Fisher (1970 [1930], pp. 485–7, 534–41) astonishingly denied that one particular price, the interest rate, measures any genuine opportunity cost.) Precisely because the expository task is such a demanding one, it is important to beware of misleading formulations or examples.

High suggests that general-equilibrium theory tends to neglect opportunity cost or to convey a conception of cost that clashes with the true subjectivist conception. This suggestion prods me to some concluding reflections. Austrians have no good reason to scorn the Walrasian and Casselian equation systems that seek to describe what an economy would look like in a state of full coordination. Pondering such a system helps one grasp the central fact of general interdependence. It helps one see how greater production of some goods and services requires lesser production of others and how, ultimately and subjectively, greater satisfaction of some desires costs lesser satisfaction of others. It helps one grasp the immensity of the task of coordination that the price system works toward performing. Of course the performance is never complete and perfect, and I would be astonished indeed if any general-equilibrium theorist ever as much as hinted otherwise. Of course general-equilibrium theory leaves room for investigating the processes at work in the real world of disequilibrium. Much needs to be said – I agree with High – about complexity, uncertainty, judgment, creativity, and enterprise. Walras and Menger are complementary goods.

I mean nothing personal – and I want to emphasize this – in my comments. Professor High's article appears to show the influence of a tendency characterizing much of present-day Austrian economics; a tendency to mistake clever verbal maneuvering for substantive analysis. Yet High and other Austrians do have much of substance and of value to say, including much about the subjective aspects of cost. They will do better conveying their findings and their insights if they shun factitious quarrels, contrived paradoxes, and misleading terminology and take pains to present their message in straightforward language.

REFERENCES

Buchanan, James M. (1969), *Cost and Choice*, Chicago: Markham.

Fisher, Irving (1970), *The Theory of Interest*, New York: Kelley. (Reprint of 1930 edn.)

High, Jack (1987), "A Note on the Cost Controversy," *Market Process* **5**, Spring, 8–10, 26–7. (Reprinted as Chapter 9 of this volume.)

Yeager, Leland B. (1987), "Why Subjectivism?," *Review of Austrian Economics* **1**, 5–31.

11. Economics, subjectivism and public choice

Jack Wiseman

It is no cause for alarm that academics should be dissatisfied with the state of their chosen discipline: doubt is the yeast of intellectual progress.

But a group of scholars can lose its way, and new kinds of doubt then develop: doubt about the nature of the intellectual problem itself or about the "right" or "best" way to study it – what might be called, parodying the jargon of the relevant philosophers, "paradigm doubt." Economics today seems to me to have all the symptoms of this condition, with its concomitant factionalism. More, the problem is not a simple one of paradigm replacement, in that the disturbance is simply a reflection of the need for time in which a new paradigm, providing generally better "explanations," can replace an existing one. I have neither time nor space to embroil myself in such issues as the status of economics as an "innovative" science. I would assert simply that our problem is not of this kind, but is rather that we have no one developed system of thought that is adequately comprehensive (embracing), and hence none which as it stands is capable of displacing the others. I do not expect to remedy this defect in a couple of thousand words. I shall content myself with an attempt to identify the reasons for our malaise, in the hope of encouraging agreement about what is wrong and what sort of remedies are needed.

Also, in the space available I can deal only in generalizations. It is consequently inevitable that my descriptions of intellectual positions will have an element of parody. But I trust, and believe, that they are neither unrecognizable nor unfair.

At this general level, it is possible to make two useful distinctions, one more familiar than the other. The first concerns the approach to the "explanation" of economic phenomena, in respect of which what has come to be known as the "Austrian School" offers formulations and insights that stand in marked contrast to those of "mainstream" or "neoclassical" economics. The second concerns the appropriate subject matter. Both mainstream and Austrian economists concentrate attention on the logic of choice as expressed through markets. Non-market choice-situations are studied only incidentally, or as "offshoots" or addenda to this central concern with the market. The development of the study of public choice is a partial response to this restriction, but, I shall argue, is itself in danger of being treated as an addendum (an obligatory chapter in a textbook of economic analysis), rather than as the general and unifying construct that I believe to be needed.

Not everyone is agreed that there are significant intellectual differences between the Austrian School and what might be called the Chicago Positivist School: distinguished members of the latter have been known to claim that there is little difference between their own intellectual position and, for example, that of Professor Hayek. My own perception is that there is one difference that is of fundamental importance, and abdications from (or misperceptions of) that difference that make the two views of the economic problem seem more similar than they in fact are, while in fact making them more difficult to integrate into a common intellectual framework. The essential difference can be put in this way: while both schools are concerned with the characteristics of human behavior in response to scarcity, they specify the characteristics of the environment in which scarcity occurs in significantly different ways. For both, scarcity obligates choice, and choice implies sacrifice. Any chosen course of action implies a necessarily sacrificed alternative course, which both schools would identify as the opportunity-cost of the implemented decision. For the Austrian, opportunity-cost is a subjective concept: the value placed by an individual on the best course of action envisaged as feasible but rejected in favor of the chosen course. So conceived, opportunity-cost has no objective manifestation: it is a "non-event" (rejected plan), whose characteristics, insofar as they can be "known" at all, can be known only to the individual decision-maker. A Chicago positivist would not necessarily reject this description. But he would give the subjective plans objective content, by way of simplifying assumptions about the knowledge (information) available to the individual decision-maker. Readers will be familiar with the devices I have in mind. The simplest one is that entrepreneurs' plans are conceived in terms of known prices. When it is acknowledged that present plans concern the future, and future prices are not "known" now, the problem is emasculated by assuming that (objective) probabilities can be attached to possible outcomes and that individual risk-preferences are somehow "known." There are sophisticated models that allow for "mistakes": but "mistake-correction" follows pre-specified "rules" so that the models "run-down" to a stable world. The most sophisticated attempts to deal with the uncertainty problem within "mainstream" economics (such as those of Arrow and Debreu) continue to depend ultimately on the assumption that the future is "knowable" (indeed, known) in the sense that someone (Walras-with-Bayes?) is apprised of all the plans that are or could be considered by all decision-makers (since the models require that the number of possible plans be "finite"). Insofar as they treat historical data as a record of successfully implemented plans (so that e.g. price series are never treated as a record of (at least partial) plan-failure) the econometric studies resting on such intellectual foundations can never permit trustworthy inferences about causal relations relevant to a decision-making world in which the future is not only unknown but unknowable, and in which the plans of individuals consequently not only produce unpredicted outcomes, but generate no particular surprise for the planners when they do so.

It is this "subjectivist insight": that the future is not only unknown but in a practical sense unknowable, that distinguishes the Austrian position. As a criticism of mainstream economics, it is difficult to answer. Indeed, I do not think it can be answered. The more usual defense is a counter-criticism: Destructive comment is one thing. But what alternative explanations can the Austrian/subjectivist school offer? Clearly, they cannot replicate the neat outcomes of the mainstream economic models, nor can they find a ready substitute for the (Paretian) efficiency concept that derives from such models. For the Austrian, the process of allocation of resources between uses is an individual decision process continuously unfolding in time. The concept of "static" allocative outcome-efficiency is not particularly interesting, even if comprehensible. Thus, the Austrian response is to change the focus of interest, from the efficient outcome of the resource-allocation process to the efficiency of the process *per se* . This follows directly from the different assumptions of the two schools about knowledge and its distribution. It produces the paradoxical situation that the Austrian specification of the problem is clearly superior in terms of realism, but lends itself less readily to sophisticated analytical manipulation or formally precise conclusions. This in no way destroys the Austrian position, in that false precision deriving from a misleading specification of the relevant problem is not itself practically helpful. Nevertheless, the desire of Austrians to preserve the purity of their specification, and the simultaneous desire to make a positive as well as a critical contribution, together perhaps with a scholarly urge to impose intellectual order on a difficult problem, can and does confuse the issue by producing the misconceptions I referred to earlier. A few illustrations may help:

I have already drawn attention to the difficulty of interpreting causally a historical record which to an unknown extent is the record of the outcome of mistaken judgments: How are we to infer causality from such data? The reaction of some Austrians is simply to reject the use of statistics. But this is surely too extreme a position. The historical record is the only record we have got: we cannot ignore it, but clearly need to find ways to interpret it better – ways that must involve abandonment of some of the neoclassical simplifications. Again, it is a virtue of the Austrian approach that it places the entrepreneur/decision-maker/innovator at the center of the economic process. But in a truly subjectivist world, all individuals are decision-makers, and it is implausible to distinguish "the entrepreneur" as a special kind of decision-maker, as is sometimes done (though it may be useful to identify "entrepreneurial decisions" with particular kinds of choice-situation). Similar objections can be taken to the use of "orthodox" (neoclassical) supply-and-demand curves to "explain" the process of price change through time. The "orthodox" curves imply the existence of "objective" market demand and supply schedules: something that denies the Austrian postulate of an unknowable future. On the other hand, it is difficult to understand why an Austrian-subjectivist should find the idea of general equilibrium of interest either of itself or as an efficiency indicator, or why any kind of equilibrium state should ever emerge from the information transmission which Austrians properly identify with competitive decision-making.

If the two schools are ultimately to be reconciled, it will have to be by way of the increasing willingness of mainstream economists to accept the superior behavioral insights of the Austrian formulation, and to direct their undoubted technical sophistication to the development of new insights within this new framework. The process would be helped rather than hindered by consistency among Austrians themselves in the interpretation of subjective cost in a truly uncertain world: a consistency which is not always apparent at present.

Such a reconciliation will become more likely if and when both schools recognise the need to broaden their subject-matter. I have already pointed out that, for both schools, the study of economics is identified for practical purposes with the study of market or market-type phenomena. Mainstream economics generally treats other institutional arrangements as "inputs" to the behavior of markets and, implicitly or explicitly, judges such arrangements, insofar as they are considered at all, in terms of their influence on the functioning of the market. The Austrian position is ambiguous: it emphasizes the embracing nature of "human action" (and the consequent unrealism of e.g. the notion of an "economic" decision), but at the same time broadly identifies the subject-matter of economics with the study of the behavior of markets.

The emergence of public choice as a sub-discipline of mainstream economics was undoubtedly influenced by a recognition of the inadequacy of this restriction, which e.g. has inhibited study of the behavior of government and its institutions. Paradoxically, it matured as a critique/extension of mainstream economics, whose importance is now generally recognised e.g. by the incorporation of a public-choice section in most standard texts. Yet the public-choice insights have always fitted easily with the neoclassical "orthodoxy": the subjectivity of the decision process, and of the nature of costs, becomes even more manifest when interest shifts from market-related to political or bureaucratic decision-making. Yet applied research in public choice still depends largely on the neoclassical model: it is surely incongruous to find the standard econometric techniques being used on public-choice problems to which they are manifestly inappropriate.

The concept of subjective opportunity costs helps with an understanding of all human decision-problems – that is, all problems requiring a choice between mutually-excluding alternatives. Mainstream economics not only mis-specifies the economic problem, but conceives the subject-matter too narrowly. It is now generally recognised that a policy-relevant economics must embrace public choice (I would personally prefer to say must be absorbed by it), and this requires embracing an "Austrian" methodology rather than persistence with the present Chicago-positivist model.

The practical problem is to develop an overarching public-choice framework for the study of decision-making in society: it is the burden of my argument that such a framework can be evolved from the Austrian School insights, but that this will need a catholic interpretation of the subject-matter, and perhaps a less defensive attitude of mind from Austrians as well as from their critics.

12. Shackle and a lecture in Pittsburgh

James M. Buchanan

It is both intellectually and emotionally stimulating to be drawn back to the radical subjectivism of G.L.S. Shackle, who has consistently exhibited the courage to state the implications of his perspective for the whole realm of scientific inquiry in economics. Along with many others among my disciplinary peers, I have found it too easy to slip into orthodox methodology when its applicability beckons, thereby implicitly expressing a lack of concern with the apparent logical incoherence that describes my work upon any inclusive evaluation. The invitation to write this short review article provides me with an opportunity to re-evaluate my own position specifically as it relates to that taken by Shackle, which is restated severally in this volume.

Business, Time, and Thought collects 20 papers, most of them short, almost all of which have been quite recently written and published, well beyond the productive years of most economists. But, as we have long been aware, George Shackle is no ordinary economist, and his ability to present even familiar ideas in a prose that sparkles with enthusiasm remains characteristic of this new volume.

I can commence my re-evaluation by a direct citation:

> The elemental thing we study is *choice*. If choice means anything, it means *origination*. The making of history (on however small a scale) is the making possible one path of affairs rather than another. By origination, I would say (and here take a decisive step outside all orthodoxy, even the Austrian) we ought to mean an act of thought that is a *first cause*, so that choice in its essential nature is unpredictable in its effects, its sequel. Many 'choices' are of course mere response or obedience to habit or simple reckoning. By choice we ought to mean a *momentous* act of thought. If such an act is truly originative, it cannot be foreknown in character or timing, and thus we are essentially denied the power to specify the sequel of any present choice as a singular path. (p. 206, original emphasis)

I want to suggest that Shackle's definition of choice, expressed here and elsewhere, tends to conflate two distinguishable mental events, both of which

Essay Review of *Business, Time, and Thought* by G.L.S. Shackle, edited by Stephen F. Frowen (New York: New York University Press, 1988).

can, with qualifications, be brought within his definition but which remain categorically different in their implications for both economic theory and the whole scientific enterprise of economists.

I propose to introduce a personal, autobiographical example to develop the distinction between the two quite separate conceptions of choice, and I hope, in so doing, to construct a bridge of sorts between the implied scientific nihilism in Shackle's position and the positivism that describes orthodox neoclassical economics.

In late 1987, an officer-agent for the National Association of Business Economists invited me to deliver the annual Adam Smith Lecture at the association's scheduled meeting in Pittsburgh in September 1988. This lecture, as delivered by me, involved two quite distinct choices that illustrate the category differences I want to emphasize. There was, first of all, a decision, a choice, made by some officer, officers, or committee, on behalf of the Association. This choice was expressed by the sending of the initial invitation to me. This choice was *creative* in that a sequence of events was made possible, a sequence that did not exist prior to choice and that was brought into being, literally, by the choice itself. This creative choice seems to be the sort that occupies Shackle's attention almost exclusively and, by inference, his treatment relegates all other "choices" to the status of behavioral responses.

I suggest, however, that the lecture, as delivered, involved a second genuine choice, this time a choice on my part concerning acceptance or rejection of the invitation. In one basic sense, my choice in this instance was not creative; it was instead, *reactive*. I found myself confronted with a modified set of environmental alternatives, but I had done nothing directly or indirectly to create the change in conditions that had brought the new opportunity into realization. Clearly, however, I did face a genuine choice that fits within the inclusive Shackle definition. I was not merely responding to a stimulus in my act of acceptance.

There is a categorical difference between *creative* and *reactive* choice when we come to the realm of predictability, the domain of scientific inquiry. My reactive choice could have been, probabilistically, predicted by those who advanced the Association's invitation. By contrast, there was no way that I could have, even probabilistically, predicted that such an invitation would have been forthcoming. The matching of the name "Buchanan" with the "1988 Adam Smith Lecture" was creative in a Kirznerian entrepreneurial sense.

I need not push the personal illustration too far. But it does allow me to clarify my own position, as expressed variously, which may have seemed to embody inconsistency by my acceptance of much of the Shackle critique while continuing to use the neoclassical framework of analysis. Neoclassical analysis is, and must be, restricted entirely to the domain of *reactive* choice, which is always predictable, at least within probabilistic limits. A genuine science of reactive choice is possible, and patterns of order can be predicted to emerge, even if each choosing participant retains the fullest Shacklian freedom to originate his own sequence of future events. The domain of reactive choice extends over a wide spectrum of possible choice settings. At the one extreme, the individual actor is genetically programmed to respond uniquely and predictably to the alternatives that are confronted; in this limit, "choice" in any meaningful sense disappears. As we move beyond this limit, *individual choice* becomes possible, and indeterminacy replaces determinacy in any attempt to predict individual behavior. Such indeterminacy need not, however, extend to *patterns* of behavior that describe the choices made by many persons comparably situated in at least some respects, or, alternatively the choices made by a single person over a whole series of comparably defined circumstances.

I should stress that the *reactive* choice of an individual may meet the Shacklian criterion for *originative* choice, when examined in perspective of the individual who chooses. Such a person does, indeed, originate the particular sequence of events that can only come into existence, *for him*, after genuine choice is exercised. In my acceptance of the invitation to deliver the Adam Smith Lecture in Pittsburgh, I originated a sequence of events, for myself and others, that would not have been within the possible had my choice been rejection. I suggest, however, that my choice in this instance was not itself *creative* because it was at least probabilistically predictable, as indeed all reactive choices must be. The *pattern* of response might have been such as to allow for my private choice to have been either one of the alternatives that I faced, while retaining some appropriate appellation of stochastic determinacy. And, of course, as we move back along the spectrum of reactive choice toward generalization over persons and over time sequences, the determinacy of reactive choice patterns increases and with this comes enhanced productivity of scientific inquiry.

All such reactive choices are, however, categorically distinct from genuinely creative choice, which does indeed bring into being a sequence of events that remains indeterminate, not only at the level of individual action but also at the level of any conceivable pattern of behavior generalized over many persons and many periods. In creative choice, the behavior of the individual is not probabilistically predictable because such choice, in itself, *creates* alternatives from which the other individuals choose. The creative chooser does not select from among competing "forks in the road" that remain "out there," thrown up to him either by natural circumstance or by the action of others, privately or collectively. The reactive choice I faced in accepting or rejecting the invitation to deliver the Adam Smith Lecture came into being by the creative decision of the agents who acted on behalf of the

Association. This choice was dimensionally different from that which I faced in reacting to the modified opportunity that I found.

The essential contribution of G.L.S. Shackle, who is surely one of the most neglected economists of this century, lies in his emphasis and insistence on the indeterminacy of choice. And the related emphasis of modern Austrian economists, notably that of Israel Kirzner, on the necessary role of entrepreneurial choice in the dynamic operation of any economy, deserves our praise. Understanding how the economic order works requires that we give due attention to both dimensions for choice, and neoclassical orthodoxy has surely neglected creative choice as the necessary complement to the reactive choice that must be its central focus. But all "choice" that deserves to be so labeled is originative, while not all "choice" is creative (entrepreneurial).

In this short essay, stimulated again by reading Shackle, I have shifted my own position toward a more catholic and less critical attitude on the orthodoxy of neoclassical economics than that expressed in separate essays published in celebratory volumes in honor of Hayek and Mises.[1] I remain a Shacklian, but I now recognize, more than before, the essential distinction between individual and pattern indeterminacy.

I apologize to those readers who might have expected me to offer a more comprehensive review of the particular contents of this new Shackle book. In terms of the central subject matter discussed, at least two earlier books by Shackle are more focused,[2] because the essays reprinted here are necessarily the sometimes unrelated reflections of a senior scholar. But it is difficult for me, here as before, to read anything by Shackle without being stimulated to reflect on issues that are, indeed, central to our whole enterprise as economists.

NOTES

1. See my (1969) "Is Economics the Science of Choice?" in Erich Streissler (ed.), *Roads to Freedom: Essays in Honor of F.A. Hayek,* London: Routledge and Kegan Paul. Reprinted in my (1979) *What Should Economists Do?*, Indianapolis: Liberty Press, pp. 39–63; and, my (1982) "The Domain of Subjective Economics: Between Predictive Science and Moral Philosophy," in Israel Kirzner (ed.), *Method, Process, and Austrian Economics: Essays in Honor of Ludwig von Mises*, Lexington, MA: Lexington Books. Reprinted in my (1987) *Economics: Between Predictive Science and Moral Philosophy*, College Station: Texas A & M University Press, pp. 67–82.
2. G.L.S. Shackle (1972), *Epistemics and Economics*, Cambridge: Cambridge University Press; (1979), *Imagination and the Nature of Choice* (Edinburgh: Edinburgh University Press).

13. Insight and the creative potential of mind

G.L.S. Shackle

A mind desires to understand its environment in order to use it, and in order to improve it. Use may allow and assist the gaining of insight into the nature and process of an unchanging environment by observation during a lapse of time. An enterprise of improvement must have some inceptive steps designed in advance of observational knowledge of their effect. If the environment is constituted in some respects by the actions of others, the knowledge that others are attempting improvements for their own purposes will make the gaining of insight more precarious. Thus the empirical view of the nature of knowledge exposes its process of attainment to essential and irremediable partial frustration by the creative potential of mind itself. However, there is another view of the nature of knowledge. If the world presents to us a set of what seem to be self-evident and irrefutable truths, and if these seem to be the entire body of such truths, it has been supposed that the whole nature and process of the world can be derived from them by reason alone. If so, the question has been asked, can any proposition so derived be regarded as new knowledge, as being synthetic in the sense that the bringing together of some ideas formerly regarded as entirely independent of each other produces a further proposition not hitherto recognized? Can there come into being synthetic propositions *a priori*? The answer must surely be that if the *a priori* basis is given and complete once and for all, everything deducible from it already in some sense exists and is not new. If there are to be synthetic propositions *a priori*, the *a priori* must itself be treated as subject to additions, to innovations, to the creative potential of mind. The Misesian view, that the *a priori* is to be found by searching examination of our minds, thus leaves the question in doubt whether the *a priori* is fixed forever by the ultimate constitution of the world, or whether it can itself be transformed.

My suggestion has been that there can be thoughts not traceable in all respects to antecedents, no matter how complete and perfect our knowledge of the antecedents is. Such thoughts if they can come into being are an *uncaused cause*, a beginning.[1] An alternative formulation could be that they are the random mutations of thought in a sense analogous to the phrase used by geneticists.

I would say that new knowledge must come either from observation or from the creative potential of mind.

NOTES

Editor's note: This is a short comment on the article by George A. Selgin entitled "Praxeology and Understanding: An Analysis of the Controversy in Austrian Economics" (*Review of Austrian Economics*, **2**, 1988).

1. G.L.S. Shackle, *Imagination and the Nature of Choice*, Edinburgh: Edinburgh University Press, 1979.

PART THREE

Money and Banking

14. The yield on money held revisited: lessons for today

George A. Selgin

INTRODUCTION

Over thirty years ago, in a volume honoring the 50th anniversary of Ludwig von Mises's receipt of his doctorate, William H. Hutt published an essay on monetary economics which has since become an "Austrian" classic. In "The Yield from Money Held" Hutt argued that writers from Aristotle to Keynes, including Locke, Smith, and Mises himself, committed crucial errors by claiming that money is "barren" – that it "has a yield of nil."[1] Because of this blunder, these writers failed to explain properly how the value of money (the "price level") is determined. Some also went on to suggest monetary policies that were seriously misguided.

Regrettably Hutt's revelations have gone unheeded by many monetary theorists since the time of the appearance of his essay. The writers continue to overlook the yield on money held. As in previous cases this error leads those who commit it into more serious theoretical and practical blunders. The purpose of this essay is to review the history of these blunders, showing how crucially they depend on the assumption that money has no yield.

THE GREIDANUS CONNECTION

That so many economists should overlook the yield on money for so long is surprising, for a recognition of that yield is essential to the successful application of subjective-value theory to money, and many economists who wrote on monetary theory after the marginalist revolution were at least *implicitly* aware of an *implicit* (non-pecuniary) return on money balances. Yet as late as 1935 John Hicks was still looking forward to a marginalist revolution in monetary theory; that theory continued to be dominated by the quantity theory, with its distinctly non-subjective notion of "velocity."[2]

According to Richard Timberlake, such circumstances should have "culminated in an epic work on the subject" of the yield on money.[3] The irony, though, is *not* (*contra* Timberlake) that such an epic work never appeared. It is that one did appear, but was entirely ignored. The work was a book called *The Value of Money* by Dutch economist Tjardus Greidanus.[4] According to Hutt, Greidanus had been the only economist before 1956 to give proper due to the yield on money as the principle factor responsible for its value.[5] Indeed, Greidanus's book, a second edition of which appeared in 1950, was probably the inspiration for Hutt's essay. Greidanus undertook a systematic critique of earlier attempts to explain the value of money, showing how most of them failed to acknowledge its yield – a return from liquidity or marketability services. Because they ignored this yield, past theorists made the mistake of identifying the marginal utility of money with the marginal utility of goods that could be purchased with it. Theories of the value of money based on this starting point were, Greidanus showed, inadequate. He then went on to elaborate in detail a "yield theory" of the value of money in which the marginal utility of money is identified with the utility of liquidity services provided by another unit of it.

Greidanus's book, which first appeared in 1932, should have been hailed as the fulfillment of Hicks's 1935 "suggestion." But instead it was ignored and then overshadowed by another important book: Keynes's *General Theory*. Whereas Greidanus succeeded in extending the marginalist revolution to monetary theory, Keynes declared that revolution a failure – largely on the basis of its inadequate treatment of monetary phenomena – and proposed a whole new revolution to replace it. Diverted by Keynesianism,[6] the profession turned its back on Greidanus's pathbreaking accomplishment .

THE "CLASSICAL DICHOTOMY"

It took almost two decades – until about the time when Hutt's essay appeared – for economists to begin returning from the "Keynesian diversion" to renew the challenge to integrate monetary theory with neoclassical value-theory. The first important steps of this so-called "neoclassical synthesis" were taken by Don Patinkin.[7] Whereas Greidanus solved the value-of-money problem following the tradition of Menger and the Austrian School, Patinkin – who does not seem to have known about Greidanus – drew his inspiration from Walras and from Walras's idea of the *encaisse désiree* applied to a general-equilibrium framework.

That the final, lasting synthesis of monetary and value theory should have to be accomplished using a general equilibrium framework is ironic, because this, of all approaches, is the most difficult one: it is most difficult to rationalize a positive demand for and value of money in a general-equilibrium framework. Patinkin himself realized this,[8] and Austrians will find Greidanus's less-Procrustean approach much more satisfying. Nevertheless Patinkin's contribution has much in common with that of his Dutch predecessor. Patinkin also understood that the problem of the value of money could never be solved as long as the marginal utility of money continued to be identified with the marginal utility of goods a unit of money could purchase.[9] In this connection he – like Greidanus before him – critically cited works by Wicksell, Fisher, Keynes, and Mises. He also declared that Mises's position was especially puzzling, because Mises had described "the liquidity advantages of holding money ... so clearly in other parts of his work."[10]

Patinkin charged the classical quantity-theorists in particular of having erected an "invalid dichotomy" of forces determining relative prices and those determining the value of money (the scale of "absolute" prices). Relative prices were, in the classical approach, supposed to be determined by the forces of supply and demand as conditioned by the subjective-utility calculations of market participants. The value of money, in contrast, was held to be determined by a set of objective factors, independent of the will of individuals, consisting of the supply of money, its velocity of circulation, and the extent of real output. Patinkin argued that this approach was theoretically "inconsistent," and that, furthermore, it did not lead to a stable solution to the value-of-money problem: it failed to explain how the value of money (the "price level"), once displaced from its equilibrium value as determined by objective conditions, would be restored to that value by market forces. The "velocity" of money, which appeared as a kind of *deux ex machina* in the classical equilibrium-solution, was – because it was "technologically given" – devoid of any power to explain equilibrating *adjustments*.

Patinkin's solution, which was to let real-money balances "enter the utility function" directly or indirectly through their influence on production, was the equivalent of Greidanus's yield approach, only tailored to fit a utility-maximization, general-equilibrium framework. By assigning a role to real (not merely nominal) cash balances in agents' utility functions, Patinkin was able to motivate a "real cash balance effect" which assured a stable equilibrium solution to the value-of-money problem. He thereby succeeded in fixing a chink in the classical armor which Keynes had tried to exploit.

Some theorists disputed the significance of Patinkin's contribution. Archibald and Lipsey, Brunner, and Valavanis all argued, contrary to Patinkin, that "a consistent monetary theory could be constructed without assigning utility to money."[11] As Harry Johnson points out, Patinkin was forced to drop the "inconsistency" charge. Nevertheless, his critics had failed to see the point.

> While a formally *consistent* theory can be constructed by interpreting velocity as an externally-imposed restraint on monetary behavior ... this treatment not only leaves velocity itself unexplained on economic grounds, but precludes any analy-

> sis of monetary dynamics and the stability of monetary equilibrium by its inability to specify behavior in disequilibrium conditions. As the better classical monetary theorists saw, these problems are most easily handled by assuming that money balances yield services of utility to their holders.[12]

Greidanus also rejected the "mechanical quantity theories" with the reliance they placed on an objectively given value for velocity.[13] Like Patinkin, he found this approach question begging. He also gave a neat demonstration showing that, in a sense, these theorists *were* "inconsistent" in using standard supply and demand explanations to explain how individual relative prices were formed while referring to "velocity" to explain the value of money.[14] Suppose, Greidanus argued, that for some definite period 1 it must be true that

$$M_1V_1 = P_1T_1$$

where V_1 is given by "technical conditions." Then, if we consider a second period which "contains the first period … plus one other transaction" consisting of a purchase of 100 bushels of corn, it must be the case for this second, longer period that

$$M_2V_2 = P_2T_2.$$

If we assume that $M_2 = M_1$ (there is no change in the money supply) and that $T_2 = T_1$ plus 100 bushels of corn, then these values, which are *given* values, together with V_2, determine P_2. But, Greidanus pointed out, V_2 is also given "by technical considerations." It follows that P_2 is fully determined by M_1, T_2 (= T_1 + 100 bushels of corn), and V_2, without being at all influenced by the will of the persons involved in the exchange of the additional 100 bushels of corn! Thus, the price of the corn, rather than being the result of supply and demand as determined by the will of the buyer and seller, is determined by "a number of quantities given by technical circumstances." Moreover "in fixing his price the purchaser has to take into account a number of data of which he does not even know the value." If, for example, M_2 is \$100 million and V_2 is 10.001, then – independent of the will of the buyer – M_2V_2 (hence P_2T_2) *must* be \$1,000,010,000. The purchaser of the corn "*must* know – though he *cannot* know – that he *must* pay \$10,000" for 100 bushels.

Like Patinkin – but many years before – Greidanus had seen that the value problem could only be solved (in a manner consistent with orthodox value-theory) by letting money in the utility function or, in other words, by acknowledging the yield on money held.

THE CIRCULARITY PROBLEM AND THE REGRESSION THEOREM

Though he insisted that the utility of money had to be acknowledged for the value-of-money problem to be solved, Patinkin denied that there was any "circularity problem" to overcome, either in theories that denied the utility of money *per se* or in others like his own (or Greidanus's) that acknowledged the utility of money services. This view contrasts sharply with views of earlier theorists. They believed either (1) that the circularity problem made application of marginal utility theory to money futile or (2) that some special approach had to be taken to get out of the "vicious circle."

What was this "vicious circle"? It was argued that the value of money depended on its marginal utility, but that this marginal utility (which was often identified with the marginal utility of goods the money could purchase) also depended on the value of money. Hence, attempts to explain the value of money by appealing to its utility or marginal utility were in effect trying to explain the value of money by appealing to that value. This was the vicious circle. Mises's "regression theorem" was an attempt to get out of the circle.[15] Mises argued that, although the value of money today depends on its marginal utility today, that marginal utility depends, not on the realized value of money today, but on the value money is *expected* to have today, which is based on its realized value *yesterday*. Rather than leading to an infinite regress (which, presumably, is no better than a vicious circle), the regression theorem implies that the value of money is ultimately linked to the pure-commodity value of the medium of exchange, i.e., the industrial or non-monetary value of the commodity for which present money can be or once could be redeemed.

The circularity problem seems more evident when the utility of money is identified with the utility of goods it can purchase than when it is identified with the liquidity services from money-holding. Nevertheless, even in the latter case it appears that the value of money ultimately depends on its possibility of resale in a manner distinct from the case with other goods; for the latter, resale possibilities *may* enter into value calculations, but they *need* not.

Though he acknowledged this peculiarity of money, Patinkin held the circularity problem to be entirely bogus.[16] Its basis, according to Patinkin, was a failure – understandable from a writer whose contribution first appeared in 1912 – to appreciate the significance of "mutual determination" in market-processes. Mises and other early writers had simply failed to distinguish between "individual experiments" and "market experiments" involved in the determination of the value of money. In the former, individuals are confronted with hypothetical "price levels" and asked what nominal quantity of money they would desire at each of these price levels. This experiment gives a set of individual-demand schedules for nominal money balances. The schedules can then be summed horizontally into a market-demand schedule, which, when combined in a "market experiment" with a schedule (usually a vertical one) showing the nominal money *supply*, gives a definite solution to the value-of-money problem. The procedure is entirely analogous to the one used to find equilibrium solutions for relative prices of other goods.

But does this prove that the regression theorem is entirely superfluous? It does not, for although a "circulatory problem" does not exist in the strict sense in which Mises conceived it, it is nevertheless still true that the expectation that money will be accepted – that it will have a positive exchange value – is essential to its having a determinate, positive market value. For if a positive value of money is not in some manner "given" to market participants *ahead of* their deciding how much of it to demand, it is doubtful whether they will demand it at all. The market can always refuse to acknowledge the "moneyness" of the good in question, using some other medium of exchange instead of it or resorting to barter.

Thus one can say of Patinkin what Mises[17] said in criticizing the quantity-theorists: that he tacitly assumes a positive value of the money-good – both a symptom of and a prerequisite for its acceptance as a medium of exchange – to be given. Indeed, in denying the necessity of the regression theorem (or something like it) for explaining the value of money Patinkin commits the same error as his critics who denied the necessity of a real-balance effect: he confuses the requirements for constructing a *logically consistent* solution to the value-of-money problem with those for explaining how the solution is arrived at by human agents in the real world. He even cuts the ground from under his real-balance effect, for if the expected value of money is never to be explained as the result of some independent expectations-formation process, but is identified with the solution to a hypothetical "market experiment," then there can be no question of any *erroneous* expectations leading to a *disequilibrium* price-level. It follows that, if the regression-theorem (or alternative explanation of how money comes to have a positive expected value) is superfluous, then so is the real-balance effect.

But let us return to our original argument. Suppose that we are about to perform an individual experiment. It is perfectly logical to imagine a demand schedule for nominal money balances independent of any particular exchange value for money. But this schedule is really only *one of two* possibilities: the other is a "schedule" that coincides with the horizontal and vertical axes of the supply and demand diagram; that is the relevant schedule for the case where the expected value of money is *zero*, i.e., where the individual does not expect the so-called "money" to be regarded as such by the rest of the community. And this expectation is a self-fulfilling prophesy if it is shared by a large number of persons.

Of course it is possible to speculate about the *potential* yield from a new, pure fiat money adopted in place of barter. This yield, if it could be realized, would be sufficient to give the money a positive value divorced from any historical exchange value. But for the yield to be realized people must believe in the money; they must first acknowledge its "moneyness." Absent some implausible (and very non-Mengerian) convention they are not likely to do so for the case of mere pieces of paper.

How, then, can the perception of a good as "money" be encouraged, so that the relevant demand-for-nominal-money schedules lie off of the axes? A necessary (but not sufficient) condition is that the good be expected to have a positive exchange value. The regression theorem is merely one way for showing how that condition might be fulfilled. As Leland Yeager notes, the need for the theorem is most strikingly apparent if we consider the fate of a pure fiat "money," with no historically given exchange value, to which the regression-theorem would *not* be applicable:

> Suppose the old commodity money were declared invalid and each person were given x units of the new money and told nothing more than to start using it. How would anyone know what prices to ask and offer for things? Would not the launching of the new money be facilitated by some indication of its initial value? If the answer is 'yes,' Mises was right.[18]

In light of this it is ironic that Richard Timberlake has chosen the case of a pure, new fiat money to show that the regression theorem "is nothing but an awkward and useless contrivance."[19] He argues that "if fiat paper money were dumped into a primitive barter economy and forced into acceptance by the impress of legal tender, its price would be established in terms of other things because of the monetary function it fulfilled and because its quantity was limited." It is hard, first of all, to see how money can be "forced into acceptance" and have its value determined by market forces at the same time. If it is forced into acceptance, it must be at *some* exchange rate, which must not be a market rate (because otherwise force would be unnecessary). But if there is no force, why should the money have a positive value at all? Is it not more likely to have a value of zero, *despite* its potential usefulness? Can anyone doubt that that would be the case if the experiment were actually tried on some isolated primitive tribe today? Not only would it be the case for a "new" paper money; it would also be the case for paper dollars, so long as their foreign-exchange value remained unknown to the tribesmen.

At best Timberlake's argument shows that the regression theorem is not the *only* auxiliary, expectations-formation hypothesis[20] useful in solving the value-of-money problem. Some kind of public acceptability – as is usually associated with legal-tender laws – for payment of taxes and the like, at pre-set rates, might also promote a good's perception and acceptance as "money."

Given a good's acceptance as money, the good can legitimately be treated as the object of individual experiments in which the demand for it is a function of its liquidity-service yield.

Significantly, in developing his yield theory of the value of money, Greidanus tacitly employs the regression theorem. In explaining how tradesmen determine how much money to hold, he assumes a gold-commodity money, noting that "at the moment when the tradesman started to use gold in his business it had a certain value in exchange, which was due to the fact that it was used for industrial purposes.[21] Later Greidanus explained that, to make his yield theory work he "had, of course, to start from the use of money of a good that already possessed value in exchange for other reasons."[22] Thus the yield theory needs something like a regression theory. That, of course, doesn't mean that a regression theory alone can explain the value of money: by itself, the regression theorem, though it might in some sense evade the "vicious circle," does so by trapping the value of money in a pure commodity-value box.

THE TOBIN EFFECT

Though Patinkin's neoclassical synthesis assigned a crucial role to the liquidity services of money balances, other developments continued to deny their importance. This was true of the bulk of the monetary-growth literature which appeared in the late 1960s, including James Tobin's pioneering study.[23] Tobin's most important and controversial finding – which came to be known as the "Tobin effect" – was that inflation, by discouraging money-holding in favor of "real saving" and capital investment, makes consumers better off.

Tobin's model, and others that followed it, suffered from a number of analytical shortcomings, including the assumption – standard to most Keynesian theory but indefensible nonetheless – that consumption can be treated as a constant fraction of income. Far more important for our present purpose, however, is the fact that these models implicitly deny the utility of money services. Thus, while the models emphasize real gains to be had from increased capital investment, they view the associated fall in holdings of real money balances as entirely costless. In other words, they assume that real-money balances, unlike capital, are not a source of utility, so that a reduction in holdings of real balances does not adversly affect consumers' welfare.

If, on the other hand, the value of money balances reflects the discounted value of their anticipated yield of liquidity services, then any policy that reduces holdings of real balances reduces consumer welfare as well. This implies that inflation, even if it increases capital investment (as it does when the savings ratio is fixed), has an *ambiguous* overall effect on consumer welfare.[24] Analytically this has been demonstrated in two ways, both of which are means for acknowledging the yield on money. One is to directly include real money balances as an argument in the utility function (as Patinkin did to provide grounds for his real-balance effect). The other is to represent money balances as an *indirect* source of utility by letting them play a role in the production function.[25] The standard Tobin-type growth model, amended by either means, leads to the same result: the Tobin effect vanishes, and another argument justifying inflation falls to the ground.

Tobin's original conclusions make for an interesting comparison with the conclusions of the "optimal quantity of money" literature.[26] In that literature, the assumption of a fixed savings ratio is not employed. At the same time, explicit emphasis is given to the yield on money. The conclusion reached is that consumer welfare can be maximized, not through inflation, but through *deflation*, which induces the public to saturate itself with welfare-enhancing, yield-producing real money balances.

OVERLAPPING-GENERATIONS MODELS

In the last two decades a new approach to monetary economics – the "overlapping-generations" method – has begun to dominate formal investigations.[27] Its proponents have already produced a number of startling conclusions. They include (1) the claim that the long-discredited real-bills doctrine is valid after all; (2) the claim that free trade with freely-floating exchange rates is not merely undesirable but "unfeasible"; and (3) the claim that money is a product of "legal restrictions" which would not exist in an unregulated setting.[28]

All of these findings have been criticized;[29] I deal with the last of them in some detail in the next section. At the moment, though, I shall concentrate on criticizing the overlapping-generations method itself by reviewing its origins. I will show how they are rooted in theorists' refusal to acknowledge the yield on money held.

Overlapping-generations theorists are fond of claiming that their models are the "only choice" for investigating monetary phenomena.[30] This claim is based on the alleged failure of conventional monetary models. The conventional approach was to model a representative, discounted-utility maximizing agent facing a finite planning horizon. However, optimizing behavior in these models was not sufficient to give rise to a positive demand for and value of money. This was because of the so-called "hot potato" problem. The problem stemmed from the premise, implicit in standard models, that the value of money in any period was identical to its expected exchange value. Because that expected exchange value would be zero in the last period of the planning horizon (the "end of the world"), it followed that the demand for money and hence its value in the next-to-last period would also be driven to zero, and so on. Thus the realization that money becomes worthless at the "end of the world" is sufficient in these models to make money worthless from the start.

One response to the hot-potato problem was to abandon the standard, finite-horizon model in favor of an infinite-horizon model with no "end of the world" in sight. This response was intuitively unsatisfactory because it made the "representative agent" immortal, which was obviously unrealistic. It also was not much better at explaining monetary phenomena than its predecessor, because it resulted in a multiplicity of "optimal" equilibrium trajectories, including some that still implied a zero demand for money.

So renewed attempts were made to construct monetary models that would motivate a positive demand for money while also allowing representative agents to be mortal. An adaptation of Samuelson's "Exact Consumption-Loan" model[31] – the original overlapping-generations model – was seen as being ideal for this. In overlapping-generations models the demand for money derives from its ability to facilitate transactions between younger and older generations, where old people cannot produce and cannot profitably carry over surplus stocks of goods they produced when they were young.

As means for explaining monetary phenomena the overlapping-generations model is subject to several fundamental criticisms. Most significant is the fact that the demand for money in such models is very tenuous, being based purely on money's ability to serve as a *store of value.* Many other non-perishable assets might also perform this role; and some of them, like interest-earning bonds, seem superior for the purpose. In fact, it turns out that money ceases to have a positive value in overlapping-generations models if any other, interest-earning or productive, non-perishable asset is assumed to exist.[32] Thus, as Patinkin observes, the overlapping-generations model "cannot deal with one of the basic questions of monetary theory: namely, why individuals in the real world hold money when they can instead hold assets that yield a higher rate of return."[33] To really explain the demand for money, Patinkin continues, one must consider its use, not just as "a store of value that can be carried over from one period [generation] to another" but also as a medium of exchange which offers "a 'liquidity service' during any given period." In short, one must acknowledge the yield on money by treating it either as a direct source of utility or as a factor of production.

One could of course modify the overlapping-generations model in light of this criticism. The result would, however, be quite superfluous, for if money is assumed to have a yield, then the "hot potato" problem of standard finite-horizon models — the problem which provided the original rationale for the overlapping-generations approach – disappears. As Patinkin explains, the fact that money is certain to be worthless at the "end of the world" will, given the new assumption, no longer imply a zero demand for it in earlier periods:

> There will in earlier periods be a positive demand (and hence a positive value) for money because of the liquidity services that it then provides – just as there is a positive demand for a machine that is productive for a finite period of time, even though it may depreciate in value to zero by the end of the period.[34]

Patinkin's rejection of the "hot potato" problem is remarkably similar to Greidanus's much earlier rejection of the same problem as posed by Bruno Moll in his *Logic des Geldes*. Like the overlapping-generations theorists, Moll argued that money is wanted for its ultimate redemption [exchange] value only, and "not as a thing that contents us in itself."[35] This, according to Moll, leads to a "problem of the end," because the circulation of money today must depend on its having a positive, expected ultimate-redemption (or gratification) value in the future:

> The certainty of the individual to be able to pass on the money rests in the end on trust ... that even the last owner of the money, who cannot pass it on, has in his possession something of value.[36]

This is, the money must be expected to have some value to its final holder independent of its ability to circulate.

In contrast to Moll, Greidanus held that it was ludicrous to believe that money was accepted in the real world because of some belief in its ultimate redemption or gratification value. "The history of the last five thousand years," Greidanus wrote, "gives me the firm and deliberate conviction that the money that I readily accept today will one day be valueless." Such expectations could not be uncommon; yet men were not prevented by this from assigning a positive value to money. The explanation was that Moll's "problem of the end," like the "hot potato" problem, was a pseudo-problem, based on failure to acknowledge the yield on money held. Whereas Patinkin makes this point by comparing money to a machine, Greidanus made it by comparing money to a house. A house, like a machine, cannot be expected to last forever; it is likely to end up as a pile of rubble. Yet rubble need not have a positive exchange-value for someone to be willing to pay a positive price for a house today:

> It seems improbable to me that people, when buying a house, are satisfied with its function of habitation and do not trouble about the 'problem of the end,' but that they should require from money, besides its function as money, another 'ultimate gratification.'[37]

Though money in use today may some day be worthless, this has an imperceptible effect on its current value, which depends on the marginal-utility of its liquidity-services:

> Whether the shilling that I accept today will be worth a shilling after a thousand years, or nothing, makes in cash value only the difference of a *small* fraction of a farthing.[38]

THE LEGAL-RESTRICTIONS THEORY OF MONEY

One product of the overlapping-generations framework has been a whole new theory of the origin of money called the "legal restrictions" theory.[39] According to this theory, the simultaneous existence of non-interest bearing money (currency) and interest-bearing bonds is paradoxical, because the latter should always dominate the former in individual portfolios. Under laissez-faire, one would expect either that the rate of interest on bonds would go to zero to end the paradox (an unlikely possibility, even according to the legal-restrictions theorists) or that money would disappear. Because money continues to be held alongside bonds in the real world, some legal restriction must be preventing market forces from functioning.

The legal-restrictions theory may be dubbed the "anti-Menger" theory of money, for while Menger argued[40] that money is a product of spontaneous evolution, and *not* a creature of the state, the legal-restrictions theory says just the reverse. Also, whereas Menger viewed the saleability of money as its essential and *unique* attribute, the legal-restrictions theory denies this. Its implicit view is that money is not inherently more "saleable" than other assets. This view does not provoke surprise since, as we have seen, it is also the starting axiom of the overlapping-generations framework. That framework assumes that money is "barren" and "intrinsically useless." Money serves a role in it only if other, durable assets that could serve as a store of value (including bonds) are excluded.

Obviously if money yields no interest and has no other advantage over bonds the demand for it must be nil. As Greidanus observed, "nobody would consent to forego the profit of the coupon on [a] bond if . . . he could enjoy the same advantages as those that he could derive from a stock of money."[41] So why doesn't this happen? The reason is that money *does* have an advantage over bonds, which is its superior marketability or saleability – the source of its non-pecuniary return. Bonds, in contrast, suffer from a critical *disadvantage* – their lack of divisibility – which renders them less marketable than money and explains why they do not entirely displace it.

But the lack of divisibility of bonds turns out to be precisely the "legal restriction" that some overlapping-generations theorists hold responsible for the "paradoxical" existence of money. That bonds are not issued in small denominations that can be used in place of currency must, according to the legal-restrictions theory, be due to some government interference. Here is where the shortcomings of the legal-restrictions theory become apparent. In the first place, given the assumptions of the overlapping-generations framework, money has no liquidity-return. To deny this is to deny the very rationale behind the use of these models. Thus to make extra denominational convenience (artificial or otherwise) a basis for the demand for money is to beg the question of the validity of the overlapping-generations approach. The authors of the legal-restrictions approach are aware of this. They observe that

> It is not entirely satisfactory to modify the environment of an overlapping-generations model by introducing a cost of inter-mediating large-denomination government liabilities. If it is costly for individuals to get together and share a government bond, then getting together for any other purpose, perhaps to exchange other things, cannot be costless.[42]

Yet one of the assumptions of the overlapping-generations approach is that transacting is costless. To abandon this assumption is tantamount to admitting that money is not "intrinsically useless" and that it can be a source of utility from liquidity services .

Putting this fundamental inconsistency aside, is it true that the absence of small-denomination bearer-bonds and hence the existence of money result from state intervention? The answer is that they do not; there have been numerous past examples of non-interest-bearing money circulating in the absence of any relevant legal-restrictions – in Scotland, Canada, China, Sweden, and the United States, to name just a few places.[43] Indeed, there was at least one historical instance when a government attempted consciously to promote the use of small bearer-bonds in place of money. This was during the First World War, when the French government issued its "*bons de la defense nationale*". Though the *bons*, according to the legal-restrictions theory, should have been preferred to non-interest-bearing currency (such as notes of the Bank of France) in every transaction, this did not happen. The *bons* were never regarded as a substitute for money.[44]

Why did this happen? Why weren't interest-bearing assignats preferred to non-interest-bearing ones? The reason is that the same features that make it possible for bonds to pay interest also make them less useful for making payments, that is, less marketable. Even though it might be *legal* for small bonds to be issued and for them to circulate, often this possibility is precluded by the fact that the *costs* of calculating and administering interest payments on frequently-negotiated small bonds outweigh the interest payments involved.[45] Thus for bonds to circulate in place of money they must cease to bear interest, whereas if they continue to bear interest they cannot circulate. So the continued use of non-interest-bearing money is explicable as a purely economic and not a legal, phenomenon.

Does this mean that there is no scope at all for the replacement of money by interest-paying assets? Not at all. One observes such replacement going on today in various ways. Checkable bank-deposits and money-market accounts serve instead of currency for many transactions while also bearing interest. But they are not *perfect substitutes* for currency, which is useful in transactions for which checks are not acceptable (and for which other assets would be too inconvenient). It is also conceivable that changes in technology could make interest-bearing currency possible in the future, especially if currency is competitively provided. This points to a grain of truth in the legal-restrictions argument. For although it is by no means true that "money" as an institution has always been a creature of the state (hence a product of legal restrictions), it is true that most non-interest-bearing money in use *today* is a product of legal restrictions. In the absence of state interference, much of this money, now issued by government banks, would be replaced by private bank-money; and competition among private issuers would perhaps lead to new innovations to eliminate non-interest-bearing money – innovations not realized by free-banking systems of the past.[46]

CONCLUSION

Reviewing the legal-restrictions theory of exchange rates, Gottfried Haberler called it an "extraordinary example of how remorseless logicians can end up in Bedlam, if they get hold of the wrong assumptions."[47] The "wrong assumptions" in this case are that money is "intrinsically worthless" and that it has no yield. As we have seen, these assumptions also lead to Bedlam in other applications. Applied to the value-of-money problem, they lead to the conclusion that the value of money must be indeterminate; applied to monetary-growth theory, they lead to the conclusion that growth is best promoted by inflation; applied to assess the quantity theory, they lead to the conclusion that the real-bills doctrine is more sound; applied to the issue of how money evolves, they lead to the conclusion that money is a creature of the state. All of these conclusions contradict a wealth of historical evidence. Moreover, the assumptions themselves are contrary to experience and common sense. That money plays a crucial role in society by serving as a generally accepted medium of exchange is manifest. Though substitutes for money can replace it to some extent, they cannot do away with the need for it entirely. That is why money continues to be a useful "good," which is valued like other goods for the stream of services it provides.

Contemporary monetary theorists who deny these truths must do so on questionable methodological grounds. Some argue that, since the role of money as a medium of exchange (and hence as a provider of liquidity services) is difficult to represent in formal models, that role cannot be a link in any "rigorous" theorizing about monetary phenomena. Perhaps this is so, but then it requires, not that we reject the view of money as a medium of exchange, which puts rigor ahead of accuracy in our view of "science," but that we do without rigor until we can have it without doing violence to the facts.

NOTES

1. William H. Hutt (1956), "The Yield from Money Held," in Mary Sennholz (ed.), *On Freedom and Free Enterprise: Essays in Honor of Ludwig von Mises*, Princeton: Van Nostrand, pp. 196–223.
2. Hicks, J.R. (1935), "A Suggestion for Simplifying the Theory of Money," *Economica*, n.s. **2**, 1–19.
3. Richard H. Timberlake, Jr. (1987), "A Critique of Monetarist and Austrian Doctrines on the Utility and Value of Money," *Review of Austrian Economics*, **1**, 86.
4. London: P.S. King & Son, 1932; expanded second edition, London: Staples Press, 1950.
5. Hutt, "The Yield from Money Held," p. 196.
6. The expression comes from Leland Yeager's paper, (1973), "The Keynesian Diversion," *Western Economic Review*, **11**(2), 150–63.
7. The results of Patinkin's work, first published in a series of articles in the 1950s, are gathered together in *Money, Interest, and Prices*, 2nd edn, New York: Harper & Row, 1965.
8. See *ibid*., p. 574.
9. *Ibid*., pp. 574–5.
10. *Ibid*., p. 575.
11. G.C. Archibald and R.G. Lipsey (1958), "Monetary and Value Theory: A Critique of Lange and Patinkin," *Review of Economic Studies*, **28**, 1–22; Karl Brunner (1951), "Inconsistency and Indeterminacy in Classical Economics," *Economica*, **14**, 152–73; and S. Valavanis (1955), "A Denial of Patinkin's Contradiction," *Kyklos*, **7**, 351–66.
12. Harry G. Johnson (1978), 'Monetary Theory and Policy," in *Selected Essays in Monetary Economics*, London: George Allen & Unwin, p. 21.
13. Greidanus, *Value of Money*, ch. 7.
14. *Ibid*., pp. 58–61.
15. Ludwig von Mises (1980), *The Theory of Money and Credit*, trans. H.E. Batson, Indianapolis: Liberty Classics, pp. 129–36.
16. Patinkin, *Money, Interest, and Prices*, pp. 115–16.
17. Mises, *Theory of Money and Credit*, p. 137.
18. Leland B. Yeager (1982), "On Individual and Overall Viewpoints in Monetary Theory," in Israel M. Kirzner (ed.), *Method, Process, and Austrian Economics*, Lexington, MA: Lexington Books, p. 235.
19. Timberlake, "Critique," p. 84.
20. The regression theorem was first interpreted as a "bold empirical hypothesis" about how agents' value-of-money expectations are formed by Laurence Moss. See "The Monetary Economics of Ludwig von Mises" in *idem* (ed.), *The Economics of Ludwig von Mises*, Kansas City: Sheed & Ward, 1976, pp. 13–49. See also the "Critical Discussion" by Karen I. Vaughn in the same volume, esp. p. 103.

    Israel M. Kirzner has also defended the regression theorem from its critics in "A Note on the Circularity Bogey in the History of the Marginal Utility Theory of Money," (unpublished ms., n.d.).
21. Greidanus, *Value of Money*, p. 255.

22. *Ibid.*, p. 316.
23. James Tobin (1965), "Money and Economic Growth," *Econometrica*, **33**, 671–84. See also *idem* (1955), "A Dynamic Aggregative Model," *Journal of Political Economy*, **63**, 103–15.
24. On this see Harry G. Johnson, "Inside Money, Outside Money, Income, Wealth and Welfare in Monetary Theory," in *Selected Essays*, pp. 252–3; also *idem*, "Recent Developments in Monetary Theory," in *ibid.*, pp. 204–205, and "Money in a Neo-Classical One-Sector Growth Model," in *ibid.*, pp. 143–78.
25. Both approaches are taken in David Levhari and Don Patinkin (1968), "The Role of Money in a Simple Growth Model," *American Economic Review*, **58**, 713–53. See also the essays by Johnson cited in the previous note.
26. See Milton Friedman (1969), "The Optimum Quantity of Money," in *idem*, (ed.), *The Optimum Quantity of Money and Other Essays*, Chicago: Aldine, Ch. 1.
27. See John H. Kareken and Neil Wallace (eds) (1980), *Models of Monetary Economics*, Minneapolis: Federal Reserve Bank of Minneapolis.
28. See Thomas Sargent and Neil Wallace (1982), "The Real-Bills Doctrine versus the Quantity Theory: A Reconsideration," *Journal of Political Economy*, **60** (6), 1212–36; John Kareken and Neil Wallace (1981), "On the Indeterminacy of Equilibrium Exchange Rates," *Quarterly Journal of Economics*, **96**(2), 207–22 and *idem* (1978), "International Monetary Reform: The Feasible Alternatives," Federal Reserve Bank of Minneapolis *Quarterly Review*, **2**, 2–7; and Neil Wallace (1983), "A Legal Restrictions Theory of the Demand for 'Money' and the Role of Monetary Policy," Federal Reserve Bank of Minneapolis *Quarterly Review*, **4**, 1–7.
29. On the real-bills doctrine see David Laidler (1984), "Misconceptions about the Real-Bills Doctrine: A Comment on Sargent and Wallace," *Journal of Political Economy*, **92**(1), 149–55; on exchange-rates see Gottfried Haberler (1981), "Flexible Exchange-Rate Theories and Controversies Once Again," American Enterprise Institute *Reprint* no. 119; on the "legal restrictions" theory see Gerald P. O'Driscoll, Jr. (1986), "Money, Deregulation, and the Business Cycle," *Cato Journal*, **6**(2), 588–91 and 597–603; Lawrence H. White (1987), "Accounting for Non-interest Bearing Currency: A Critique of the Legal Restrictions Theory," *Journal of Money, Credit, and Banking*, **19**(4), November, and Gail E. Makinen and G. Thomas Woodward (1986), "Some Anecdotal Evidence Relating to the Legal Restrictions Theory of the Demand for Money," *Journal of Political Economy*, **94** (2), 260–65.

    A good, overall critique of the overlapping-generations approach is Bennett T. McCallum (1983), "The Role of Overlapping-Generations Models in Monetary Economics," *Carnegie-Rochester Conference Series on Public Policy*, **18**, 9–44.
30. See David Cass and Karl Shell, "In Defense of a Basic Approach," in *Models*, p. 260; also M. Kareken and N. Wallace (eds), "On the Indeterminacy," p. 208.
31. Paul A. Samuelson (1958), "An Exact Consumption-Loan Model of Interest with or without the Social Contrivance of Money," *Journal of Political Economy*, **66**, 467–82.
32. This implication leads directly to the view that money is a result of "legal restrictions," which is criticized below.
33. Don Patinkin (1983), "Monetary Economics," in E. Cary Brown and Robert M. Solow (eds), *Paul Samuelson and Modern Economic Theory*, New York: McGraw-Hill, p. 161.
34. *Ibid.*
35. As cited in Greidanus, *Value of Money*, p. 85.
36. *Ibid.*, p. 88.
37. *Ibid.*
38. *Ibid.*
39. See Wallace, "Legal Restrictions Theory."
40. See Carl Menger (1892), "On the Origin of Money," *Economic Journal*, **2**, 239–55.
41. Greidanus, *Value of Money*, p. 313.
42. Kareken and Wallace, "Introduction," in their *Models of Monetary Economics*, pp. 8–9.
43. On Scottish note issues see Lawrence H. White (1984), *Free Banking in Britain*, Cambridge: Cambridge University Press; on Chinese note issues see G.A. Selgin (1987), "Free

Banking in China, 1800–1935," (unpublished ms.); on Swedish note issues see Lars Jonung (1985), "The Economics of Private Money: The Experience of Private Notes in Sweden, 1831–1902," paper prepared for the Monetary History Group Meeting, London. References to competitive note-issue in Canada and the US are numerous.

44. See Makinen and Woodward, "Anecdotal Evidence."
45. For a simple demonstration of the prohibitive costs of paying interest on circulating transactions-media see White, "Accounting for Non-Interest Bearing Currency.'
46. One possible innovation, suggested by Hugh McCulloch, would be for banks to pay "interest" on competitively-issued notes by holding weekly note serial-number lotteries and paying the interest to the lucky holder of the winning note as a prize.
47. Haberler, "Flexible Exchange-Rate Theories," p. 44.

15. Prices, the price level and macroeconomic coordination: Hutt on Keynesian economics

Steven Horwitz

The science of economics and the cause of liberty have lost an exemplar of scholarship, integrity and courage with the passing of William H. Hutt. At a time when macroeconomics was Keynesianism, Hutt stood his ground and defended his understanding of the classical world-view with a force and sophistication perhaps unmatched since. While Richard Ebeling has provided an overview of Hutt's contributions and a recent article by Morgan O. Reynolds (1988) provides an excellent and complete bibliography, my focus here will be to examine a particular contribution of Hutt's in more detail – namely, his critique of the orthodox Keynesian explanation of unemployment. Hutt's powerful challenge has been lost in the history of economic thought and the time has come to retrieve it.[1] With 50 years of Hutt's own subsequent elaborations, we can now recast Hutt's original argument in light of certain advances in economics which underscore the importance of subjectivism and knowledge for economic coordination in the market process. Hutt's critique of Keynesianism provides the basis for understanding the microfoundations of the macroeconomic market process.

The key to Hutt's argument lies in the old aphorism that the forest can sometimes hide the trees. Many critics have complained that one major problem with Keynesian macroeconomics is its overaggregation. Action occurs at the individual level, so economic analysis must take account of individual actions. However, that in itself is not enough. What is it, exactly, that is going on at the individual level that is obscured when we are preoccupied with aggregates? One answer, perhaps the most important one, is the role that relative prices play in coordinating action. What entrepreneurs and consumers use to guide their actions are prices, and it is prices that ultimately matter for economic coordination. The difficulty with aggregates is that they gloss over the information that actors in the market place need to guide their actions and promote economic coordination. Keynesianism's overemphasis on aggregates allows it to ignore questions about correctness of individual relative prices, which are precisely the questions, according to Hutt, that classical economics was concerned with.

THE KEYNESIAN PROBLEM

In Hutt's eyes, the nature of the Keynesian thesis can be summarized rather briefly. Unemployment and depression are caused when the real wage (w/p) is stuck at a level higher than can clear the labor market. At this "too high" real wage, more labor is being offered to employers than they can afford to hire. The result is that many who want to work cannot – unemployment. If we could somehow bring (w/p) to the level consistent will full employment, we could solve the problem. For Keynes, the level of real wages is what ultimately determines the level of employment, which in turn determines total national income/output.

A crucial plank in the Keynesian argument is the denial of Say's Law of Markets. For over a hundred years economists had broadly accepted the notion that a general glut of goods could not occur, because (as it is put colloquially) "supply creates its own demand." Any good supplied to the market would generate revenues sufficient to purchase existing goods, making an excess supply of goods impossible. Excess supplies of one good had to imply excess demands for other(s). The Keynesian concept of "unemployment equilibrium," however, has to rest on the possibility of a general glut.

There are two ways that Keynesians could explain the supposed failure of Say's Law. The one that will concern us here is, again, a nominal wage stuck too high.[2] Suppose all is proceeding along normally and Say's Law is holding. Now suppose entrepreneurs are stuck by a wave of pessimistic expectations. Prices fall and production slacks, but the nominal wage remains high, leading to lay-offs. Previously produced goods sit unbought as consumers (due to unemployment) have insufficient current income to purchase previously produced goods. A general glut occurs and the sticky nominal wage (too high real wage) causes Say's Law to be invalidated.

Posing the problem this way (which I do not believe is a drastic misrepresentation of Keynes), suggests two possible solutions. As is true of any fraction, there are two ways to reduce the real wage: we can lower the numerator or raise the denominator. If the level of real wages is too high, either lower nominal wages or increase the price level. In Hutt's view, Keynes's mistake was to take the latter way out. Instead of allowing wages to adjust, Keynes's choice was to inflate his way back to full employment by pushing up the price level, until real wages fell sufficiently.

Reasons for preferring this strategy are fairly straightforward. The main justification rests on psychology. Workers will resist cuts in their nominal wage rate, but will not notice cuts in real wages if they are done through inflation. Workers get fooled by changes in the price level. They don't notice the fall in real wages until it is too late and the inflation has done its job.[3] For Keynes this was much less messy than the potential labor unrest that would follow if employers tried to cut wage rates across the board. As Hutt argued (1977 [1939], p. 209; emphasis in original), Keynes thought that the solution could "be obtained only through 'real' rates of earnings of labor being reduced in a *tactful* way… by inflating prices through monetary policy." In an era of strong unions and the breezes of socialism, anything that could be done to lessen labor unrest may have seemed politically preferable.[4]

Inflating one's way out certainly solves the problem at the aggregate level. The level of real wages is back to where it should be, and the lower real wage brings workers that were previously unemployed back into the market. But health at the aggregate level can mask disease underneath, and this is precisely what Hutt sees as the problem with the Keynesian solution. While inflation can coordinate the levels of wages and employment, it decreases coordination among the millions of relative prices that make up those levels. And it is these individual prices that ultimately matter for the strength of the economy and for the ability of individuals to coordinate their actions. Inflation gives us "crude coordination" (Hutt, 1979, p. 158 *et seq.*), rather than the more refined coordination that flexibility in nominal wages would achieve. Hutt's argument is that raising the denominator solves the aggregate problem, at the cost of a worse problem with relative prices, and it therefore should be rejected. In addition, the Keynesian solution implicitly acknowledges the validity of Say's Law and a proper understanding of it can subvert the Keynesian argument before it gets started.

RELATIVE PRICES AND ECONOMIC COORDINATION

Underlying the Huttian response is the important recognition that it is relative prices that guide actors in their allocative decisions in the market. What prices do is allow actors to coordinate their actions. Prices adjust to reflect changes in consumer tastes and preferences, in entrepreneurial preferences, and in the availability of resources. Higher prices indicate increased scarcity relative to consumer wants, while lower prices reflect decreased relative scarcity.[5] Beyond just coordination, prices reflect and convey knowledge. Human tastes, preferences, and skills are often such that they cannot be communicated. (Try to describe exactly what you do when you ride a bicycle.) The whole process of competition allows this knowledge to be passed in the market through acts of buying and selling. Actions in the market communicate this knowledge in a way that language often cannot.

Of course the process of competition is about individual prices. Buying and selling bicycles affects their prices. So ultimately it is these individual prices that convey knowledge and facilitate coordination. If we want to ask whether a particular resource is better allocated than another, the answer will rely heavily on information about this price. Individual actors care whether the prices they pay or charge are profitable, not whether the price of "consumer goods" as a whole is right. McDonald's cares mostly about the price of Big Macs not about the price of "food" in the abstract. The price of food is not relevant to the plans of either McDonald's interests or to consumers. By overemphasizing aggregate prices, Keynesians ignore the fundamental issues concerning the coordination that takes place below.

What economies "do" is coordinate actions through prices. With this view, it is easy to see why macroeconomic problems are really microeconomic problems. What causes unemployment is faulty relative prices in numerous labor markets, not simply inaccurate wage levels as a whole. To quote Hutt (1979, p. 111).

> It was partly through the clumsiness of the macroeconomic approach that Keynes came to believe that the idleness of [labor] is caused by factors other than the mispricing of the flow of services and products. For instance, the clumsy concept of the price of labour… [W]hen Keynes did think in terms of this "price" having a crucial task, he seemed to assume that the adjustment required to induce full employment is an equal percentage reduction in all wage rates and secondly to assume that rises and falls in the general level of wage rates correspond to rises or falls in the general flow of wage receipts. [This] assumption is [not] acceptable.

It is the individual wage rates (and other prices) that matter for economic coordination, not the accuracy of a wage level.

Given this, Hutt, argues that the way to relieve the unemployment problems that concern Keynesians is to allow nominal wage rates to adjust to coordinate labor markets. As was his call for his entire career, Hutt pointed to institutional impediments as the main source of trouble. Minimum wage laws, for one, prevent wages in many service markets from properly coordinating labor supply and demand. Unions, backed by governmental protection of strikers, can also prevent wages from adjusting appropriately. Certainly psychological and other factors make prices less than perfectly flexible, and Hutt recognizes this,[6] but he insists that there is no reason to make matters worse with additional institutional impediments.

Once such restraints are removed, wages will be free to adjust to change from both the consumer and producer sides of the market. With improved (though not perfect) flexibility, wasteful unemployment should decrease and many of the Keynesian worries can be overcome. Unemployment is a pricing problem, not a "macroeconomic" one.[7] When relative prices in the labor market are more accurate, unemployment is reduced. "When the coordinative role of price adjustment is understood…all the principle Keynesian theses seem to dissolve" (Hutt, 1979, p. 85).

Hutt's line of reasoning also provides a vindication of Say's Law. Rather than the oversimplified "supply creates its own demand," Hutt (1979, p. 160) prefers to view Say's Law as "the principle that the demand for any commodity is a function of the supply of non-competing commodities."[8] The Keynesian story of recession can occur only under particular institutional arrangements, i.e., when nominal wages are made artificially sticky. Say's Law is still valid; in fact it explains why the high real wage causes problems. An artificially sticky wage closes some number of laborers out of the market, and they are then unable to exercise demands for non-competing commodities. When the wage is flexible, and a coordinating real wage is obtained, the additional labor actually supplied can then be turned into money, which will then constitute demands for non-competing commodities and the "glut" can be purchased. Say's Law is always operating, but its efficacy depends upon the institutional environment in which it acts.[9]

Not only is Say's Law valid, but Hutt argues that the Keynesian solution of inflating down real wages presupposes its validity. The typical Keynesian multiplier story shows this. As the price level rises, real wages fall and unemployment picks up. The newly employed workers spend their additional income on goods and services, driving up demand for those products and the demand for labor in those industries. More people get hired and more goods get bought and the glut is solved. Using inflation to solve the problem implies a Say's Law-like process. To quote Hutt (1979, p. 228): "[This] dynamic factor toward which Keynes seems to have been groping – what I shall call 'the true multiplier'…is actually nothing more than Say's Law." Whether through institutional reform or through inflation (it appears), the inexorability of Say's Law will make itself felt. Hutt effectively rescued it from the dustbin of intellectual history.

Yet the question remains: why not inflate? Why bother with the admittedly politically difficult institutional changes needed to do things Hutt's way, when inflation can solve the problem more easily? The answer lies in a deeper understanding of the inflation process and the ways in which inflation can further distort relative prices, even as it crudely coordinates the real wage.

INFLATION AND RELATIVE PRICES

The problem with inflation as a solution is that the process by which excess supplies of money enter the market process itself affects relative prices. The standard view on inflation simply argues that an increase in the money supply will cause an increase in the price level and leaves the discussion at that. The Keynesian solution is relying on this kind of thinking. If an increase in the price level will reduce the real wage enough to increase employment to the desired amount, we only need increase the money supply by some amount and all will be solved. What this ignores is the process by which increases in the money supply become increases in the price level and the fact that this process must take place through changes in relative prices. Money enters the market process in particular places at particular times and therefore alters the structure of relative prices depending on which industries feel the influx of new money the most. To assume that the various relative wage rates will remain constant during the inflation process is to assume away the entire problem.

The importance of the ragged process by which new credit enters the economy is that it alters the flow of resources throughout the capital structure. The specific goods and services whose prices increase relatively more will find that more resources are being devoted to their production due to the increased opportunity for profits that the rise in price indicates. This will ripple through the capital structure as entrepreneurs adjust production processes to meet the increased demand for the now more desired products. Given that capital goods are scarce, this implies a reduction in resources applied to alternative final goods, which in turn changes the price and profit structure in those industries.[10] The inflation process itself affects the allocation of resources, both at the level of final consumer goods and ultimately at the level of the capital goods that produce them.

The inflation process also affects the dynamics of Say's Law. For Say's Law to operate at its best, particular institutional arrangements need to hold. One of these is that the money supply is "correct." The importance of money lies in the fact that it is the means by which the supply of one commodity becomes the demand for non-competing ones. We cannot directly purchase goods with our potential labor power, we need to turn labor power into money into goods.[11] Ultimately the ability to purchase goods derives from productive abilities (supply), not money. Money is only the form in which demand is expressed. Changes in the supply of money can only "determine the number of containers [in which] purchasing power [resides]" (Hutt, 1977 [1939], p. 259). Inflationary increases in the money supply can only redistribute existing purchasing power, they cannot create it.

Ideally, money allows the Say's Law process to operate smoothly. Money (as claims to resources) is possessed by those who earned such claims by supplying desired goods to the market. If this condition is met, then the unfolding of a macroeconomic market process in a money economy will allow for economic coordination. When inflation occurs, not all demands derive from previous supplies; now recipients of the excess dollars obtain purchasing power (money) at the expense of existing holders.[12] Simply being at the right point in the money supply process brings claims to resources to some people, which in turn allows them to affect the direction of future resource allocation. This disrupts economic coordination as goods no longer accrue to those who have produced desired goods, but to those who benefit from the politicized process of money creation.[13] Inflation also disrupts the effective operation of Say's Law, the coordination achieved through the Huttian solution is preferred to that of the Keynesians.

The inflation process puts political preferences into the knowledge generating and conveying prices of the market, which reduces their ability to accurately coordinate the actions of economic actors and reflect economic scarcities. Entrepreneurs now are faced with deciding whether price changes reflect true shifts in relative scarcities or the effects of inflation. This additional, and unnecessary, complexity can only lessen the ability of entrepreneurs to take coordination-promoting actions. For Hutt, the best that inflation can do is the crude coordination of the level of real wages and employment, at the cost of the coordination that really matters – that between individual consumers and producers.

"MY ENEMY'S ENEMY IS NOT MY FRIEND"

One interesting aspect of Hutt's critique of Keynesianism is that it applies with equal force to the successors to Keynesian orthodoxy, the New Classical response to Keynesianism. Agents, if they are rational, will have rational expectations and will use all relevant information available in deciding what to do. One such piece of information is the rate of inflation. Thus, unless workers are assumed to be rational, they will learn the rate of inflation, will realize that their real wages are being lowered, and will bargain for a higher nominal wage, negating the intended effect of the Keynesian inflation. Inside the neoclassical paradigm of rational utility-maximizing agents, this is a devastating critique. But with fallible human actors and real-world financial institutions, it is no better than Keynesianism.

The problem is once again over-aggregation. The New Classical story relies on several questionable assumptions,[14] one of which is that new issues of money are received by agents in patterns identical to the existing distribution. In other words, it is as if we simply tacked on an extra zero to everyone's currency holdings and bank balances. By assumption, the New Classical view of inflation ignores the possibility of the relative price changes stressed by Hutt.[15] In doing so it oversimplifies the nature of the coordination that has to take place in a complex economy.

The problem that confronts actors in a real-world inflation process is how to know the precise effects that the path of the inflation will have on them.

While a worker may know that the rate of inflation as a whole is 5 percent, that does not tell her what its relative effect on her particular industry would / will be. If she is in an industry that attracts much of the new money, the "proper" adjustment for her nominal wage may be higher than the average level of inflation. It is these adjustments that have to occur, in Hutt's view, for economic coordination to take place.

The difficulty is that the economy is so complex that no one mind or group of minds can follow the precise path that every excess dollar follows. The millions by millions matrix that is the price system is beyond detailed human comprehension. Even the most extreme assumption of rationality pales in comparison to the knowledge needed to completely trace an inflation process.[16] Having rational expectations about the aggregate level of inflation is not enough, since what matters for economic coordination is individual relative prices. And no economic agent is able to precisely trace the effect that inflation has on each and every one. Economics is not about the correctness of aggregates, but rather the accuracy of the myriad of individual price signals that guide human action. By looking at aggregates, modern macroeconomics, both Keynesian and New Classical, overlooks the Huttian concept of economic coordination as the fundamental problem and thus misses the Huttian solution.

Hutt's emphasis on the fundamental role of price coordination and its relation to macroeconomics provides a foundation on which to rehabilitate much of pre-Keynesian economics. Along with developments since, many of them due to Hutt, we also have the beginnings of a sound macroeconomics of the market process. Wherever good macroeconomic thinking ends up, it will owe a huge debt, both theoretically and personally, to the ideas and role model of W.H. Hutt.

NOTES

Thanks to Don Lavoie for his comments on an earlier draft. Thanks also to W. H. Hutt for his ideas, his integrity, and his inspiration.

1. The exception to this banishment is David Colander's (1986) macroeconomics textbook which gives Hutt a fair amount of attention.
2. The other possibility is that an excess supply of goods is due to an excess demand for money. This deflationary (or monetary disequilibrium or effective demand failure) story is the Keynes seen by Yeager (1973) and Leijonhufvud (1981), though not really by Hutt. While this is not the place to debate both interpretations of Keynes and the merits of the effective demand failure stories, the relevant questions seem to concern the banking system. Why is there an excess demand for money? Why are the banks unable to supply a sufficient amount of money? This interpretation of Keynes has to move to a discussion of monetary theory and institutions.
3. It is, of course, this exact point where the Monetarist and New Classical counter-

revolution has responded to Keynes. To the New Classical economist, it makes no sense for rational, utility-maximizing agents to be "fooled" by something that it is within their ability to gain information about. In a world where people have rational expectations, the rate of inflation would be known, and agents would plan accordingly and not be fooled. This neutralizes the effect of Keynes's strategy.

4. See Hutt's (1971) book, *Politically Impossible...?* for an elaboration of this point.
5. The classic here is Hayek (1945). Though also see Lavoie (1986) and Hutt's own discussion in (1979, ch. 7).
6, "[The Classical] view did not (as Keynes alleged) rest on an 'assumed fluidity of money wages'. It could be said to have rested in part on a belief that if such 'fluidity' of wage rates were achieved, the system would work better and wasteful layoffs of workers would occur less frequently." (Hutt, 1979, p. 77).
7. That macroeconomic problems should fall back to an incorrect price is nothing new to non-Keynesians. The Mises–Hayek theory of the trade cycle is ultimately an explanation based on a wrong price, in this case the interest rate. Because of its connection with money and monetary institutions, incorrectness of the interest rate has widespread repercussions and triggers the trade cycle.
8. For an elaboration of this version, see Hutt's (1975) book on Say's Law.
9. Such institutions include monetary ones as discussed below.
10. Hayek (1941, p. 374) argues that the "given" of scarce capital goods is precisely what Keynes denies: "[Keynes] has given us a system of economics which is based on the assumption that no real scarcity exits, and that the only scarcity with which we need concern ourselves is the artificial scarcity created by the determination of people not to sell their services and products below certain arbitrarily fixed prices." Though Hayek's focus is different, his critique of Keynes seems complementary to Hutt's.
11. See Robert Clower's (1983 [1969], p. 100) famous constraint "Goods buy money and money buys goods – but goods do not buy goods in any organized market."
12. This is the process of forced savings. Non-recipients of new money have their purchasing power diluted by the additional purchasing power acquired with the influx of new money. This represents a forced abstinence on the part of non-recipients, which is transferred to new recipients. See the discussion in Selgin (1988, pp. 60–3).
13. See the discussion in Wagner (1977).
14 For an excellent summary of the issues, and a critique of rational expectations that is complementary to the argument below, see Rector (1990).
15. For a more sympathetic view of non-Keynesian inflation stories and their relationship to relative prices, see Humphrey (1986).
16. There is an Old Testament story that illustrates this point in another context. A rabbi decided to teach a town gossip a lesson about the unintended effects of gossip. He told him to rip up a feather pillow and scatter the contents in the wind and then come back in two weeks. When the man returned, the rabbi told him to try to collect all of the feathers and bring them back.

    The unintended consequences of inflation are even more complex since they are not even directly observable in the way that feathers are.

REFERENCES

Clower, Robert T. (1983 [1969]), "Introduction to Monetary Theory: Selected Readings," in Donald A. Walker (ed.), *Money and Markets*, Cambridge: Cambridge University Press.

Colander, David (1986), *Macroeconomics*, Glenview, IL: Scott Foresman and Co.

Hayek, F.A. (1945), "The Use of Knowledge in Society," *American Economic Review*, **35**(4), September.

Humphrey, Thomas M. (1986), "On Nonneutral Relative Price Effects in Monetarist Thought: Some Austrian Misconceptions," *Federal Reserve Bank of Richmond Economic Review*, May/June 1984. Reprinted in Humphrey, *Essays on Inflation*, 5th edn, Richmond, VA: Federal Reserve Bank of Richmond, 1986.
Hutt, W.H. (1971), *Politically Impossible*...? London Institute for Economic Affairs.
—— (1975), *A Rehabilitation of Say's Law*, Athens, OH: Ohio University Press.
—— (1977 [1939]), *The Theory of Idle Resources*. Indianapolis, Ind.: Liberty Press.
—— (1979), *The Keynesian Episode: A Reassessment*, Indianapolis, Ind.: Liberty Press.
Lavoie, Don (1986), "The Market as a Procedure for the Discovery and Conveyance of Inarticulate Knowledge," *Comparative Economic Studies*, **10**(1), Spring.
Leijonhufvud, Axel (1981), "Effective Demand Failures," in *Information and Coordination*, Oxford: Oxford University Press.
Rector, Ralph (1990), "The Economics of Rationality and the Rationality of Economics," in Don Lavoie, (ed.), *Economics and Hermeneutics*, New York: Routledge.
Reynolds, Morgan (1988), "Selected Contributions of Professor W. H. Hutt," *Austrian Economics Newsletter*, Spring/Summer.
Selgin, George (1988), *The Theory of Free Banking*, Totowa, NJ: Rowman & Littlefield.
Wagner, Richard (1977), "Economic Manipulation for Political Profit: Macroeconomic Consequences and Constitutional Implications," *Kyklos*, **30**.
Yeager, Leland (1973), "The Keynesian Diversion," *Western Economic Journal* (11), June.

16. Misreading the "Myth": Rothbard on the theory and history of free banking

Steven Horwitz

INTRODUCTION

In recent years, discussion among Austrian monetary theorists concerning the monetary system most desirable under laissez faire seems to be limited to agreeing on what we don't want. The essays collected in Siegel (1984) and Rockwell (1985) show great diversity of opinion, even though almost all of the authors concur that government central banking is the problem to be overcome. The focus of the debate among Austrians has been over the question of 100 percent reserve, gold standard banking versus a fractional reserve commodity standard with competition in note issue. One major contribution to the fractional reserve side of this debate was Lawrence H. White's *Free Banking in Britain* (1984), which argued that Scottish banking from 1721 to 1845 was a successful example of an actual free banking system. This triggered suspicion from 100 percent reserve theorists, who have argued that any form of fractional reserve banking is both fraudulent and inflationary.[1] Their position is exemplified by Murray Rothbard's recent (1988) analysis of White's book in the *Review of Austrian Economics*, "The Myth of Free Banking in Scotland," which repeats both of these contentions, in addition to questioning White's reading of the historical record.

My purpose in this essay is to try to clear up some of the issues raised in Rothbard's critique of White. Three points need to be dealt with. First, Rothbard and other opponents of free banking have committed a logical error in the way in which they argue from the history of Scottish banking to the theory of free banking. Second, Rothbard sees free bankers as inflationists because he fails to understand the monetary theory behind their view. Rothbard and White have different definitions of what inflation is. A short excursion into the realm of monetary theory can resolve these problems. Finally, Rothbard believes that fractional reserve bank notes are fraudulent. Even if they were beneficial, he would contend that a properly functioning legal code would not recognize such notes as legitimate. However, this argument is inconsistent with another of Rothbard's own positions. Rothbard's review, though it fails to refute the free banking argument, is a good launching point for the clarification of these issues.

THE LEAP FROM HISTORY TO THEORY

Implicit in Rothbard's attempt to refute the validity of Scotland as a historical example of successful free banking is the following syllogism:

- Scotland's success or failure determines whether the system outlined in the theory of free banking is a workable goal.
- Scotland was, in fact, not much of a free banking system.
- Therefore, free banking theory is invalidated.

The premise is incorrect. Why should *one* historical case study invalidate a theoretical development that does not rest on any particular historical manifestation? Free banking theory did not develop out of any particular historical studies, though such studies have extended and illuminated it. It is the development of a long line of argument by many distinguished monetary theorists. In the text of his first chapter, entitled "A Theory of Free Banking" (which, incidentally, is not mentioned in Rothbard's review), White (1984, pp. 1–22) does not cite any historical evidence, reserving it for three tangential footnotes on the last two pages. George Selgin (1988) also provides an analysis of free banking that is clearly independent of any particular historical manifestation.

This is not to say that historical evidence has no relevance. On the contrary, individual case studies are crucial to expanding our understanding of how free banking systems can go right and wrong.[2] They can even direct our research in directions not previously considered. But no particular case can bring down the whole theory. Unless we can find a perfect example of such a system fulfilling every assumption contained in the theory (which is extremely unlikely) and demonstrate that it failed for reasons that the theory has not considered, we still have grounds for holding the theory to be valid.

It is ironic, considering the current debate about the relationship between theory and history in Austrian economics, that Rothbard would attempt to make a historically based argument. (See Boettke *et al.*, 1986.) Elsewhere (Rothbard 1985, p. 6) he has vigorously defended the strict separation of history and theory, arguing that modern Austrians who do not accept this dichotomy are historicists or institutionalists, incapable of generating valid theory. He has also argued that Austrian theory is immune from historical or empirical tests (p. 5). Theory can be used to interpret history, but history can never generate or vitiate theory. For Rothbard, the validity of praxeological theory is a matter of correct axioms and logical deduction; historical cases may only be better or worse *exemplifications* of theory. What then of his argument against White? By Rothbard's own admission, he cannot use his supposed refutation of White's historical case as a weapon against White's theoretical framework. Free banking theory is as much a praxeological theory as any other part of Austrian economics. It is not historicist. By his own rules, Rothbard can only offer an *a priori*, deductive, theoretical refutation of free banking theory. If anything, Rothbard is the historicist since here, at least, he has given us only history.

This is not to say that only theory matters. Both theoretical and historical evidence need to be brought to bear though no single example of either can be conclusive. The theory of free banking is a powerful tool for interpreting historical cases such as Scotland, and this type of work needs to be continued. In addition, nobody has ever argued that the Scottish system was perfectly free. The fact that it wasn't perfect is exactly why it cannot be used to refute or falsify free banking theory. There was government interference with the system, for example, the prohibitions on small-denomination notes and "option clauses." White (1984, pp. 29–30, 39, 54) recognizes this. The restrictions, though relatively minor, limit the relevance of the Scottish system as an example of free banking. The first part of Rothbard's article documents other examples of interference. If Rothbard is correct about them, we should look more skeptically at Scotland as an example. But noting the existence of government interference cannot by itself defeat the theoretical argument. The Scottish banks were neither perfectly free nor a conclusive test case. The theory of free banking still stands, and its opponents need to tackle it on *both* the historical and the theoretical level to refute it.

THE "NEEDS OF TRADE," MONETARY EQUILIBRIUM, AND INFLATION

To the extent that Rothbard offers a theoretical argument, he claims that both White and the British monetary theorists White defends are inflationists. Though Rothbard does not offer a definition of inflation himself, he argues that White's problems center around his endorsement of the so-called "needs of trade" doctrine (Rothbard, 1988, p. 239). However, White's acceptance of the doctrine is not inflationary given White's interpretation of the "needs of trade," which is driven by a theoretical framework that Rothbard never elucidates. Part of being a good critic is to make every attempt to see things as others do. Rothbard fails to do so, and winds up criticizing what he evidently does not understand.

Rothbard's interpretation of the "needs of trade" doctrine is that "bank notes simply expand and contract according to the 'wants of trade' and that, therefore, issue of such notes, being matched by the production of goods, could not raise prices" (Rothbard, 1988, p. 238). Rothbard interprets the doctrine to mean that the supply of notes should correspond to changes in the production of goods. This resembles the so-called "real bills doctrine," which holds that the supply of notes should correspond to the amount of real commercial bills presented at banks. Both views link money with the amount of trade being undertaken. Under *this* interpretation both views are inflationary, as is recognized by a long line of monetary theorists, including White himself (1984, p. 122) and Selgin (1987a).

Taking the "needs of trade" to mean the amount of real bills of exchange (i.e., bills representing actually produced goods) presented to the banks leads to inflationary banking for two reasons. First, linking the volume of money to the nominal (dollar amount) quantity of bills of exchange leaves the price level undetermined, because the nominal amount of *bills* depends on the volume of money and the prevailing price level. Any price level is consistent with the real bills doctrine. As banks issue money, the nominal quantity of bills increases, leading the banks to issue more money and so on. Second, the amount of bills presented depends to some extent on the discount rate chosen by banks. Therefore banks can issue an excess supply of money (at the current price level) by keeping their discount rate low. Both of these possibilities lead to the inflationary aspects of the real-bills doctrine.

This is *not*, however, the view that White holds. He explicitly rejects the real-bills doctrine and endorses a different version of the "needs of trade" idea. For him the "needs of trade" means *the demand to hold bank notes* (White, 1984, pp. 123–4). On this interpretation, the doctrine states that the supply of bank notes should vary in accordance with the demand to hold notes. As I shall argue, this is just as acceptable as the view that the supply of shoes should vary to meet the demand for them.

Some years ago Rothbard (1963, p. 307 n. 8) defined inflation as "an increase in the money supply not consisting of an increase in the money metal."[3] By this criterion any increase in fiat money is inflationary, as is any increase in the supply of bank notes under free banking not matched by an equal amount of the base metal. As long as all notes are 100 percent backed by specie, they cannot be inflationary, and any notes not so backed are inflationary.

Missing from this account is any mention of the demand for money. When we ask what the optimal shoe supply should be, our first reaction is to ask what the demand for shoes is. Why not do the same for money? To put the question another way, what if the demand for money were to suddenly rise? By Rothbard's definition, an attempt to increase the amount of bank notes to match the increase in demand (assuming no change in gold reserves) is bad policy because it is inflationary. Is it also bad policy to meet increases in the demand for shoes by increasing the supply?

The usual response of 100 percent advocates is to argue that money's unique role as a medium of exchange means that the effects of changes in its supply are far broader than those for any other good. Instead of the supply of money increasing, they say, prices should fall, bringing the real supply of money in line with the real demand for money. The problem with this view is that it ignores the difficult and possible adverse consequences of a deflationary fall in prices. In the opposite case, a fall in the demand for money, 100 percent reserve theorists argue that prices should rise to adjust the real demand and supply of money. While long recognizing the problems with inflation, many Austrians, including Rothbard, have been far too quick to dismiss the effects of deflation.[4] Deflation as well as inflation can lead to macroeconomic miscoordination (see Leijonhufvud, 1981 and Yeager, 1986).

The theoretical position of most free bankers is somewhat different. It is that instead of tying the money supply to 100 percent reserves of gold, thus only allowing increases or decreases as gold goes in or out of the system, bankers should attempt to match the supply of money to the demand. This view is known as monetary equilibrium theory. (See Selgin, 1988 and De Jong, 1973.) Rather than the price level doing all the adjusting, it is the nominal quantity of notes that should adjust, which minimizes the possibly miscoordinating effects of changes in the price level. Monetary equilibrium theory defines inflation as an excess supply of money in the broad sense (primarily bank credit), i.e., a situation where there are more notes issued than people wish to hold. Accordingly, the proper policy when faced with an increase in money demand is to increase the nominal supply. To the monetary equilibrium theorist, this is not inflationary. In the case where money demand falls, to do *nothing* would be inflationary; the proper response is to decrease the nominal supply of notes.

Because Rothbard attempts to link 100 percent reserve banking with Mises's banking theory (Rothbard, 1988, pp. 234, 235, 240, 243 nn. 16, 18) it might be of interest to see what Mises himself had to say about inflation. In his classic contribution to monetary theory, *The Theory of Money and Credit,* Mises argues that "in theoretical investigation there is only one meaning that can rationally be attached to the expression inflation: an increase in the quantity of money (in the broader sense of the term, so as to include fiduciary [fractional] media as well), that is not offset by a corresponding increase in the need for money (again in the broader sense of the term)" (Mises, 1980 [1912], p. 272. Also see *ibid.*, p. 263). Clearly Mises is adopting a monetary equilibrium theory view of inflation. Increases of the supply of money need not be inflationary, even those that are in excess of increases in the monetary metal. Whatever the merits of Rothbard's (or Mises's) view, Rothbard is not very "Misesian" in his definition of inflation.

White's interpretation that the "needs of trade" means the demand for notes underlies his categorization of the various theorists of the British debate, which Rothbard claims is confused. Rothbard (1988, pp. 233–4), following Vera Smith, explains their views with the use of a two-by-two matrix that has free banking and central banking on one axis, and Currency School (100 percent reserve) and Banking School ("needs of trade") on the other. White, on the other hand, divides them into only three categories: Banking School, Currency School, and Free Banking School. Rothbard praises the Currency School writers, even though most advocated central banking, because they favored 100 percent reserves (p. 234). He thinks they were simply mixed up about the best means to that end. The Banking School were all wrong *a priori* because they allowed for fractional note issue, even though they often opposed central banking. Rothbard charges that White's categorization overlooks the hard money/soft money distinction among free bankers.

White does not overlook this distinction. While it is true that many Free Banking School writers favored soft money and were unclear on the "needs of trade" issue, White's emphasis is on writers who avoided such gross errors, whose ideas can be extended and corrected. His purpose in classifying some writers as an independent Free Banking School is to call to our attention that they had some concept of monetary equilibrium and realized that some version of free banking was the best means to that end. They were not always correct, but they were on the right path. Rothbard (p. 238) argues that James William Gilbart, whom White calls a free banker, has always been viewed as a member of the Banking School. Gilbart believed in the needs of trade doctrine and opposed a central bank. But, according to Rothbard, since Gilbart was not a 100 percent reserve man, he and others who shared his views on the needs of trade were inflationists. Rothbard offers neither a theoretical justification of his own position or a refutation of White's, and brands White as an inflationist for agreeing with the Free Banking School (p. 239). The problem is not White's conflation of the two groups of free bankers, but rather Rothbard's inability to see why White's framework is what it is, and his failure to explain why he thinks White's theory is wrong.

A concern Rothbard and many Austrians have is whether increases in note issue that the monetary equilibrium theory considers legitimate will generate the business cycle. Mises and Hayek thought that unwanted increases in the supply of bank credit lower the market rate of interest below the natural rate. The lower rate of interest fools entrepreneurs into thinking that sufficient real savings exist to finance longer-term capital projects. It represents not real savings, but inflationary bank credit. When the new credit stops, consumers reassert their true savings–consumption preferences and the newly undertaken projects are found to be unfinishable because the real level of savings is too low. This is the bust phase of the business cycle.

Under a monetary equilibrium-oriented free banking system, appropriate increases in the money supply should not generate such effects. The rate of interest results from the interplay of the time preferences of savers and investors. It is through bank intermediation that these savers and lenders are brought together. Banks accept deposits (savings) and make loans (investments). When banks increase the liability side of their balance sheets by the creation of demand deposits, or by issuing new notes, they are increasing the amount of investment in the loanable funds market. To keep the market rate of interest (the rate on those loans) equal to the natural rate (the true savings–consumption preferences of consumers), new investments have to be matched by an increase in savings. Where will new savings come from?

The answer lies in recognizing that the act of holding a bank liability (note or deposit) is an act of saving (Brown, 1910). The demand for money is a demand to *hold* it. The services money provides, and that determine its value, result from people wishing to hold it (Hutt, 1956). When a bank liability is held and not spent, it allows the bank to use the "unclaimed" specie to create new loans. If the demand for bank notes rises, banks have a larger amount of excess reserves to loan out, i.e., savings have increased. The appropriate response to maintain the proper relationship between the market rate of interest and natural rate is to increase investment, i.e., increase the supply of bank liabilities. The trigger of the Austrian business cycle is the artificial lowering of the market rate below the natural rate. Monetary equilibrium theory explains why not all increases in the money supply need cause intertemporal miscoordination.

Under a free banking system, true inflation by any particular bank is quite unprofitable. Defining inflation as an excess supply of bank liabilities, imagine a situation where a bank creates new liabilities without any change in the demand to hold them. In such a case, recipients of the new liabilities (which, let us assume, are all notes) will not want to hold them and will spend them or deposit them at a bank. If spent, of course, they will wind up at a bank eventually. As the receiving banks return them to the issuing bank for redemption, the issuing bank will see its reserves shrink, inducing it to reduce the amount of liabilities it is issuing. Any note issue beyond what people want to hold will return to the issuing bank for redemption, draining a source of liquidity (and therefore profit) – its reserves. (See White, 1984, p. 126 and Selgin, 1987b, pp. 438–440 on the so-called "law of the reflux" or the "law of adverse clearings.") Of course, such overissues are inflationary in the technical sense, and in a worst-case scenario might cause locally rising prices and a small degree of malinvestment. The costliness of inflationary overissues is ample incentive to prevent them from occurring with any frequency. However, if such overissues occur, they will be quickly stemmed and localized to the offending bank. Free banking, then, has advantages over both central banking and 100 percent reserve banking in that it tends to prevent both inflation and deflation.

Free banking theory is not inflationist. It understands that a bank's job is to serve as an intermediary for lenders and borrowers and to supply a generally accepted medium of exchange in accordance with the need for such media. A free banking system promotes economic growth and provides strong profit incentives against inflation and deflation.

ARE FRACTIONAL RESERVE BANK NOTES FRAUDULENT?

Let us now discuss the legal–moral argument against fractional reserve banking, which claims that the notes and deposits free banks issue are fraudulent. If a bank issues \$1000 in notes but only has \$100 in reserves, it has supposedly issued \$900 in fraudulent claims, because if everyone tried to redeem simultaneously only \$100 of claims could be immediately satisfied. Debate among free-market monetary theorists has raged on this point for quite a while. While most agree that fractional reserve notes are acceptable, and always have been, a few stalwarts hold out, among them Rothbard (1988, p. 235).

Bank notes and deposits have historically been understood to be payable "on demand," meaning that if a bank did not pay reserves when presented with a claim, it was guilty of fraud. Nowhere was there any notion that banks had to hold 100 percent specie reserves. When people deposited gold and got bank notes in return, the notes did not guarantee that that very gold, or an equivalent amount, would always be kept waiting in a drawer with the depositor's name on it. Such notes were not warehouse receipts and would not be under a future free banking system. As long as a bank can pay specie on demand, it fulfills its legal obligation.

It is worth remarking that, to the extent that 100 percent reserve banks are warehouses, they cannot afford to attract deposits by paying interest. If banks are simply warehouses, their role as financial intermediaries disappears. It is not clear what supply of savings would be forthcoming if savers received no interest. What would make banking a distinctive activity? Why wouldn't savers store their gold with private security companies instead? Of course, banks could be pure brokers, simply matching up savers and borrowers and taking a fee for the service. But historically and theoretically, banks can safely do much more by using fractional reserves to expand the available supply of credit. Banks have always acted as intermediaries in this way because that is what has satisfied the needs of the market. Outlawing fractional reserve banking would leave the business of banking without a clear purpose and reduce banks' ability to supply the appropriate amount of credit for economic growth. Rothbard's view turns banks into mere passive mechanisms for matching the supply and demand of loans. Instead we can view the banking industry as part of a creative, open-ended market process, free to adjust to the diverse tastes and preferences of market actors.

The premise of fractional reserve banking is no different from that underlying bridge-building. No bridge is constructed with the expectation that everyone in the country will want to use it at once. Is it fraudulent to build a bridge and promise that it can transport people across and then have it collapse when 20 million people pile on it? Human institutions are centered around norms of behavior. Bridge builders can safely assume that only some number of people will ever want to cross the bridge simultaneously. In the same way, bankers can safely assume that only some number of people will demand reserves on any given day. If we outlaw fractional reserve banking, its proponents argue, then we should outlaw bridges that cannot handle 20 million people at once.

Rothbard has a response to this argument; he claims that those trying to cross the bridge "are simply requesting a service; they are not trying to take possession of their lawful property, as are the bank depositors." He offers an analogy of his own: supporting fractional reserve banking is like defending "embezzlers who would never have been caught if someone hadn't fortuitously inspected the books. The crime comes when the theft or fraud is committed, not when it is finally revealed" (Rothbard, 1983 [1963], p. 309 n. 28). But is this consistent with other parts of Rothbard's vision? Under laissez faire, Rothbard has argued (correctly, I believe) that there is no such thing as a crime against society. For a crime to occur there has to be a victim. If no one comes forward to file charges and attempt to obtain restitution, there has been no crime. How then can a bank that has fractional reserves but always redeems on demand be guilty of a crime when there's no victim? As Rothbard says, the crime comes when committed. The problem is defining the crime and finding a victim. As far as note holders are concerned, the crime is failure to redeem, not the "potential" of failed redemption. Banks should be held strictly liable when they fail to redeem on demand, but not before. Fractional reserve bank notes are not fraudulent.

CONCLUSION

While Rothbard may have legitimate complaints about the real freedom of the Scottish banks, and White's measures of their economic success, his argument fails to dent the theoretical case for free banking. Where is the *argument* for the other side? Rothbard's review seems to be an example of impatient dogma overriding good scholarship. Fractional reserve free banking is neither inflationary nor a generator of business cycles. When understood as an application of monetary equilibrium theory, it is a workable and reasonable means to dampening, if not eliminating, inflation and cyclical fluctuations. Yes, it may be complicated and require an effort from the reader to understand it, but so does much of economics. Rothbard refuses to try. Free banking theory deserves better, and so do Austrian monetary theorists.

NOTES

I would like to thank George Selgin, Kurt Schuler, and Don Lavoie for their comments on an earlier draft. The usual caveat applies.

1. Interested readers might also want to see the contribution of White in Siegel (1984) and the papers by White and Rothbard in Rockwell (1985).
2. Free banking theorists have found other favorable examples in China (Selgin 1986), France (E.N. White, 1987), and Sweden (Jonung, 1975).
3. See also Rothbard (1962, p. 851 and p. 940 n. 106).
4. The usual explanation of this one-sidedness is that, since politicians control the world's banking systems and the incentives facing them are to inflate, inflation is far more common in practice than deflation. Though this is certainly true, under a 100 percent reserve system deflation might be relatively more of a concern. This would especially be true in the case of a rise in money demand, with no change in the nominal supply. Aside from all of this, theoretical completeness should demand that we fill in both the inflation and deflation sides of the story.

REFERENCES

Boettke, Peter, Horwitz, Steven, and Prychitko, David L. (1986), "Beyond Equilibrium Economics: Reflections on the Uniqueness of the Austrian Tradition," *Market Process,* **4**(2), Fall. (Reprinted as Chapter 6 of this volume.)

Brown, Harry G. (1910), "Commercial Banking and the Rate of Interest." *Quarterly Journal of Economics*, (24).

De Jong, Fritz (1973), "J.G. Koopmans' Concept of Monetary Equilibrium," in *Developments of Monetary Theory in the Netherlands*, Rotterdam: Rotterdam University Press.

Hutt, W.H. (1956), "The Yield from Money Held," in Mary Sennholz (ed.), *On Freedom and Free Enterprise*, Princeton, N.J: Van Nostrand.

Jonung, Lars (1975), "The Economics of Private Money: The Experience of Private Notes in Sweden, 1831–1902," paper presented at the Monetary History Group Meeting, London, 27 September.

Leijonhufvud, Axel (1981), "Effective Demand Failures," in *Information and Coordination*, Oxford: Oxford University Press.

Mises, Ludwig von (1980 [1912]), *The Theory of Money and Credit*, Indianapolis: Liberty Press.

Rockwell, Llewelyn (ed.) (1985), *The Gold Standard: An Austrian Perspective*, Lexington, MA: Lexington Books.

Rothbard, Murray N. (1962), *Man, Economy, and State*, Los Angeles: Nash Publishing.

—— (1983 [1963]), *America's Great Depression*, New York: Richardson & Synder.

—— (1985), "Introduction," in Ludwig von Mises, *Theory and History*, Auburn, AL: Ludwig von Mises Institute.

—— (1988), "The Myth of Free Banking in Scotland," *Review of Austrian Economics*, vol. 2, Lexington, MA: Lexington Books.

Selgin, G.A. (1986), "Free Banking in China: 1800–1935," unpublished ms., George Mason University.

—— (1987a), "The Analytical Framework of the Real-Bills Doctrine," unpublished ms., George Mason University.

—— (1987b), "The Stability and Efficiency of Money Supply Under Free Banking," *Journal of Institutional and Theoretical Economics*, **143**(3), September.

—— (1988), *The Theory of Free Banking*, Totowa, NJ: Rowman & Littlefield.

Siegel, Barry N. (ed.) (1984), *Money in Crisis: The Federal Reserve, the Economy, and Monetary Reform*, Cambridge, MA: Ballinger Publishing.

White, Eugene Nelson (1987), "Free Banking During the French Revolution." Working Paper No. 5, Financial and Monetary History of the French Revolution Project, Rutgers University.

White, Lawrence H. (1984), *Free Banking in Britain*, Cambridge: Cambridge University Press.

Yeager, Leland B. (1986), "The Significance of Monetary Disequilibrium," *Cato Journal*, **6**(2), Fall.

PART FOUR

Current Methodological Questions

17. Storytelling and the human sciences

Peter J. Boettke

INTRODUCTION

Where have all the interesting stories gone? The use of economic storytelling comprised a large portion of the staple diet of classical political economy. Adam Smith taught us about the benefits of specialization through the story of a pin factory,[1] David Ricardo used the story of the international market for wine to present the law of comparative advantage,[2] and J.B. Say appealed to the economic activity of the city as opposed to the country to elaborate his law of the market.[3] In more modern times, this use of a good story as a persuasive device was utilized by Carl Menger to explain the principle of marginal utility by reference to the uses of alternative bags of grain by a farmer.[4] Eugen Böhm-Bawerk employed the horse market to discuss price determination,[5] while Alfred Marshall invoked the fish market to elucidate the logic of price adjustments.[6] And perhaps the most interesting story of all was F.A. Hayek's tale about the market for tin and the communicative role of the price system.[7]

But within current economic literature stories have been relegated to principles, textbooks and classes. We use interesting stories to teach undergraduates but seldom to communicate among ourselves, either in journals or at workshops. Stories are seldom greeted by applause at the sacred level of "Theory," and those that do receive approval are typically uninteresting (unconvincing tales about two-good-worlds and finite games). Why has storytelling disappeared from our scholarly discourse? Why is economics at its highest level of theory so uninteresting?

Donald McCloskey has tried to answer these questions in his *Rhetoric of Economics.* Most reviews of the book have concentrated upon its philosophical argument, which rests upon the work of the likes of Stephen Toulmin, Michael Polanyi, Paul Feyerabend and, most directly, Richard Rorty.[8] McCloskey's philosophical approach challenges the modernist methodology of economics in a manner that is most convincing. While making for interest-

Essay Review of *The Rhetoric of Economics* by Donald N. McCloskey (Madison: University of Wisconsin Press, 1985).

ing reading, this emphasis in the various reviews does injustice to McCloskey's work. His book is much more than a summary of the philosophy of science literature, that has so completely dethroned modernist methodology in the past 25 years, applied to economics – it is a book about economic arguments. It is this aspect of McCloskey's work that I wish to discuss.

McCloskey sees his work as that of a literary critic of economic texts and a great deal of his book is dedicated to the critique of some of the most "successful" texts written under the guise of modernism. McCloskey successfully demonstrates the use of, and dependence upon, rhetoric in the works of such prominent neoclassical economists as Paul Samuelson, Gary Becker, John Muth and Robert Fogel. Hiding behind the veil of modernism does not (and cannot) emancipate these authors from the strictures of human thought. With this, McCloskey takes one giant step towards a humanistic economics.

But how good a critic is the critic? His own postmodernist method, I argue, will bolster his task as literary critic beyond where McCloskey has, so far, been willing to go. I wish to convince McCloskey (or McCloskeyites) that his case about economic reasoning goes far beyond pointing out that we all attempt to persuade one another and rather points to an economics that can recapture those good stories. In other words, rather than criticizing McCloskey for an alleged "anything goes mentality" as have his other critics, I wish to suggest that, as represented in his book, McCloskey is far too favorable to the existing body of neoclassical thought and that his own methodology points to a more critical approach.

EMPIRICISM AND FORMALISM AS MODES OF PERSUASION

"Economic science," McCloskey tells us, "must use rhetoric and might as well be aware that it must" (p. 87). But what does this mean? To McCloskey it means we must pay attention to the style as well as the content of arguments. In fact, style and content work together for one and the same purpose – the attempt to persuade your audience. McCloskey's message is well taken. We, as academic economists who make a living by writing, should learn to write clear and concise arguments. If we recognize that what we are trying to do is convince others of the relative merits of our ideas over alternatives, and in the process we resort to mathematical formulations, statistical tests or scholarly traditions as rhetorical devices to make our case, economics scholarship would be better off.

To McCloskey economic argumentation is similar to the presentation of a legal case. This does not mean we reduce economic arguments to courtroom tactics or clever plays on words. That, in fact, goes on now whenever an economic scientist "data mines" to fix his statistical test or makes hidden assumptions to help build his model or utilizes hidden ethical arguments to generate his welfare conclusion. The rules of methodology do not protect us from such abuse. Only meta rules of good behavior do that. "It is people, not intellectual devices," McCloskey points out, "that are good or bad. *Good science demands good scientists – that is to say, moral, hard-working scientists – not good methodologies"* (p. 37, emphasis added).

The meta rules of good behavior are all we have.[9] That much said, McCloskey does advocate a sort of anarchism, but I believe it is not methodological anarchism (that is: anything goes and every argument is of equal value). Rather, McCloskey's anarchism is one of scientific organization. It is like what Marx called the "anarchy of capitalist production," and it should be contrasted not with reason, but with the idea of a centrally planned science. In other words, the anarchy McCloskey envisions is the orderly process of scientific inquiry (cf. pp. 40 ff.). Ordered anarchy is the (unintended) result of various and diverse individual scientists pursuing their own methods to arrive at truth, not the (planned) methods that each scientist deploys. The truth is, in fact, that ordered anarchy, whether in economics or scientific production, is not only possible, but desirable.

Critics charge that McCloskey's methodological anarchism implies that truth is unobtainable and, therefore, all arguments are reduced to equally valid opinions. In such a scenario the rhetoric of economics becomes "mere rhetoric" and nihilism does rule. But this is *not* McCloskey's position. For McCloskey is a noble defender of the truths of economics. Demand curves slope downward, McCloskey argues. And if someone suggested that they sloped upward he would inform them they were wrong. Viewing demand curves as downward-sloping is justified on a whole variety of pragmatic grounds.[10] Viewing them this way works; it illuminates market activity. The proposition that as the price of a good rises the quantity demanded of the good falls is persuasive and its truth does not depend upon statistical tests or mathematical proof – we know its truth through experience, examples, and intuition.[11]

But what of the economics of the mainstream? All economists use rhetoric, McCloskey convincingly demonstrates, but does that mean that their arguments are good? Paul Samuelson, for example, uses many rhetorical devices within his quintessentially modernist tome, *Foundations of Economic Analysis*, but is it "mere rhetoric" or good rhetoric? The same can be asked of Gary Becker, John Muth or Robert Fogel. Yes, empiricism and formalism do employ rhetorical devices – there can be no doubt about that after McCloskey. But is their economics properly rhetorical? The appeal by Samuelson to the elegance of mathematics, for example, might suggest that the criteria of modernism is not being strictly enforced. But does that mean that Samuelson's appeal is persuasive as an argument about economic activity? Becker may employ the metaphor of durable goods to explain investment in children, but the usefulness of the metaphor can be questioned. And the same goes for Muth and Fogel. Simply because they employ rhetorical devices does not mean they meet the criteria suggested by classical rhetoric for a good argument. That is the role of the literary critic, and in that role, McCloskey does not always succeed. He is much too sympathetic a critic. Yes, all economists use rhetoric, but some are engaging in mere rhetoric, even if it is hidden behind mathematical models or reams of statistical paper. Their arguments are often rather bad and their results unilluminating. Their work is wrong-headed from both a rhetorical standpoint and a pragmatic appeal to use-value.

Research on the Soviet system, for example, suffers severely under the yoke of modernism. Economic studies of the Soviet system focus on metaphors like economic "growth" and "productivity." While the draconian methods of Stalin are generally recognized, economists usually escape quickly behind the veil of value freedom (another rhetorical device of modernism) and argue about the great growth rates achieved under Stalinization.[12] The implied (and not so subtle) message for economic development is that forced collectivization and industrialization were unpleasant, but necessary to overcome economic backwardness. But economists who merely focus upon growth rates, output figures, or some measure of economic efficiency simply cannot understand the Soviet system or its history. Yes, they do employ rhetoric to make their arguments about the system, but it is bad rhetoric. As one profound literary critic of Soviet studies, Alain Besancon, states:[13]

> The Soviet economy is the subject of a considerable volume of scholarly work which occupies numerous study centres in Europe and the United States and which provides material for a vast literature and various academic journals. But those born in the Soviet Union or those who approach Soviet society through history, literature, travel or through listening to what the emigres have to say, find that they *cannot recognize what the economists describe. There seems to be an unbridgeable gap between this system, conceived through measurements and figures, and the other system, without measurements and figures, which they have come to know through intuition and their own actual experience.* It is an astonishing feature of the world of Soviet affairs that a certain kind of economic approach to Soviet reality, no matter how well-informed, honest and sophisticated, is met with such absolute scepticism and total disbelief by those who have a different approach that they do not even want to offer any criticism – it being impossible to know where to begin.

But the field of Soviet studies is just a microcosm of the broader problem of economic argumentation in general. The world of the economist's model cannot be recognized by those who approach the subject with human beings at the center of the analysis. In other words, the very humanism that McCloskey calls upon offers a serious criticism of the rhetorical model of Paul Samuelson, Gary Becker, Robert Fogel or John Muth. The economic model of modernism, under the influence of formalism and empiricism, forgot the very thing it was supposed to study – man.

HUMANISM AS AN ANSWER

McCloskey understands that the study of man entails the adoption of humanism. In fact, he would go further, arguing that even the natural sciences are fundamentally humanistic. "The claim here," he states, "is not the vulgar figure of logic that economics is mere humanism because it is a failure as a science. The claim is that all science is humanism (and no 'mere' about it) because that is all there is for humans" (p. 56). But it does not seem to have been carried through to his literary criticism of economics. Modernism did not just negatively affect the way we argue amongst each other. And it is not just a problem of not discussing values. It is not naive literary criticism to "second guess Samuelson" (p. 182), as McCloskey suggests. The imperative of a good critic is to question and second guess.

What was (is) the opportunity cost of modernism? McCloskey argues that "modernism was a bad idea, no more than going to elementary school was a bad idea," it served its purpose (*ibid.*). But at what cost to human understanding? If humanism suggests that the creative human mind must be the focal point of analysis, then why settle for the "mechanomorphism" of mainstream economics?[14] The very model of textual criticism that McCloskey suggests, i.e., that of critical history of thought, suggests that dead-ends reveal that there were roads not taken.[15]

And this explains the loss of good stories. For example, the good Chicago tradition of price theory, represented in Simon's *Syllabus* or Frank Knight's *Risk, Uncertainty and Profit*, or Armen Alchian and William Allen's, *University Economics*, is non-existent in the world of Gary Becker. The Chicago applied-price-theory approach, which McCloskey represents, was killed by modernism. Instead of telling good stories about the operation of real-world market processes, the modern Chicago School informs us of optimal love-making (Gary Becker) and vacations during the Great Depression (Robert Lucas). One wonders if Aaron Director could motivate the current crop of students to tackle the questions that generated the law and economics movement a generation ago.[16] In three words: scientism kills science.[17]

Perhaps Michael Polanyi describes this paradox best. Modernism, with its emphasis upon formalism and empirical tests, has reduced the social sciences to a compilation of uninteresting details. "If the scientific virtues of exact observation and strict correlation of data are given absolute preference for the treatment of a subject matter which disintegrates when represented in such terms, the result will be irrelevant to the subject matter and probably of no interest at all."[18] Modernism fails not only because it is a model which we cannot live up to, but because in its hands the human sciences become nothing of interest. Moreover, modernism, Polanyi argues, threatens the very basis of scientific inquiry itself. It not only hinders human understanding, but challenges the meta rules of good science. As Polanyi writes;[19]

> This is how a philosophic movement guided by aspirations of scientific severity has come to threaten the position of science itself. This self-contradiction stems from a misguided intellectual passion – a passion for achieving absolutely impersonal knowledge which, being unable to recognize any persons, presents us with a picture of the universe in which we ourselves are absent. In such a universe there is no one capable of creating and upholding scientific values; hence there is no science.

Edmund Husserl raised similar concerns over the rise of modernism and its effect upon science, suggesting that the modernist idea of science "excludes in principle the questions which man…finds most burning."[20]

Humanism not only informs the meta rules, it suggests what are good and bad questions to ask. Methodology, therefore, must maintain an important role in economic science. Though it is more descriptive as opposed to prescriptive, there are some prescriptions that follow. In the human sciences the most fundamental prescription that follows is that questions or techniques which obscure man's human existence are not useful and do not belong in the "sciences humane."[21]

CONCLUSION

McCloskey's book does its job of criticizing the modernism of economics very convincingly, and for this we should all be grateful. But he does not take the criticism one step further and show why work that is justified on modernist grounds is bad economics. McCloskey does not fulfill his role as the literary critic of economics.[22]

Modern economics is the result of the importation of a naive philosophy of science. It is not enough to state that science has never lived up to the model of the philosophers. A stronger argument must be made. The social sciences lost whatever scientific results they had achieved as a result of the adoption of this model. Knowledge that was possessed was lost, and knowledge that could have been discovered has been postponed. The opportunity cost of modernism has been huge. We, as economists, are no longer interesting or appealing. Our interpretive skills have deteriorated and, as a result, we are incapable of illuminating the human condition. The public does not read our books and students dread our classes. Economics has truly become the dismal science, but of its own accord. Books like McCloskey's are changing that. That alone is a tremendous accomplishment.

NOTES

I would like to acknowledge Matthew B. Kibbe and Don Lavoie for their helpful comments on an earlier draft. Responsibility for remaining errors is solely my own.

1. *An Inquiry into the Nature and Causes of the Wealth of Nations*, Chicago: University of Chicago Press (1976 [1776]), pp. 8–9.
2. *On the Principles of Political Economy and Taxation*, New York: Cambridge University Press (1981 [1817]), pp. 128 ff.
3. *A Treatise on Political Economy*, 4th edn, New York: Augustus M. Kelley (1971 [1821]), pp. 132, ff.
4. *Principles of Economics*, New York: New York University Press (1981 [1871]), pp. 114 ff.
5. *Capital and Interest* (3 vols), South Holland, IL: Libertarian Press (1959) vol. 2, pp. 220 ff.
6. *Principles of Economics*, New York: Macmillan (1971 [1890]) pp. 302 ff.
7. *Individualism and Economic Order*, Chicago: University of Chicago Press (1980 [1948]) pp. 77 ff.
8. See the reviews by Mark Blaug, "Methodology with a small m," *Critical Review*, **1**(2), Spring (1987) pp. 1–5; Uskali Maki, "How to Combine Rhetoric and Realism in the Methodology of Economics," *Economics and Philosophy*, **4** (1988) pp. 89–109; Steven Rappaport, "Economic Methodology: Rhetoric or Epistemology?," *Economics and Philosophy*, **4** (1988) pp. 110–28; and Alexander Rosenberg, "Economics is too Important to be left to the Rhetoricians," *Economics and Philosophy*, **4** (1988) pp. 129–49. Also see McCloskey's reply, "Two Replies and a Dialogue on the Rhetoric of Economics," *Economics and Philosophy*, **4** (1988) pp. 150–66.
9. See Frank Van Dun, "Economics and the Limits of Value-Free Science," *Reason Papers*, Spring (1986) for an excellent discussion of the values underlying science.
10. Ludwig von Mises ultimately defended the propositions of praxeology and methodological dualism on similar pragmatic grounds. "Granted that science cannot give us truth – and who knows what truth really means? – at any rate it is certain that it works in leading us to success." It is precisely this "Pragmatic Point of View," Mises continues, that reveals the fallacy of positivism.

    > [T]he principle according to which the Ego deals with every human being as if the other were a thinking and acting being like himself has evidenced its usefulness both in mundane life and in scientific research…It is beyond doubt that the practice of considering fellow men as beings who think and act as I, the Ego, do has turned out well; on the other hand the prospect seems hopeless of getting similar pragmatic verification for the postulate requiring them to be treated in the same manner as the objects of the natural sciences.

    See *Human Action: A Treatise on Economics*, 3rd. rev. edn, Chicago: Henry Regnery (1966 [1949]) p. 24.

11. This kind of knowledge, referred to as "knowledge from within," has been defended as a scientific source of knowledge throughout the history of the Austrian school. This is not the isolated introspection of one individual, but the common-sense and intersubjective knowledge of the "life world." "The starting point of praxeology," Mises stated, "is not a choice of axioms and a decision about methods of procedure, but reflection about the essence of action" (*Human Action*, p. 39). And knowledge about the essence of human action is derived from our shared understanding of everyday life. It rests fundamentally upon "the intersubjective validity of logic and thereby the reality of the realm of the alter Ego's thought and action, of his eminent human character" (*ibid.*, p. 24).
12. For example, Michael Ellman calmly states that the "period of collectivization appears as a process which enabled the state to increase its inflow of grain, potatoes and its stock of urban labour, at the expense of livestock and the rural and urban human population." It's just a matter of costs and benefits. See "Did the Agricultural Surplus Provide the Resources for the Increase in Investment in the USSR during the First Five Year Plan?," *Economic Journal*, December (1975) p. 859.
13. "Anatomy of a Spectre," *Survey* **25**(4), Autumn (1980) p. 143; emphasis added.
14. See Karl Mittermaier, "Mechanomorphism," in Israel M. Kirzner (ed.), *Subjectivism, Intelligibility and Economic Understanding*, New York: New York University Press (1986) pp. 236 ff.
15. One comes right to mind. In 1947 with the publication of Samuelson's *Foundations* the economics profession chose to pursue the formalization of economics. At the same time in 1949, Ludwig von Mises offered the profession *Human Action*, a treatise on economics that was fundamentally humanistic in its method and humanitarian in its concern. But it was the path forgone. McCloskey's model of humanism for the sciences does suggest something about the make-up of the sciences.
16. That Chicago tradition lives on today, but in the work of the members of the Virginia school of political economy in Fairfax, far removed from the cool winters of Chicago or the sun of Los Angeles – it never did make it up north to Cambridge. Why such a geographical reallocation? Because Buchanan was never fully convinced by the onslaught of modernism; his works have always sought to explain man, either in his economic or political nexus. One could argue that Buchanan might not always have been correct, but he always sought to illuminate man's condition in the world. Knight's healthy cynicism toward scienticism rubbed off. See Frank Knight, "What is Truth in Economics?," *On the History and Method of Economics*, Chicago: University of Chicago Press (1956) p. 151 ff.
17. See F.A. Hayek, *The Counter-Revolution of Science: The Abuse of Reason*, Indianapolis: Liberty Press (1979 [1952]).
18. *Personal Knowledge*, Chicago: University of Chicago Press (1963) p. 139.
19. *Ibid.*, p. 142.
20. *The Crisis of European Sciences and Transcendental Phenomenology*, Evanston: Northwestern University Press (1970 [1934]) p. 6.
21. This is similar to Aristotle's plea that the methodological guideline for science is prudence in the choice of method – choose those methods of analysis which fit the subject matter under study. Thus, in economic science, where the questions concern human interaction, it was most unfortunate that the model of physics was imported to explain equilibrium states of affairs. As a result, exclusive emphasis was placed upon p and q vectors that produced a stable equilibrium – bumbling and erring man, creative man, was intentionally removed from the analysis. But "Economics is not about goods and services, it it about the actions of living men. Its goal is not to dwell upon imaginary constructions such as equilibrium. These constructions are only tools of reasoning. The sole task of economics is analysis of the actions of men, is the analysis of processes" (Mises, *Human Action*, p. 357).
22. Except, of course, those modernists he so thoroughly brings into disrepute. But for scholars interested in Austrian economics McCloskey has done a tremendous service by putting Austrians upon the playing field of economic scholarship. It is now up to those of us who argue that the Misesian tradition represents the most consistent humanistic approach to economic analysis to do the rest.

18. Splenetic rationalism: Hoppe's review of chapter 1 of *The Rhetoric of Economics*

Donald N. McCloskey

The Rhetoric of Economics has been reviewed by Austrian economists three times to my knowledge; by Tom G. Palmer in the *Humane Studies Review* (vol. 4, winter 1986–7), by Peter J. Boettke in *Market Process* (vol. 6, no. 2, fall 1988; reprinted as Chapter 17 of this volume), and at much the greatest length by Hans-Hermann Hoppe in the *Review of Austrian Economics* (vol. 3, 1989). The reviews by Palmer and Boettke were not as favorable as my mother would have written, alas, but they engaged the book seriously, which is all an author in these days of the paper blizzard can reasonably expect. Among other things, they said that I had not taken my own argument far enough, that "rhetoric" was a characterization of economics favoring Austrian over conventional neoclassicism. I am beginning to think they are right. To be sure, critics of the mainstream such as Palmer and Boettke tend to overlook the sweet currents of Real Keynesianism or Good Old Chicago, taking what is so ill-advisedly taught to first-year graduate students nowadays as being the whole of neoclassical economics. A candid rhetoric would favor Axel Leijonhufvud, Theodore Schultz, Robert Solow, James Buchanan, and the like over people who think that economics is merely Max Exp U(X,Y) s.t. k = k(X,Y). But Palmer and Boettke are right that a candid rhetoric would favor the opener kinds of Austrianism, too.

Hoppe's long piece, however, failed to engage the book, and in fact advocates a backward step. To answer it I have to turn away from the direction I am moving. Palmer and Boettke will understand, I am sure, if I leave most of my reply to them implicit in recent and forthcoming writings. They will see the influence of their kind of Austrian thinking more and more in my lucubrations.

It seems to this sympathetic outsider that Palmer's or Boettke's Austrianism is very different from Hoppe's. Hoppe's seems to deny at the outset the high valuation of discovery that is so central to Austrian thinking. Facts of the world beyond cloistered intuition or philosophies of science beyond Immanuel

Kant do not seem available to Hoppe. Neither intuition nor Kant is to be disdained, Lord knows. But discoveries from numerous entrepreneurs of intellect have taught us still more, and perhaps it should be put to use. Even Max Exp U(X,Y) has a thing or two worth using.

Hoppe's long piece will leave a strange impression of *The Rhetoric of Economics*. The book has ten chapters, most of which are "close readings," as the literary people say, of arguments made by economists. Chapter 5, for instance, examines the metaphors in Samuelson, Becker, and Solow; Chapter 6 examines the style of John Muth's paper on rational expectations; Chapter 7 is an analysis of the rhetoric in a few pages of Robert Fogel's book on American railways; Chapters 7 and 8 examine in detail the rhetoric of quantification in economics.

The main point of the book, in other words, is to use a literary criticism of economics to make plainer the "rhetoric" of the field – that is, to make plainer the way economists argue, badly and well. The first few chapters try to establish that the way economists argue is primarily not a matter of epistemology but of fact. The later chapters, and the bulk of the book, claim to provide some of the facts.

But Hoppe, like quite a few other methodologists, has seized on the early and conventionally philosophical chapters, especially Chapter 1. It is comfortable to construe the book as a piece of philosophy, then to write philosophically. This is a pity, because the book is not a work of philosophy, as Boettke and Palmer realized. It argues – first by precept and then most fully by example – that philosophy without rhetoric is a poor guide to how economists behave.

Hoppe does not join the argument. His interest in the book flags after a few pages out of the first of the ten chapters. Since Chapter 1 with a couple of other slices was the bulk of an article published in 1983, I would hazard the guess that Hoppe did once in 1983 cast his eye over the original article, with damage to his spleen, but has not found the time to read the book. This is my fault entirely: an author who cannot keep the reader's attention beyond the first half of the first chapter has no one to blame but himself. The book is qualitatively different from the article, being largely an empirical rather than a methodological study. I had the chance as the author to get this point across to Hoppe. But I muffed it. I apologize.

The length of Hoppe's review of portions of Chapter 1 out of 10 is strange, if flattering. But the length does not come from a complexity of argument; it comes from the repetitions of four simple points. The piece may be heard as a fugue with four themes, each repeated ten or a dozen times:

1. McCloskey shares "relativism" with some other misled people, none of whom see that "relativism" is self-refuting (pp. 179–85 of Hoppe's piece and elsewhere throughout).

2. McCloskey attacks empiricism, which is a good thing to do, but does so in a way annoying to someone who prefers the *a priori* (pp. 185–92 and elsewhere).
3. McCloskey does not consider methodological dualism (pp. 192–8).
4. McCloskey attacks the possibility of prediction (near the end of Chapter 1), and even quotes Mises, but he should have pushed further into the *a priori* (pp. 198–206).

A point of context will be helpful: Hoppe's piece is long and repetitious because he is on a big game hunt. The little McCloskey-beast could hardly inspire such an expedition. Right from the beginning it is plain that his targets are Feyerabend, Rorty, Gadamer, and Derrida. I am flattered to be put in such company. Although, shamefully, I have not read a single page of Gadamer or Derrida, I have read many pages of Feyerabend and Rorty, with pleasure and profit; and I count Rorty a personal friend. I would rather not be saddled, though, with every imagined disability of these eminent men. My poor argument has enough real disabilities, worthy of criticism and quite unrelated to what some philosopher has said, that a critic does not need to turn to imaginary ones. Much of Hoppe's argument, to put it another way, is irrelevant to the book I actually, clumsily wrote. Much of his argument is based on a misreading of Richard Rorty or of Paul Feyerabend, not on a misreading of Donald McCloskey.

Hoppe has a fine passion for ideas. But his passion has led to certain extraordinary misreadings, on which his argument turns.

First, I am not a "relativist," nor is the book "relativistic," if relativism is taken to mean what Hoppe wants it to mean. Hoppe wants it to mean the philosophy of a Valley Girl: anything goes, arguments are all equal, scholarship does not advance, we have no way of reaching common ground.

I believe, on the contrary, that good scholarship must force its arguments over many difficult hurdles, that good and bad arguments are often easily distinguished, that scholarship does and will advance, and that scholars have numerous ways of reaching common ground, if they will stop yelling at each other and take them. Since I have actually written (in British economic history) some science following these principles, I could scarcely oppose them.

In one of Hoppe's numerous returns to this first theme he remarks "such relativism would once more literally be impossible to adopt, because it is incompatible with our nature as acting talkers and knowers" (p. 191). I entirely agree, and say so to the Valley Girls in my classes. Chapters 2 through 10 of the book argue that our nature as acting talkers and knowers is crucial to economic sciences. Non-rhetorical approaches to science ignore our nature as acting talkers and knowers. Since they too would be incompatible with our nature, Popper's refined positivism or Hoppe's splenetic rationalism or various other versions of science simpler and meaner than life itself would be impossible to adopt.[1]

Nor, second, am I a skeptic, as could be affirmed by people who know me or have read my books, including the one Hoppe is talking about. In politics, if you care, I am an anarchist, but am certainly very far from being a nihilist. In politics and in science I have a standard of truth. It is the same one that Hoppe advocates. He uses many times the metaphor of a "common ground as the basis for objective truth." That is fine with me. The book says the same – though not in the chapter Hoppe studied – quoting for instance the mathematician Armand Borel: "something becomes objective...as soon as we are convinced that it exists in the minds of others in the same form that it does in ours, and that we can think about it and discuss it together" (p. 152). Chapters 8 and 9 of the book are about "truth based on common, objective grounds," namely truth in statistics, and how such truth depends on the common ground for comparison that we as acting speakers and knowers have occupied. Hoppe and I entirely agree that the purpose of science and scholarship is nothing like "entertainment" but rather is the serious job of attaining common ground for action. His notion of "the common ground of terms being used and applied cooperatively in the course of a practical affair, an interaction" (p 183) is fine. He goes on to note that "Talk, whether fact or fiction, is inevitably a form of cooperation" (*ibid.*). Admirable. As Palmer put it, the "elevation of conversation to the ethical standard by which rationality is to be judged" leans McCloskey toward classical liberalism, "for the market economy is a kind of grand conversation, a forum for persuasion" (p. 13). We all agree. It's in the book.

Nor, third, do I wish to "keep the conversation of economists going without ever claiming to say anything true" (p. 186). Hoppe says that McCloskey "wants to replace this permissiveness [of bad positivism] with an even greater one. He wants us to engage in talk, endless and unconstrained by any intellectual discipline whatsoever" (p. 189). That's not right, and knowledge of my person, or more to the point, knowledge of my book would not suggest it. On the contrary, I have no wish for conversations to go on forever, aimlessly, and I have never raised such a strange ideal. I wish conversations to end when they should. I wish merely that they would end rationally, as too often they do not. (It might be worth noting that the *Review of Austrian Economics* has evinced little interest in the rational truncation of conversation.)

Many conversations in economics are of course truncated by bad arguments, such as the conversation between some Austrian economists and the rest of the profession. Hoppe reads my opposition to bad arguments as advocating never-ending conversation. In particular he misreads my remarks about "conversation stoppers." I never would say that there do not exist proper conversation stoppers, for some arguments. It would be silly to say so. (People who have studied a lot of modern philosophy have a weakness for the rhetorical ploy of rewriting what someone has said in a new, silly form, in order to simplify the job of refutation.) Obviously, there are plenty of conversation stoppers, such as the rhetorical *tu quoque* I am going to use a little later, or the request that philosophers actually lay out their three aces of justified true belief.

I suppose if Hoppe thought about it he would want to withdraw the suggestion that I or any other moderately rational person would deny that conversations do end: "You don't think it's raining? Well, look outside" or "You think arithmetic is complete? Well, look at Gödel's proof." When I refer to "conversation stoppers" in economics it is not in aid of endless conversation. It is in aid of getting the stopping optimal. Maybe even Hoppe would agree that it is not correct to stop a conversation among economists by shouting "But Mises says you are wrong!" If Hoppe would read Chapters 8 and 9 he would see this, because there I examine the silliest of modern conversation stoppers in economics, one that Hoppe too would find silly, I think: significance testing.

Nor, fourth, do I wish intellectual constraints to be loosened. It is harder, not easier, to take into account all arguments, up and down. Scientific life is easier, not harder, if by contrast we are satisfied merely with observable implications or synthetic *a priori* or any other slogan. The book, and especially Chapter 1, criticizes 3×5-card philosophies of science. The wonder is that philosophers have been able to sell them.

What is getting in the way of Hoppe's understanding of Chapter 1 is his adherence to what might be called Hoppe's Lemma (the honor of the name could be shared, since it is the commonest argument against pragmatists and rhetoricians): if you are not a rationalist you are an irrationalist. Irrationalists, it says, are mere feelers and jokers. According to the Lemma, a non-rationalist indulges in *mere* rhetoric, and has no standards of truth. You must either do what we philosophers claim to be doing or we will declare that you are interested merely in *entertainment* (to use Hoppe's indignant italics). There are two modes of mental activity, according to Hoppe: on the one hand science following rationalist postulates and on the other hand entertainment, emotion, mere opinion, chatter.

I am surprised at Hoppe's suggestion that novels and poetry are "entertainment" in such a sneer-provoking sense that *War and Peace* would rank with "Wheel of Fortune." This cannot be what he means. The word "entertainment" must be a mistake, and cannot summarize his real beliefs about literature and philosophy. According to the crude dichotomy of science and entertainment, either there is first-order predicate logic combined with *a priori* knowledge or there is mere gab. Surely there is a lot in between.

Philosophical argument would be one candidate, *War and Peace* another. To use the philosopher's favorite rhetorical device, saying that "entertainment" covered such a large area would leave philosophy with no account of its own activities. It would put philosophy into the category of (mere) entertainment. (The argument is a variant of the usual reply to Hume's peroration about casting metaphysics into the flames: Hume's book would be the first to go.) But that cannot be right. Something is wrong. Philosophy is serious, not flameworthy. The point is that most modern philosophy does not fit into its own account of knowledge. It does fit a rhetorical account of knowledge. This being the case, philosophy should perhaps relax its 2400-year old sneer at rhetoric.

Hoppe believes his Lemma that anti-rationalism equals irrationalism because he has convinced himself, as many philosophers and their students have, that philosophy is a bulwark in defense of truth. The fuzziness of their rhetoric shows in their overlooking of the distinction between truth and Truth.

Small-t truth is what we use every day to get across the street or to detect another subatomic particle. By contrast Big-T Truth is a philosopher's construct, justified true belief. When I say, as in Chapter 1, that the philosopher's construct of Big-T Truth is of no use to economic science, and that it in fact infects economics with the sneering rhetoric of modern philosophy, the philosopher (and Hoppe) turns to the audience and says, in effect, "You see: McCloskey is against truth [small-t: DNMc]. He can't hold such a position and still make it across the street."

There's a lot of evidence in Hoppe's piece that he doesn't grasp the distinction between truth and Truth and therefore is not aware of his own rhetorical move. He would have done well to read Chapter 3. When he quotes me advocating a rule of conversation, "Don't lie," he adds *sotto voce*, "how could we, if there were no such thing as objective truth?" (p. 189). Well, there *is* such a thing as objective truth, the agreement we all make for purposes of navigating the world and society. We know when we are lying about the air temperature outside or the rational choice inside. The problem is that there doesn't seem to be any way of knowing whether we have hold of Objective Truth, capital-O, capital-T. Its presence or absence would seem to be knowable only to God. No one from Plato down to the present has been able to say how we mortals would know a Big-T Truth when we saw it.

I've said that I agree with Hoppe's pragmatic criterion of truth (he will be angry that I call it "pragmatic," because any deviation from his way of talking makes Hoppe angry; the anger, though, may at least send him to the texts about pragmatism). But he wants to build a bridge from this pragmatic and sensible position to his favored ontology, Reality (with a capital R). Understand: like you, I live squarely in a world of reality, small-r, a world in which it rains sometimes in Iowa and in which the IRS has unconstitutional powers. What is at issue here is the philosopher's construct, Reality, which may or may not exist, like Truth. I don't know, though I reckon God does. In contrast to Hoppe, I claim only to know about reality and truth.

But I do know from the history of philosophy that, unfortunately, there does not seem to be any way of getting from Truth in epistemology to Reality in ontology. We all wish there was, and many thinkers since Plato have contributed to floating logs and tossing bricks into the river to build a bridge between the two. But empirically speaking the bridge looks like a hopeless job. If you try to walk across the few finished pieces you fall right in. The construction time has exceeded that of a new defense system: at present, reckoning from the pre-Socratics, 2500 years and counting. As an empirical scientist I have to conclude that further investment in the bridge is not a high priority.

The philosophers claim that their notions of Truth and Reality and a Brooklyn Bridge between the two are necessary to prevent "permissiveness" and, as they invariably put it, "anything goes" (I myself never said such a thing as "anything goes," and never would). The philosophers should reflect coolly on their worries (Chapter 3 again may be therapeutic here). They will see that their fears about "permissiveness" and lack of discipline are perhaps neurotic and surely authoritarian, an appeal for a central planning of the intellectual marketplace.[2]

Scrutiny of how people actually argue will persuade the philosophers that their constructs do not play a foundational role in mathematics or science or married life or common law or other species of practical reasoning. The philosophical definitions of Truth and Reality play "merely" rhetorical roles. It is crucial for the aggrieved husband to claim that his view of the marriage is Reality. No biologist is going to want to claim anything less than Truth for her version of cell chemistry. But when it gets down to deciding who is going to take out the garbage or what the next experiment on crab glands is going to be, then lower-case, garden-variety reality and truth do the job just fine, thanks.

I do not say that good philosophical work cannot be done about lower-case truth and reality. It can, and has been. But to get the whole story the philosophers are going to have to examine all the arguments, not merely the ones that suit a crystalline realm of Truth and Reality.

So Hoppe is quite wrong when he summarizes my argument as "Economics, too, is merely rhetoric… [The conversation of mankind] exists not for the sake of inquiring about what is true, but for its own sake; not in order to convince anyone of anything based on objective standards, but in the absence of any such standards, simply in order to be persuasive and persuade for persuasion's sake" (p. 180). His "merely" in "merely rhetoric" is the problem, and shows how little he grasps the point of the book. Repeatedly he uses the metaphor of the rhetorical approach ending up "in mid-air." "If statements are merely and exclusively verbal expressions hanging in mid-air, what reason could there be for any one statement to ever give way to another?!" (p. 190).[3] He then broadens the attack to Kuhn and Feyerabend (which illustrates his tendency to wander off the subject of the book) by reducing their position, and (he thinks) mine, to the transparently silly assertion that science is "merely and exclusively verbal expressions hanging in mid-air." Having made the reduction his remaining task is easy: just sneer. (As I've said, much of modern philosophy depends on this rhetorical device.) Of course one need not bother to give reasons why such a silly statement about science should be replaced by another, non-silly, Hoppean statement.

Among the commonest of rhetorical turns in philosophy is the *tu quoque*, that is, the demonstration that someone is doing or using X at the very time he argues against X. Hoppe adopts the *tu quoque* in attacking his straw man of "relativism." A "relativist" who says,

1. "It is true that there is no truth," is contradicting himself: at the very time he argues against truth he is using the concept of truth. Hoppe believes, although he does not argue the case, that my position about economics being rhetorical has the self-defeating character of "relativism. " It does not. A technical reply is that Hoppe here again cannot see the difference between truth and Truth. It is not self-refuting to say,
2. "It is true that there is no [sublunary standard for judging our access to God's own] Truth." In this form the assertion has always been an objection to philosophy in the style of Plato. You can see why Platonists like Hoppe cannot bring themselves to treat their opponents with civility: it seems so *obvious* to them that (2.) is the same as (1.) and that (1.) is self-refuting. But there is a more important reply. To assert that the statement,
3. "Economics is rhetorical," is in some way self-contradictory (the assertion I repeat is not argued; Hoppe merely lays statement (1.) next to statement (3.) and asserts that they are somehow connected) *is itself self-contradictory.* Why? Because the assertion uses rhetoric at the very time it argues against rhetoric. One commits a contradiction weighing at a higher level against one's argument if one argues that there exists a contradiction weighing against a rhetorical approach to argument. So there.

My reply is not a piece of "mere" rhetoric; or at any rate, it is no more "mere" than is the Philosophers's Friend, the assertion of self-contradiction. Both are instances of the figure *tu quoque*. The reply is a variation on the earlier rhetorical argument that a philosophy spurning rhetoric in favor of a radically narrower conception of argument is left with no account of its own arguments, which are not in fact narrow. In the midst of tossing his straw man of "relativism" about the room in mock combat, for instance, Hoppe says that "One cannot argue that one cannot argue" (p. 181). Startlingly, he does not see the self-contradiction in this, that he is arguing (rhetorically) that one cannot argue that one cannot argue (narrowly and anti-rhetorically). His footnote 6 comes close to self-awareness on the matter, but does not arrive.

Hoppe's piece, then, does not exhibit much skill at reflecting on its own philosophy or reporting on other philosophies, setting aside that the book is not chiefly philosophical. Hoppe's understanding of the philosophical traditions under attack is surprisingly shallow. I've mentioned that the piece exhibits no familiarity with pragmatism, which precisely asserts as Hoppe does that "observations as well as words are constrained by action." Not reading Dewey, James, and Peirce is going to make it hard for Hoppe to read Rorty or even McCloskey with much understanding.

Another problem with the piece is the blurring of categories for attack. I am called a "hermeneuticist," which would surprise students of the subject. The word is as close as Hoppe can get to the right one, "rhetorician." The two traditions are related (as are others such as pragmatism, pragmatics, semiotics, informal logic, communication studies, and literary criticism). But it shows how little Hoppe has studied the traditions he thinks he disagrees with that he cannot keep them straight.

I must defend hermeneutics, though, from one of Hoppe's calumnies. Though its main literature is in German he has apparently understood little of it. No one who had read as much as an encyclopedia entry on the subject could characterize it as "an uncritical appeal to and acceptance of authority" (p. 198). It is of course exactly the reverse. Hermeneutics came out of the aptly named "critical" tradition of biblical interpretation, the "high criticism" that so radically undermined the authority of the Christian Bible in the early nineteenth century; which was in turn a result of ("lower") Latin and Greek textual criticism since the early Renaissance, critical and emendatory of classical texts. In English the word "critic" is first used c. 1600 in this sense, and especially to mean one who judges unsympathetically.

But I'll let Don Lavoie and others show in detail how little Hoppe understands the "hermeneutics" he and Murray Rothbard attack with such unrestrained animosity.[4] My chief concern is Hoppe's treatment of the tradition of rhetoric. Many philosophers reviewing the book have felt comfortable in their ignorance of rhetoric. How do they know how to behave towards rhetoric? Plato told them. Such appeal to a narrowing authority is I am afraid typical of modern philosophy, which less and less takes knowledge as its realm. Have the philosophers who are certain they know what they don't like read Aristotle's *Rhetoric*, for instance? Have they taken the first steps in understanding the other half of our intellectual culture, for example, by looking at Cicero, Quintilian, Augustine, or the modern masters such as Burke, McKeon, or Perelman?[5]

The rhetorical tradition, the philosophers should realize, is the main alternative to the philosophical one, and encompasses it. The academic study of rhetoric has been in disfavor since the seventeenth century, but survives unnamed in departments of literature, communications, and law. Our lives depend on rhetoric – how arguments are made, good and bad, and how to distinguish them. A philosopher will offer the ignorant reply, "But that's the job of logic." He has not heard that logic is a subset of rhetoric and he does not realize that human argument, even in philosophy, must be wider than one formalization of logic. It is most distressing to see people sneering at something they seem to know so little about. We professors are not supposed to act that way.

Professor Hoppe's tone in the piece is of more than local interest. The hackers say that they "flame" when attacking someone else's item on a computer bulletin board with foul temper and foul language. Hoppe has flamed on my book. I object to the flaming, not for myself (if you can't stand the flame, get out of the kitchen) but on behalf of our traditions of civility. Hoppe wears proudly the badge of "extreme" rationalist – the position, worthy of respect if in the end hard to use for life, that such important matters as economic science are to be based on the *a priori*. But the churlish form he has given to it suggests that a better description would be "splenetic" realism.

Aren't we all tired of such yelling and sneering in academic prose? And wouldn't we all prefer even the sanitized formulas of official scientific writing to productions like Hoppe's? His piece is strewn with hysterical overstatements, the academic equivalent of yelling in the face of one's opponent. A mild instance among many: "McCloskey's first round against empiricism then is a complete failure" – he wrote these intemperate words a few pages after conceding that even in his strange reading of the book "McCloskey's first criticism is well-targeted." Would Hoppe advocate talking like this to his wife? To his colleagues? To a mass rally?

Yelling and sneering, sadly, is characteristic of modern philosophy. It comes from ignorance of rhetoric. If I were a philosopher I would be worried that my field finds it impossible to remark on other traditions or even other philosophers without descent into abuse of rhetoric. The philosopher Stanley Rosen begins his book *The Limits of Analysis* by noting of the dominant, analytic school that it evinces "a general failure to understand the rhetorical nature of its own justification… [T]he typical practitioner of analytic philosophy…[succumbs] to the temptation of confusing irony for a refutation of opposing views."[6] That seems to be right. The philosopher Clark Glymour begins his book on *Theory and Evidence* with the following *jeu d'esprit*, a model for open-minded inquiry: "If it is true that there are but two kinds of people in the world – the logical positivists and the god-damned English professors – then I suppose I am a logical positivist."[7] Similarly, another eminent American analytic philosopher said proudly to me that he had never read a page of Hegel and furthermore (he added with a smile) proposed never to do so. Young philosophers are amused by such behavior on the part of their elders, which testifies to its emotional function: erecting barriers and defining the barbarians, to whom we philosophers need not pay serious attention.

The sneer has spoiled academic life, which could if it wished exhibit the morality of conversation at its best. Professors use the sneer and get away with it, perhaps because in lecturing to sophomores they do not have to hold themselves to high intellectual standards; or because more and more these days the professors feel no need to speak to the department next door. The mathematician sneers at the political scientist, the physicist sneers at the chemist, the economist sneers at the sociologist, and the philosopher sneers at everybody.

The sneering and yelling is often defended as fair in war. The battle of the books has always been a scholarly amusement, though always and properly seen as ridiculous by outsiders. From the first page of his piece Hoppe reveals the intellectual world in which he lives, a world in which academic discussion is a matter of "attack," "gaining ground," and being "ready to invade," divided into "soft" and "hard." Such a world is needlessly mean-spirited and ugly. But worse it is a world in which it is hard to get anywhere.

Hoppe's is a European, even Central European, world of discourse. I am disoriented by the irrational violence of his sneering and posing and ranting and viewing with alarm. Even some familiarity with British academic life does not prepare me. Welcome, I suppose to the *Review of Austrian Economics*. May I suggest to the *Review* Austrians, as a mildly sympathetic outsider, that they really must do something about their tone?

Hoppe delights for instance in tarring people with Nazism. Indeed he actually *does* go "so far as to smear everyone committed to [any other position] as a dangerous, potential dictator – revealingly, without ever going to the trouble of explaining what the ethical or methodological principles *are* whose *a priori* grounding allegedly implies such a threat" (p. 207). Why hasn't it occurred to European intellectuals who use this and similar rhetorical devices that their intemperate speech is overheard, and used to justify literal thuggery? How many real nihilists have been inspired by professor-talk about West Germany being "fascist" and capitalism being "exploitative?" The danger from the left and right is Hoppe's poisoned world of discourse, not the tolerant pragmatism or the cultivated hermeneutics or the reasonable rhetoric at which he flails.[8]

One source of Hoppe's fury against me in particular seems to be that I do not know German and have not read his works.[9] Therefore, instead of complaining about what is in the book (most of which has nothing to do with philosophy) the piece complains repeatedly about the German-language philosophy neglected in the book. I am ashamed that I do not know German, and will undertake to learn it as soon as the great pressure of other ignorances allows. Perhaps Hoppe will take a similar vow concerning Italian, Greek, and the rhetorical tradition.[10]

The other source of Hoppe's fury is the suspicion that I and people like me do not believe in synthetic *a priori*. Even paranoids have real enemies, of course, and the abusive way in which some of the less polite Austrians defend *a priorism* does in fact produce quite a few enemies. Portraying McCloskey as an enemy of Austrian economics, however, is at best peculiar. I am a supporter of many Austrian positions, on prediction, for example;[11] the revaluation of introspection in the book could be construed as sympathetic with some Austrian positions on method; I agree with the anti-statism of many Austrians. I am in short an ally. That I might possibly have unsound views on synthetically *a priori*, one might think, would be a venial sin, a worry to the editors of the *Review of Austrian Economics* but not perhaps as serious to other Austrians as Hoppe makes it out to be.

But no: Hoppe, in the style of fanatics left or right, cannot bear the slightest deviation from his line. When I make a Misesian argument about prediction, and then – unlike the rational expecters and random walkers employing the argument – actually do mention the great man, does Hoppe welcome me as a comrade in arms? Not on your life. He quotes at length the very passage I advert to, as though he, not I, had first made use of it. He then proceeds to rant about my deviationism. His chief anger is reserved for those closest to his position (Hayek among them, at whom he also sneers).[12]

For instance, when I have bad words for bad empirical work in economics Hoppe is temporarily mollified, because he misunderstands my words as philosophical objections. He thinks I would agree that "Empiricism [by which he appears often to mean empirical work, not merely the narrowing doctrine of empiricism, of which we both disapprove] is a methodology suited to the intellectually poor" (p. 188). "Austrian" arguments like this give Austrian economics a bad name. Surely it is unreasonable to dump Kepler, Darwin, and numberless historians into the category of "intellectually poor." Philosophy commonly has such bizarre effects. By crippling our capacity to examine all the reasons it makes us less reasonable.

Hoppe's one mention of the book beyond Chapter 1 is a refutation of my views on why economists believe the law of demand. Again his argument consists of stating my position and then asserting the contrary, leaving argument to another occasion. He presumably would not deny the empirical fact that economists are persuaded that the law of demand is true (small t) by econometrics and introspection. His objection appears to be that their persuasion is not "founded." The word "founded" has special force in Hoppe's world. It means something like "providing a justification according to epistemological criteria." What are epistemological criteria? Those arguments of which Hoppe approves. One begins to wonder if Hoppe has forgotten what an argument is. Perhaps he has lived too long among students and colleagues who agree with him, and has forgotten that arguments are supposed to persuade doubters, not merely to embolden the faithful in the pursuit of heretics.

There is something in the make-up of what Eric Hoffer called true believers that impels them to attack their natural allies. Thank the Lord. If the true believers cultivated allies with anything approaching social competence the register of crimes, follies, and misfortunes of mankind would be still more crowded with their names.

I wrote the book because, yes, I am tired of academic discourse such as Hoppe's, and want to bring that sort of "conversation" to an end. I would expect the many reasonable people among Austrian economists to agree. The philosophical point of the book – recall that the philosophy is mainly confined to Chapter 1 and a few later scraps…is that the Valley Girl madness of anything goes is in fact a consequence of ignoring rhetoric, not of recognizing it. Sadly, anything does go in an argument that refuses to recognize and control its rhetoric. If one refuses to recognize that human argumentation is rich and complex the arguing does not merely disappear. It goes underground, to emerge as sneers and yelling and intolerance. The most unrestrained and irrational rhetoric, I am saying, comes from those most hostile to the idea of rhetoric.

NOTES

I would like to thank Don Lavoie, Harold Leiendecker, and Matt Kibbe for helpful comments on earlier drafts.

1. See my "Sartorial Epistemology in Tatters: A Reply to Martin Hollis," *Economics and Philosophy*, 1, April (1985) 134–7.
2. Do philosophers realize how much they sound like parodies of sadomasochists when they talk about "discipline" and "permissiveness"? John Cleese as The Philosopher.
3. Incidentally, the sentence quoted is a case of Hoppe's method of argument, down to the punctuation. When Hoppe used a "?!" in his manuscript he was signaling his unwillingness to argue; he was pounding the table; he likes pounding tables.
4. See Don Lavoie (ed.) (1990), *Hermeneutics and Economics*, New York: Routledge.
5. See John Nelson, Allan Megill, and D.N. McCloskey (eds.), *The Rhetoric of the Human Sciences*, Madison: University of Wisconsin Press (1987).
6. New York: Basic Books (1980) p. xiii.

7. Princeton: Princeton University Press (1980) p. ix.
8. I must defend Bruce Caldwell and his version of tolerant pluralism, mugged in Hoppe's footnote 10. Hoppe's idea of an argument, I have noted, is to put exclamation points after his sentences! This is characteristic of modern philosophy, especially in its central European mode! Hoppe's conception of "founding" an ideology is surprisingly narrow! In a paragraph that makes wild comparisons between Mussolini and modern pluralists he nonetheless does not see that the main argument for the pluralism he so despises is moral and political! But perhaps the oversight is unsurprising in one so comfortable with methodological authoritarianism!
9. Hoppe goes so far as to correct my use of "Doktor Herr Professor." "The Correct nomenclature," he barks, "is 'Herr Professor Doktor'" (p. 209).
10. And economic history. He makes an argument heard frequently that I hope is not typical of the grasp of economic history *chez* Rothbard: that "hand in hand with [the] development [of natural sciences] went a steady, universally recognized process of technological advancement and improvement" (p. 24). Such an argument for science is vulgar; and it has supported the excesses of Big Science. But mainly it is historically mistaken. I realize that everyone who is not a historian of the matter thinks it is true, this correlation between scientific and technological advance. We all get it in the newspapers. But few historians of science or of technology or of the economy believe it. Modern economic growth had been going on for a century or longer before science had any but a tiny effect on technology. The earliest date of a significant effect for science would be 1900, on a generous reckoning. A more rigorous dating would be the 1940s, with an antibiotic that for the first time made medicine good for patients rather than bad, a practical use of airplanes (*viz*., bombing), the universalization of radio, and so forth.
11. Incidentally, Hoppe's elevation of the issue of prediction to a major role in the argument is out of proportion to its place in the book. The disproportion shows how closely he adheres to the usual philosophical questions and how little he had read beyond Chapter 1. Alexander Rosenberg, another philosopher, makes a similar mistake, and no economist reviewing the book has, which suggests to me that it is the importance of prediction and control in the received philosophy of science that is causing the misreading. See "Two Replies and a Dialogue: Rosenberg, Rappaport, and Maki," *Economics and Philosophy* 4 (1988): 150–66. I have elaborated a few thoughts on the matter of prediction in "The Limits of Criticism: If You're So Smart Why Ain't You Rich?" *The American Scholar* 57 (Summer, 1988): 393–406. But it is not important in *The Rhetoric of Economics*.
12. Hoppe condemns Hayek for his "deviations" from what was originally a "much more Misesian methodological position" (pp. 208–9).

19. Hermeneutical integrity: a guide for the perplexed

G.B. Madison

As *Maclean's* magazine remarked in its coverage of the 1987 annual meeting of the Learned Societies of Canada, "hermeneutics" is a "buzz phrase currently fashionable – and controversial – in intellectual circles."[1] That there is currently much talk about hermeneutics is certainly not to be denied. From its home base in philosophy it has crossed interdisciplinary boundaries and is now a common subject of at least occasional concern in all the human disciplines, even economics. Like many "new" developments it has provoked perplexity as to what it is all about. It has also provoked opposition, some of it extremely strident (often by people who have only the vaguest knowledge of it). In the hope that it will simply fold up and go away, a number of its opponents seeks to portray it as nothing more than the latest of "nonrational intellectual fads" to invade the intellectual scene.

It is ironic that hermeneutics, which embodies a general theory of human understanding, should be utterly misunderstood by many. It is certainly misunderstood when it is portrayed as a passing fad. Hermeneutics is anything but new. What currently goes under the heading of "philosophical hermeneutics" (represented most notably by Hans-Georg Gadamer and Paul Ricoeur) has roots reaching deep into our intellectual tradition.[2] Hermeneutics is not just another new *school* of thought. It would more properly be characterized as a general movement, one which, while resting on a long tradition, is yet internally diverse and in the process of continual development. Unlike some doctrinaire schools of philosophical or economic thought, hermeneutics does not seek to preserve inviolate the received wisdom of patron saints and to maintain a strict orthodoxy in regard to their teachings. Nor has hermeneutics ever sought to institutionalize itself by adopting all trappings of a formal establishment. As a general movement of thought, hermeneutics draws together some of the most innovative thought-currents of our times, not the least of which is the hermeneutical approach to the philosophy of science instigated by Thomas Kuhn. This is no doubt why many present-day readers, including Kuhn himself, have the impression, upon reading thinkers like

Gadamer or Ricoeur, of (to borrow a phrase from Maurice Merleau-Ponty) "not so much of encountering a new philosophy as of recognizing what they had been waiting for."

Access to basic hermeneutical theory is, nevertheless, not always easy. The major reason for this is that while people may find in hermeneutics what they had been waiting for once they have breached the barrier of understanding, the requirement for breaching this barrier is to overcome a number of culturally inherited (and extremely tenacious) epistemological and ontological prejudices, the artificiality and groundlessness of which – and thus the reason for abandoning – become fully apparent only once they have been seen through with the aid of hermeneutics. In this piece I shall attempt to make hermeneutics a bit less perplexing and a bit more accessible by deconstructing some egregious misunderstandings that surround it. Some of these misunderstandings are, so to speak, honest ones, stemming from the aforementioned difficulty. Others are, quite frankly, dishonest ones, obstacles deliberately thrown in the path of the uninitiated by opponents of hermeneutics who have every interest in slowing its progress. Let us then zero in on some of the more widespread misunderstandings of hermeneutics. In attempting to understand something new, it is always very useful to understand what that thing is *not.*

HERMENEUTICS AND REASON

Hermeneutics is not a form of irrationalism and does not entail a rejection of reason. Misunderstandings in this regard may be due to this philosophy's thoroughgoing critique of all forms of *rationalism.* By the latter term I mean the position that has dominated philosophy since the time of Plato, which holds that human beings are endowed with a special kind of faculty called reason by means of which they can intuit or otherwise discover absolutely indubitable, eternally valid, objective truths. Hermeneutics strenuously objects to such a belief (which, in any event, cannot *itself* be demonstrated), since it believes that claims to have access to unimpeachable truths – by means of reason, revelation, or mystical insight – are incompatible with the maintenance of a free and democratic society. Since hermeneutics views the conception of reason upheld by rationalists as a perverse and dangerous distortion of authentic reason, it is fully understandable that rationalists should retaliate by accusing hermeneuticists of advocating irrationalism. But (and this is crucial) to reject rationalism is not *necessarily* to reject reason – an elementary point in logic that the anti-hermeneuticists generally overlook.

On what it means to be rational, hermeneutics has in fact a great deal to say. We shall have occasion in what follows to see a little of what is involved here. For the moment let us simply note that hermeneutics holds to a fallibilist and pluralist view of reason: fallibilist in that it believes that no truth-claim can ever be immune from criticism such that there would no longer be any need to carry on the "conversation of mankind"; and pluralist in that it believes that there can be no single, privileged "rational method" for deciding upon what is "true."

In regard to pluralism, the criticism hermeneutics makes of rationalism ties in with its criticism of what Hayek so aptly referred to as "scientism" or the "scientistic prejudice": the "slavish imitation" on the part of the human sciences of the concepts, methods, and goals of the physical sciences – the human sciences' attempt to mimic the objectivity thought to characterize the natural sciences.[3] The belief that one is rational only when one adheres to the scientific method as positivists understand it is what Hayek, like the hermeneuticists, calls an "abuse of reason." In its defense of a nondogmatic, pluralist conception of reason, hermeneutics entails a critique of scientific reason (what Gadamer would term "method"). The purpose of this critique is not to do away with method altogether so as to open wide the door to all manner of subjective whim and fancy. There is no attempt here to substitute empathetic intuition for acts of rational cognition, as some uninformed critics of hermeneutics maintain. Its purpose is, rather, to combat methodological imperialism ("unified science") and to safeguard that form of rationality specific to the human sciences. The longstanding debate over the relation between the natural sciences and the social sciences, between "explanation" and "understanding," and the rejection of the positivist Natural Science Ideal (as Lewis White Beck called it) has been one of the central issues in hermeneutics. Austrian economists, who have long insisted upon the irreducibility of the human to the natural, of economics to a kind of physics – the attempt, as Mises put it, "to study the behavior of human beings according to the methods Newtonian physics resorts to in the study of mass and motion"[4] – will find in the hermeneutical critique of rationalist "objectivism" a natural ally.

Related to this issue, and of direct relevance to economics, is the question of what it means to speak of "rational man." The object of economic science is the rational behavior of human agents in the realm of the economic. If, as hermeneutics maintains, reason cannot be reduced to calculative, instrumental, efficiency-oriented rationality, or what Israel Kirzner calls Robbinsian optimizing, it follows that the human agent which is the proper object of economics is not reducible to *homo economicus*. By that I do not mean a creature whose sole motivating force is supposed to be economic gain or greed, which is one of the meanings commonly attached to the term. The sense I intend is a quite different one, having to do not with passion or interest but rather with reason itself. I am referring to a particular conception of rational man, very widespread in contemporary economic theory, according to which rationality is interpreted solely in terms of the logico-mathematical disciplines of decision theory and game theory. According to this form of rationalist reductionism, reason, whether it operates in the service of economic or other interests, is essentially nothing more than a utilitarian calculus of optimal maximization, mere means-end rationality. Kirzner[5] has rightly criticized this way of viewing economic activity, since it renders something as integral to the understanding of a free enterprise economy as entrepreneurship absolutely impossible to understand. As far as the issue of rationality is concerned, it is apparent that there is a natural affinity between philosophical hermeneutics and Austrian economics.[6]

HERMENEUTICS AND RELATIVISM

Hermeneutics does not entail relativism. The belief that it does is perhaps the most widespread of all misunderstandings. There is something of a parallel here with the notion that hermeneutics is a form of irrationalism. In both cases, when hermeneutics rejects one thing, its critics (who seem to be locked into a restrictive either/or mentality) accuse it of embracing the opposite. Since hermeneutics rejects rationalism it must *ipso facto* advocate irrationalism. Similarly, since hermeneutics is opposed to all forms of metaphysical and epistemological *absolutism* it must endorse relativism, or so its critics say. I admit, though, that the critics' mystifying endeavors are facilitated by certain writers speaking in the name of hermeneutics. I am thinking in particular of Richard Rorty, whose *Philosophy and the Mirror of Nature* did much to further discussion of hermeneutics in Anglo-Saxon circles. While hermeneuticists working out of the phenomenological tradition have welcomed Rorty's critique of foundationalism (i.e., absolutism) and his deconstructive attack on epistemology, since it fits in very well with their longstanding critique of philosophical modernity, they are not at all prepared to embrace what they perceive to be Rorty's relativism. Reason's claim to universality is something that thinkers like Gadamer and Ricoeur are not in the least prepared to relinquish. For this they themselves have come under heavy attack from other anti-objectivist schools of philosophy such as deconstructionism of Jacques Derrida, whom – irony of ironies! – some lampooners of hermeneutics would enroll in the hermeneutical camp, all the better to give the impression that hermeneutics is complete nonsense.

Since the hermeneutical position on the relativism issue is neither a simple nor a simplistic one, it can easily be the source of honest difficulties for those seeking to understand it. The difficulty is in a sense intrinsic to the hermeneutical position itself. For unlike the absolutist, who has nothing else to do than to wage a constant, single-minded battle against all who contest the existence of his timeless verities, the hermeneuticist is constrained to do battle on two fronts at once. He or she must contest those who claim that they have discovered the Truth (the absolutists or dogmatists) as well as those who deny the existence of truth altogether (the relativists), while at the same time defending what might be called the *pursuit* of truth, i.e., an understanding of things that is animated by a drive for universality, a universality which must nevertheless remain always only presumptive. "We are born to seek after truth," Montaigne wrote; "to possess it belongs to a higher power."

If we consider for a moment what for hermeneutics functions as a paradigmatic case of interpretive understanding, namely, the understanding of texts, it should be easy to see that hermeneutics does not furnish a license for "anything goes" relativism. The basic hermeneutical principle in this regard can be stated quite succinctly. While it is impossible ever to claim legitimately to have discovered *the* correct meaning of a text (the corollary to this is that a text does not have a definitive meaning), nonetheless, at any given moment, it can legitimately be maintained that some interpretations are decidedly better than others. In interpretation, truth is never an all-or-nothing affair, nor is it a matter of *approximating* to some absolute criterion. Truth has nothing to do with *corresponding* to some objective fixed reference, such as authorial intention. (A claim to objective adequation is just that, a claim, which is always open to dispute.) Truth is, rather, a matter of the persuasiveness of an interpretation that can appeal to certain commonly or communally accepted criteria as to what counts as a rational argument, as for instance those are defined by a community of working scientists or, in general, by a certain speech community.[7] There are no free-floating, timeless standards of rationality divorced from the discursive practices of a historical community of men, but this does not mean that choice between textual interpretations (or scientific theories) is purely arbitrary and subjective. Generalizing, we could say that while an apodictic Science of reality (the Truth) is an impossibility, at least as far as finite human beings are concerned, some statements or interpretations of the world are, at any given time, better, more rational (more arguable) and thus "truer" than others. Hermeneutics may consider absolute truth to be a nonsensical ideal, but it most certainly does not license an all-pervasive intellectual permissiveness, as immoderate critics would have us believe.

From what has just been said, it should be apparent that hermeneutics also does not deny the existence of common grounds; it does not plunge us into an abysmal nihilism. Yet this is precisely what some critics assert, without the slightest of textual grounds to go on. For hermeneutics, dialogue is not mere talk, mere entertaining, cocktail chitchat. For hermeneutics conversation is not an aimless *passe-temps*; it has a goal (although not in a metaphysical teleological sense, i.e., one which could ever be definitively reached, once and for all). This goal is understanding, self-understanding, and mutual understanding or agreement. The purpose of dialogue in either the ordinary conversational sense or in the forms it assumes in various specialized disciplines – the object of the pursuit of truth, in other words – is to arrive at a common agreement on a certain issue. The important thing to note, since it definitively sets to rest the charge of groundlessness, is that the search for common agreements itself presupposes the existence of prior agreements or common understandings. In the absence of some common, antecedent, "grounding" standards one could never reach new meaningful, intelligible agreements; in that case the conversation could not even (if I may be permitted the expression) get off the ground. Progress in understanding, in science, for instance, would be impossible. Accordingly, when people with different backgrounds find themselves engaged in a dialogical encounter, they will, if motivated by good will and the desire to reach an agreement, attempt to discover the grounds they do share (*loci commune*) and on whose basis a consensus can be built.

One is perfectly at liberty to call such common grounds or shared standards "objective" if one so chooses. The epithet would be especially appropriate if the grounds in question were common to an entire discipline or, even more, an entire cultural tradition. Yet only dogmatic rashness could justify one in thinking that a common ground of whatever kind could ever be some sort of metaphysical, extratemporal, superlunary Archimedian point, which seems to be what dogmatists have in mind when they speak in hushed reverence of "objectivity" or the "objective world" (sometimes also referred to as the "external world"). It is really difficult to know what some critics have in mind when they appeal to absolute ("objective," in their sense) grounds. An absolute ground would have to be a ground which does not itself have a ground, a groundless ground, which sounds like a meaningless notion, "mere talk," as they themselves might say, or, to use Hegel's words, "the night in which all cows are black." When hermeneuticists say that all understanding occurs within (and is, in this precise sense, dependent on) a context, they are not saying as relativists do that we are imprisoned in closed, incommensurate universes of discourse; they are simply saying that in our ongoing search for ever greater understanding we are not supported in this endeavor by *nothing*. A groundless ground, an *Urgrund*, is the same thing as an *Abgrund*, an abyss.

The more desperate critics of hermeneutics are victims of what Richard Bernstein has diagnosed as "Cartesian anxiety."[8] This is the fear some people are inordinately prone to that if somewhere or other there is not some absolute foundation on which to anchor human endeavors, then everything becomes subjective, idosyncratic, and relativist; truth no longer exists, everything becomes relative and meaningless. It must be admitted that this is a fear human beings are naturally prone to (which, accordingly, it is one of the principal goals of absolutist rhetoric to excite), but it is a fear which is quite groundless, actually. In spite of all the efforts that have been expended to date by metaphysicians and epistemologists, not to speak of religious cult leaders and mystics of all sorts, we have yet to discover any metaphysical or epistemological absolutes that can compel general agreement, *and yet* we as individuals and as communities do manage to pursue meaningful courses of action in the world and to arrive at meaningful understandings of things. We do find ourselves in the possession of certain truths. In the last analysis, hermeneutics, as a general discipline, is nothing other than the attempt to bring to reflexive awareness exactly what it is that has happened whenever we do so arrive at an understanding of things, the world, our products, ourselves – when, in other words, we find ourselves "in the truth."

WHAT RELEVANCE FOR ECONOMICS?

Hermeneutics is not an arcane philosophical doctrine irrelevant to the work of economists. The more vociferous critics of hermeneutics inform us that while hermeneutics may have some idle entertainment value as a mode of armchair philosophy, it has nothing whatsoever to say to practicing economists. As evidence they point out that neither Gadamer nor Ricoeur has written on economic issues. This argument is such as to perplex even a hermeneuticist, who is not a person to scorn the virtues of rational argumentation. If the issue is the relevance of hermeneutics to economics, then it is obviously quite *irrelevant* whether Gadamer or Ricoeur has or has not written on economic issues. In that case it is up to other people, economists in particular, to draw out the relevant implications. There is no reason why economists should not try their hand at this (as indeed they have!), since the practitioners of many other human sciences, from anthropology to sociology, have done the same for their own disciplines and have in the process revitalized them.

The critic will perhaps retaliate by saying that hermeneutics does not *mandate* a particular view of economic method. In so saying he would of course be right. In this respect hermeneutics contrasts sharply with logical positivism, Popperian theory, and other such theories of knowledge in that it does not seek to lay down from on high normative, prescriptive, methodological criteria that must be rigorously adhered to if the practitioners of a given discipline are to put forward legitimate claim to being "scientists." (Most working scientists ignore such criteria with no apparent detriment to the quality of their work.) What Gadamer sought to accomplish in his major work, *Truth and Method*, was something altogether different. His aim was "not to develop a procedure of understanding, but to clarify the conditions in which understanding takes place."[9] He sought to elaborate a general, descriptive (i.e., not prescriptive) theory of human understanding whose purpose was to elucidate all the various forms in which our understanding of the world manifests itself and which was concerned with "all human experience of the world and human living."[10] If hermeneutics does indeed provide us with a general theory of human understanding of universal scope, then it follows that it is at least in principle relevant to economics, since economics is not only *qua* social science a mode of understanding, but also has for its object the understanding that economic agents *themselves* have of what as economic agents they do. Like all the other human disciplines, economics is a discipline which is *doubly* interpretive.

It is above all Paul Ricoeur who over the years has sought to establish a dialogue between philosophical hermeneutics and those other interpretive, hermeneutical endeavors that constitute the human sciences. In his essay, "The Model of the Text: Meaningful Action Considered as a Text," Ricoeur sought to show the relevance of hermeneutics, taken in a narrow sense as the theory of textual interpretation, to the understanding of human *action,* the proper object of the various human sciences. Ricoeur's suggestions have been taken up by a great number of social scientists, for instance Clifford Geertz, from whose work in interpretive anthropology economists could no doubt borrow a page or two.

The relevance of hermeneutics to economics can be summed up in the following twofold way. In the first place, the general theory of human understanding embodied in hermeneutics has, so to speak, a "negative" overall value for economics *qua* discipline. Were economists to draw the appropriate lessons from the hermeneutical critique of objectivism – the natural science ideal – they would find themselves in possession of a means for overcoming the positivism still rampant in economics; economics would be *freed* to become what it ought to be if it is to be a genuinely *human science*. I refer to this as a "negative" contribution since freedom itself – the highest of all values, according to Gadamer – is in its authentic sense (as Hayek has convincingly shown), something negative, i.e., freedom *from* coercion, *in*dependence.

In the second place, while hermeneutics does not, as I have pointed out, mandate a method or set of methods for any discipline, it nonetheless does have something important to say on the issue of methodology. Aristotle long ago observed that every science should adapt its method to its object, that the object under study should determine the method of studying it. Gadamer's critique of the modern conception of universal, standardized "method" was precisely an attempt to remind us of this dictate of intellectual prudence. Now, if we hold that the proper object of economics is human *subjects,* is the *meaningful* behavior of human agents, it follows that we cannot get hold of our object in appropriate manner unless we have a means for incorporating into our scientific accounts the understanding that the agents themselves have of their own action, since this is, in the case of humans, constitutive of the meaning of the action itself. A purely "objective" approach can never do justice to the object of economics.

Hermeneuticists are not, of course, the only people to have elaborated a critique of scientistic objectives such as are found in the attempt to reduce economics to a kind of physics. However, they differ from many other critics of objectivism in a way that highlights a methodological point of direct relevance to economics. Hermeneuticists reject as untenable the modernist, Cartesian split between mind and body, as well as that between man and nature. Accordingly, they do not argue that the objective measuring techniques, model-building, and mathematical devices characteristic of the physical sciences have no place at all in the study of man – as if there existed an ontological chasm between the natural (understood as the realm of determinism) and the human (understood as the realm of freedom). As far as hermeneutics is concerned, there is no reason to outlaw objective techniques in the study of human action; they constitute one legitimate segment of what Ricoeur has called the "hermeneutical arc," the overall understanding process. Indeed, in the eyes of the hermeneuticist, inflexible opposition to the use of such techniques in economics (as in the social sciences generally) is not only methodologically inappropriate but, more seriously, tends to render opposition to objectivism irrelevant and ineffectual, since most people are not likely to renounce objective techniques altogether. That having been said, it is equally important to emphasize that from a hermeneutical point of view objective measuring techniques, statistical correlations, or econometric devices are of strictly limited usefulness and validity. To become fully intelligible (that is, to enable us to understand the *meaning* of human action), the results of such techniques must ultimately be incorporated into a wider approach which seeks not merely to "explain" (in the usual scientistic sense of the word) the phenomena but to "understand" them.

This is what traditionally has been referred to as the method of *Verstehen.* Economists need to work out means for making intelligible the actual life-world of real businessmen and other economic agents, for instance by undertaking detailed historical case studies. It was precisely a *general hermeneutics* that Frank H. Knight was calling for in the 1940s when he wrote (in an attack on T.W. Hutchison's positivism): "the need is for an interpretative study (*verstehende Wissenschaft*) which, however, would need to go far beyond any possible boundaries of economics and should include the humanities as well as the entire field of the social disciplines."[11] What we are witnessing in the 1980s, as a result of the increased attention accorded hermeneutics on the overall intellectual scene, is perhaps the beginning of a response by economists to Knight's call. Certainly, Austrians will find in hermeneutical theory a powerful conceptual tool for reinforcing positions they have long defended, perhaps influencing thereby the course of economic science in what Ludwig Lachmann has described as "a tempestuous season."[12]

CONCLUSION

It could be said that hermeneutics is basically a call for intellectual honesty or integrity. What this entails can best be appreciated if we return to the paradigmatic instance of textual interpretation. When we seek to understand an ancient text, say a text of Plato or Aristotle, honesty demands that we make an attempt to penetrate into the particular universe of discourse of the text and seek as much as possible to understand it on its own terms. We must avoid simply reading our own presuppositions, prejudices, and biases into the text. We need to *listen*. "The work," Gadamer says, "issues a challenge which expects to be met. It requires an answer..."[13] At the same time, however, hermeneutical integrity demands that we realize that all understanding involves what Gadamer calls "application" or "appropriation." That is, we must not pretend that in this attempt we can extricate ourselves from our own particular historical and cultural situation in such a way as to step, Manchausen-like, out of our own subjectivities and attain to a pure, unsullied objectivity. The meaning of the text itself is its meaning *for us* ("appropriation" means "to make one's own"). Our response to the text must be our "own, given actively," Gadamer says; "the participant belongs to the play." It would be fundamentally dishonest to pretend that one's own necessarily perspectival reading of the text is nothing less than the absolute truth itself. What objectivists forget is that, however much we must respect what Gadamer calls the "autonomy" of the text, it is nevertheless we ourselves, individual human subjects, who must make a decision as to the meaning of the text – and must assume the responsibility for defending it. This does not in any way authorize us to project onto the text our own fanciful interpretations.

As a final irony of hermeneutical misunderstanding, it is interesting to note that some of the more vituperative critics of hermeneutics, in rejecting it wholesale, discard in the process all claims to intellectual integrity. When, for instance, one critic seeks to portray the hermeneutical approach to texts as "wholly egocentric" and asserts that the hermeneuticist looks to texts of others in order only "to contemplate the reflection of his own more lovely features," one is inclined to ask that he first take the time to read what it is that hermeneutics in fact says – that he listen first and not so unabashedly read his own prejudices into the texts of others. It is unlikely that a call for honesty and openness (i.e., truthfulness) will be heeded by people like these, who have their own vested interests to defend and their own philosophical axes to grind. The misunderstandings of hermeneutics that will continue to result from this refusal of hermeneutical integrity on the part of some of its critics nonetheless have hermeneutical usefulness. In piercing through them we may be able to overcome some honest perplexities and understand a bit better what hermeneutics most definitely is *not*. That in itself would be a considerable plus.

NOTES

1. *Maclean's*, 15 June 1987, p. 42.
2. For the historical background of contemporary phenomenological hermeneutics see Richard E. Palmer (1969), *Hermeneutics*, Evanston, IL: Northwestern University Press. For a useful survey presentation of hermeneutics see the introduction to B. R. Wachterhauser (ed.) (1986), *Hermeneutics and Modern Philosophy*, Albany: State University of New York Press.
3. See F.A. Hayek (1979), *The Counter-Revolution of Science: Studies on the Abuse of Reason*, 2nd edn, Indianapolis: Liberty Press, p. 24.
4. Ludwig von Mises (1976), *Epistemological Problems of Economics*, New York: New York University Press, p. xiii.
5. See Israel Kirzner (1979), *Perception, Opportunity, and Profit*, Chicago: University of Chicago Press, pp. 108–9, 226 ff.
6. This affinity is also historical, as, for instance, the personal relationship between Mises and the phenomenologist Alfred Schutz testifies.
7. For a further treatment of these issues, see my essay, "Method in Interpretation," in Madison (1989), *The Hermeneutics of Postmodernity: Figures and Themes*, Bloomington, IN: Indiana University Press.
8. See Richard J. Bernstein (1983), *Beyond Objectivism and Relativism: Science, Hermeneutics, and Praxis*, Philadelphia: University of Pennsylvania Press.
9. Hans-Georg Gadamer (1975), *Truth and Method*, New York: Seabury Press, p. 263.
10. *Ibid.*, p. xviii.
11. Frank H. Knight (1956), *On the History and Methods of Economics*, Chicago: University of Chicago Press, p. 177.
12. One area of possible dialogue between hermeneutics and Austrian economics, as yet unexploited, would compare the hermeneutical attempt to disclose various universal structures of human understanding and Mises's attempt to set out the *a priori* of human action. Discussion on this subject could be extremely productive.
13. Hans-Georg Gadamer (1986), *The Relevance of the Beautiful and Other Essays*, Cambridge: Cambridge University Press, p. 26.

PART FIVE

Modern Political Economy and the Austrian School

20. Recent developments in social choice theory

Tyler Cowen

Although social choice theory was once almost exclusively associated with such problems as the Arrow Impossibility theorem, the field of social choice has considerably widened its scope in the last decade. The so-called "new welfare economics" that originated in the 1930s no longer comprises the cutting-edge of social choice theory.

A number of factors are behind the demise of the "new welfare economics." One influence has been the work of Sen, who has argued that this framework imposes an analytical straightjacket upon the analysis of interesting normative problems. Also important has been the influence of such philosophers as Nozick, Parfit, and Rawls, who have drawn the attention of economists to questions that lie outside the scope of older versions of Paretianism.

Among welfare theorists, Paretian analysis has been supplanted by a variety of approaches embodying distributional considerations, interpersonal utility comparisons, and the use of non-utility information. Other strands in current work have been characterized as "meta-welfare economics," as they attempt to analyze the strengths and weaknesses of different welfare standards themselves. While Paretian constructs are found often in these analyses, such constructs are used to organize one's thoughts or analysis. This is in contrast to Paretian theory as a monolithic normative standard.

The majority of economists who are not welfare specialists still restrict their attention to the "naive" version of Paretianism represented by the Kaldor–Hicks criterion. The volumes under examination in this review can be considered an excellent introduction to post-Paretian developments. Many of the essays examine the compatibility of Paretian theory with different ethical norms. In other cases, welfare economics is now being extended to areas which had previously been ignored or considered disreputable. This includes

Essay Review of *Foundations of Social Choice Theory*, edited by Jon Elster and Aanund Hylland (Cambridge University Press, 1986); *Social Choice and Welfare*, edited by Prasanta Pattanaik and Maurice Salles (New York: North-Holland, 1983); *Choice, Welfare and Measurement*, by Amartya Sen (MIT Press, 1982).

such issues as endogenous preferences, theories of rights or "agent-relative" constraints, and optimal population theory.

Despite these developments, many social choice theorists are intent of filling out every nook and cranny in the issues surrounding the construction of a social welfare function. Far too often, this process of exploration has been concerned with mathematical detail at the expense of substantive normative economics. A similar reservation is expressed in the Elster and Hylland introduction to their book – "Today social choice theory may be approaching the baroque stage. Breakthroughs are dwindling, while minor embellishments are accelerating. Formalism is gaining the upper hand, as in what Ragnar Frisch used to refer to as 'playometrics.'" With this point in mind, Elster and Hylland have produced a volume which addresses the foundational issues underlying social choice. An emphasis is placed upon rethinking problems rather than simply modifying existing models.

Sen's "impossibility of a Paretian liberal" result receives considerable attention in this volume. This result supposedly demonstrates the impossibility of a social welfare function that satisfies the properties of Pareto optimality, unrestricted domain, and liberalism. Since many individuals consider the latter two conditions desirable properties of normative orderings, this may imply significant restrictions upon the use of the Pareto principle. Even when social orderings escape the problems raised by Arrow, they may still violate liberal principles.

Dating from a 1970 article by Sen in the *Journal of Political Economy* ("The Impossibility of a Paretian Liberal," reprinted in the Sen volume), this literature often revolves around Sen's well-known example of reading D.H. Lawrence's *Lady Chatterly's Lover*. Sen postulated the existence of Prude and Lewd. Prude would like most of all that no one reads the book, but would rather have to read the book himself than contemplate the idea that Lewd is being exposed to such filth.

Lewd would like most of all that both read the book, but barring this possibility, he feels that a good dose of Lawrence would do Prude more good than it would do himself. This gives us the following preferences:

	Prude	Lewd
1.	No one reads the book	Both read the book
2.	Prude reads the book	Prude reads the book
3.	Lewd reads the book	Lewd reads the book
4.	Both read the book	No one reads the book

The outcome where Prude reads the book is clearly Pareto superior to the outcome where Lewd reads the book. Yet the liberal principle, or at least

Sen's interpretation of it, requires that only Lewd read the book, as each individual should be allowed to decide his own reading matter. Sen's statement of the liberal principle requires that each individual have freedom of choice in states of affairs that concern only himself, such as what he reads or what color he paints his ceiling.

There are many different attempts to resolve the Paretian liberal paradox (an essay in Sen's book provides a survey). The concepts of liberalism and Pareto optimality are either modified or discarded in these solutions. Brian Barry's excellent essay "Lady Chatterly's Lover and Doctor Fischer's Bomb Party: Liberalism, Pareto Optimality, and the Problem of Objectionable Preferences" in the Elster and Hylland volume is one of the best extant attempts to clarify the issues involved.

Barry argues that the paradox disappears once we allow the individuals to trade with each other. Under the above-specified set of preferences, Prude will offer to read the book if Lewd promises not to read the book and both optimality and the liberal criterion (or at least one version of it) will be satisfied. As Barry (p. 19) notes, "Liberalism is, indeed, a principle that picks out a protected sphere, but one that is protected against unwanted interference, not against use in trading with others ... surely we are more free to choose if we can trade a decision over something we have a right to control in return for control over a decision that we value more."

Of course, it is possible that transactions costs may prevent such a trade. When viewed in this light, Sen's paradox of the Paretian liberal collapses into the Coase theorem. In the presence of transactions costs, decentralization of economic decision-making is incompatible with Pareto optimality. This is not a startling result and has been known since the socialist calculation debate between Mises, Hayek, Lange and Lerner.

If, like some Chicago School economists, we define Pareto optimality relative to transactions costs, then we are always in the Pareto optimal state and Sen's paradox becomes trivial. The cost of this intellectual solution, however, may be quite high. The incompatibility between ethical norms and welfare economics is resolved by eliminating the possibility of normative economics.

The above reference to the socialist calculation debate may provide a more fruitful direction for generating further results from Sen's paradox. If transactions costs (i.e., problems of knowledge and information) are the source of conflicts between the liberal principle and optimality, then we ought to seek a constitution which, over time, will best allow citizens to deal with knowledge problems and reduce transactions costs. An important message of Sen's paradox is that such dynamic considerations involving knowledge may be more important than whether the constitution satisfies the static ranking criteria outlined by Arrow's Impossibility Theorem.

Sen does not accept the view that the "impossibility of a Paretian liberal" result can be reinterpreted in terms of the Coase theorem. His response to this argument can be found in his essay "Liberty as Control: An Appraisal," (*Midwest Studies in Philosophy*, 1982) and his set of comments at the end of the Elster and Hylland book. Sen argues against the conception of liberty as giving someone moral "control" to determine a particular state of affairs, as the control conception of liberty does not succeed in capturing many important aspects of what freedom means.

Sen is denying the above-cited view of Barry that "we are more free to choose if we can trade a decision over something." This kind of critique has been developed at length by political philosopher Michael Walzer in his *Spheres of Justice.* Walzer argues that societies have not (and should not have) given their members the right to trade away many rights. Few philosophers, for instance, would defend the right of an individual to sell himself into slavery. Other examples given by Walzer include selling the right to raise a child, selling body organs and selling the right to sue. If we look askance upon such trades, the Sen paradox reappears, as the "control" conception of liberty would be neglecting certain elements of the concept of freedom. For Sen, rights are not only a "protected sphere" against outside encroachment but also a protected sphere against certain types of self-chosen voluntary exchanges.

Similar considerations can be applied to the issue at hand. Sen argues that a Lewd–Prude trade would require the constable to stand over Prude's shoulder in order to ensure that he reads Lawrence with a sufficient amount of lasciviousness. Another possibility arises if the traders themselves have a preference against such exchanges; Lewd may feel that reading the book helps Prude only if he reads it of his own volition and with enthusiasm. "Reading the book with enthusiasm" is thus not a commodity that can be traded, as enthusiasm may exist only when one need not be paid to perform the action.

Although Barry defends liberalism on the *Lady Chatterly's Lover* issue, he questions liberalism through his own example of Dr Fischer's bomb party. Taken from a Graham Greene novel, Dr Fischer is a rich Swiss doctor who enjoys placing other human beings in humiliating situations. Dr Fischer decides to throw a Christmas party where each invitee is given a present whose contents consist of either a sizable monetary reward or a small bomb. This is done for the express purpose of placing party participants in a degrading situation. Dr Fischer enjoys degrading others so much that he dines upon caviar while his guests eat porridge.

Even though attendance at this party is voluntary and thus *ex ante* Pareto optimal, Barry feels that it is not consistent with true liberalism because it degrades other human beings. Perhaps the objectionable feature of this exchange is that one side of the exchange reaps virtually no consumer surplus, a feature of many types of exchange that Walzer (and perhaps Barry?) consider dehumanizing. Barry would probably not consider the party degrading if the attendees were only required to tell Dr Fischer that his house was very beautiful (a small concession).

In practice, determining the consumer surplus resulting from an exchange is an extremely difficult matter. Other standards for measuring "degrading" exchanges also experience difficulties with implementation. Furthermore, even if we can clearly define "degradation" within the context of voluntary exchange, not allowing individuals to equate wealth and degradation at the margin may also be a violation of human dignity. I therefore remain unconvinced of the practical importance of the examples of Barry and Sen. Their concerns, however, are far from nonsensical, a view that was my initial reaction upon reading this material.

A merit-goods approach to the Sen paradox and several related problems is directly developed by Robert Goodin's interesting essay "Laundering Preferences." Goodin argues for solving such problems by developing standards for which preferences should be allowed to count in social decision-making. This is not a plea for totalitarianism; Goodin points out that it may further individual sovereignty in many situations. An individual, for instance, may have a higher-order preference that some of his lower-order preferences be overridden, as in the case of many smokers. Such situations are obscured by traditional utility theory which reduces preferences to a single set of non-conflicting rankings. (This criticism has also been made by Thomas Schelling – see his *Choice and Consequence*, Harvard University Press, 1984.)

A theme running throughout this volume is a defense of traditional or "classic" political philosophy at the expense of social choice theory. Social choice theory is essentially a procedure for generating rankings of outcomes. Barry, Elster and John Roemer each argue that there is far more to political philosophy than such rankings. Barry sees the missing variable as individual rights. Viewing individual rights as a value implies that the endeavor to aggregate preferences may be misguided in principle. Although it might be possible to express our notion of a right in the language of social choice theory, Barry doubts that this would shed any light upon the important questions of political philosophy, a theme which has also been emphasized by Robert Sugden.

Elster ("The Market and the Forum: Three Varieties of Political Theory") argues that social choice theory does not capture the instrumental nature of politics. Building upon the work of John Stuart Mill and Jürgen Habermas, Elster claims that the goal of politics is not merely the ranking of outcomes but also the transformation and education of its participants. Like the ancient Greeks, Elster views participation in the political process as itself part of the good life because it elevates its participants, both intellectually and morally.

This view has certain similarities with the emphasis upon knowledge problems found in such economists as Richard Nelson and Sidney Winter. Viewing the problem of social choice in terms of rankings assumes that the relevant alternatives are already known and comprehended. Elster's theory of politics views the political arena as a discovery process, much as Hayek views the market as a discovery process. In addition, Elster views the discovery process itself as morally desirable.

Elster's work is always lucidly written and demonstrates a remarkable breadth and depth of scholarship, and this essay is no exception. Nonetheless, I would be inclined to turn Elster's conclusion on its head. The political process certainly transforms and educates, but in many different directions. To the extent that political participation is motivated by rent-seeking, the political process may be part of the "bad life." Economic science can demonstrate which constitutions encourage rent-seeking and which discourage it. The constitution that does the most to discourage rent-seeking will improve the moral climate of society, a theme that has been emphasized by James Buchanan. Elster's work thus needs to be supplemented with a public choice perspective.

Like Habermas, Elster may be visualizing a notion of "politics" and "political discussion" that differs radically from the status quo. Nonetheless, I am not convinced that it is possible for "politics" to morally elevate itself much beyond the current level of discourse in Washington. Current political discussions have obtained their often "sickly" character because of the incentives built into the political process and altering this incentive scheme would be quite difficult.

John Roemer ("A Historical Materialist Alternative") argues that welfare economics and social choice theory are defective because they cannot come to grips with the concept of exploitation. Roemer proposes the alternative criterion of self-actualization, but I do not find his taxonomy of exploitation a useful basis for analyzing this issue. Instead, I prefer the theories of self-management developed by Elster (*Ulysses and the Sirens*, Cambridge University Press, 1979) and Thomas Schelling (*Choice and Consequence*, 1984) as a starting point. These approaches could be used to analyze how different political constitutions generate different patterns of self-actualization through the mechanisms of (a) incentives and (b) the types of knowledge that are made available for utilization.

The final topic taken up in this volume is interpersonal utility comparisons. Due to the positivistic influence of the Chicago School and the "logic of choice" influence of Lionel Robbins and Ludwig von Mises, most economists view interpersonal utility comparisons with scorn. Yet belief in the meaningfulness of such comparisons has virtually become the orthodoxy in modern welfare theory. Both Allan Gibbard and Donald Davidson present strong arguments for this view in their essays in this book. (On this point the Sen volume offers a number of important contributions as well.)

Opponents of interpersonal comparisons often attack a caricature by visualizing a central planner hooking electrodes up to people's brains and choosing social policy by summing "utils." Others tend to dismiss the issue by invoking what I see as artificial distinctions between "science" and "non-science" or "normative" and "descriptive." The essays by Gibbard, Davidson and Sen are useful antidotes to such points of view. I see a strong case for the view that interpersonal comparisons are "descriptive" (I use the word with reservations) without involving actual measurement. Nearly all judgments of well-being involve such comparisons to some degree and such judgments should not be immediately dismissed as "non-scientific."

I do not believe that interpersonal comparisons of welfare are the best tool for normative analysis, although I think they are a possible tool. A section of my dissertation ("Essays in the Theory of Welfare Economics," Harvard University, 1987) is devoted to arguing against the use of such information for choosing an economic constitution. Nonetheless, the challenge offered by the "New New Welfare Economics" (as it is sometimes called) is a real one and cannot be readily dismissed. The above-mentioned essays provide an excellent introduction to this approach and deserve the attention of the skeptics.

The second volume under consideration, *Social Choice and Welfare*, edited by Prasanta Pattanaik and Maurice Salles (North-Holland, 1983) is more technical in nature. Many of the essays in this book represent the sort of "baroque" developments criticized by Elster and Hylland.

A number of essays in this book concern themselves with the Arrow Impossibility Theorem. This result can be interpreted on a purely ethical level. It shows that certain value judgments are logically inconsistent if we use them to rank alternatives. These value judgments are the Pareto condition, non-dictatorship, transitivity and the irrelevance of independent alternatives.

The Arrow Impossibility Theorem has never been lacking in commentors. Gordon Tullock, in his book *Towards a Mathematics of Politics* (University of Michigan Press, 1967), characterizes the theorem as "irrelevant." Paul Samuelson has argued that the theorem is false by constructing social welfare functions which satisfy the intra-profile but not the inter-profile condition (i.e., a SWF does not violate the Arrovian conditions for a given set of tastes, although it might violate the conditions under other sets of tastes.) Other strands in the literature have attempted to salvage the social welfare function by relaxing Arrow's original conditions. 'The reader is referred to the Sen volume for a masterful survey and critique of the literature on the Arrow Impossibility Theorem. The professional consensus regards the Arrow Impossibility Theorem as an insuperable obstacle to the aggregation of ordinal preferences.

For an interpretation of the Arrow Impossibility Theorem one must look to Sen's book, specifically his essay "Social Choice Theory: A Reexamination." Arrow's work demonstrates that it is impossible to aggregate preferences if we restrict our inputs to the utility information which can be derived from ordinal preferences. Considering other types of information, however, such as preference intensities or non-utility information (e.g., rights or equity considerations) may allow for a solution. Tor this reason Sen refers to Arrow's work as the General *Possibility* Theorem. Much recent work in social choice theory has been concerned with spinning out such possibility results – Kevin Roberts's articles in the 1980 *Review of Economic Studies* are a good introduction to a rapidly expanding research program.

Despite its "baroque" tendencies, there are a number of interesting essays in *Social Choice and Welfare*, and these essays make the book a valuable collection. Yew-Kwang Ng, the inveterate defender of classical utilitarianism, offers some interesting insights about social choice theory ("Some Broader Issues of Social Choice"). Ng draws a distinction between ordinal preferences and cardinally measurable welfare. Not only are conflicts possible between the two concepts, but Ng believes that normative priority ought to be given to the latter. This is the case not only with irrational preferences but also with interdependent preferences, which are treated differently by ordinal and cardinal theories.

Ng's discussion points out that all ordinal theories must implicitly take account of interpersonal comparisons if they include the strictly ordinal preferences of altruistic individuals (who make "personally valid" interpersonal comparisons on a regular basis). Failure to acknowledge this fact can result in contradictions, as individuals now have preferences as to how wealth is distributed across other individuals. So-called neutral lump-sum transfers may be unambiguously welfare-increasing or decreasing when this form of altruism is present.

The second half of Ng's paper consists of an interesting discussion of normative population theory and reproduces an exchange between Ng and John Harsanyi on whether the principle of average or total utility should be used to determine the optimal population.

In "Ex-post Optimality as a Dynamically Consistent Objective for Collective Choice Under Uncertainty," Peter Hammond of Stanford University offers an extension of his arguments for evaluating actions by their *ex post* results, rather than by their *ex ante* evaluation. The two standards may differ even when individuals perceive probabilities correctly. An *ex ante* standard, for instance, will include risk aversity, whereas an *ex post* standard will not. Economists tend to intuitively defend the inclusion of risk aversity in normative evaluations, but the case for this view has not been clearly made. The anxiety and planning uncertainty effects of assuming risk are quite different from von Neumann–Morgenstern risk aversity. Furthermore, no social risk is involved in many instances; the only issue is the distribution of the unfavorable outcomes. Why shouldn't we simply count the results of a policy in our evaluations, rather than *ex ante* evaluations? Invoking contractarianism begs the question, as Hammond's arguments are a case against a contractarian standard (which is *ex ante* by nature).

The difference between *ex ante* and *ex post* standards is relevant for the literature on optimal income distribution. Certain types of risk-taking (perhaps not buying catastrophic health insurance) may appear acceptable (i.e., utility-improving) *ex ante*, even though the resulting *ex post* distribution will not conform to certain standards of equity. Since markets operate on an *ex ante* standard, both for efficiency and distributional matters, Hammond is offering a significant critique of private sector decision-making.

This critique is another way of expressing some of the concerns of Sen, Barry, and Walzer. Even if an individual is willing to accept an exchange *ex ante*, the *ex post* consequences may be "socially unacceptable", requiring constraints on which exchanges should be allowed. Perhaps the best-known attempt to respond to this argument can be found in Robert Nozick's critique of "end-state" theories of justice in his *Anarchy, State, and Utopia*. If "justice" is defined strictly in terms of the process generating the outcomes, rather than in terms of the outcomes themselves, then Hammond's *ex post* standard should be discarded.

Another interesting article in this volume is Paul Grout's fascinating "Welfare Aspects of Naive and Sophisticated Decision-making." Much of the literature on self-management assumes that consistency of a single individual's plans is a virtue and that "sophisticated" (i.e. rational expectations) decision-making algorithms will welfare-dominate "naive" decision-making algorithms. Building upon the work of Kydland and Prescott (*Journal of Political Economy*, 1977), Grout demonstrates that "naive" decision rules may actually be welfare-superior where dynamic inconsistency is a problem. Non-rational expectations give the individual the ability to "fool himself" and this ability can prove quite useful in a number of self-management problems. The threat of dynamically inconsistent punishments (why punish oneself once the sin has been committed?), for instance, becomes more credible and this allows for better self-management. Grout's Essay is highly recommended for those interested in the literature on what Thomas Schelling has called "egonomics."

This essay has provided intermittent commentary on Amartya Sen's *Choice, Measurement and Welfare*, but a few additional words on this book are necessary. Sen's work spans the entire range of welfare economics and this book is one of the best places for an interested reader to start. It is also one of the best books for the welfare specialist to re-read several times. Although

Sen probably has more critics than allies, he is widely recognized as one of the great economic minds of our generation. The essays in this book are a collection of many of Sen's most important essays: essays that have revolutionized welfare economics in the last fifteen years.

The reader is referred to Sen's book for the specifics of his views but Sen's central conclusion focuses upon the poverty of a normative approach to decision-making, which he calls "welfarism." The philosophy of welfarism enables us to use only information about utilities in ranking outcomes. Welfarism is thus a broader version of utilitarianism, which specifically recommends the summation of these utilities. (Other forms of welfarism might still allow for such factors as the distribution of utilities.)

Sen's work in development economics, growth theory, the theory of income distribution and welfare economics is all part of a larger view of economics and its place in the social sciences. According to Sen, we must drop some of the "tight priors" or Lakatosian "hard-core" of economics if we wish to talk meaningfully about human welfare. Although this point is far from new, Sen is the first to make it across a wide range of issues in convincing and rigorous fashion. Even those who are not completely convinced by either Sen's critique or his suggested alternatives should find his attack on the traditional method of economics a stimulating challenge.

21. J.M. Buchanan and F.A. Hayek: the thought of two Nobel Laureates

Viktor Vanberg

Among all his predecessors, the one with whom the 1986 Nobel Laureate in Economic Science, James M. Buchanan, has most in common is, without doubt, Friedrich A. Hayek, the laureate of 1974. Buchanan's work, like Hayek's, keeps a critical distance from both the standard themes and the formalism of mainstream economics. It is informed by the same interest in broader social theoretical issues, in particular in the institutional foundations of social order, and it defies, like Hayek's work, the artificial disciplinary boundaries which have come to slice up the social sciences. Both Hayek and Buchanan have contributed eminently to the modern intellectual revival of classical liberalism and classical political economy, and they have done so in ways that in crucial respects complement each other.

Hayek's system of ideas centers around the notion of *spontaneous order*. This notion is as central to his explanatory social theory as it is to his normative philosophy of liberty. With regard to Buchanan's work much the same can be said for the notion of *voluntary agreement*. The difference between the two notions is a matter of emphasis rather than theoretical principles. They can be consistently combined and, in combination, they allow for a more powerful approach to the explanatory as well as the normative issues of social order than each one on its own.

Hayek has viewed much of his work as a systematic restatement and elaboration of an idea which had been stressed by the eighteenth century's founders of classical political economy, by David Hume, Adam Smith and other Scottish moral philosophers. It is the idea that many obviously beneficial aspects of social reality, like language, law, or "the wealth of nations," are not, as one might be inclined to assume, the result of somebody's purposeful making, but, rather, an unintended social outcome of individual actions which were carried out for much more narrow purposes. Stated in other terms, it is the idea that, what looks like *teleology*, can be systematically translated into *causality*, an idea which Darwin successfully applied to biology. In Hayek's view, to provide an "invisible-hand explanation" of social order, to show how social order can emerge as an unintended outcome of separate individual choices, is the most challenging task for social theory. And, as a consequence, his analytical interests have been concentrated on the principles of spontaneous social order. This is not to say that Hayek simply ignores the role of "non-spontaneous" forces. In fact, he has elaborated very carefully on the general theoretical distinction between the "two kinds of social order," the spontaneous order and the organized, deliberately created order. Yet the latter appears in his writings mainly as a negative foil against which the spontaneous order is contrasted, without being systematically analyzed in its own right. The Hayekian system is, in a sense, "one-sided." It provides a quite elaborate theory of spontaneous social order, but it leaves the principles of organized, collective action largely unexamined.

Buchanan's work is part of the same intellectual tradition as Hayek's. Buchanan, no less than Hayek, views his approach as restating and extending on the theoretical program of classical political economy. Yet, without ignoring the significance of the spontaneous order idea, his emphasis is somewhat different. What Buchanan stresses as the classical heritage is the general principle of explaining social phenomena as the outcome of individual actions, a principle that can be applied to all kinds of social settings and, thus, be the basis for a systematic comparative analysis of alternative institutional arrangements. Buchanan's specific interest is in systematically extending the individualistic paradigm that informs the spontaneous order theory into the realm of organized, collective action. In other words, his approach aims at bringing the study of the other "kind of order" under the same theoretical umbrella as the study of spontaneous social order. In Buchanan's view, the notion of *voluntary agreement* which, embodied in the notion of voluntary exchange, is central to our understanding of the spontaneous order of the market, can serve as a fruitful theoretical concept in our understanding of organized, collective action as well. It is a notion that focuses our attention on the issue of what promotes and what inhibits people's potential for realizing mutual gains from cooperation. Gains from cooperation can be realized through trade and exchange, and they can be realized through organized, collective action. And the notion of voluntary agreement can provide a useful theoretical benchmark for analyzing systems of organized action – whether clubs, firms, or states – no less than it does for the analysis of decentralized systems of exchange transactions.

Just as Buchanan's and Hayek's theoretical perspectives can be integrated into a coherent individualistic theory of the "two kinds of order," so can their normative conceptions be considered as supplementing each other. The difference between their views on the normative significance of the notion of individual liberty is, like the difference between their social theories, a matter of emphasis rather than of conflicting principles. As mentioned above, it is the spontaneous order notion which is as central to Hayek's normative as to his theoretical conception. His view on the normative significance of liberty is closely related to his arguments on the superior performance characteristics of the spontaneous order of the market which are attributed, in particular, to its capacity for utilizing dispersed knowledge and to the role of competition as a discovery process. The emphasis in his conception of liberty is on the beneficial consequences that can be expected to emerge if individuals are free to choose, provided there exists a framework of general rules which impose "appropriate" constraints. In this context, the spontaneous order notion carries its normative meaning on two levels, with regard to the process of social interaction within a given framework of rules and with regard to the process in which the rules themselves are generated. On both levels the above-mentioned arguments on the superior performance characteristics of spontaneous processes are central to Hayek's normative conception.

Hayek does not suppose that spontaneous processes necessarily produce "good" outcomes, neither for the within-rules nor for the rule-generating level. Nor does he suppose that outcomes of spontaneous processes are necessarily superior to the results of organized, collective action. Yet the thrust of his arguments is, without doubt, that spontaneous arrangements represent, as a rule, the superior "kind of order." What is, in the present context, more important, the other kind of order – i.e. the organized, collective variety – appears in Hayek's normative system mainly as a negative foil against which the spontaneous order is contrasted, but which is not examined in its own right – analogous to what has been said above about his positive system. Since the principal locus of individual liberty is seen in the spontaneous order context and outside of collective, organized arrangements, organizations – whether business firms or governments – remain essentially an alien element in Hayek's conception of a "good society." Of course, Hayek recognized the role of firms and he talks about "legitimate functions" of government, but his arguments on these issues do not appear to be systematically integrated with his normative spontaneous order conception.

Buchanan's view on the normative significance of the notion of individual liberty does not deny or diminish the validity and relevance of Hayek's arguments on the performance characteristics of the spontaneous order of the market or spontaneous processes in general. Though Buchanan emphasizes, more than Hayek does, that spontaneous processes may very well produce undesired outcomes, the greater optimism or pessimism of their respective views is not the essential issue. Where they differ is rather in the systematic role they assign to "individual liberty" as a normative criterion. As indicated above, Hayek's argument has an instrumental drift. His emphasis is on the beneficial outcomes that can be expected to emerge if individuals are free to choose. An order of liberty qualifies as a "good" order because of its positively valued working properties, a judgment that can be made from an outside observer's perspective. The emphasis in Buchanan's argument is characteristically different. It is not on the consequences that result if people are free to choose – though Buchanan is hardly in disagreement with Hayek's view on these matters. His emphasis is on the role of "free choice" as a normative criterion in and of itself. According to Buchanan, the subjective individualism of classical liberalism implies that people's free choice is the ultimate criterion against which the "goodness" of a social order is to be judged. There is no criterion for judging the "goodness" of social transactions or arrangements independently of the choices of the parties involved. If a "good" social transaction or arrangement is one which allows the parties involved to realize what they want, then the focus of normative judgment has to be on whether the respective transactions or arrangements reflect the parties' free choices, or, in other terms, whether they are based on voluntary agreement. The criterion of voluntary agreement generalizes the normative thrust of the concept of individual liberty, extending its application from in-period choices, i.e. choices within a defined set of rules, to constitutional choices, choices among different sets of constraints. It provides a criterion of evaluation that can be consistently applied across the two kinds of order, to its decentralized, spontaneous as well as to its organized, collective variety.

The relation between the contributions of J.M. Buchanan and F.A. Hayek to the modern traditions of classical political economy and classical liberalism has, in recent years, repeatedly been a subject of inquiry. My purpose in this somewhat sketchy essay has been to provide some suggestions for how the views of these two scholars may be fruitfully combined, their theoretical as well as their normative conceptions of social order. Sharing the same individualistic paradigm, but systematically extending it into somewhat different directions and applying it to somewhat different issues, Buchanan and Hayek have helped to shape an analytically powerful general conception of social order that offers new prospects for a theoretically integrated social science, a modern political economy.

22. Can democratic society reform itself? The limits of constructive change

Karen I. Vaughn

This paper argues that constitutional reform, reform of the basic rules of the game in a democratic society, is fully compatible with an evolutionary view of social change. It further argues that constitutional reform can only take place piecemeal and at the margins of governmental procedures if the reform has any hope of being beneficial. There is no trick to getting bad reforms. Indeed that seems to be the specialty of twentieth-century democracies. But if the aim is to institute political reforms that enable men to more effectively pursue their purposes in peace with their neighbors, then there are definite limits to the amount of reform that can successfully be accomplished in a modern, stable western democracy. In order to support this, however, it is first necessary to show that the idea of reform itself is an acceptable one to those of us imbued with the Hayekian spirit.

Buchanan and others have recently pointed out a possible inconsistency between Hayek's emphasis on the gradual evolution of spontaneous orders in society on the one hand, and his call for reforms of the legislature and of the money supply on the other.[1] Buchanan, who in his work over the last ten years or so, has consistently called for constitutional reform of the role of government in the economic order, has criticized those who might display a too faithful adherence to some possible implications of Hayek's evolutionary theory of social institutions. If one takes too seriously the argument that social institutions contain a spontaneously developed wisdom in their traditions, one might be led to a "council of despair,"[2] a feeling that any rationally conceived social change is necessarily "constructivist rationalism" leading inexorably to a worsening of whatever problem it was constructed to solve. Clearly, Hayek himself does not believe that, nor could anyone who expends breath or energy in trying to change people's minds about the nature of an ideal society. Yet neither Hayek, nor others that I know of in the broadly liberal tradition, has spent much time discussing how reform is possible, or, even more generally, how change takes place in social institutions. This is the question I will address here. More specifically, I will question (a) how does social and political change come about? (b) what are its limits? and (c) what are the chances that future social change can be in the direction of the "good society" as conceived by one who values freedom? We focus on reform in a democratic society, as Hayek points out, because democracy is the only political tradition so far in which there is a mechanism for peaceful change in government.[3] Obviously, political reform can be brought about by armed revolution, but our interest is in political reform that occurs through peaceful and willing acquiescence to change.

THE EVOLUTIONARY MODEL OF SOCIAL CHANGE

One of the persistent themes of Hayek's *Law, Legislation and Liberty* is that the rules of social behavior encompass more knowledge than can be possessed by any one participant in that society. These rules evolve gradually. They are never fully articulated by any one, nor are they in principle articulatable, yet they are understood and obeyed implicitly. Further, they serve purposes that are often unknown but important to the survival of the community. Hayek's explanation for this phenomenon is that these "rules of behavior" have evolved along with man and in a sense define what man is. Man and culture develop together, man did not evolve first and then create culture to suit his purposes. He is not a purely rational being who can exist or even think completely apart from his culture. He chooses his purposes within the context of his culture.[4]

Hayek's vision seems to be of a primitive time, an early pre-history of humanity in which language, social customs, religion, trade, money, sexual mores all evolved as adaptive responses to the exigencies of a difficult natural environment. In this early time, man fought an evolutionary battle with both other species and other cultures. Those institutions and mores which represented more successful behavioral strategies won out relative to others, and became dominant. The more successful strategies became embedded in tradition, and the original survival value of the behavior was lost to conscious knowledge, if it ever had been consciously recognized in the first place. In this way, tradition developed as the repository of unarticulated knowledge that contributed to successful culture.

Hayek uses this conjectural history to elucidate his concept of spontaneous order. Spontaneous order arises as the unintended consequences of human action. The individual actions themselves are directed at particular purposes, but the order that results serves no purpose designed by any one human mind. The ultimate "purpose," success of the culture, emerges solely through the agency of some sort of process of natural selection.[5]

While the evolutionary model of human development does seem to suggest a gradual building up and tearing down of traditions over long stretches of time, even gradual change has an ultimate source. Evolutionary models of spontaneous orders need to incorporate a means of change in order to be complete. The theory of biological evolution relies on mutation or genetic accident to explain species creation; theories of social evolution must have some comparable instrument of introducing novelty into the society. The possible agencies of change one can suggest for human society are divine intervention, genetic accident or human creation – either intentional or inadvertent. Of the three, the only acceptable source of change in society to a social scientist would seem to be human action. I emphasize this because the term "spontaneous" in spontaneous order can be misleading if not carefully defined. It conjures up visions of spontaneous combustion or spontaneous generation – things that seem to spring up without explanation. Yet even in Hayek's version of spontaneous order, the order is an unintended result of an intended action. Hayek focuses on the unintended result. I wish to focus on the intentionality. Humans, after all, have as part of their genetic make-up the ability to learn and to transmit ideas and ways of doing things. They also have the ability to imagine futures different from the past. It is this ability that accounts for innovation and discovery, and it is innovation and discovery that is the well-spring of social change.

HUMAN ACTION AS THE SOURCE OF CHANGE IN SOCIETY

Social change is a tension between human creativity and daring and human reluctance to disturb the known patterns of their lives. Man is part dreamer and part follower of rules. Hayek has emphasized the important implications of man the rule-follower, but he has surprisingly down-played the role of man the dreamer in bringing about the desirable social change. Consider for example Hayek's explanation of how common law (rules of just behavior) develops. Common law develops on a path conducive to spontaneous order because common law judges do not believe they are making law but discovering it. The underlying presumption of the judges is that what constitutes law exists independently of their ideas, and their task is to discover the implications of the law for any particular case they are called upon to decide.[6] Hayek points out that in the process of trying to render judgments in hard cases, the abstract concept of what the law is may well change, but this is an unintended consequence of a judicial process, that is, a process of applying abstract, incompletely articulated rules to particular concrete cases.[7] This kind of process can also explain the development of human conceptions of morality and ethical behavior. Where the "correct thing" is in dispute among men who share a basic commonality, the very notion of "correct" will undergo gradual change.

This gradualist version of the evolution of rules of behavior is an appealing one. It is consistent with how humans think and use language. Language is imprecise and words have shades of meaning, sometimes encompassing ambiguities and ambivalences that make language only an imperfect proxy for the thought underlying it. The very notion of searching for an abstract rule within the confines of language seems to guarantee a social process of dispute, compromise, resolution and gradual change of shared ideology. Yet even in this extreme gradualist explanation of social change, someone has to originate a new idea, a new interpretation or new vision. Man is a rule-follower once he understands the rules. It is man the dreamer who fashions the rules for himself and others to follow. The real question Hayek is asking in *Law, Legislation and Liberty*, and the real question in all "conservative" theories of social change, then, is how can man the dreamer channel his dreams into socially desirable ends?

To explicate the problem, I turn back to the biological theory of evolution once again. The biologists tell us that in any species, genetic mutations occur with surprising frequency, but most mutations are evolutionary dead-ends. They are either irrelevant to the organism, or harmful in some way. Organisms that suffer from serious mutations are usually physically defective and/or sterile and hence present no danger to their species from interbreeding with normal individuals. Where the mutation does get passed on, if it is of some benefit, it confers a competitive advantage on those individuals who inherit it, and they tend to dominate the species.

In human culture, innovations, the "mutations" of social change, are also more likely to be harmful to the society than beneficial. The introduction of social novelty is probably not as random in effect for society as a whole as genetic accident is for a biological organism since social novelty is introduced by a thinking, planning being. But even though individuals have rational minds, their ability to perceive the effects of deliberate innovation is limited by the competence of their models of social reality and by the irremedial uncertainty of a non-preordained future. In such a world, a conservative attitude toward social change can be a valuable survival technique for any group. This is especially true of primitive societies which have very little margin for error in their struggle so close to the edge of survival. Rule-following makes sense when the consequences of deviations can be disastrous for one's group. Yet without the ability to adapt to changing circumstances, and without the ability to introduce novelty where the novelty can improve the chances for survival, a particular culture can easily stagnate and eventually die out. Somehow, the prudential features of social conservatism must be combined with a certain amount of willingness to take risks on innovation for a society to remain viable. One technique available to social orders to test out innovation in a relatively low-cost manner is to somehow isolate the intellectual "mutant" until the worth of his suggested innovation is evaluated. If this can be done, a social order can increase the probability of embracing beneficial change while rejecting innovation that would prove disadvantageous to society.

One possible way a social order might isolate the innovation from contaminating the group until its worth is proven is to socially ostracize the innovator who refuses to follow some of the established rules. For relatively innocuous deviations, isolation can take the form of social disapproval, not being treated as a social equal, being shunned by one's neighbors. For more serious deviations, it can take the form of expulsion from the group. Expulsion is the ultimate group protection from a failed innovation, but it also insulates the group from any possible benefits from new ideas. If ostracism were the only means society had to protect itself against dangerous novelty, one would expect innovations to be incorporated into cultures at an excruciatingly slow pace.

We contrast the technique of social ostracism to another technique that has evolved to isolate the innovator – to internalize the costs and benefits of his activities: the technique of residual claimancy in a market economy based on private property. The entrepreneur is the residual claimant in a market economy and he is also the source of innovation in a market order. Schumpeter, interestingly, saw him as a "creative destroyer" who disrupts established patterns to introduce progress as he searches for personal gain.[8] Kirzner sees him as essentially an arbitrager alert to profitable opportunities others fail to perceive.[9] The crucial feature of the entrepreneur for our purposes here is as the earner of profit and loss. His personal financial stake in the outcome of his venture is what isolates the effects of his innovation until the worth is proven to society. If the entrepreneur makes an error, the consequences are limited to his own personal wealth loss (and perhaps some external effects within his immediate neighborhood). If his visions and judgments are correct, he profits personally from his actions and his success encourages others to imitate him thus disbursing his innovation throughout society. Because of the ability of the market order to isolate the entrepreneurial experiment until the test results are in, this kind of order can afford to assimilate change of a much larger magnitude and at a much faster rate than would be possible in a more communal environment. Perhaps this helps to explain the great economic progress of western civilization that takes place alongside a depressingly stagnant set of ideas about political and social relationships.

SPONTANEOUS ORDER AND CONSTRUCTIVE REFORM

I have tried to establish so far that in an evolutionary theory of society, change normally takes place only gradually and at the margins of accepted rules of behavior.[10] Errors are costly to the group, and unless a mechanism, such as a market order, arises to internalize the errors of innovators, gradual change is a valuable survival strategy (except obviously in the case of catastrophic environmental changes that must be adapted to rapidly). Further, I have argued that even in evolutionary theories of social orders such as Hayek's, the agent of social change is still some intentional human action. The order may evolve as an unintended consequence of that action, but to the extent that a change is intended, all change is constructivist in some sense.

The problem this paper addresses, however, is not the possibility of any kind of change in society, but a particular kind of change – reform. Reform does not fit easily into an evolutionary theory of society. Reform seems to imply a discrete jump of some kind, a conscious break with an established tradition. Even if the reform is intended to return to an earlier way of doing things, a return is still a conscious break with the present. The problem here is, can a general theory that stresses the unintended outcomes of individual human actions also encompass conscious reform? More specifically, does the fact that orders arise from the unintended results of human action limit or nullify the possibility of reform?

There are two problems buried in this question. The first is positive: Where human actions have unlooked-for consequences, can there ever genuinely be a constructed reform that achieves a desired end? The second is normative: Even if reform is possible, is it desirable or is it merely a destructive influence in a benign social process?

Hayek has justly denounced a particular kind of reform he calls "constructivist rationalism." Constructivist rationalism refers to the attempt to sweep away all or most existing institutions and to replace them with a new set that is the product of someone's model of how society *should* be. Society is mentally rebuilt from the ground up so to speak in an attempt to clear away the inefficiencies and immoralities inherent in the existing set of institutions. Looked at in this way, constructivist rationalism is simply a product of human intelligence (or hubris) and human longing for improvement. Rational constructivism would seem to be a temptation particularly of intellectuals who specialize in allowing their imaginations free reign to contemplate the "good life," but any human being could well become afflicted. Merely reflecting on the evils of present day society – any present day society – leads one inexorably to explain the evils and to design ways of correcting them.

This longing for a better way has manifested itself in a long history of utopian thought and utopian action. A large number of philosophical writings consist of this kind of rational constructivism from Plato's *Republic* and More's *Utopia* to Nozick's *Anarchy, State and Utopia*. And there have been throughout history many attempts by individuals to put their alternative visions into practice through voluntary means. Religious orders, religious sects that have formed quasi-governmental structures, attempts at communal living, are all examples of experiments in rational constructivism. As we implied earlier, these social experiments probably serve an important service in introducing and testing particular kinds of social deviations at minimum cost to the larger group. Because of the inherent conservative bias of human beings, only a few participate at any one time, and hence errors in construction are borne by members of the group. To follow our analogy above, the "mutation" is isolated until its worth is proven, and society gains in knowledge. As a practical matter, such experiments are usually dismal failures to the extent that they attempt to change too many customary institutions too radically, but where the changes are at the margins, the experiment may lead to discovery of a social improvement (or at the least, an equally acceptable way of doing things). Obviously, this kind of constructivism is simply an instance of the evolutionary model of society. When a utopian group attempts to force its vision on an unwilling population, however, a harmless social experiment can become a deadly virus infecting the social order.

Hayek's objection to constructivist rationalism is really an objection to the *forced* imposition of a comprehensive new set of social institutions that are designed of a piece by some social reformer. As an historical note, Hayek first became aware of the problem of rational constructivism during the economic calculation controversy of the 1920s. That controversy involved a group of "market socialists" who wanted to eliminate private ownership of the means of production and the market exchange private ownership implies, and to replace it with a form of central direction they believed would duplicate the successes of the market while correcting its failures. Hayek centered his criticisms of the socialist schemes around the problem of information in the market economy. On one level, he argued that the advantage of private property and markets rests with the fact that it allows people to take advantage of a specialization of knowledge that could not exist in a centrally planned economy. On a more abstract level, however, he also argued that no one mind could understand all the complex functions existing economic institutions served and hence no one mind could possibly design a system to take care of all the potential problems existing institutions evolved to solve.[12] While Hayek's arguments were not taken seriously at the time he wrote, events in soviet-type economies have certainly borne out Hayek's view of the importance of the division of knowledge to economic efficiency. Even more to the point, Communist China under Mao and more recently, Cambodia under Pol Pot have borne out Hayek's more general view of the knowledge limitations that doom rational constructions on a grand scale. Indeed, Cambodia is a tragic example of what any sane person should call "irrational destructivism," the forcible tearing away of all civilized customs and institutions to replace them with the nightmare visions of a demented mind.

The difference between a New Harmony[13] and a Pol Pot is, of course, one of voluntarism. An experiment like New Harmony, as we have shown, is part of a process of acquiring knowledge from voluntary attempts in alternative life-styles that do not threaten the overall fabric of society. Decentralization of experiments serves to limit the consequences of a failed vision. Pol Pot forces everyone into his mold of a "good life" and thereby threatens the entire society if his mold is defective. The unrestrained power of government is the power to turn constructivist dreams into the reality of oppression. But where government is seen as the guardian of independently existing rules of just conduct, the dangers from the Pol Pot kind of rational constructivism are minimal. This is the crux of Hayek's distinction between the rule of law and the rule of men. The rule of law serves to constrain the power of political leaders to enforce their will on an unwilling population. Constitutional democracy is a form of government that peacefully limits the degree to which any guardian of the rule of law can violate his trust.

GOVERNMENT VERSUS SPONTANEOUS ORDERS

In a sense, Hayek's objections to constructivist rationalism are not directly relevant to the problem of reform as conceived here. The question addressed is "Can Democratic Society Reform Itself?" The title should read, "Can Democratic Government Undergo Genuine Reform by its Citizens?" Is reform something that one group somehow imposes on the political process, or is reform something that emanates from within the process itself? Is government itself part of the grand spontaneous order that describes the evolution of human societies or is it an impediment to that order? In what sense, in simpler language, do people get the government they deserve?

One can agree that orders exist that obey no known purpose, that these orders evolved through no conscious design of any one mind or group of minds, and also believe that government itself is not primarily a spontaneous order. Government is then conceived of as being imposed upon spontaneous orders affecting the way in which orders evolve and function. This is largely the view Buchanan espouses. He sees government as the result of a social contract, an agreement men enter into to submit to a shared set of rules that set the framework within which voluntary orders can arise.[14] Hayek similarly sees government as the forum for articulating rules of just conduct and imposing the rules on a more or less willing society. One needs government because the application of abstract rules to particular instances is not above dispute, and because not everyone is equally scrupulous in following the abstract rules that are accepted by the group.[15]

Both Buchanan and Hayek, then, view government essentially as an organization with a definable purpose that is in some sense agreed to by the population it serves.[16] The problem the society subject to a particular government faces is that a "spontaneous order" develops within the structure of government which in many instances runs contrary to the stated purposes of the organization. Indeed, that is the theme of most public choice literature from Mises's *Bureaucracy* through *The Calculus of Consent* to the present esoteric works on agenda control. But the governmental "order" develops after the imposition of the organization on the social structure, and it affects how the organization performs its designed functions. The order within government – the way things are *really* done as opposed to how they are supposed to work – is actually an unintended product of the organizational design itself. This seems to dictate the conclusion that perverse consequences resulting from organizational design can only be corrected by some kind of constructivist redesign of that organization. Once a particular design is in place, however, redesign may be extremely difficult. Our modern dilemma is how to redesign our present governmental organization to overcome obvious faults despite the fact that many individuals profit from those faults and most people do not recognize the faults for what they are.

When it comes to the question of how to redesign our current political institutions, an interesting paradox presents itself in the work of Hayek and Buchanan. Buchanan the social contractarian rests his hopes for reform on a quasi-spontaneous process leading to agreement on the rules of the game while Hayek the evolutionist draws a blueprint for the design of good government. The paradox is only apparent, but it is an interesting one to dissolve.

Buchanan believes that reform must emerge from a genuine social contract. Good political institutions can only emerge when men choose them without regard to their place within a particular society.[17] Buchanan does not actually imagine any population actually sitting around behind a veil of ignorance deciding on a just set of political institutions to govern them.[18] Rather, he uses this construct as a model for evaluating particular sets of institutions. In an analogy with Pareto optimality in the theory of exchange, Buchanan offers only those institutions that could emerge from agreement within the genuine social contract as candidates for an acceptable set of rules of the game.[19] This criterion does not dictate any one set of institutions – the ignorance of any one man or group of men about the consequences of their decisions precludes the prediction of which institutions might emerge – but it does delineate a range within which political reform can rationally and honorably take place. Within this range, the fact that a set of rules could emerge from agreement will insure that the polity will serve the social order rather than the social order exist only for the sake of the polity.

Buchanan's model is a good starting place for intellectually choosing among political institutions. However, it suffers from being essentially a static model of political organizations. Once the social contract is entered into, Buchanan pays no attention to provisions for maintaining the abstract rules agreed upon. This is particularly disturbing because historically the United States had an acceptable social contract – The Constitution – which was gradually transformed into the sorry competition of special interests we see today. Hence, while Buchanan describes a method of choosing among reforms, he has not turned his attention to the problem of how to bring about needed reform or how to protect the social contract from another process of decay.[20]

Hayek shares Buchanan's view that political institutions are necessary to set the rules within which the spontaneous orders within society can flourish, but his emphasis has been on articulating an ideal organization of government that will interfere least with the order of society. Hayek recognizes that the "rules of just behavior" are subject to continual re-evaluation and reinterpretation in human life. Hence, he has designed a political organization that will institutionalize the re-evaluation process to ensure that it is done in a manner that comes close to duplicating Buchanan's genuine social contract. His scheme is to set up a bicameral legislature where one house is concerned solely with articulating the rules of just conduct while the other is concerned solely with matters of political organization. Hayek offers no suggestion about how we might approach such an ideal constitution however and, indeed, he discourages anyone from using his blueprint to undertake major reform in a country with an established constitution.[21] While Hayek's reluctance to endorse major reform is understandable, if we are not to give up hope of better government even in the relatively free countries of the West, we need some theory of how we can at least approach the ideal.

POLITICAL REFORM IN A DEMOCRATIC SOCIETY

In attempting to answer the question "How do we get from here to there?" I really have only two insights to call upon. The first is drawn from Buchanan's call for constitutional reform. This suggests that human intelligence must be involved in the designing of man's political institutions. To rely on the long sweep of cultural evolution is to consign intelligent men to evolutionary traps and dead-ends within losing cultures. The second insight is drawn from Hayek's theory of the gradual evolution of social orders. This suggests that any designed change in political organizations must be gradual and at the margins of existing organizations if it is to be both acceptable to an inherently conservative population and beneficial in its unintended consequences. Hayek convinces us that no matter how careful our designs, no human intelligence can foresee all of the consequences of an imagined course of action. Even the most carefully thought-out changes in the "rules of the game" will have unexpected results if for no other reason than that people are creative in finding ways to use rules to their own advantage, a fact that partly explains our drift away from the old "implicit constitution." Gradual reform allows us to catch our errors before they lead us too far away from our original intention while minimizing the wealth loss to those who have learned to function honestly within the old rule.[22]

The paradox that remains is this: Although in practice, gradual reform is required to minimize our chances of still greater error, reform in a direction libertarians and conservatives would favor, toward greater personal liberty under a rule of law, will not come about unless committed individuals have a clear idea of the nature of a fully constructed, radically free society. One *must* be a constructivist rationalist in the sense of carrying a vision around in one's mind in order to have any hope of achieving the rules we desire in a society that chooses through democratic means.

Reform in a modern democratic society where outcomes depend in large measure on convincing others to agree with the reformers requires the activities of ideological entrepreneurs. People don't vote exclusively according to their self-interests. They vote for political packages that have mixed implications for their own wealth positions. Hence, they have to make judgments among candidates on some ideological basis that encompasses both a view of how the world works and a set of moral judgments about the rightness of a policy. This composite view is what ideological entrepreneurs sell. They sell consensus, and in this way ideological entrepreneurs are the political counterpart to the economic entrepreneurs who coordinate activities and bring about change in the economic order. However, although they both bring about "reform" in some sense, they achieve social change in ways that are diametrically opposed to each other.

The economic entrepreneur acts to achieve his own purposes which generally involve increasing his pecuniary wealth. He acts on the basis of particular knowledge of specific circumstance – he possesses knowledge of "time and place" to use Hayek's phrase[23] – which enables him to take advantage of opportunities others miss. He operates to coordinate small pieces of the economic order, but his individual efforts cojoin with those of other entrepreneurs to bring about an overall coordination of the economic order intended by no one conscious being. Actions in the small bring about coordination in the large. The entrepreneur himself has no need for an awareness of his role in the grand design and indeed, most entrepreneurs have no idea of their value or place in bringing about catallactic order. They are unconscious agents of Adam Smith's "invisible hand" who serve the common good through no intention of their own.

The ideological entrepreneur, on the other hand, does have an awareness of a grand design. That is why he is valuable. He has visions of how society should be, of how all the pieces fit together and of how it can be guided or molded to the ideal shape. In having such a vision, he shares some of the characteristics of the constructivist rationalist Hayek decries, but his vision might easily be one of competing spontaneous orders that does not partake of the constructivist fallacy. He is entrepreneurial in that he takes advantage of numerous small opportunities to bring about the larger end he desires. The economic entrepreneur lacks a grand vision, but because he sees the small opportunities for gain, he helps to bring about a larger end. The ideological entrepreneur can only act to bring about his larger end because he has the vision that enables him to take advantage of small opportunities. He cannot identify the small opportunities without the larger vision. The irony is that the economic entrepreneur who recognizes only small opportunities for gain, by his actions inadvertently brings about an overall order. The ideological entrepreneur begins with the grand design, but because of the nature of the democratic process, he can only hope to bring about marginal changes in the political organization.[24]

Ideological entrepreneurs have existed throughout history (I am reminded most forcefully of Beatrice and Sidney Webb), but even if they did not exist, we would have to invent them to bring about the political reform we desire. In a democracy political change rests on agreement, and agreement on the constitutional level, as Buchanan calls it, will not come about spontaneously as humans independently recognize the same sources of evil and the same methods for institutionalizing the good. Even in relatively homogeneous societies, individuals differ both in their values and in their understanding of the social order.

It has been said that people want to do right and they want to do well. They have values and they have interests. To be able to know what actions will help them fulfill either one or both of these aims, they must rely on their own observations, the knowledge transmitted by their teachers and the moral instruction meted out in their lives – religious and otherwise. They have to be convinced that any particular kind of reform is possible, practical and "fair." This means communicating a particular model of the social order and invoking a shared sense of values that the order supports. The ideological entrepreneur, then, must be part teacher and part preacher.

It must be further recognized that there are all kinds of ideologies for sale and as many entrepreneurial efforts aimed at selling them. Unfortunately, in any competitive struggle, the "best" does not automatically win and "right" does not always triumph without efforts directed toward ensuring its triumph. Ideological entrepreneurs expend those efforts. The successful ones will have to combine plausible arguments with correct models; good ideas with good packaging. And being in the right place at the right time is as much an asset to the ideological entrepreneur as it is to his economic counterpart.

In this competitive struggle of ideologies, those who believe in the value – the rightness – of political freedom and the rule of law will have to grab entrepreneurial opportunities to proselytize for their program. Successful proselytizing however requires that there be a consistent, coherent program to present to the public on all levels. To develop it, we need to study the principles of a free society, the history of its emergence and recession, and to explore possible practical means for its restoration. But over all, we need to understand the moral basis of the free society since it is on the moral arguments that the principles of freedom generally lose to the easy fallacies of the left.

The moral justification of a free society is far less articulated than the economic justification, although ultimately it will prove to be far more profound when fully understood. It will be a moral justification that takes account of man's individuality in an uncertain world, that judges processes rather than outcomes. In charting this moral argument, we will have to take care to address the hard questions that too often have been sloughed over in the past. For example, it does no favor to the ideal of freedom to pretend that freedom yields only winners and no losers.[25] And it does no good to the cause of free markets to pretend that self-interested businessmen are altruists after all.[26] There are always individual costs to any change in social structure, there are mean ends and noble ones, there are always injustices and accidents of fate. We live in an uncertain world which by its nature can never live up to any human conception of perfection. Hence, we need to develop a morality that accepts the fact of uncertainty, revels in it and places its faith in the ability of humans to plot a course through the unknown.

NOTES

This paper was awarded first place in the N. Goto prize contest sponsored by the Mont Pelerin Society at their meeting in West Berlin in September, 1982. The Mont Pelerin Society holds copyrights.

1. James M. Buchanan, *Cultural Evolution and Institutional Reform*, working paper (Center for the Study of Public Choice, George Mason University, 1982). See also "Law and the Invisible Hand," in *Freedom in Constitutional Contract* (Texas A&M Press, 1977).
2. Buchanan, *Cultural Evolution and Institutional Reform*, p. 3.
3. *Law, Legislation and Liberty*, vol. 3 (Chicago: University of Chicago Press, 1979), p. 4. (Hereafter, *L.L & L*).

4. *L.L & L*, vol. 1, *Rules and Order*, ch. 1 "Reason and Evolution."
5. "The Error of 'Social Darwinism' was that it concentrated on the selection of individuals rather than on that of institutions and practices, and on the selection of innate rather than on culturally transmitted capacities of the individuals" (*ibid.*, p. 23).
   Buchanan is much less sanguine about the outcomes of a natural selection process among institutions. The natural selection model is consistent with the survival of many different cultures enjoying very different levels of material success. As Buchanan has pointed out, above a very minimum level of subsistence, there is a great latitude of material wealth that can support a human culture. As long as differing cultures are isolated from each other, relatively more successful and relatively less successful ones can exist simultaneously. Obviously, there is no basis for arguing, then, that survival in itself is a criterion for judging a "good" culture relative to a bad culture. The same can be said of institutions existing within a culture (*ibid.*, pp. 6–8). See also Buchanan, *Freedom in Constitutional Contract*, p. 31.
6. *L.L & L*, vol. 1, *Rules and Order*, pp. 76–8.
7. *Ibid.*, pp. 81–2.
8. Joseph Schumpeter, *Capitalism, Socialism and Democracy* (New York: Harper & Row, 1950).
9. Israel Kirzner, *Competition and Entrepreneurship* (University of Chicago Press, 1973).
10. Obviously, change also follows great cataclysmic upheavals, but it might be argued that after the first shock of cataclysm subsides, society once again reverts to a form of "business as usual."
11. *L.L & L*, vol. 1, *Rules and Order*.
12. Karen Vaughn, "Economic Calculation Under Socialism: The Austrian Contribution," *Economic Inquiry*, **XVIII**, October (1980), 535–54.
13. New Harmony was a well-known social experiment based on the ideas of Robert Owen in the nineteenth-century American midwest.
14. Buchanan, *Freedom in Constitutional Contract*.
15. *L.L & L*, vol. I, *Rules and Order*, pp. 43–6. Hayek's argument for why a society resorts to government is very Lockean. Although Locke believed a natural law exists and is discoverable by reason, he also believed that there would be hard cases where the abstract rules would not be easily applied to particular property disputes and an official arbiter would have to be imposed. He also suggested that men were not given to strict observance of the rule of law when their own interests were in dispute. See Karen Vaughn, *John Locke: Economist and Social Scientist* (Chicago: University of Chicago Press, 1980), pp. 94–5.
16. Hayek distinguishes between orders which have no purpose of their own other than the individual purposes of the participants in the order, and organizations that are designed to serve a particular end. My argument here is that government is an organization that is imposed on order. See *L. L & L*, *Rules and Order*, ch. 2.
17. Buchanan, *Freedom in Constitutional Contract*, pp. 128–30.
18. "Individuals do not participate in a 'social contract' that involves organizing everything from scratch. They do participate in social decision processes that involve changes in organizational structure, changes from what exists to what might be" (*Ibid.*, p. 278).
19. *Ibid.*, pp. 223–5.
20. Buchanan does recognize the problem of gradual decay of the social contract and regards this as an unintended result of the political process that requires reform to correct (*ibid.*, pp. 174–275).
21. *L.L & L*, vol. 3, "The Political Order of a Free People", pp. 105–27. "I certainly do not wish to suggest that any country with a firmly established constitutional tradition should replace its constitution by a new one drawn up on the lines suggested" (p. 107).
22. People have capital value accumulated in understanding a given system. To change that system too rapidly depreciates their capital and imposes wealth losses on essentially innocent victims caught in a change. The possible way to deal with this problem is to buy off the losers in some way, but the information problems inherent in this course of action may frequently be insurmountable. Gradual change still imposes losses, but gives people more time to learn new strategies to offset the obsolete strategies they once followed.

23. Hayek, *Individualism and Economic Order* (Chicago: University of Chicago Press, 1948) p. 80.
24. The idea of the ideological entrepreneur was inspired by Buchanan's discussion of the difficulties of the usual kind of entrepreneurial behavior in bringing about structural social change. See *Cultural Evolution and Institutional Reform*, pp. 15–18.
25. This is the naive interpretation of consumer sovereignty that overlooks such obvious facts as that some renters gain from rent control and some workers gain from minimum wages. A moral basis for free markets must show how those particular kinds of gains are not only inefficient in some sense but also unfair.
26. This is the startling claim made by George Gilder in *Wealth and Poverty* (New York: Basic Books, 1981). To argue that entrepreneurs are really altruistic muddies the notions of altruism and self-interest. It would be far more satisfying intellectually to argue that there are spillover benefits from self-interested behavior.

23. Virginia political economy: a view from Vienna

Peter J. Boettke

INTRODUCTION

George Mason University provide a unique institutional environment for exploring the relationship between the "Virginia" or public choice school of political economy and Austrian economics. The strength of this relationship becomes particularly apparent if we consider the branch of public choice economics associated with James Buchanan. The other branch of the Virginia school, which derives its research program mainly from Gordon Tullock, is, I would argue, more consistent with the neoclassical paradigm than the Austrian one, though of course there is much Austrians can learn from the Tullockian branch of public choice analysis. As Buchanan (1986a, p. 26) states:

> I think it is accurate to say that my own emphasis was on modeling politics-as-exchange, under the acknowledged major influence of Knut Wicksell's great work in public finance. By comparison (and interestingly because he was not initially trained as an economist), Gordon Tullock's emphasis (stemming from his own experience in, and his reflections about, the bureaucracy) was on modeling public choosers (voters, politicians, bureaucrats) in strict self-interest terms. There was a tension present as we worked through the analysis of that book [*The Calculus of Consent*], but a tension that has indeed served us well over the two decades since initial publication.

There are other important links, for example, by way of Sweden (via Wicksell, who undoubtedly also influenced the Austrians) or London (via the LSE cost tradition and Hayek), but the best way to get from Vienna to Virginia is by way of Chicago. Frank Knight, the great Chicago School economist, is an important link between Buchanan and the Austrians.

The tempestuous relationship between Knight and the Austrians on capital and interest theory is well documented, but on the nature and significance of economic science Knight and the Austrians are, I will argue, close indeed. The Chicago School today does not derive its methodological inspiration from Frank Knight so much as from Milton Friedman and George Stigler. It is the Virginia School, exemplified by Buchanan, which inherited and extended the Knightian tradition. This displaced Knightian tradition, with its emphasis on action within an uncertain world, is what students and colleagues of Buchanan are exposed to in his classes, his writings and seminars. And it is against this Knightian background that one can best see the "Austrian" strengths of the Virginia school.

FRANK KNIGHT AND SUBJECTIVIST ECONOMICS

I was fortunate enough to have had the opportunity to take courses with two of Knight's most prolific students, Kenneth Boulding and Buchanan, during the spring semester of 1986. Boulding as it happens was visiting George Mason University as a Robinson Professor and as a guest of the Center for the Study of Conflict Resolution. He taught a "great books" class in economics while Buchanan was teaching his course on constitutional economics. Knight's influence on Boulding and Buchanan was apparent throughout the courses. Boulding often referred fondly to Knight, describing him as "an engine of creativity without a clutch." Buchanan taught his class in what I understand is the typical Knightian fashion,[1] by analyzing Adam Smith's deer and beaver model and deriving the "simple economics of natural liberty" (cf. Buchanan, 1987b).

It is no accident that Boulding and Buchanan advanced very similar arguments about the inadequacies of standard economic analysis. Standard economics is trapped within a static framework that can not deal with the important issues of political economy. As a result, modern economics seems to be losing its ability to shed light on economic problems and in the process losing the meaning of its mission. To correct for these problems, both Boulding and Buchanan have advocated rethinking and restructuring the foundations of economic analysis. Boulding, in *The Image* (1961), advances a general theory of knowledge distribution and conveyance that is quite consistent with the Austrian understanding of the nature of choice and the discovery process of the market. He says, "If we are to have a theory of economic behavior or a theory of economic dynamics an explicit recognition of the importance of the image is necessary" (1961, p. 97). Buchanan in *Cost and Choice* (1978 [1969]) and *What Should Economists Do?* (1979), and in particular in the essay "Natural and Artifactual Man," (from *What Should Economists Do?*) has also advanced the thesis that sound economic reasoning must be based on a subjectivist understanding of human action.

As Knight argued in the chapter entitled, "'What is Truth' in Economics":

> Concrete and positive answers to questions in the field of economic science or policy depend in the first place on judgments of value and procedure, based on a broad, general education in the cultural sense, and on "insight" into human nature and social values, rather than on the findings of any possible positive science. *From this point of view the need is for an interpretive study* (verstehende Wissenschaft) *which, however, would need to go far beyond any possible boundaries of economics and should include the humanities as well as the entire field of the social disciplines*. (1956, p. 177; emphasis added)

Both Boulding and Buchanan have also gone far beyond the usual disciplinary boundaries in their research, and both have advanced a non-positivistic approach to economics in much of their work.[2] The Knightian aspects of Buchanan's thought, which he shares with Boulding, are also the aspects he shares with the Austrian School.

ELEMENTS OF PUBLIC CHOICE

The basic principles of public choice follow from a direct application of economic reasoning to political activity. By examining politics as an exchange process, analogous to the market, public choice theorists have been able to render government policies intelligible. This is most evident in the analysis of deficit financing, but public choice insights apply to the general pattern of political activity as well. Governmental bias toward short-term policies, the nature of the voting process, the role of special interests and the economics of bureaucracy are intertwined to produce an alternative understanding of political processes that is both logically coherent and more persuasive than the standard public interest view of the legislative process.

Any theory of collective or public choice must account for the fact that "government is a mechanism, like markets, through which individuals act collectively to improve their private utility" (Samuels, 1980, p. 57). The institution of government will be used, within the political exchange process, to promote the interest of those in charge of the apparatus of government. Economic policy, therefore, can not be modeled with the assumption that government is operated by a benevolent despot. Recognition must be made of the fact that politicians, like the rest of us, are purposive actors pursuing their own self-interest.

The fundamental concept of the economic way of thinking is to explain how it is that under a system of freedom of exchange and production individuals pursuing their own self-interest will be led to promote the interest of "society" as a whole. The task of the economist, from an Austrian perspective, is twofold: (1) to render economic phenomena intelligible in terms of purposive human action, i.e., to get at the meaning individuals attach to their actions, and (2) to trace out the unintended consequences, both desirable and undesirable, of human actions. When analyzing political exchange, the economist's task is not altered. Rather, he must take on the same twofold task with respect to the different institutional environment and its incentives structure. The traditional "public interest" view of government fails to account for the nature of political action and instead focuses on putting "good" people in office. But public-spirited individuals are at a comparative disadvantage in political markets.

Certainly one of the chief goals of any politician has to be to obtain election or re-election. The politician, therefore, must seek votes. Political markets are characterized by the interaction of rationally ignorant voters and rationally less ignorant special-interest groups. In the market for goods and services individuals choose between consumption bundles, and there is a direct link between their expenditure and the benefit they receive. Individuals voluntarily decide to buy some goods and forego others, they bear the costs and reap the benefits of their actions. In the political market, though, voter rewards are less direct (and often non-existent). The expected marginal benefit of casting a vote or being informed on the issues is very small because an individual's vote is only decisive in the unlikely case of a tie prior to the final vote. But the cost of being informed on political issues is high. For example, if the state of Virginia were to pass a bill raising the salaries of state university professors by $1 000 per year, the cost to individual voters to be informed on the issue would most likely be greater than the expected benefit. The bill might increase an individual's state income taxes by $5 per year, but the time and effort expended to be informed on the issue and block its passage would be greater than $5. On the other hand, university professors may well have a lot to gain from the bill and it will be in their interest to be knowledgeable about it and to work for its passage. Political exchange, then, is characterized by such activity and vote-seeking entrepreneurs will find it in their interest to cater to the well-organized and informed. This is the logic behind the governmental bias toward concentrated benefits and dispersed costs.

BUCHANAN AND THE BURDEN OF PUBLIC DEBT

Buchanan, since his discovery of Wicksell's principle of just taxation, has challenged his fellow economists to stop treating economic policy as if it were implemented by a benevolent despot. Instead, economists should examine the political exchange nexus within which policy decisions are made. Buchanan employed these ideas in his research in public economics – welfare economics and public finance – and challenged traditional economists to postulate a theory of the state that was consistent with the workings of politics. In this regard Buchanan was influenced by earlier Italian theorists of public finance. "Real rather than idealized politics, with real persons as actors – these were the building blocks in the Italian constructions, whether those of the cooperative-democratic state or the ruling class-monopoly state" (Buchanan, 1986b, p. 356). Exposure to the Italians, Buchanan argues, enabled him to escape the utilitarian mindset that dominates the field of public economics.

Public Principles of Public Debt (1958) was Buchanan's first book. This book applied the general understanding of political processes he had begun to develop, along with an insistence that economic analysis must discuss the relevant choice alternatives that real individuals face, to demonstrate the fallacies of the Keynesian orthodoxy. The Keynesian revolution, and specifically Abba Lerner's development of the concept of "functional finance," provided intellectual justification for abandoning the balanced budget orthodoxy (cf. Lerner, 1987 [1943]). With the acceptance of this new view, deficit financing came to be regarded as a tool for demand management instead of the result of budgetary mismanagement.

Buchanan questioned the main propositions of the "new" orthodoxy that: (1) creation of public debt does not transfer a real burden through time to future generations, (2) the analogy between private debt and public debt is fallacious, and (3) there is an important distinction between internal and external public debt. His argument was essentially a methodological criticism that hit at the core of Keynesian fiscal policy. First, Buchanan argued that there was no recognition on the part of the fiscal theorist that the government he is proffering advice to is made up of individuals within a political process, not some "organic" group. Secondly, this focus on the organic group produced a level of aggregation in the new orthodoxy that strained the imagination, violated the political norms of a democratic society, and fundamentally misconstrued the nature of the debt burden. Buchanan's argument against aggregation focused on the fact that groups, such as a nation, do not reap gains or suffer losses. Individual decision-makers in their capacity as government officials or political critics enjoy the benefits or suffer the losses of actions. "It is misleading to speak of group sacrifice or burden or payment or benefit," Buchanan states, "unless such aggregates can be broken down into component parts which may be conceptually or actually imputed to the individual or family units in the group" (1958, p. 36). By confining their focus to the aggregate unit, fiscal theorists were unable to address the problem of who will have to pay for the creation of public goods and when payment will be made. "The fact that making guns 'uses up' resources in years of war tells us nothing at all about *who* must pay for those guns, and *when*" (Buchanan, 1986b, p. 366). The problem with fiscal theory, therefore, was a misunderstanding of the basic principles of opportunity cost and economic decision-making.

The controversy over Buchanan's book led him to re-examine the doctrine of cost. *Cost and Choice*, Buchanan's most Austrian book, was the result of his attempt to clarify the issue of the burden of public debt. The main problem with most fiscal theorists was that they were viewing debt burden in terms of commodities rather than in utility terms, he argued. As a result, they failed to understand how the burden of public debt is shifted from one group of individuals to another.

E.G. West (1987 [1975]) has tried to clarify Buchanan's position in the debt controversies of the 1960s by concentrating on the meaning of cost. "In retrospect," he argues, "Buchanan's position in the debt controversy would have been considerably clarified had he used his most recent separation of subjective cost into 'choice influencing' and 'choice-influenced' cost" (p. 109). Both concepts of cost are subjective, reckoned in the utility, not the commodity, dimension. Choice-influencing costs are born solely by the decision-maker at the moment of decision and cannot be shifted onto others. Choice-influenced costs differ mainly in that they are shifted to the future. The subjective opportunity cost of present-day decisions is the cost in the future when the consequences of those decisions must be reckoned with. The burden of current deficit financing is, therefore, passed on to the future generations who have to pay the taxes.

PUBLIC POLICY OF THE PUBLIC DEBT

The issue of public debt has not received much attention from modern Austrian economists.[3] But the debt problem might be one of those issues, like the stagflation of the 1970s, that could lead to paradigmatic revolution and it seems that Austrians might have something to say on the social consequences of deficit financing, and possible solutions to the problem. Buchanan's analysis on the debt burden provides a natural "in" for a subjectivist analysis of the economic coordination problems associated with mismanaged fiscal policy. Buchanan, in fact, has addressed many of these issues in *Democracy in Deficit* (1977), co-authored with Richard Wagner, though the analysis may be said to underestimate the social consequences of inflation and monetization of the debt. Wagner and Robert Tollison (1987 [1982]), however, building on the earlier analysis of Buchanan and Wagner, as well as the Austrian theory of the inflation process, recognize the macroeconomic coordination problems that result from activist monetary and fiscal policy. They do not limit themselves to discussing the "shoe-leather" costs of inflation, but recognize that, since new money works its way through the economic system by incremental changes in the relative price structure, changes in the nominal money supply can have real effects on the distribution of resources and property in an economic system (pp. 188–91).

Perhaps the most promising area for merging the public choice perspective on the political economy of deficit financing with Austrian macroeconomics concerns the issue of capital consumption through public debt and positive solutions to this problem. Public choice theory, in the hands of Buchanan and his followers, has been able to understand why we are faced with the current fiscal dilemma, but it is not clear that it offers viable solutions to the problem. Public choice theory might be in the same situation with respect to the debt issue that Mises and Hayek found themselves in the 1930s with respect to business cycles. They were able to understand why the Great Depression occurred, and, in fact, were able to provide an explanation of the cluster of errors that characterize monetary disturbances, in general, that was quite convincing. But they did not provide a policy solution that was viable given the nature of the political control of money. As a result, Keynes's economic ideas were accepted and implemented. Buchanan and public choice economics might confront a similar problem in the 1990s in regard to public policy of the public debt.

James Bennett and Thomas DiLorenzo (1983) have shown that many government expenditures occur in the off-budget sector. Off-budget enterprises allow the elected official "to preach fiscal conservatism to his constituents while simultaneously increasing the size and scope of the public sector" (Bennett and DiLorenzo, 1983, p. 33). The constitutional constraints proffered by Buchanan, such as a balanced budget amendment to the constitution, intend to change the rules of the game, the constraints within which political exchange processes occur, so that the natural proclivities of politicians to spend rather than tax are checked. Given the ability of politicians to go off-budget, a balanced budget amendment may be a necessary condition for fiscal reform, but it is certainly not a sufficient one. A federal tax limitation would also have to be passed. But even if both balanced budget and federal tax-limit amendments were passed, politicians could still procure resources for spending through money creation. This again is a point where combining Virginian and Austrian themes could add something to the practical policy discussions.

While in the 1930s the Austrians did not offer any radical policy solutions to the economic problems, it seems that later theoretical developments have laid the ground for a positive cross-fertilization of a public choice understanding of politics and Austrian research on money and banking. Research by Lawrence H. White (1984) and George Selgin (1987) has demonstrated, both theoretically and historically, the viability and desirability of a monetary system of competitive note issue. Such a system would reduce monetary disturbances by taking away the government monopoly of money and prevent the government from raising funds through the hidden tax of inflation. Recognizing that, historically, government monopoly over note issue has grown from government's need to finance its expenditure (usually military), free banking theory removes the possibility of the political manipulation of the monetary system that public choice theorists have documented (Wagner, 1986 and Grier, 1986). By combining public choice analysis of the deficit with free banking theory, Austrians can offer a positive solution to the problems created in the political struggle over fiscal and monetary policy.

SOCIAL CONTRACT THEORY, PERFECT COMPETITION AND THE STATE

The *locus classicus* in public choice theory is *The Calculus of Consent* (1962), co-authored by James Buchanan and Gordon Tullock. As its subtitle suggests, the book explored "the logical foundations of constitutional democracy." Buchanan and Tullock sought to explain the existence or potential existence of democratic institutions as the result of contractual agreements among the participating individuals.

Any theory of constitutions, they argued, must rely on the postulates that the society is composed of free individuals, or at least ones free from deliberate political exploitation, and that the state can be used for deliberate political exploitation. "Were it not for the properly grounded fear that political processes may be used for exploitative purposes, there would be little meaning and less purpose to constitutional restrictions" (Buchanan and Tullock 1962, p. 13). They attempted to defend the Madisonian ideal of constitutional democracy.

> The determination of the degree of correspondence between this theory and the theory implicit in the American Constitution is left to the reader. Insofar as such correspondence emerges, however, this would at least suggest that Madison and the other Founding Fathers may have been somewhat more cognizant of the economic motivation in political choice-making than many of their less practical counterparts who have developed the written body of American democratic theory. (p. 25)

Buchanan's influence on this project, as pointed out above, was to emphasize politics as exchange. He has continued in this research direction which he calls constitutional economics ever since. Buchanan has made contributions in constitutional economics to both our understanding of the pre-constitutional and post-constitutional stages. He has discussed how it is that individuals would come to agree to a constitution and what are the likely outcomes of political activities within certain constitutional constraints. Both projects have been aided by Buchanan's use of game theoretic models. These constructs were useful to the public choice school in their contractarian discussion of the reason of rules and the economic theory of anarchy.

In the early 1970s, perhaps influenced by the political and social turbulence of the previous decade or the writings of libertarian anarchists, Tullock and Buchanan focused their attention on the economics of the original contract – the leap out of the Hobbesian jungle. Tullock had a manuscript circulating for some time on the economics of war and revolution, later published as *The Social Dilemma* (1974b), and it stimulated discussion that led to the publication of two small volumes of essays: *Explorations in the Theory of Anarchy* (1972) and *Further Explorations in the Theory of Anarchy* (1974a). It should be mentioned that besides Buchanan and Tullock, Winston Bush was also a major contributor to this literature (Bush 1976).

Economic exchange and production depends upon enforceable and exchangeable property rights. The absence of such rights would lead to a destruction of production and exchange. Public choice theorists attempted to explain the origin of these rights, which underlie market exchange and production and maintain social order. They questioned any explanation based on natural rights, and sought instead to build a contractarian justification. Buchanan *et al.*, therefore, embraced the theoretical construct of the Hobbesian jungle, where there was no "mine or thine" and the life of man was "solitary, poor, nasty, brutish and short" and sought to explain the process by which the leap out, by way of a social contract, is achieved. This exercise reached its most advanced discussion in Buchanan's *Limits of Liberty* (1975). This book serves as the theoretical backdrop for much of Buchanan's later work in constitutional economics, such as his two books with Geoffrey Brennan, *The Power to Tax* (1980) and *The Reason of Rules* (1985).

But was the effort successful? Were their goal to explain the origin of real-world property rights, the Hobbesian apparatus would certainly be inappropriate. They admit that this construct is ahistorical and that the social construct serves as a mental experiment. It is fair to ask, however, how useful such experiments involving ahistorical "start-states" are. The Hobbesian jungle can be a trap for political theory analogous to the one economists have set for themselves with their equilibrium end-states. As Tullock puts it, "there is no implication that some time in the ancient past, man lived in a 'state of nature'… Indeed, insofar as we can tell man developed from an ape which *was already social.* Hobbes's 'war of all against all' was *not part of human history*, although we can make use of it for analytical purposes" (1974b, p. 9; emphasis added).

The Hobbesian construct misleads the theorist in treating man in an atomistic, rationalist fashion, even while we admit that man is a social animal, conditioned by his culture and language. The primary task for the social theorist, it could be argued, is not to construct the leap out of this imaginary jungle into society, but to recognize the fact that man is already "thrown in" to a social life-world. Mises's discussion of Ricardo's Law of Association and social cooperation or Hayek's various treatments of common law might provide a more fruitful framework.

This seems apparent if we consider that the analogy Buchanan draws between the emergence of norms through the social contract and economic theory is the model of perfect competition. In his essay "Ethical Rules, Expected Values and Large Numbers," Buchanan (1977) argues that the dilemma of large numbers in ethical systems is directly analogous to the free-rider problem and inversely analogous to the theory of perfect competition. Whereas in ethical situations the desired change is toward smaller groups or structuring the rules of the game so that small group results emerge, in the model of perfect competition efficient outcomes rely on large number dilemmas. The analogy may cause problems if we view the market as a competitive discovery process.

The large number of other participants in the perfect competition model prevents any one individual buyer or seller from affecting price; a similar situation prevents any one individual from altering ethical rules. In perfect competition price is treated as a parameter; in large number social models, ethical rules are a parameter. The perfectly competitive model, since everyone is assumed to be a price-taker, can not explain how markets adjust through price changes (cf. Israel M. Kirzner, 1973; 1979; 1985). If everyone is a price-taker how does price change? Standard economics solves this problem by postulating the extra-economic entity: the Walrasian auctioneer, who insures that supply meets with demand. Similarly, the large number social dilemma faces the same problem. If everyone is assumed to treat ethical rules as given, how is it that rules ever emerge or change? Buchanan seems to postulate an extra-human entity: the sovereign, who ensures that rules are enforced and order is maintained. There is no way that the individuals within the model can develop rules; they must rely on something outside of the model. But if the model was supposed to explain the emergence of rules then should not the model be able to explain the emergence of rules within the model?

Recent research has shown that cooperation can emerge in these large number dilemmas without recourse to an external authority. The prospect of reciprocity can overcome many of the problems that large numbers appear to present. The problem with the earlier public choice analysis was that it was limited to one-run prisoner's dilemma games, where it was easy to see the individual short-run benefit of non-cooperation. If the game is modeled as an iterative process, though, cooperation seems to be the most truly self-interested behavior (Robert Axelrod, 1984). This idea of social cooperation without command has also been discussed by David Lewis (1969), Michael Taylor (1976), Edna Ulman-Marglit (1977) and, most recently, Robert Sugden (1986) and Ulrich Witt (1986). As Tullock himself has pointed out, "Black market dealers and professional gamblers are very, very careful to keep a good reputation because it is their reputation for prompt payment which makes it possible for them to continue in business. They are, indeed, probably more careful about prompt performance than a businessman who can make a contract which will be enforced by the courts" (1972, p. 69). The reason for this, as he explains, is what Adam Smith called the discipline of continuous dealings (Tullock 1985). Tullock states,

> It is likely that almost all interactions between human beings can be drawn as prisoner's dilemmas because it is possible for one party, or all parties, to make a one-time gain by cheating. In practice, almost no one ever thinks of this opportunity in a competitive market in which he intends to remain for a while because the cost of getting a reputation for cheating is too high… Under these circumstances, the cooperative solution is usually an optimum. (1985, p. 1079)

Even under the strictest assumptions of self-interest the prisoner's dilemma problem can be overcome in practice.

Cooperative behavior and the ethical norms that govern human behavior can be more fruitfully discussed as a result of purposive human action, though not of human design. Norms governing social cooperation are not so much arrived at through rationalistic calculation as they are discovered in the process of social interaction and accepted. Robert Tollison has summarized the important contribution the Austrians can make in this regard to public choice theory:

> Spontaneous orders embody the outcome of individual problem solving over time. Constructed orders involve the product of individual reason in drawing up a social contract. The latter approach parallels much current work in public choice theory, for example, all the concern given to John Rawls. The Rawlsian decision maker is every man and thus no man; his reason is sufficient to deduce the first principles of every society. What is missing in this highly rationalistic approach is the superman who is supposed to possess the incredible amount of information necessary to choose first principles and yet be blinded by a veil of ignorance to his future. While all this makes for great intellectual fun, like it or not there is just no substitute for spontaneous orders, and a major importance of the Austrians is their stress on seeking more innovative ways in which individuals can pursue their own private ends to the benefit of everyone. (1978, p. 130)

Indeed, men do not meet behind the Rawlsian veil of ignorance and reach unanimous agreement (conceptual or not) concerning the rules which govern human interaction. This fiction is not only historically inaccurate, it may be analytically inappropriate for understanding the human condition.

The conventions that govern human behavior arise through the socialization process of human evolution. Traditional values are conveyed in the social language of the community. We, as human beings, do not leap out of some pre-social environment by contracting with the sovereign. There is no primordial Hobbesian jungle. Instead, man is a social being who comes to consciousness, language and rationality from within an already-cooperative order.

THE POST-HAYEKIAN REALM

In a talk at the Institute for Humane Studies' 25th anniversary shortly after he was awarded the Nobel Prize, Buchanan analyzed what he termed the delusion of the Kennedy administration and the disillusionment of the Reagan administration. The delusion of Kennedy was a result of viewing political agents as benevolent despots, and the "pretense of knowledge" that characterized the Keynesian revolution and Paretian welfare economics. Theories went from the university blackboards at Harvard, MIT and Yale to the economic policy drawing boards in the federal bureaucracy, in the utopian belief that their implementation would rid the world, through the judicious use of Science, of economic disturbances. Twenty-five years later, however, the traditional Keynesian model has suffered intellectual bankruptcy (brought on by the stagflation of the 1970s), and there appears to be no clear-cut alternative to lay claim as the "new" macroeconomics (cf. Arjo Klamer, 1983). On the other hand, the Reagan administration, with its promise of a new age, has produced no structural changes in the political arena (cf. Milton and Rose Friedman, 1984). The disillusionment results from the apparent empirical generalization that principle always loses out to expediency in Washington. Washington is just the bastion of rent seekers. Moreover, if we take into account the fact that much of the public choice analysis of rent seeking is confined to the static model of perfect competition, then the costs of rent seeking might be even higher than traditional public choice theorists have suggested (cf. DiLorenzo 1987).

Buchanan suggested that the solution might lie in the intellectual pursuit in the "post-Hayekian realm of ideas." We must, as Buchanan argues, dare to "dream attainable dreams, and to recover the faith that dreams can become realities" (1986c).

The brilliance of Buchanan lies in the questions he asks, or leads others to ask. Characteristically, he ended his Nobel lecture with a question: "How can we live together in peace, prosperity and harmony, while retaining our liberties as autonomous individuals who can, and must, create our own values?" (1987a, p. 250). This question, informed by the public choice revolution, might present a serious problem for the traditional classical liberal faith in democracy. Classical liberalism is a doctrine which defends the right of private property, upholds the principles of non-interventionism and advocates the night watchman ideal of limited government. This vision of the "good" has informed thinkers from Adam Smith to Thomas Jefferson. Economists such as F.A. Hayek, Milton Friedman and Buchanan are modern proponents of classical liberalism. Their work, however, may point beyond itself to an alternative vision of the "good society," a vision which accounts for the contradiction between the idea of democracy and the practice of democracy.

Hayek has recently come to the position that government monopoly over money has led to the monetary corruption we have witnessed in this century. "The basic tools of civilization – language, morals, law and money," Hayek argues, "are all the result of spontaneous growth and not of design, and of the last two organized power has got hold of and thoroughly corrupted them" (1979, p. 163). Hayek has advocated the elimination of monopoly in money (cf. 1978), and this has led to young scholars pursuing research that was unthinkable a decade ago.

The positive argument for denationalization of economic affairs centers on the Austrian understanding of the competitive market process as a discoverer and conveyor of dispersed and local knowledge. But this argument can be generalized beyond strictly defined economic concerns, and be applied to understand the coordinating role that institutions like language, moral traditions or law play in society.

The negative case against government monopoly over such institutions, therefore, has two aspects. First, even assuming he is a benevolent despot the government official, regulator or planner does not possess the knowledge necessary to plan the socioeconomic system. Secondly, political agents are not benevolent despots; they are, like the rest of us, concerned with promoting their own self-interest. Thus, for reasons stated above, the practice of democracy can not live up to the ideal of democracy. Legislation, more often than not, is the result of special interest group efforts and not of policies intended to promote the public interest.

Both the knowledge and public choice arguments have been used to support deregulation and privatization of monetary affairs, but until recently Hayek's arguments have not been applied to other social institutions. Scholars such as Viktor Vanberg (1986) and Randy Barnett (1985; 1986) are extending the insights of Buchanan and Hayek to critically analyze the moral and legal order of the liberal society. Their research, along with that of many others who have been dually influenced by Buchanan and Hayek, might provide the intellectual framework "to change history in the direction of a society that combines liberty of person, prosperity and order" (Buchanan 1986c).

CONCLUSIONS

Austrian economists have much to learn from the work of the Virginia School. Buchanan, especially, has left a legacy of research projects that affect both our understanding of the nature and significance of political economy as well as practical problems of public policy. By merging public choice insights with Austrian analysis – a framework in which Buchanan fits quite comfortably – Austrians can improve their understanding of political economy and buttress their case for individual liberty. Some Austrians, such as Murray Rothbard, have argued that Buchanan and Tullock have misunderstood politics because they model the political process as if it consisted of voluntary exchanges (cf. Rothbard, 1977). While Rothbard is correct in pointing out the coercion of political activity, he does injustice to the contribution Buchanan and Tullock have made to political economy. The Virginia School holds that political exchange processes are fundamentally different from voluntary market processes; politics involves the use of force to transfer privilege from one group to another. There is no *a priori* reason, though, why this understanding of politics as power cannot be incorporated into a politics as exchange paradigm. It simply requires the theorist to recognize the institutional environment in which political activity takes place and where political economy decisions are made. Political action, like economic action, is purposive and the social analyst must pierce the surface and get at the meanings of the agents, and from these meanings the theorist must trace out the unintended (both desirable and undesirable) consequences of human actions. In this regard, Buchanan, and Virginia political economy in general, has provided indispensable insights into our quest for "attainable dreams."

NOTES

I would like to acknowledge Don Lavoie and Kurt Schuler for helpful comments on an earlier draft. Responsibility for existing errors is, of course, my own.

1. Boulding justified the length of time we spent discussing Adam Smith's deer and beaver model in his class by explaining that Knight spent half of his history of thought class discussing the history of religion and the other half analyzing deer and beaver.
2. Boulding, who is known for his wonderful sense of humor, once commented in a conversation that the only reason everyone became a logical positivist is because no one wanted to be accused of being an "illogical negativist." This statement takes on a new significance if we reflect on the sickly state of the present-day economic conversation.
3. This is perhaps because, for better or worse, the majority of younger Austrians have some leaning toward radical libertarianism, and examining the public debt seems to them like examining the books of the Mafia. See however the note by Roger Garrison (1984) on empirical testing of the relationship between deficits and inflation, and his review of Robert Eisner (Garrison 1987). Also see Boettke and Ellig (1987), and Sennholz (1987).

REFERENCES

Axelrod, Robert (1984), *The Evolution of Cooperation*, New York: Basic Books.

Barnett, Randy (1985), "Pursuing Justice in a Free Society – Part One: Power vs. Liberty," *Criminal Justice Ethics*, Summer/Fall.

—— (1986), "Pursuing Justice in a Free Society – Part Two: Crime Prevention and the Legal Order," *Criminal Justice Ethics*, Winter/Spring.

Bennett, James and DiLorenzo, Thomas (1983), *Underground Government*, Washington: The Cato Institute.

Boettke, Peter and Ellig, Jerome (1987), "The Business of Government and Government as a Business," in Fink and High (eds).

Boulding, Kenneth (1961), *The Image*, Ann Arbor: The University of Michigan Press.

Buchanan, James (1958), *Public Principles of Public Debt*, Homewood, IL: Richard D. Irwin.

—— (1975), *Limits of Liberty*, Chicago: University of Chicago Press.

—— (1977), *Freedom in Constitutional Contract*, College Station, TX: Texas A&M University Press.

—— (1978 [1969]), *Cost and Choice*, Chicago: University of Chicago Press.

—— (1979), *What Should Economists Do?*, Indianapolis: Liberty Press.

—— (1986a), *Liberty, Market and State*, New York: New York University Press.

—— (1986b), "Better Than Plowing," *Banca Nazionale del Lavoro Quarterly Review*, December.

—— (1986c), "Quest for a Tempered Utopia," *Wall Street Journal*, Friday, 14 November.

—— (1987a), "The Constitution of Economic Policy," *American Economic Review*, **77**(3), June.

—— (1987b), "Towards the Simple Economics of Natural Liberty," *Kyklos*, **40**(1).

Buchanan, James and Brennan, Geoffrey (1980), *The Power to Tax*, New York: Cambridge University Press.

—— (1985), *The Reason of Rules*, New York: Cambridge University Press.

Buchanan, James and Tullock, Gordon (1962), *The Calculus of Consent: The Logical Foundations of Constitutional Democracy*, Ann Arbor: University of Michigan Press.

Buchanan, James M. and Wagner, Richard (1977), *Democracy in Deficit: The Political Legacy of Lord Keynes*, New York: Academic Press.

Bush, Winston (1976), *Essays on Unorthodox Economic Strategies*, edited by Arthur Denzau and Robert Mackay, Blacksburg, VA: University Publications.

DiLorenzo, Thomas (1987), "Competition and Political Entrepreneurship: Austrian Insights Into Public Choice Theory," *Review of Austrian Economics*, **2**.

Fink, Richard H. and High, Jack C. (eds) (1987), *A Nation in Debt*, Frederick, MD: University Publications of America.

Friedman, Milton and Friedman, Rose (1984), *Tyranny of the Status Quo*, New York: Harcourt Brace Javanovich.

Garrison, Roger (1984), "Deficits and Inflation: A Comment on Dwyer," *Economic Inquiry*, **XXII**, October.

—— (1987), "Review of Robert Eisner's *How Real is the Federal Deficit?*," *Southern Economic Journal*, January.

Grier, Kevin (1986), "Monetary Policy as a Political Equilibrium," *Cato Journal*, **6**(2), Fall.

Hayek, F.A. (1978), *The Denationalization of Money,* London: Institute for Economic Affairs.
—— (1979), "Three Sources of Human Values," in *Law, Legislation, and Liberty*, vol. 3, Chicago: University of Chicago Press.
Kirzner, Israel M. (1973), *Competition and Entrepreneurship*, Chicago: University of Chicago Press.
—— (1979), *Perception, Opportunity and Profit*, Chicago: University of Chicago Press.
—— (1985), *Discovery and the Capitalist Process*, Chicago: University of Chicago Press.
Klamer, Arjo (1983), *Conversations with Economists*, Totowa, NJ: Rowman & Allanheld.
Knight, Frank (1956), *On the History and Method of Economics*, Chicago: University of Chicago Press.
Lerner, Abba (1987 [1943]), "Functional Finance," reprinted in Fink and High (eds), 1987.
Lewis, David (1969), *Conventions*, Cambridge: Harvard University Press.
Rothbard, Murray (1977), *Power and Market*, Kansas City: Sheed Andrews & McMeel.
Samuels, Waren (1980), "Toward Positive Public Choice Theory," *Review of Social Economy*, **XXXVIII**, (1), April.
Selgin, George (1987), *The Theory of Free Banking*, Totowa, NJ: Rowman & Littlefield.
Sennholz, Hans F. (1987), *Debts and Deficits*, Spring Mills, PA: Libertarian Press.
Sugden, Robert (1986), *The Economics of Rights, Cooperation, and Welfare*, New York: Basil Blackwell.
Taylor, Michael (1976), *Anarchy and Cooperation*, New York: John Wiley & Sons.
Tollison, Robert (1978), "Review of Gerald O'Driscoll's *Economics as a Coordination Problem*," *Public Choice*, **33**(3).
Tullock, Gordon (1972), "The Edge of the Jungle," in Tullock (ed.).
—— (ed.) (1972), *Explorations in the Theory of Anarchy*, Blacksburg, VA: Center for Study of Public Choice.
—— (ed.) (1974a), *Further Explorations in the Theory of Anarchy*, Blacksburg, VA: Center for Study of Public Choice.
—— (1974b), *The Social Dilemma*, Blacksburg, VA: Center for Study of Public Choice.
—— (1985), "Adam Smith and the Prisoner's Dilemma," *Quarterly Journal of Economics*, **C**, supplement.
Ulman-Marglit, Edna (1977), *The Emergence of Norms*, Oxford: Oxford University Press.
Vanberg, Viktor (1986), "Spontaneous Market Order and Social Rules: A Critical Examination of F.A. Hayek's Theory of Cultural Evolution," *Economics and Philosophy*, **2**.
Wagner, Richard (1986), "Central Banking and the Fed: A Public Choice Perspective," *Cato Journal*, **6**(2), Fall.
—— and Tollison, R. (1987 [1982]), "Balanced Budgets, Fiscal Responsibility, and the Constitution," reprinted in Fink and High (eds).
West, E.G. (1987 [1975]), "Public Debt Burden and Cost Theory," reprinted in Fink and High (eds).
White, Lawrence H. (1984), *Free Banking in Britain*, New York: Cambridge University Press.

Witt, Ulrich (1986), "Evolution and Stability of Cooperation without Enforceable Contracts," *Kyklos*, **39**(2).

24. Socialism as Cartesian legacy: the radical element within F.A. Hayek's *The Fatal Conceit*

David L. Prychitko

> Virtually all the benefits of civilization, and indeed our very existence, rest, I believe, on our continued willingness to shoulder the burden of tradition. These benefits in no way "justify" the burden. But the alternative is poverty and famine. (F. A. Hayek, 1988 p. 63)

> [I]f it were the case that there were no single locus of solidarity remaining among human beings, whatever society or culture or class or race they might belong to, then common interests could be constituted only by social engineers or tyrants, that is, through anonymous or direct force. But have we reached this point? Will we ever? I believe that we would then be at the brink of unavoidable mutual destruction. (Hans-Georg Gadamer, letter to Richard Bernstein)

INTRODUCTION

During the spring of 1989 dozens of internationally recognized Marxist philosophers met for two weeks in Dubrovnik to re-examine the potential of the Marxist critique of capitalism and its corresponding vision of socialism. As with any intellectual conference of this sort, there were sharp differences of opinion over particular details of Marxist and post-Marxist thought.

Nevertheless, most, if not all, were willing to completely abandon the goal of comprehensive planning and concede that the "anarchy" of market processes delivers both economic rationality and political freedom. Karl-Otto Apel's session was the most telling. Apel argued that the vision of Lenin, Mao, and the others suffered from what he called "the great pretension." The market system, he maintained, is a great evolutionary achievement of mankind, much more complex than the utopians and Marxists could ever imagine. Albrecht Wellmer, the chair, smiled, nodded his head in agreement, and symbolized the consensus of the audience.[1]

Socialism is clearly on the run. The experiments, the "real existing socialisms" of our time, are a collective failure. The intellectuals, such as those who gathered in Dubrovnik, now leap from the crumbling foundation upon which they once steadfastly stood. The Hayekian overtones of many of their arguments – Apel's for instance – are striking.

Hayek, in fact, deserves partial credit for the intellectual disillusionment within socialism. His writings, which span over 60 years, represent one scholar's indefatigable defense of the market as a system to which advanced society owes its *raison d'etre*. The University of Chicago Press has recently published Hayek's latest statement, written in his eighties, which summarizes his lifelong argument against socialist planning. Hayek's *The Fatal Conceit: The Errors of Socialism*, the first of a projected 22 volume collection of Hayek's works, represents a serious scientific challenge to those intellectuals who believe a deliberately guided society is more rational than a spontaneously evolved one. Moreover, Hayek's summary may also challenge classical liberals as well. Some seem to believe that Hayek has caved in, in the sense that he may now grant too much to the forces of tradition, and too little to the potential of human reason to shape our future.

Hayek's classical liberal critics maintain that his argument may allow for only a very small role for the critical scrutiny of tradition, and little prospect for the ability to use reason to overcome the growing problems of our age.[2] Does Hayek's recognition that it is impossible to emancipate ourselves from tradition necessarily imply a conservative defense of existing society? I wish to show, to the contrary, that Hayek's case against socialism and his corresponding defense of the market derive from a sophisticated epistemological research program, one that points toward a realizable political radicalism.

THE EPISTEMOLOGICAL ERROR OF SOCIALISM

Hayek argues that the problems of socialism go well beyond incentive problems, motivation problems and social choice problems. Certainly those specific problems exist, and much interesting research is being undertaken to explain their origins and persistence. But the whole notion of socialism, Hayek believes, is founded upon a factual error.

That error is based upon a misconception of the way knowledge is distributed and used in society. The knowledge necessary to coordinate the complex activities in advanced society cannot be given in complete and objective form to a single mind or even a committee of minds that occupy a central planning bureau. Certainly data, such as information pertaining to historical prices and quantities of material goods produced, technical information relating to actual production processes used in the past, the various outlays by consumers on final goods and services, and so forth, can be collected by a vast computer network for the planner's examination. But data only partially corresponds with the type of knowledge that lies at the basis of economic decision-making.

Statistical data is the measurable result of individuals following their own clues and judgments, judgments which, when combined with monetary price signals, allow individuals to integrate their plans into the overall market order. Data does not, however, encompass the entire realm of knowledge. The actual knowledge necessary to coordinate interlocal and intertemporal production and consumption plans is never available in its totality. Rather, it is dispersed among hundreds of thousands of individual minds in the form of local contextual knowledge, knowledge which is largely embodied in the form of individual skills and tacit know-how. The blueprints of socialism, as well as the standard models of capitalism, are questionable because they tend to assume that the relevant knowledge is given and known, or that it can be obtained if one is willing to bear the transactions costs of collection. Both the neoclassical theory of Walrasian *tatonnement*, and the socialist's assumption that the central planning board would be able to gather the relevant information as efficiently as an entrepreneur, is mistaken, at least if either theory is understood to be a description of the real world or a practical possibility.[3]

Whether the formal theorist is a proponent of the market or planned economy, he or she conceals if not misunderstands the discovery process of the market system: "the problem is not how to use given knowledge available as a whole," Hayek argues, "but how to make it possible that knowledge which is not, and cannot be, made available to any one mind, can yet be used, in its fragmentary and dispersed form, by many interacting individuals – a problem not for the actors but for the theoreticians trying to explain those actions" (Hayek, 1988, p. 99).

The epistemological mistake of socialism appears in the long-held socialist hope to abolish the market institutions of property, commodity production, and the general medium of exchange in order to realize social and economic justice through a unified, comprehensive plan. The traditional socialist belief that our advanced society could be "emancipated" from the ungoverned market process – by transforming principles used to organize relatively simple phenomena for the organization of complex social phenomena as a whole – is the basis of what Hayek calls "the fatal conceit." Comprehensive planning sought to replace *ex post* discovery based upon rivalry, or the inevitable clash of millions of often conflicting plans, with *ex ante* coordination based upon scientific reason. Any attempt to consciously engineer society must end in utter failure, because it presupposes that the knowledge required to accomplish that task can be captured outside the extended order established by voluntary competition and cooperation. Socialist theory has traditionally failed to understand the knowledge-disseminating character of spontaneous social orders:

> The efforts of millions of individuals in different situations, with different possessions and desires, having access to different information about means, knowing little or nothing about one another's particular needs, and aiming at different scales of ends, are coordinated by means of exchange systems. As individuals reciprocally align with one another, an undesigned system of a higher order of complexity comes into being, and a continuous flow of goods and services is created that, for a remarkably high number of participating individuals, fulfills their guiding expectations and values. (Hayek, 1988, p. 95)

Because socialists did not understand that the spontaneous order of the market system is the very basis of advanced society, and that such an ordering process cannot be abolished without destroying the future reproduction of society, they erroneously believed they could choose between a spontaneously ordered system and a comprehensively planned system:

> The demands of socialism are not moral conclusions derived from the traditions that formed the extended order that made civilisation possible. Rather, they endeavour to overthrow these traditions by a rationally designed moral system whose appeal depends on the instinctual appeal of its promised consequences. They assume that, since people had been able to generate some system of rules coordinating their efforts, they must also be able to design an even better and more gratifying system. But if humankind owes its very existence to one particular rule-guided form of conduct of proven effectiveness, it simply does not have the option of choosing another merely for the sake of the apparent pleasantness of its immediately visible effects. The dispute between the market order and socialism is not less than a matter of survival. To follow socialist morality would destroy much of present humankind and impoverish much of the rest. (*Ibid*., p. 7)

SOCIALISM AS CARTESIAN LEGACY

Hayek maintains that the error of socialism is an intellectual error whose roots trace well back to Descartes's philosophy of knowledge. Hayek does not make the wild claim that Descartes was a socialist, or that contemporary socialists are self-proclaimed followers of Descartes. There is no need to. Instead, Hayek argues that socialism's assumptions about the nature of knowledge are based upon similar premises and presuppositions as Cartesian rationalism. They have their origins in Cartesian rationalism.

In its attempt to uphold the products of human reason as the highest form of rationality, Hayek maintains that Cartesian rationalism misunderstands the nature of our reason. Logically, it leads to constructivism, which abuses reason. How can that be?

Descartes strove to attain pure reason. In the *Meditations Concerning First Philosophy*, for example, Descartes writes: "Since reason already convinces me that I should abstain from the belief in things which are not entirely certain and indubitable no less carefully than from the belief in those which appear to me to be manifestly false, it will be enough to make me reject them all if I can find in each some ground for doubt" (Descartes, 1964 [1641], p. 75). He explicitly sought the Archimedean point upon which to ground our knowledge claims. Claims to knowledge outside pure reason, those under the influence of opinion, prejudices, authority, or tradition were, to Descartes, mere nonsense. Prejudices, authority, and tradition are said to block one's reason. They are considered obstacles which must be overcome in our search for truth. We must emancipate ourselves from these constraints by way of a proven method in order to achieve pure reason, for, if we do not succeed, Descartes feared, we will wallow in the waters of relativism.

This may sound reasonable to many still today, for it characterizes the knowledge claims of modernity. Hayek argues, however, that this epistemology is "plainly false" (1988, p. 49), a "product of an exaggerated belief in the powers of individual reason and of a consequent contempt for anything which has not been consciously designed by it or is not fully intelligible to it" (1946, p. 8). Hayek is not alone in that respect. With Hayek, a growing body of literature in hermeneutics argues that the dichotomy between reason and tradition, between objectivism and relativism, is untenable. The dichotomy does not enhance reason and objectivity. It unintentionally destroys it.[4]

The continental philosopher Hans-Georg Gadamer argues that Descartes's attempt to design a methodology that would overcome prejudices, authority, and tradition was futile. He sought a method that would "safeguard us from all error," a goal which erroneously presupposes a "mutually exclusive antithesis between authority and reason" (Gadamer, 1985, p. 246). Richard Bernstein, following Gadamer's observation, remarks that Descartes's *Meditations* exemplifies the modern quest for a "foundation" upon which to support knowledge claims, and the parallel belief that, without an objective foundation, we will succumb to relativism. He has dubbed that belief the "Cartesian Anxiety," an intellectual fear associated with what is now considered a very misleading and debilitating notion of reason and rationality (Bernstein, 1983, pp. 16–20).

Cartesian rationalism, or "constructivism," as Hayek also puts it, assumed that the institutions which benefit society have been consciously created by the power of human reason. Its goal was to overcome the spontaneous processes of historical evolution. This goal was expressed by the utopian socialists such as Saint-Simon and Fourier, and later by Marx and his followers. They all sought to overthrow the "anarchy" of the market system with a scientifically determined comprehensive plan.[5]

Marx in particular faced a similar anxiety: without a comprehensive plan to ground and guide society, he believed, people will be estranged from their species-potential. They will be victimized by alienation. Understandably, the anxiety spread from Descartes's theory of knowledge to Marx's theory of history. More specifically, what originated as a method which tried to ground knowledge and produce epistemological certainty, Hayek shows, led to a method which tried to order society and design institutions for the benefit of humanity. It logically led to the call for the conscious ordering of society.

In sum, just as Descartes argued that man must overcome tradition, authority, and prejudices in order to attain pure reason, so Marx would later argue, man must be emancipated from the alienation and false consciousness of markets in order to "return" to himself (Marx, 1964 [1844], p. 135). Man cannot "return" to himself, i.e., he cannot become a whole, fully creative being, until he develops a method – a comprehensive plan – by which to overthrow the entire market system. For Marx, "The life-process of society, which is based on the process of material production, does not strip off its mystical veil until it is treated as production by freely associated men, and is consciously regulated by them in accordance with a settled plan" (Marx, 1906 [1867], p. 92). This is a specific example of what may be called the "Constructivist Anxiety."

It makes sense that both the Cartesian quest for pure reason and the socialist search for rational social construction are motivated by the same type of anxiety. Hayek's profound insight that the spirit of Cartesian rationalism logically leads to socialism seems to be an insight, however, that many classical liberals would like to do without. For it may also radically challenge their own intellectual presuppositions.

IF REASON CANNOT OVERCOME TRADITION…? THE CLASSICAL LIBERAL ANXIETY

Hayek's stance against socialist pretension, first popularized in *The Road to Serfdom* some 50 years ago, has certainly garnered a respectable following. But to some classical liberals, Hayek's emphatic synopsis in *The Fatal Conceit* may have hit negative returns. That is, Hayek's final summary of his six decades of research may do more harm than good. Specifically, some seem disenchanted with Hayek's final statement because it is now quite clear that his criticism of socialism has really been a criticism of rationalist philosophy. There is a growing anxiety among classical liberals themselves that Hayek's critique may imply that reason and rationality are in fact powerless in the face of authority and tradition.

It is a reasonable apprehension. Consider, for instance, Hayek's following remarks:

> Learnt moral rules, customs, progressively displaced innate responses, not because men recognized by reason that they were better but because they made possible the growth of an extended order exceeding anyone's vision, in which more effective collaboration enabled its members, however blindly, to maintain more people and to displace other groups. (1988, p. 23)

> The idea that reason, itself created in the course of evolution, should now be in a position to determine its own future evolution (not to mention any number of other things which it is also incapable of doing) is inherently contradictory, and can easily be refuted... It is less accurate to suppose that thinking man creates and controls his cultural evolution than it is to say that culture, and evolution, created his reason. (1988, p. 22)

Would it not be ironic, indeed, if one of the leading exponents of classical liberal philosophy, a philosophy which sprang forth during the Enlightenment, now maintains that humankind must blindly submit to tradition and prevailing authority? Can we not question the rules and social institutions in society in order to improve the lot of humankind? What, in fact, is Hayek's case for reason and rationality? As James Buchanan puts it, "Is the implication that we must remain quiescent before the forces of cultural evolution?... Despite his earlier denial, is Hayek, after all, a conservative?" (1988–9, pp. 4, 5).

Every reader must interrogate *The Fatal Conceit* with this very question. I believe, however, that the contemporary hermeneutics literature helps overcome the anxiety that the nature of the question elicits. Let's therefore consider Hayek's discussion of the role of cultural evolution and tradition in a bit more detail.

Hayek maintains that morality is not the product of deliberate consideration. People were never so intelligent as to be able to consciously design a system of rules by which to guide society for the better. It may appear "as if" humankind had the foresight to establish rules of several property, honesty, the social division of labor, monetary exchange, and so on. But this interpretation is very misleading. In fact, nothing of the kind occurred. Rather, those groups that first adopted practices such as the use of several property probably did so accidentally. Nevertheless, they had a better chance to prosper compared to those that did not. These practices enhanced the wealth of the small bands of people, which further allowed them to multiply their numbers. They acquired rules and characteristics, which, even though they were not fully understood, were passed from generation to generation through imitation. Our moral heritage is not the product of rational foresight, but of cultural evolution.

Hayek has extended his discussion of market competition as a discovery procedure to human history in general. Market competition selects particular individuals who are economically efficient, while cultural evolution selects overall groups which follow practices that increase the wealth prospects for the average member. Both selection processes disseminate primarily inarticulate knowledge to individuals through space and time.

While Hayek considers this an extension of his earlier work, others argue that it conflicts with his earlier methodology. For example, John Gray and Viktor Vanberg suggest that Hayek's emphasis on the selection of groups rather than individuals represents a departure from the principle of methodological individualism.[6] But it is not clear what they mean by methodological individualism. If it is understood as a position that studies human action in an isolated context (the Robinson Crusoe approach to economics), then it is true that Hayek's approach differs dramatically. Hayek moves well beyond a naive, atomistic individualism, and accounts for human action in a social context. For Hayek, society is composed of individuals who are not immune to, nor can they fully transcend, the influence of language, economic institutions, and other rule-guided practices of which they may be only faintly aware. Nor can they fully account for the effect of their actions on others. Hayek's approach to methodological individualism is sophisticated, and suggests that the study of individuals in isolation cannot account for the development of rules through time. It seems to successfully break from atomistic individualism without adopting the opposite extreme of a naive holism which posits a group mind approach to history and institutions, an approach that has proven to be dangerous.

Socialism failed to understand the historical basis of our extended market order and consequently tried to overthrow the rule-guided practices of several property, monetary calculation, and so forth. In other words, its futile hope to uncouple society from the "economic base" of capitalism is a direct result of the fallacious notion that reason can criticize the totality of human history. Socialism not only failed to recognize that the market system acts as an indispensable discovery procedure. In addition, it did not understand that crucial knowledge is also communicated from generation to generation through tradition itself.

Perhaps now we may be in a better position to understand Hayek's claim that we must still be willing to "shoulder the burden of tradition" (1988, p. 63). Hayek argues that we owe our very intelligence to that realm between instinct and reason which is tradition (1988, p. 21). Tradition is the undesigned result of a process of selection from among rival beliefs. By the same reasoning that the market economy gives rise to a level of intelligence far beyond the capability of an individual human mind, so tradition is "in some respects superior to, or 'wiser' than, human reason" (1988, p. 75). "The whole of tradition is," Hayek argues, "so incomparably more complex than what any individual mind can command that it can be transmitted at all only if there are many different individuals to absorb different portions of it" (1988, p. 79).

The knowledge problem argument holds in both cases. In the economic sphere, the efficiency and compatibility of certain production plans can be judged only within a concrete market process, as opposed to some abstract theoretical standard. Economic activities comprise, of course, only a portion of a much larger social domain which consists of art, politics, science, family relationships, etc. If economic plans must be rationally appraised within the context of the market process, then it follows that social interaction in general can be rationally understood and criticized only from within: "The only standard by which we can judge particular values of our society," Hayek writes, "is the entire body of other values of that same society" (1970, p. 19).

We cannot transcend all of society, for we exist only within society. That may sound either trivial or redundant. One is reminded, however, of Marx's notion of the economic base and superstructure. Marxism understood itself to pierce through the veil of the superstructure, or social consciousness, by fully explaining the realm of material production, the base. But if ideas were to some extent determined by the base, as Marx argued, then why weren't Marx's own ideas also determined by the base? What gave Marx the remarkable ability to rise outside society itself?

Hayek's words seem right on target: "The picture of man as a being who, thanks to his reason, can rise above the values of his civilisation, in order to judge it from the outside, or from a higher point of view, is an illusion. It simply must be understood that reason itself is part of civilisation" (1970, p. 20).

If the basic Hayekian insight into the market order is correct, that there is no Archimedean position by which to judge the rationality of economic activities, and that the spontaneous ordering of economic activities is defined only within the process of its emergence, then it sensibly follows that there is no objective framework by which to judge human history itself.

There is no fundamental difference between Hayek's claim and Gadamer's notion that "we stand always within tradition" (Gadamer, 1985, p. 250; cf. p. 324). In particular, like Hayek, Gadamer argues that tradition is not an object that can be overcome in the name of enhancing knowledge:

> That which has been sanctioned by tradition and custom has an authority that is nameless, and our finite historical being is marked by the fact that always the authority of what has been transmitted – and not only what is clearly grounded – has power over our attitudes and behaviour. (p. 249)

In Hayekian fashion, Gadamer concludes that "The validity of morals, for example, is based on tradition. They are freely taken over, but by no means created by a free insight or justified by themselves. This is precisely what we call tradition: the ground of their validity" (1985, p. 249).

Equally important, Gadamer makes it clear that real authority is based upon reasoned judgment and not blind obedience, something one should keep in mind when reading Hayek:

> It rests on recognition and hence on an act of reason itself which, aware of its own limitations, accepts that others have better understanding. Authority in this sense, properly understood, has nothing to do with blind obedience to a command. Indeed, authority has nothing to do with obedience, but rather with knowledge. (Gadamer, 1985, p. 248)[7]

The hermeneutical understanding of knowledge suggests that authority enables rather than debilitates human intelligence. It suggests that the appeal to authority is a fundamentally rational act, and that the prejudice against all authority rightly understood is a misleading and dangerous pretension. If true, then the recognition of authority does not necessarily lead to uncritical conservatism. Hayek understands that authority is based upon knowledge, and now explicitly links the division of knowledge to the division of authority (1988, p. 77).

OVERCOMING OUR ANXIETIES

The anxiety some of us face has its origins in the belief that reason can and must overcome authority and tradition. But that fear is based upon a misunderstanding of human reason. To believe that we actually can break with the whole of tradition is to believe that we can leap outside time and history. It is utopian in the strict sense of the term. Although it is a burning desire among modern scientists and intellectuals, such an idea remains an utter impossibility in the here and now of human existence.

It may be worthwhile, by the way of conclusion, to recall an aspect of the celebrated Habermas–Gadamer debate. It seems that the early Habermas, like Marx before him, wanted to subject all of tradition at once to unrelenting criticism, in order to penetrate what he perceived to be dominating interests and false consciousness. Gadamer argued that Habermas's project was futile, an epistemological impossibility. Gadamer also maintained, however, that although authority and tradition communicate indispensable knowledge among peoples and generations, that by no means precludes the possibility of critique. In particular, Gadamer argued that "our human experience of the world, for which we rely on our faculty of judgement, consists precisely in the possibility of our taking a critical stance with regard to every convention. In reality, we owe this to the linguistic virtuality of our reason and language does not, therefore, present an obstacle to reason" (1985, p. 496). We can question everything, Gadamer concluded, but not all at once.

Hayek concurs with Gadamer. We stand within tradition. We cannot escape it. Nor can we fully explain it, because the totality of tradition is at a higher level of complexity than that of the individual human mind. Hayek has, truly, extended his Goedelesque argument that the human mind can never be capable of fully explaining itself (1963, esp. pp. 184–90) into the domain of human history itself. Reason is incapable of fully explaining or criticizing human history. And like Gadamer, Hayek also argues that we can question everything, but not all at once. Although traditions are passed down because they tend to enhance human survival, Hayek is quick to point out that recognition "certainly does not protect those rules from critical scrutiny" (1988, p. 20). "[W]e are indeed called upon to improve or revise our moral traditions," Hayek assures us. As opposed to critical scrutiny from some exterior, utopian position, our task must be "based on immanent criticism" (1988, p. 69).

Hayek's research program develops a profound account of the errors of truly utopian reasoning. It is a criticism of a major element, a tradition, as it were, of modernity. The spirit of Hayek's research suggests that the alternative to utopianism does not have to be conservatism at all:

> I must warn you… that the conservatives among you, who up to this point may be rejoicing, will now probably be disappointed. The proper conclusion from the considerations I have advanced is by no means that we may confidently accept all the old and traditional values. Nor even that there are any values or moral principles, which science may not occasionally question. The social scientist who endeavors to understand how society functions, and to discover where it can be improved, must claim the right critically to examine, and even to judge, every single value of our society. The consequence of what I have said is merely that we can never at once and the same time question all its values. Such absolute doubt could lead only to the destruction of our civilisation and – in view of the numbers to which economic progress has allowed the human race to grow – to extreme misery and starvation. (1970, p. 19)

One does not have to be conservative if one jettisons the utopian project, whether that project is associated with Descartes, Marx, or Habermas. It seems to me that, beyond a non-human utopia and a reactionary conservativism, there lies a sophisticated radicalism waiting to be explored. Hayek points us in that direction. It's up to his students to continue the quest.

NOTES

I thank James Solan for helpful comments. The usual caveat applies.

1. The conference I refer to is "Philosophy and Social Science: The End of Utopia?" Inter-University Center for postgraduate studies, Dubrovnik, Yugoslavia, 27 March–7 April 1989. Apel's session was entitled "Critique of Utopian Reason." Unfortunately, the paper

he prepared for the session was confiscated by Italian customs police while Apel was en route to Yugoslavia.

2. This is apparent in some of the essays written for the special Hayek symposium issue of the *Humane Studies Review*, vol. 6, no. 2 (Winter 1988–9).
3. To be sure, contemporary neoclassical theorists do not defend the formal equilibrium model as a practical possibility or even an accurate description of real world markets. While it is true that many in the past had once argued that the market really does solve a system of excess demand equations (cf. Patinkin, 1965, pp. 38–9), most, following Arrow and Hahn (1971), understand that the standard model is only about the imaginary construction of equilibrium as such, and not about the actual operation of real existing markets. Others, following Friedman (1953), justify the assumptions of the model on the grounds that unhampered markets perform "as if" the relevant information is given and known and market participants behave like price-takers. But this still does not help us understand the following question: how is society possible in light of the fact that the knowledge necessary to achieve any degree of order is dispersed among many people? With this question in mind, Hayek's discussion of the knowledge problem is at once a criticism of the socialist attempt to comprehensively plan society and a criticism of the standard theory of the market system. It is no exaggeration to say that Hayek's earlier articles about the knowledge problem (1937; 1945; 1948b; 1968) are as much a criticism of standard economic theory as they are a criticism of the assumptions of socialism.
4. I specifically have in mind Gadamerian-type hermeneutics. For a good introduction see Weinsheimer (1985) and Bernstein (1983). Rabinow and Sullivan (1979) provide a good representation of original essays on the major themes of hermeneutics in general and its implications for the human sciences.
5. Wrote Hayek:

   > Rationalism in this sense is the doctrine which assumes that all institutions which benefit humanity have in the past and ought in the future to be invented in clear awareness of the desirable effects that they produce; that they are to be approved and respected only to the extent that we can show that the particular effects they will produce in any given situation are preferable to the effects another arrangement would produce; that we have it in our power so to shape our institutions that of all possible sets of results that which we prefer to all others will be realized; and that our reason should never resort to automatic or mechanical devices when conscious consideration of all factors would make preferable an outcome different from that of the spontaneous process. It is from this kind of social rationalism or constructivism that all modern socialism, planning and totalitarianism derives. (1965, p. 85)

6. Cf. Gray (1984, pp. 45–55; 1988–9) and Vanberg (1986). Also see Hayek's earlier statement about cultural evolution in the epilogue of his *Law, Legislation, and Liberty*, vol. 3 (1979).
7. Also cf. Gadamer (1985, p. 524, n. 187). The insight that authority is based upon a division of knowledge in society rather than command was in fact recognized by one of the earliest critics of Marxism, the anarchist Michael Bakunin, over a century ago. See his brilliant passage in Bakunin (1970, pp. 32–5).

REFERENCES

Arrow, Kenneth, and Hahn, F.H. (1971), *General Competitive Analysis*, San Francisco: Holden-Day, Inc.

Bakunin, Michael (1970), *God and State*, New York: Dover.

Bernstein, Richard J. (1983), *Beyond Objectivism and Relativism: Science, Hermeneutics, and Praxis*, Philadelphia: University of Pennsylvania Press.

Buchanan, James (1988–9), "Hayek and the Forces of History," *Humane Studies Review*, **6**(2).

Descartes, Rene (1964), *Philosophical Essays*, New York: Bobbs-Merrill Co.

Friedman, Milton (1953), "The Methodology of Positive Economics," in *Essays in Positive Economics*, Chicago: University of Chicago Press, ch. 1.

Gadamer, Hans-Georg (1985), *Truth and Method*, New York: Crossroad.

Gray, John (1984), *Hayek on Liberty*, New York: Basil Blackwell.

—— (1988–89), "Evolutionary Functionalism," *Humane Studies Review*, **6**(2).

Hayek, F.A. (1937) "Economics and Knowledge," in Hayek (1948a), pp. 33–56.

—— (1945), "The Use of Knowledge in Society," in Hayek (1948a) pp. 77–91.

—— (1946), 'Individualism: True and False," in Hayek (1948a) pp. 1–32.

—— (1948a), *Individualism and Economic Order*, Chicago: University of Chicago Press.

—— (1948b), "The Meaning of Competition," in Hayek (1948a) pp. 92–106.

—— (1963), *The Sensory Order*, Chicago: University of Chicago Press.

—— (1965), "Kinds of Rationalism," in Hayek (1967) pp.82–95.

—— (1967), *Studies in Philosophy, Politics, and Economics*, Chicago: University of Chicago Press.

—— (1968), "Competition as a Discovery Procedure," in Hayek (1978), pp. 179–90.

—— (1970), "The Errors of Constructivism," in Hayek (1978) pp. 3–22.

—— (1978), *New Studies in Philosophy, Politics, Economics and the History of Ideas*, Chicago: University of Chicago Press.

—— (1979), *Law, Legislation, and Liberty*, Chicago: University of Chicago Press.

—— (1988), *The Fatal Conceit*, Chicago: University of Chicago Press.

Marx, Karl (1906 [1867]), *Capital*, Vol. I, Chicago: Charles Kerr & Co.

Marx, Karl (1964 [1844]), *The Economic and Philosophical Manuscripts of 1844*, New York: International Publishers.

Patinkin, Don (1965), *Money, Interest, and Prices*, New York: Harper & Row.

Rabinow, Paul, and Sullivan, William M. (eds) (1979), *Interpretive Social Science: A Reader*, Berkeley: University of California Press.

Vanberg, Viktor (1986), "Spontaneous Market Order and Social Rules: A Critical Examination of F.A. Hayek's Theory of Cultural Evolution," *Economics and Philosophy*, **2**.

Weinsheimer, Joel C. (1985), *Gadamer's Hermeneutics*, New Haven: Yale University Press.

25. A political philosophy for the market process

Don Lavoie

What sort of political philosophy fits best with the understanding we get from the economics of market processes? I mean "fits" here in two different senses, one philosophical or methodological, and one substantive. Methodologically the question is: which approach to political issues conforms to the general philosophical perspective which market-process economists take on the nature of the human sciences? Substantively the question is what kind of political institutions are most conducive to the flourishing of the creative entrepreneurial process which market-process economists study? These are difficult questions about which the readers and writers of *Market Process* differ, but it is fair to say that classical liberalism, broadly defined, has historically been the political orientation most market-process economists have favored. A good place to start, if one wants to learn about the philosophy of classical liberalism, would be Gary Madison's book. Although the bulk of this book appears to be a simple restatement and endorsement, with generous quotations, of the great contributors of classical liberalism, the book is far more than a summary of old ideas. It points beyond the eighteenth-century social theory it sometimes seems to be complacently defending, toward a fresh new alternative for today. Implicitly throughout the first nine chapters, while the old tradition is being summarized, the book is deliberately selecting those passages from the classics which cohere into a consistent vision. The last two chapters articulate a substantially revised version of classical liberalism, and defend it against alternative positions labeled conservatism and socialism. Only upon finishing these last chapters does the reader fully realize that this is no mere apology for the "founding fathers." An exciting new perspective is being introduced into contemporary political discourse, however much it may owe to its honorable precursors in the classical liberal tradition. And in my view this new version of liberalism presents us with a politics that, in both senses, best fits the market process.

Essay Review of G.B. Madison's *The Logic of Liberty* (New York: Greenwood Press, 1986)

The old classical liberal position went into rapid decline toward the end of the nineteenth-century and until the last couple of decades had virtually disappeared. The dominant political alternatives had become conservatism and socialism, or what's worse, the terrifying combination of the two that was fascism. The word "liberal" has come to mean a moderate and inconsistent variation on "socialism," advocating economic policies which interfere with and distort the workings of the market process. Conservatism, on the other hand, opposes socialism only by advocating a moderate and inconsistent variation of state capitalism, which it turns out is guilty of advocating pretty much the same kinds of distorting policies. These old words capitalism and socialism are misleadingly attached to the kind of interventionist system defended by both modern socialism and conservatism. They suggest modern conservatives and socialists are more different from each other than they appear from the market-process perspective. Both advocate a policy of active government intervention into the workings of market processes, an approach which tries to exert direct control over economic outcomes. Both are suspicious of the sort of protection of individual liberty which liberalism seeks, and which market-process economics considers necessary for the exercise of entrepreneurship.

To Madison "liberalism" represents a political philosophy which steers between the overly pessimistic view of human nature proper to conservatism and the overly optimistic view proper to socialism. While conservatism seeks to constrain the (inherently wicked) individual to obey the dictates of traditional authorities, socialism seeks to liberate the (inherently perfectible) individual from any constraints of law, and permit democratic institutions full sway in the shaping of the direction of social change. In effect, conservatism is afraid that the freedom of individuals sought by liberalism will lead to disorder, while socialism is afraid that such individual freedom will obstruct the collective and democratic aspirations of society. Both conservatism and socialism seem to fear that a regime oriented to the protection of individual liberty will fail to be properly "social" and lead to either atomistic chaos or private selfishness. Whereas conservatism leaves no room for democracy, socialism sets no limits to majority rule and degenerates into a tyranny over minorities. Madison argues that in fact only a liberal society can achieve both the order desired by conservatism and the democracy desired by socialism.

Classical liberalism promotes a kind of policy that does not try to directly control economic outcomes but instead tries to set in place general rules within which an essentially uncontrolled entrepreneurial process can work. These rules, often misleadingly called "private property rights" are to be devised such that the initiative of market participants is allowed to be freely exercised. The rules need to be fairly stable, based on intelligible principles, so that the members of society can generally tell in advance of their actions which are likely to be "violations" of the rules and which are not. From the point of view of market-process economics, this policy orientation seems very conducive to the workings of creative discovery processes.

The problem with classical liberalism is that, despite its substantive advantages as seen from the market-process economic perspective, it has had some very serious philosophical disadvantages. The viewpoint declined and disintegrated into versions of socialism and conservatism for definite reasons connected with problems in its political philosophy and it is unlikely to become a major force again unless it can overcome these philosophical difficulties. The older form of classical liberalism relied on a natural-rights approach based on metaphysical arguments concerning such things as the "essence" of man. This position, which essentially takes the rule of law to be imposed by God from outside of human society, leaves no room for democracy, for the participation by the members of society in the setting and revising of rules. It thus belongs naturally to conservatism. The later utilitarian version had its own difficulties, not least of which was the questionableness of its claim to be a value-free way of dealing with value-laden policy issues. Utilitarianism takes the rule of law to be nothing but whatever the majority of the moment decides it to be, and thus sets no limits to democracy. It belongs naturally to socialism. Classical liberalism needs to have its own philosophical justification which can leave room for true democracy without turning into a tyranny over minorities.

This is where Professor Madison's moderately couched, but in fact profoundly radical, revisions to classical liberalism come in. His approach shares with utilitarian critics of natural rights a healthy pragmatism and distrust of metaphysics. On the other hand it shares with natural-rights critics of utilitarianism a healthy insistence on universal principles and a distrust of narrow expediency. But the approach he develops turns out to be completely different from either traditional version of liberalism.

With respect to natural rights he argues that "When it abandons the notion of natural law and the idea of natural rights, liberalism becomes a much more coherent, and thus defensible, philosophy" (p. 132–3):

> [A] coherent liberal philosophy would do best simply to view this unwritten law of nature which exists nowhere but in the murky and private minds of men as a not-so-useful fiction and, accordingly, make the least possible use of it when it is a matter of arguing for an open and public space in which people may coexist in peace and freedom. People may think that they should enjoy certain basic rights, but it is not thinking that makes them have these rights. Only positive law can make them exist in the only area where they amount to anything at all, that of institutionalized social praxis.

As for utilitarianism, Madison argues that "there is perhaps nothing more damaging to the liberal cause than the attempt to justify liberal values on utilitarian grounds." From the quotation that opens the book, taken from philosopher Hans-Georg Gadamer, which begins "There is no higher principle of reason than that of freedom," Madison makes it clear that in his view freedom is not of merely instrumental value. To reduce freedom to a mere subjective preference, he argues, is to condemn political philosophy to "pure arbitrariness and ethical relativism" (p. 268).

> By making "utility" or "pleasure" the criterion of what is supposed to be a value, one is in effect denying that value any universal status, and thus any genuine normative status at all, for what is useful or pleasurable to one person need not be such to another... If individual liberty is a fundamental value, it is not because it contributes to an individual's private "happiness" or "pleasure," but because it is the necessary condition for implementing the principle of human dignity...
>
> Anyone who would prefer slavery to freedom (for the security it offers, perhaps) would thereby demonstrate, not that freedom is not a supreme value, but only his own deficiency as a human being.

In his last two chapters Madison sketches a kind of philosophical "grounding" of classical liberalism which its classic philosophical defenses sorely lacked. One may wonder, indeed, whether Madison's liberalism is really "classical" any more. He sketches a vision of political philosophy which, in my view, fits both methodologically and substantively with market-process economics. He has outlined a political philosophy which can support the kind of rules-based policy approach which market-process economists are looking for.

At the heart of Madison's reformulation of liberalism is the notion of free speech. Although nearly everybody in contemporary political philosophy pays lip service to free speech, it is usually perceived narrowly as simply one among several civil liberties which need to be defended. In practice its narrowness results in its being interpreted as a special privilege for the scientific community and the intellectuals without any general implications for the freedoms of everyday citizens. In this form, freedom of speech refers only to the right of citizens to criticize their government, a freedom that is admittedly important, but which in practice is exercised by a rather small minority of people in most societies.

For Madison free speech serves as a foundational principle, as a paradigm of freedom itself. A liberal society is one wherein "everybody is expected voluntarily to renounce the use of force in the pursuit of their own interests and to seek instead to resolve their differences and to solicit the uncoerced agreement of others through open dialogue carried on in the spirit of good will" (p. 208). *Persuasion* as occurs in a reasonable dialogue among people is to replace *coercion* as the main device for achieving political influence over others in society.

The basis for Madison's reformulation of liberalism is the idea of "communicative rationality," that is, a critique of what Hayek calls Cartesian rationalism. He identifies as the most serious problem of traditional liberalism its lack of an adequate theory of reason, and suggests that on the basis of a communicative notion of reason an adequate philosophical defense of liberal values can be constructed.

> [T]he various values defended by liberalism are not arbitrary, a matter of mere personal preference, nor do they derive from some natural law existing independently of the reasoning (communicative) process, such that they would be discernible only by metaphysical insight into the "nature of things." Rather they are nothing less and nothing more than what could be called the operative presuppositions or intrinsic features and demands of communicative rationality itself. In other words, they are values that are implicitly recognized and affirmed by everyone by the very fact of their engaging in communicative reason. (p. 266)

The title of the book has to be understood as not a strict "logic" of liberty in the Cartesian rationalist sense, but rather in the Greek sense of a *logos* of liberty. It is not logic so much as the "art of discourse" that is taken as the foundation of liberal politics. The reason we are called human beings, what really separates us from other animals, is our ability to speak, to "relate to one another by means of reason, the *logos*" (p. 265).

> Fundamental principles and values can be ascertained, affirmed, and applied only through unimpeded rational dialogue and the free exchange of reasoned opinions. People are truly rational, and thus truly human, only when they possess the freedom to reason together. (p. 210)

Madison distinguishes this view of communicative reasonableness with the rationalist notion of reason. His discussion of this contrast will sound familiar to market-process economists, for the rationalist notion is essentially an end-state oriented, equilibrium idea, while communicative reason is a process-oriented view. Since humans "simply have no access to absolute truth" reasonableness demands "the willingness to search for solutions through a reasoned exchange of opinions and arguments which itself requires that all participants to the dialogue renounce any privileged access to truth" (pp. 210, 212). Just as no one mind could be expected to intelligently shape an economy's direction of future investment, for reasons market-process economists have shown, so no single mind should be expected to guide the political process.

> For the liberal the "good society" is not the "perfect" or perfected one; on the contrary, it is one which is in constant and unending mutation, but also one wherein changes come about through the peaceful reconciliation of opposing interests and conflicting opinions as to what constitutes the "good life." (p. 215)

Communicative reason, Madison argues, "is not a form of intellectual problem-solving which seeks to 'discover' supposedly objective truths or values, ones, that is, which are believed to exist prior to, independent, or outside of the reasoning process itself" (p. 217). Rather it is the discursive process of consensus-formation among subjective minds itself which constitutes the standard, not some absolute, final target of objective truth toward which this process is supposed to be tending. He quotes Frank Knight and James Buchanan in support of this radical position to the effect that here "truth means agreement." Madison does not shy from the most stark and apparently extreme implications of this "genuinely revolutionary" concept of truth.

> The important thing to note in this context is that in communicative rationality the "truth," that is, the agreed-upon, is not extrinsic to the reasoning process itself (to say that the "truth" is the product of an agreement, that it exists as soon as an agreement is reached, that it is expressive of nothing other than the fact that an agreement has been reached means that it is not "discovered," for this would imply that it existed prior to the agreement). In communicative reason there is, in other words, no distinction between the substantive and the procedural, between ends and means. That is "good" or "true" which is the outcome of a dialogical process aiming at consensus. Here there can be no criterion for assessing the appropriateness of the result apart from the means of attaining it. (p. 218)

Madison confronts directly the objection critics of this position raise, that this "truth as agreement" position amounts to "the elimination of the universally valid in favor of the subjectively arbitrary." The charge, if it can be sustained, would undermine the whole notion of the rule of law, understood as a set of universal principles of just behavior. If truth is arbitrary, then we "open the door to legal positivism" and the "politically expedient" (p. 220–21). Indeed Madison at times seems to suggest that truth is arbitrary when he says it "is expressive of nothing other than the fact that an agreement is reached." The point is, however, that already within the notion of a "reasonable agreement" is contained a whole set of ethical implications. Truth isn't "nothing but agreement" because agreement itself isn't really "nothing but agreement." Agreement in this sense refers not just to whatever people actually agree to, but only to what they can come to a reasonable agreement together about. That is, "an agreement, to count as 'reasonable,' must be one which, being general, is also, to that degree, generalizable."

> This is to say that when a group of people assert something as a general principle, they are in effect recognizing that the principle is as binding on them as on anyone else. The reasonable person is therefore one who recognizes that no agreement can lay claim to argumentative validity which favors some at the expense of others. What could be called the *reciprocity principle* or the *principle of*

> *universalizability* is the core of all rational argument aiming at general agreement. (p. 223)

Indeed Madison argues that "all forms of communicative rationality have for their object the establishment of general principles or rules" (p. 221). To uphold what he calls the "essential link between the reasonable and the universalizable," Madison (p. 225) quotes the famous theorist of rhetoric, Chaim Perelman:

> A principle of action which others would consider acceptable and even as reasonable cannot arbitrarily favor certain people or certain situations: What is reasonable must be able to be a precedent which can inspire everyone in analogous circumstances, and from this comes the value of the generalization or the universalization which is characteristic of the reasonable.

This ideal of universalizability is not secured by an arbitrary "veil of ignorance" procedure, as in the contractarian approach of John Rawls, which Madison argues, falls into "pure and simple idealism." For reason or justice to prevail it is not necessary, Madison argues, "that the discussants have no special interests or, what comes down to the same, be unaware of them" (p. 230). This focus on an unreal "original position" deprives Rawls's theory of "any real empirical relevance, as well as any conceptual value" (p. 231) and is unnecessary to support a conception of reasonable political discourse.

> When people engage in communicative rationality, they do not do so out of ignorance of their differences but in spite of them – the difference is all-important. The most important feature of communicative or contractarian theory is that it allows for agreement or consensus among people who are not *de facto* equals at the stage of deliberation. (p. 232)

We don't need a politics for abstract, homogeneous "people" who lack any particular purposes or history, and who are somehow supposed to decide on rules of fairness without the benefit of concrete ethical experiences. We need a politics for people as they really are, diverse and situated in specific contexts, equipped with particular orientations and goals. The theory of communicative reason offers a way to get to universalizable principles without resort to mysterious veils. The ignorance real people face is the actual uncertainty of human action, the circumstance that "they do not know how future turns of events will affect their private interests" (pp. 232–3). Again, parallel to the market-process economist's concern to develop an economics for real people, we have here a politics for people as they really are. That is, it is a politics for people who lack neither the *ability* to learn (as in traditional Keynesian models) nor the *need* to learn (as in many neoclassical models where the agent already knows everything he needs to know) but who are realistically knowledgeable.

Thus this communicative approach leads us to "consider the kinds of arguments that are likely to produce agreement among parties who find themselves in disagreement on a specific issue or course of action to be taken" (p. 222). Not any arbitrary rule is likely to win such consensus. For example, if we debate directly the issue of who should have more wealth, it would seem unlikely that we could reach a reasonable agreement. For this reason it is necessary to aim political discourse at the establishment of general rules, for example, rules concerning which ways of obtaining wealth are to be counted as legitimate and which are to be called theft. Madison shows how Hayek's work in particular points the way to a conception of the rule of law upon which a communicative liberalism can be developed.

Although Madison's book provides a great deal of evidence that many elements of this communicative approach to politics can be found throughout the writings of classical liberalism, he understates the extent to which what he provides in this book is a radically new perspective. In my view liberalism has never been so persuasively defended in political-philosophic terms as it is in this important work. Madison puts the politics of liberalism in terms that can be defended in the context of contemporary social theory, and thus has done an inestimable service to those in other fields, such as economists, who have been lacking a persuasive political justification for their generally liberal orientation.

But the importance of Madison's failure to show how far he has come from traditional liberalism goes beyond the fact that he is too modest about his own originality. There are some aspects of his argument which I think suffer from his mistakenly supposing himself to be merely defending an already existing doctrine instead of charting a path to a whole new world-view. The book too often reads like a conservative tract, defending the American "founding fathers" as if they had it all right. Madison, you might say, is too comfortable with Madisonianism. Those of the eighteenth-century founding fathers such as James Madison and Thomas Jefferson who deserve the honorable label of classical liberalism had enormous differences with one another, and would hardly have considered their general position a completed doctrine. Even if they occasionally made gestures in a direction we could now identify as communicative liberalism, there is no getting away from the fact that they grounded their beliefs in a natural-rights perspective most modern political philosophers, including Gary Madison himself, can no longer defend. And of course many of the leading political figures of the revolutionary period cannot really be called classical liberals at all. Many students of American history will find disturbing Madison's fondness for Alexander Hamilton, for example, who is uncritically lumped together with Jefferson and James Madison.

And what's worse, there are places in this book where we find Madison not only uncritically defending the ideals of the founding fathers, but even defending the actual policies of the United States government, as if it were an already achieved liberal utopia, instead of, perhaps, a relatively more liberal society than most. When, for example, Madison applies his principles of communicative liberalism to Lincoln's reasoning against the secessionists in the Civil War, as if the Union were already a genuinely liberal society whose rules the South was bound to obey, the confusion between his ideal and reality becomes a serious problem. (Not to mention that Madison's particular argument against the right of groups or individuals to secede from a polity whose rules they dislike is in my view completely unpersuasive and inconsistent with his otherwise principled defense of individual rights.) There are many important ways, of course, in which American politics – not only today, but throughout its history – diverges profoundly from the ideal of communicative liberalism this book is trying to describe. The book would have been more persuasive if it had consistently presented communicative liberalism as an as-yet unachieved future possibility, rather than a reality that the founding fathers had already achieved but have now lost.

Most importantly, if the fact that communicative liberalism is an unachieved ideal is kept clear, we are more likely to realize just how much work needs to be done to develop this philosophical position. Again, despite the many hints of this ideal in classical liberal writings, the fact is that Madison's formulation of liberalism is new. Of particular importance, for example, is the question of exactly how democratic institutions can be so constructed as to permit both a reasonably stable rule of law, and a reasonably effective process of participation by the citizenry in the making and revision of this law. How can democratic participation in the setting and revising of laws be genuine and yet still be sufficiently constrained to avoid sabotaging the rule of law? These are difficult questions which classical liberalism never adequately resolved, and which its contemporary defenders had better take seriously.

Perhaps if Madison were less susceptible to such conservative tendencies, he would have dealt a bit more sympathetically with a particular school of neo-Marxism which comes surprisingly close to his own position. As some readers will have noticed, much of what Madison is saying sounds just like the kind of argument that such contemporary "leftist" social theorists as Jürgen Habermas and Karl-Otto Apel have been making. Habermas in particular has written extensively on the idea of communicative rationality, and although at times, for example in his depiction of an "ideal speech community," he may be said to suffer from the kind of idealism for which Rawls is criticized, by and large his contribution is quite close to Madison's. This similarity is all the more important because Habermas, unlike Madison, shows no particular fondness for market institutions, and thus those who would like to integrate market-process economics with a communicative notion of politics have a responsibility to answer Habermas's position.

Madison is aware of the similarity between his own and Habermas's position, and allows that Habermas is "to be commended for drawing the attention of much of the public" to the idea of communicative reason. But his main reaction is merely to insist that classical liberals had the idea first, devoting an appendix to establishing that non-Marxists (such as Frank Knight) have said before much of what Habermas is saying now.

It seems to me that Madison here misses an important *communicative* opportunity. An extended critique of Habermas, which tried to show why, properly understood, market institutions are fully consistent with a communicative notion of rationality, would have been far more valuable than a mere assertion that we classical liberals said these things first. Classical liberalism in general is all too often identified with conservatism, and although Madison goes to great lengths to try to distinguish his position from conservatism, even he slips in that direction now and then. If the philosophy is to be revived, as Madison's own book begins to do, it is necessary that the political spectrum be fundamentally re-divided so that the communicative liberal alternative to both socialism and conservatism is given room to breathe. The way to do that may well be for pseudo-conservatives such as Madison to join forces with pseudo-socialists such as Habermas, and come to realize how much they have in common with each other, and how little they share with the ideology out of which their views have evolved.

The point is not that Madison and Habermas are saying the same thing. On the contrary, the kinds of Hayekian insights Madison provides in this book could in my view teach the Habermasians a great deal that they do not seem to already know. But there might be a thing or two conservatively oriented classical liberals like Madison could learn from the Habermasians as well. Habermas has drifted as far from traditional socialism as Madison has from traditional conservatism. Perhaps it is time for these more liberal elements of the left and right sides of the old political spectrum to transcend the confines of these obsolete ideologies and work together to articulate a new vision of the free society.

Madison's *The Logic of Liberty* is not what it pretends to be, an argument that we can solve our modern problems by simply "going back" to traditional classical liberalism. But what it is is far more valuable. It is a first step toward a major reformulation of liberalism, a reformulation that can stand up to the best arguments in contemporary political philosophy. It injects a new voice into modern social theory which suddenly makes liberalism look not like an old, failed idea, but like a fresh new one with a promising future. Corresponding to the process-oriented content of its message, it does not really offer an end to political discourse that points back to already achieved solutions, but a new beginning that points ahead to future, as yet uncertain, possibilities in political philosophy. Not this book itself, but perhaps the dialogue with contemporary social theory it could help launch, may show us a way to transcend the unsatisfactory alternatives that have been offered by the politics of conservatism and socialism. The market process throughout the world has been severely constrained by interventionist political institutions, derived from conservative and socialist ideas, with which it does not fit. Madison's book is a very important step in the direction of outlining the kind of political institutions that could truly fit with the market process.

PART SIX

Conclusion

The future of Austrian economics

Peter J. Boettke and David L. Prychitko

When Frank Knight was asked to define economics, he merely quipped, "Economics is what economists do." Because we wish, by way of concluding this book, to speculate over the future of Austrian economics, a definition of Austrian economics appears to be in order.

But that is not so easy. If Knight had difficulty defining economics as a whole, we humbly admit that it is even more difficult to define Austrian economics. We hesitate to say, for example, that "Austrian economics is what Austrian economists do." The movement ignited over a century ago by Menger and his students now attracts many more American, German, and British scholars than it does Austrians. In fact, none of the authors in this book is Austrian. On the other hand, there is something distinctively "Austrian" about the preceding essays, especially when juxtaposed against mainstream analyses of the market system. Surely it amounts to something more than "verbal, free market economics," as some critics are apt to say.

Rather than define contemporary Austrian economics, we instead shall briefly reiterate what we believe to be its defining characteristics, its overarching methodological and theoretical presuppositions – much of which was implicit or explicit throughout the previous chapters. Once we accomplish that, we will be better prepared to speculate over the future of Austrian economics.

DEFINING CHARACTERISTICS OF AUSTRIAN ECONOMICS

Austrians have long championed a peculiar methodological foundationalism that consists of individualism, subjectivism, deductivism, and value freedom. This has implications for their rejection of both mathematics and econometrics in theory building and empirical testing. And, contrary to some widespread beliefs, Austrian economics does rely heavily on equilibrium analysis. Let us consider each in turn.[1]

1. Methodological Individualism

Austrian economists have claimed that the unit of analysis is the individual actor, the chooser. The goal of theory is to explain the evolution and maintenance of market institutions as a result of individual human actions, though not necessarily the result of any willed, purposive design. Accordingly, Austrians have dismissed explanations of the market system that rely upon teleological forces of history (as in orthodox Marxism) to explain the market system's emergence, or aggregative analysis (such as Keynesianism) to explain the trade cycle and other system-wide distortions.

2. Radical Subjectivism

Of course, methodological individualism *per se* does not distinguish Austrians from, say, Chicago-School price theorists, or even their Rational Expectations offspring. Austrians differ from other methodological individualists in that they weave a methodological subjectivism deeply into their analysis of acting individuals. They go well beyond the standard claim that value is something "subjective," a matter of individual taste and preference, something that can be conveniently assumed behind indifference analysis or Lagrangian technique. Instead, Austrians adopt a more radical approach: economic theory, for them, is an analysis of acting minds, of individuals attempting to switch their present states of affairs for imagined better states. This invariably links methodological individualism with the concepts of time (in the sense that Henri Bergson popularized) and genuine uncertainty (as opposed to mere risk, or formal, probabilistic "uncertainty").

Austrians have therefore traditionally rejected calculus, topology, and other mathematical methods on philosophical grounds, rather than for "humanistic" reasons or for some irrational fear of, or unwillingness to learn, mathematics. The key questions of Austrian analysis – the analysis of individuals acting under the inescapably subjective conditions of time passage, ignorance, and genuine uncertainty – cannot be meaningfully captured nor understood through mathematical technique.

3. Formal, Deductive Theory

Moreover, Austrians generally share a commitment to deductive methodology. Mises and Rothbard are exemplary in their defense of praxeology: a strictly formal, logically deductive approach to economics that starts from allegedly self-evident axioms (such as the claim that individuals act purposively), and attempts to derive apodictically certain (logically irrefutable) conclusions. The deductive, or praxeological approach strives to create a purely formal theory of not only the market system, but of human action in general. In other words, it purports to develop a universally valid theory. This very commitment to a highly formal deductive methodology has led Austrians to traditionally reject not only econometrics as a test of theory, but also any historical methodology, including the use of anecdotal accounts, case studies, descriptive statistics, and surveys as empirical *tests* for theory.

Again, this extreme stance among many Austrians is defended for philosophical reasons: a praxeological economic theory which is grounded upon an absolutely true axiom (or set of axioms) generates absolutely true conclusions, as long as those conclusions follow laws of logic and reason. Historical events, collected by case, survey, or regression can never provide an empirical testing ground for Austrian economic theory so derived: pure logic provides the only test of theory. It would be absurd to gather historical data to test the claims of a theory which are logically derived from self-evident axioms.

That is not to say that history plays no role in Austrian economics. In the end, the whole value of deductive theory is to render human history intelligible in terms of human action. History is not a means to test theory; rather, deductive theory is the means to understand history.

4. Value Freedom

From this perspective, formally deductive economic theory is independent of history, and yet it is nevertheless essential for our attempt to understand history. Austrian economic theory purports to offer a true, transcendent framework to correctly interpret contingent, everyday reality. Thus, it is also considered to be value-free. Although they have very different reasons for doing so, Austrians claim, like their neoclassical colleagues, that economic theory must be distinguished as a positive, *Wertfrei*, contribution to knowledge, wholly separate from personal judgment or normative application.

5. The Method of Imaginary Constructions: Equilibrium Versus Market Process

This is not to say that every conceptual tool behind Austrian theory is perfectly true. Methodologically, Austrian economists rely heavily upon the notion of the *Gedankenexperiment*, the use of imaginary constructs. For example, Austrians have developed the Evenly Rotating Economy (a timeless, static economy in general economic equilibrium) as a thought experiment to illustrate the significance of market institutions. By first studying general equilibrium – an imagined world without time, uncertainty, action – we may gain some insight into the role that money, firms, markets and a panoply of other institutions play in the everyday world.

Hence, Austrians differ from their mainstream colleagues in that they consider general equilibrium to be a subsidiary tool of analysis, rather than the focus of theoretical inquiry. At best, Austrians have traditionally claimed that an unhampered market process tends toward a general economic equilibrium, but it never reaches it in the everyday world due to the dynamic changes and the persistence of ignorance and uncertainty. The Austrian criticism of mainstream equilibrium theory is not that it is false – any imaginary construct is descriptively false – but that it fails to get on with studying the very processes (rivalry, entrepreneurship, etc.) that tend, in principle, toward equilibrium. By focusing exclusively on the formal conditions of general equilibrium, mainstream theory has failed to develop a theory of the market as a process, and a sophisticated understanding of the way markets work when the assumptions for a general economic equilibrium do not hold. Austrians believe that mainstream economists tend to confuse the tool (the fictitious world of general competitive equilibrium) with the object of analysis (empirical market processes).

THE RESURGENCE OF AUSTRIAN ECONOMICS, AND ITS FUTURE

If the above represent the "foundations" of modern Austrian economics, then the School's ability to prosper into the twenty-first century will depend ultimately upon the "ruggedness" of its foundations (i.e., the School's ability to withstand sustained, sophisticated criticism), and the School's ability to attract a growing number of students who are interested in developing and applying the foundations of Austrian theory to successfully understand, if not remedy, events and problems of the everyday world.

Let us discuss the latter issue first. Considering the resurgence of interest in Austrian economics since the late 1960s, students seem to be attracted to the School for two reasons: they have either become disenchanted with the tremendous degree of abstraction and mathematical rigor of mainstream neoclassical economics, and/or they have been lured by the generally strong free market ideology behind the School's leading exponents, from Hayek's restatement of classical liberalism to Mises's uncompromising defense of the minimal state to Rothbard's libertarian anarchism.

We believe that the ideological aspect of Austrian economics cannot sustain the resurgence of interest in the School in the longer term. Faced with tremendous – and still growing – pressure to meet the formal, positivistic canons of the mainstream, Ph.D. candidates and especially untenured economists still committed to free market liberalism tend to switch their human capital investment to neoclassicism, to create and maintain a relative degree of professional respectability and acceptance. For example, for all its free market aura, the Chicago School has nevertheless enjoyed much greater respectability within the profession compared to the Austrians. Time and again young intellectuals born from the ideological womb of Austrian economics mature years later as scholars in the halls of the University of Chicago or UCLA. Reswitching back to Austrian economics seems all too costly once one's professional reputation has been established.

Those students and already established economists who have become disenchanted with positivist, mainstream methodology may find some solace in the Austrian methods and methodology mentioned above, and the Austrian criticism of the mainstream. But they shall also find a growing number of competing alternatives – including Institutionalism, Post Keynesianism, Radical Political Economy – that demand, and are worthy of, close attention. Austrians have traditionally considered these alternative schools of thought hostile competitors, and have been most inclined to hold them in even lower esteem than the mainstream – largely for ideological reasons.

Let us now consider the "ruggedness" of the foundation of modern Austrian economics. The explosion in post-positivist, Continental, and pragmatist thought that has emerged since the 1960s has created nothing less than a revolution in the philosophy of science. Although the mainstream has yet to feel the sting, the philosophical pretenses behind neoclassical economics – and positivist and formalist systems of thought in general – has been all but shattered. This has helped buttress, to a small extent, the Austrian resurgence through the 1980s. After all, the key characteristics of the School stem from a Continental, anti-positivist tradition.

But we also believe that it will become increasingly difficult for Austrians to defend the foundation of their approach in light of contemporary developments in the philosophy of science, including phenomenology, hermeneutics, and critical theory. The methodological foundations of Austrian economics have failed to keep up with the times. Indeed, in the 1990s, foundationalist thought itself is in trouble.

Despite Austrian arguments to the contrary, many versed in contemporary philosophical developments might find the Austrian defense of methodological individualism atomistic, unable to capture the action of truly social, culturally-situated persons, and its notion of rationality to be too narrow and instrumental, unable to cope with the rich complexity of everyday choice. Although Austrians can claim a phenomenological component to this, their understanding of phenomenology may appear stuck with the early Husserl, or, at best, with Schutz. Austrian subjectivism, even in the most "radical" variety, appears to go little further than Dilthey's nineteenth-century interpretive methods to analyze meaningful human action. The traditional claims of the apodictically certain (and value-free) theory, developed through strict deduction from self-evident axioms, appear unfounded in light of the past 30 years of scholarship in phenomenological hermeneutics, let alone critical theory and pragmatism.

Now it may be that hermeneutics and critical theory and pragmatism and the rest is ultimately flawed. We are still awaiting a verdict. But Austrians who make philosophical claims about the nature of their discipline must nevertheless come to terms with this literature. Simply repeating past arguments will get them nowhere.

More practically minded Austrians may wish to avoid all the murky epistemological waters and instead continue their work, both theoretical and applied. This, we believe, will become the most attractive alternative: doing "verbal" analysis with little or no sophisticated philosophical justification. (It is easy to rationalize this: the profession, anyway, is not concerned with philosophical rhetoric.) However, the best in the profession do know something about equilibrium. And the theoretical methods of Austrian economics have come under great scrutiny in the past decade: the Austrian theory of the market process seems to be all too wedded to equilibrium constructs, implicit or explicit (consider Austrian business cycle theory, for example, and, indeed, many of the chapters throughout this book). We contend that Austrian theorists actually have much to learn from standard neoclassical economists here: compared to the Austrian notion of the Evenly Rotating Economy, the standard model of general competitive equilibrium (particularly the well-articulated Arrow–Hahn-Debreu framework) provides a much clearer, if not more consistent, picture of the nature of abstract market equilibrium. To the extent that Austrian theory is founded upon the belief that, although it may never reach equilibrium, the market process at least tends toward general economic equilibrium, then Austrians are making an empirical claim. We believe it has become much more difficult for Austrians to defend that claim in light of the voluminous research on the hopelessly unrealistic nature of general equilibrium. If we are correct in our contention that Austrian theory is tied to equilibrium much more than Austrians wish to admit, then the theory itself will face future, stronger charges of inconsistency. And that, of course, renders the traditional Austrian defense of free markets quite problematic.

WHERE WE STAND

Perhaps we have just created what many Austrians would consider only a worst case scenario. After all, we point to the possibility of a thoroughgoing shaking, if not crumbling, of the foundations of modern Austrian economics. What arises from that – if anything – may no longer look like traditional

Austrian theory, but may combine more of the Institutionalists' work on historical and cultural analysis, more of the Post Keynesians' subjectivism, more of the Radical Political Economists' focus on power, to mention only the most obvious. And who knows what we may learn from other social scientists, from sociologists and organization theorists to ethnographers and anthropologists.

Now, if contemporary Austrians really do stand upon a solid methodological and theoretical foundation, then future criticism can only strengthen that foundation. Alternatively, if it proves to be no secure foundation at all, it is best that Austrians realize that, and the sooner the better. Either way, we believe a more open, interdisciplinary dialogue between Austrian economists and their intellectual neighbors can only strengthen the insights of the Austrian understanding of market processes. We believe, in fact, that such an interdisciplinary dialogue (which, arguably, emerged in the pages of *Market Process*) has already borne fruit. For example, many younger Austrians have rekindled interest in applied comparative systems research, sociology, and political economy, broadly conceived. The 1980s and 1990s have witnessed growing philosophical sophistication among some Austrians interested in methodological issues, as well as a quest for a more integrated, Weberian conception of the social sciences.

Perhaps, more than anything else, the success of this new wave in Austrian economics requires a good dose of intellectual and disciplinary humility. We are reminded especially of the gracious example of Kenneth Boulding, whose actions fit perfectly with his words written for the preface to his 1950 book, *A Reconstruction of Economics*: "I have been gradually coming under the conviction, disturbing for a professional theorist, that there is no such thing as economics – there is only social science applied to economic problems."

NOTE

1. We should be clear from the outset that not all economists who consider themselves "Austrian" would adhere fully to each of the following characteristics. The Austrian School, like any other intellectual community, is neither perfectly homogeneous nor in full agreement on either methodological, theoretical, or policy issues. The characteristics we list are those that an "ideal-typical" modern Austrian would defend, and we would consider Mises and Rothbard to be empirical examples.

Index